SCHUBERT

A Critical Biography

Da Capo Press Music Reprint Series

MUSIC EDITOR
BEA FRIEDLAND
Ph.D., City University of New York

This title was recommended for Da Capo reprint by
Frank D'Accone, *University of California at Los Angeles*

2

10.

SCHUBERT

A Critical Biography

BY

MAURICE J. E. BROWN

DA CAPO PRESS · NEW YORK · 1977

Library of Congress Cataloging in Publication Data

Brown, Maurice John Edwin.
  Schubert: a critical biography.

  (Da Capo Press music reprint series)
  Reprint of the ed. published by Macmillan, London.
  1. Schubert, Franz Peter, 1797-1828. 2. Com-
posers—Austria—Biography.
[ML410.S3B7 1977]   780'.92'4 [B]   77-4160
ISBN 0-306-77409-7

This Da Capo Press edition of *Schubert: A Critical Biography* is an
unabridged republication of the first edition published in London
and New York in 1958. It is reprinted by arrangement with the
author's executors and The Macmillan Press Ltd., London and
Basingstoke.

Published by Da Capo Press, Inc.
A Subsidiary of Plenum Publishing Corporation
227 West 17th Street, New York, N. Y. 10011

SCHUBERT

Also by Maurice J. E. Brown

SCHUBERT'S VARIATIONS

SCHUBERT: THE MEMORIAL BUST BY JOSEPH DIALER
Historische Museum, Vienna

SCHUBERT

A Critical Biography

BY

MAURICE J. E. BROWN

LONDON

MACMILLAN & CO LTD

NEW YORK · ST MARTIN'S PRESS

1958

MACMILLAN AND COMPANY LIMITED
London Bombay Calcutta Madras Melbourne

THE MACMILLAN COMPANY OF CANADA LIMITED
Toronto

ST MARTIN'S PRESS INC
New York

PRINTED IN GREAT BRITAIN

To

OTTO ERICH DEUTSCH

CONTENTS

CHAPTER		PAGE
FOREWORD		ix
I.	1797–1814	1
II.	1815–1817	32
III.	1818–1819	78
IV.	1820–1823	99
V.	1824–1825	146
VI.	THE ARTIST	194
VII.	1826–1827	233
VIII.	1828	281
IX.	HIS CENTURY AND OURS	312

APPENDICES

(i) The 'Gmunden-Gastein' Symphony	354
(ii) Works not included in the 'Gesamtausgabe'	362
(iii) The works in chronological order	368

INDICES

(i) General Index	399
(ii) Index of Works:	
1. Vocal Music	407
2. Instrumental Music	411

ILLUSTRATIONS

1. SCHUBERT (the memorial bust by Dialer) *frontispiece*

2. STRING QUARTET no. 2, in C: slow movement
facing page 20

3. TITLE-PAGE of MATIEGKA'S 'NOTURNO'   36

4. FERDINAND, COUNT TROYER   148

5. SCHUBERT (Passini's engraving, after Rieder)   196

6. SCHOOL REPORT OF FRANZ THEODOR
SCHUBERT   260

7. RONDO in A, Op. 107   292

8. FERDINAND SCHUBERT   340

FOREWORD

An attempt is made in this biography of Schubert to present the composer in the light of a century of discovery and research, not only in so far as the discoveries concern him directly, but also in so far as they concern the aims and ideals of modern biography in general.

The views of nineteenth-century biographers on human nature and personality seem to us, today, to be altogether too naïve and superficial. Where the creative artist is concerned, their wholehearted acceptance of the 'artist as hero', as a pure channel through which heaven's inspiration might flow, belongs, in our view, more to the realm of fairy-tale than to life itself. Schubert has suffered perhaps more than his fellow composers from this fairy-tale approach to the musical creator. We ask today for an interpretation of his character based on something deeper and more suggestive than that of the simple-hearted but idle Viennese Bohemian, who composed in a state of 'clairvoyance'.

The chance to present the interpretation was first given to the Schubert biographer by Otto Erich Deutsch in his great collection of the documents of the composer's life, a book which is discussed fully later on in this biography. Because those documents have now, at last, been so fully given to the world, it has not been felt necessary when quoting from them to do so *in toto*. I have, on the contrary, sought to digest the mass of records and filter the essential from the immaterial, to suppress, and even to destroy when desirable, the doubtful documentary addition which merely obstructs our view of the composer.

The reader who wishes to refer to original documents in their entirety will seek them in Deutsch's collection, and not in the pages of this particular biography, which seeks to go beyond the document or record to the interplay of motives behind it, and which attempts also an assessment of the composer's craft and achievement.

The term 'critical' of the subtitle gives the clue to the kind of biography I have attempted to write. I have, I realise, run the danger of failing to achieve either true biography or true aesthetic appraisement. Nevertheless, it is the kind of book on Schubert which I felt impelled to write, and I could not write it in any other way. We read again and again in the columns of reviewers that the fusion of 'Life' with 'Works' is an unsatisfactory solution. With Schubert, however, the two are so inextricably bound up that without the 'Works' the 'Life' is almost nothing. On the other hand, the 'Works' without the 'Life', of which we have had several examples in recent years, must deal with categories, e.g. PF. Music, Church Music, etc., and Schubert's artistic growth cannot then be fully examined. In this biography the reader must be prepared to encounter the major compositions twice in the course of a chapter: first as the biographical fact, then as the subject of musical analysis and appraisement.

I have not followed the accepted modern practice of giving a 'Bibliography' at the end of the book for the simple reason that every book and article on Schubert of importance will be found mentioned in the text and particulars are given there.

A number of items are published for the first time in this book, and others for the first time in any Schubert biography in English. I wish especially to thank Dr. O. E. Deutsch for personal encouragement, for several items of fresh information incorporated in the text, and particularly for permission to give an English translation of the recently recovered letter from Doppler to Schubert in Chapter III. Another letter, from Schubert to Anna Hönig, appears for the first time with the kind permission of Major S. L. Courtauld of Umtali, S. Rhodesia. Konsul Otto Taussig, Malmö, has kindly allowed me to reproduce the School Report from the hand of Schubert's father, and a page from the score of the String Quartet no. 2, in C major. I am also grateful to the 'Deutsche Staatsbibliothek', Berlin, to the 'Stadtbibliothek' and the 'Historisches Museum', Vienna, for permission to reproduce various manuscripts and pictures in their possession.

Extracts from contemporary documents, other than Schubert's own letters, are quoted from Deutch's 'Documentary Biography' by kind permission of its publishers, J. M. Dent & Sons, Ltd., London. The American Edition, entitled *A Schubert Reader*, is published by W. W. Norton & Co., Inc., New York, and to these publishers also I express thanks for their kind permission to quote from the book.

Whenever necessary for the purpose of exact identification of a particular composition, I have quoted the number of the work in the Deutsch 'Thematic Catalogue', another invaluable book of reference for the Schubert scholar which is fully discussed on a later page. Such a reference appears as, for example, D. 570. In time, no doubt, the 'Deutsch' numbers will displace all other means of reference to the works of Schubert, although, at present, certain well established opus-numbers may possibly be more convenient to the reader. I have left song-titles in the original German. There are no generally accepted equivalents amongst the several English versions of these titles, and to give yet more, and still different, English titles seemed more likely to confuse, than to clarify the position. Only in the case of the universally used *Erlking* have I felt that it would be pedantic to restore the original German.

Schubert has been for thirty years, and will be for forty years to come, spared the attention of centenary celebration, with its unavoidable exaggerations and distortions. The portrayal of the composer in the following pages is, as far as I have been able to make it, a true picture of how he appears to the musical world of the mid-twentieth century. It is a different picture from those of the nineteenth century, and it will differ in the same degree from those which will be drawn in the next hundred years. It is to be hoped, paradoxically, that the farther he recedes in time, the nearer each successive portrait may come to the truth.

M. J. E. B.

MARLBOROUGH
February 1957

I

1797-1814

I

Three aspects of Schubert's life give it a unique place in the annals of creative artists. It has, to begin with, no elements in it of the success story; no climax of recognition of his genius, or acknowledgement of it, breaks the continuous obscurity of his years. Hence the biographer of Schubert cannot achieve readability in his pages by holding out the promise of eventual, even if delayed, success. There is no gathering darkness to make the dawn so welcome, for there is no dawn. A contributory cause is that he made no public appearance as a performer or conductor. He had not, in any case, the ability to do so as a keyboard player, since the charm and expressiveness of his playing were not alone sufficient to impress the public. It is surprising when one reviews the lives of the great composers to realise that *all* of them, without exception, first impressed patron or public as performers or conductors. Schubert could not gain recognition in that way. There have been attempts recently to prove that recognition did come, in the end, by composition alone, and as evidence, reviews of his work from musical journals in Leipzig, Berlin and Dresden have been quoted. But notices of his songs and pianoforte pieces in the provincial press of Germany are only such as we find accorded to every young composer's work; it is misleading to quote them in isolation. Amongst the multitudinous reviews of new music in all the newspapers of Germany and Austria they would make no showing. It is sufficient to recall that the young English musician Edward Holmes, a friend of Keats and a biographer of Mozart, passed the spring of 1827 in Vienna, and there moved in musical circles\determined to find out all that was worth finding out; and in his records he does not once mention Schubert's name. Yet, in

1827, that name was almost at the summit of what renown it was ever to have in its owner's lifetime. Three years later, in 1830, that is, after the death of Schubert, the French scholar Fétis published an article on the state of music in Germany in his 'Curiosités Historiques de la Musique'; there is not one mention of Schubert's name throughout.

In the second place, Schubert was never able to free himself entirely from *necessity* in composing; that is to say, throughout his life he composed because he strove for a foothold. He was never to know, except in the modest way which any of us can know, what it was to compose for an audience which would attend to his music with the anticipation and respect always given to the established artist. Instead, outside the immediate circle of his friends, he was given a polite, even patronising, interest: not unfriendly, but containing a hint of 'Is this not the carpenter's son . . . ? ' about it. And because the musical world of Vienna was never sure of him, he could never be entirely sure of himself. That is why he could not wholly succeed in discarding the influence of the older masters on his work. An artist who is still struggling for recognition is bound to retain a tentative streak in his work. This is certainly not to imply that there is anything tentative in the great C major Symphony, or in the 'Death and the Maiden' String Quartet. But as a tendency in his work its presence cannot be denied. It does not seem to have occurred to his critics that the reason for the late development in his instrumental works, late, that is, in comparison with his songs, is that he would not let himself *be* himself in these works. He was still trying to be Haydn or Mozart or Beethoven—or even Hummel and Kozeluch. It is obvious, to give a concrete example, in the last of his early string quartets, the one in E major of 1816 (Op. 125: no. 2). Time and again the real Schubert appears, tender and imaginative, but is swept aside by the merest aping of the Beethoven externals. Even in the works of his last years, in the Mass in E flat, or in the Sonata in C minor, he is prone to revert to Beethoven's mannerisms. Accordingly there is no phase in Schubert's composing career in which he is, in the best sense of the term, the self-conscious artist, determined, in the first place certainly, to please others, but also to please himself. And at no time, as a result of this, is he self-conscious about his finished work: he never catalogues, nor records and documents it as all other composers have done.

The third, and most remarkable, aspect for the Schubert biographer, is the almost impenetrable obscurity which descended at his death, and which persisted, with so little mitigation, for forty or fifty years. The outcome of that obscurity was that Schubert's compositions, apart from his lyrical songs, never really became part of the nineteenth century's international heritage of music until that century was nearly passed, nor did he, as a composer, become part of that century's musical thought and philosophy. It is a commonplace to encounter the names of Bach, Mozart, Beethoven, Berlioz, Liszt, Wagner, and others, in the criticisms and philosophical essays of non-musical writers, that is, of writers not primarily concerned with music; the name of Schubert could not occur there. And because his work has not influenced, nor been illumined by, the intellectual writings of the nineteenth century, nor has it, by some queer form of exclusiveness, found its rightful place amongst musico-scholarly writings either. The musical scholar and critic, priding himself, rightly, on his acquaintance with non-musical criticism and philosophy, is never led to Schubert by any of it. The case of Berlioz illustrates the point. The extraneous problems and exploits of that composer's 'Romanticism'—extraneous, so to say, to the actual corpus of his music, fascinated the literary figures of his day. The result is that Berlioz's music is lifted to cognizance by two factors quite apart from what it achieves by its own intrinsic worth: the attention given to him by contemporary literary figures, and the interest aroused since then in critics, musical and otherwise, by the references to it in the writings of the poets, and novelists, and essayists, and diarists of Berlioz's time. Schubert's obscurity leaves no possibility of this happening to him. Dates in isolation rarely mean very much; let us illustrate a chosen one in the nineteenth century—1865. In that year the 'Unfinished' Symphony was brought to light and performed in Vienna; the symphony which, to most people, means 'Schubert'. In 1865, Mendelssohn

and Schumann, both always ardently ready to disseminate knowledge of new Schubert works, had been dead for many years.
Neither knew the symphony: neither knew even that it existed.
By 1865, Berlioz's work was finished, Wagner had composed
'Tristan' and 'Die Meistersinger', and Sibelius was born. And not
until that year, two thirds of the way through the century, was
the 'Unfinished' Symphony played for the first time.

In reading Schubert's life, these three facts should be remembered; otherwise that life offers many puzzles, and presents all
kinds of difficulties. And one of the chief of these is to see the real
Schubert through the fog of sentimental distortions which has
arisen from the efforts of Victorian biographers, who, because of
his posthumous obscurity, were obliged to rely too much upon
anecdote and reminiscence, because manuscript and document
were not available. The matter will be dealt with more fully later,
when Schubert's art is considered more closely, but one point at
least, may be made here. We read again and again in the pages of
Kreissle, Grove, Reissmann and other biographers, and in numerous short, critical essays in musical periodicals, of Schubert's
rapidity and ease in writing: we read that he never sketched, was
impatient of revision, and composed, as it were, by improvising
on paper. It is a false picture. Certainly Schubert had a fluent pen,
and he composed quickly, because, when he was engaged on a
composition, he could devote undistracted days to the work and
did not spare himself till it was done. But such feats of rapidity
lost nothing in the telling, especially by the friend or acquaintance
to whom the business of composition was such an arduous and
prolonged process that Schubert's fertility and energy impressed
deeply—Lachner, Doppler, Randhartinger and the rest. In a few
cases the anecdotes deriving from these acquaintances are obviously, demonstrably, pure inventions: proved to be so when
documents have made an incredibly delayed appearance. The
truth, which is, of course, less sensational, shows that the accounts
of Schubert's lack of preparation can be ignored; and the truth is
the discovery—still continuing today—of innumerable sketches
(the adjective is not lightly used) for the finished compositions.
Songs, PF. Sonatas and dances, symphonies, chamber music,

operas, Church music, there are sketches for all these works, and in the case of the songs as many as four versions before he was satisfied. The sketches for the 'Unfinished' Symphony are, most happily, preserved. Those for the C major Symphony, which were probably begun at Gastein in 1825, are lost. Ignorance of such matters is bound to produce erroneous conclusions in writing of the composer himself, his procedures, and his music.

II

Schubert was the fourth surviving son of a schoolmaster in Vienna. Both his parents had come to the city from northern provinces in Austria; that may have been a factor in drawing them together. His father, Franz Theodor Schubert (1763–1830), was born in Neudorf, a village in Silesia; at the time of his marriage, he was teaching in the Leopoldstadt suburb of Vienna. His mother, Elisabeth Vietz (1756–1812), was in domestic service (there is no definite evidence for the information occasionally given, that she was a cook) in the nearby Liechtental district. The memorial tablet for her birthplace in Zuckmantel, Silesia, was for many years affixed to the wrong house! They were married on 17 January 1785 in the parish church of Liechtental, a small but most attractive baroque church which we encounter many times in Schubert's boyhood and youth. Schubert was, it will be seen, of Silesian peasant origin, and the firmly rooted legend of his being Vienna's 'one native composer' must give place to a more temperate view. He, just as Beethoven, Haydn, Mozart and the rest had done, came to Vienna from outside provinces. His nature responded to the stimuli of Vienna's gaiety and melancholy in so far as those elements were present in him, but as for his being an embodiment of her virtues and characteristics, a native of the capital born to give her a voice and an utterance, this is only a half-truth. His nature had depths, epic and tragic, not characteristic of Vienna, whereas her passivity, her *laissez-faire*, were largely unknown to him. And has not Vienna always subconsciously realised this? Not Schubert, but Johann Strauss is her favourite composer, her darling. And it is the strains of the Strauss waltz, not of the Schubert song or symphony, which she uses as the expression of her rejoicing at national fête-days.

What kind of a Schubert should we have had if his parents had returned to Silesia when he was a child? A great composer, of course; but we can assess Vienna's contribution to his genius if we see it as an enriching, stimulating and provoking influence rather than as a fundamental element. It is the non-Viennese part of his nature that responded so readily to the appeal of German literature; his song-texts alone could call the 'native Viennese' theory into question.

Just over a year after his marriage, in June 1786, Franz Theodor was appointed to a school of his own in the Himmelpfortgrund, a small district in the Liechtental parish whose name is preserved today by a short flight of stone steps called the 'Himmelpfortgrundstiege'.

New facts have recently come to light about the school and its story under the care of Schubert's father. It had been founded many years before in a house called 'Zum roten Krebsen' ('The Red Crab') in the main street now known as Nussdorferstrasse. It was originally no. 42; this was changed to no. 72 a year before Schubert's birth, and is, today, no. 54. Schubert's father occupied the schoolhouse as early as 1786, not, as hitherto supposed, in 1796. The house was typical of the terribly overcrowded neighbourhood; it contained sixteen 'dwellings', on ground and first floor, each comprising one room with a kitchen. The Schubert family (for two children, Ignaz and Elisabet, were born by then) had two of these dwellings and in these two large and two small rooms a school of several classes was accommodated, and Schubert's mother bore twelve children and brought up the five who survived infancy. They were Ignaz (b. 1785), Ferdinand (b. 1794), Karl (b. 1795), Franz Peter (b. 31 January 1797) and Maria Theresa (b. 1801). Today the birthplace is a Schubert Museum, preserved by the City Authorities of Vienna. It is exquisitely 'groomed' and contains much of interest in the way of pictures including the original of Moritz von Schwind's drawing A Schubert Evening at Spaun's'. The courtyard, into which one

steps with surprising suddenness from the busy Nussdorferstrasse, is, one imagines, very like what it was in Schubert's own
day, and private dwellings lead off from it still. In the house
itself it is still possible to identify in the structure, though it
has been somewhat altered, the original one-room-plus-kitchen
scheme of the many family apartments of those far off times.
The 'alcove', Schubert's actual birth-room, according to his
sister Maria Theresa, was clearly one of the 'kitchen' rooms.

When Schubert's father took over the school it had a bad
reputation; but in a few years' time all this was changed. One
cannot but admire the industry, tenacity and spirit of this man.
Fees were very low and not paid regularly; as numbers increased
he was obliged to have a two session day, and to make ends meet
gave private coaching as well. When his school had lived down
its bad name, and more and more boys came to him, frequently
from distant suburbs, the extra assistants he had to employ swal-
lowed up the increased income. It is not difficult to see why he
persuaded his sons, as they grew old enough, to become assistants in his school. When Schubert was born there were nearly
200 boys in his father's charge. In 1801, by means of a mortgage,
Schubert senior bought and moved into a bigger (though still
small enough) house in a nearby side-street called the Säulengasse.
This house still stands in Vienna—it is a garage, called by some
quirk of deference, 'Schubert-Garage'. It is like the birthplace in
the sense that a small courtyard is surrounded by a two-storey
building; but it is crumbling and decayed. Nevertheless, if one is
allowed to mount the stone stairway and stand in the room over
the gateway, one is surrounded by the small rooms where the
schoolboys—Schubert among them—were taught; there is no
groomed look about the tall houses beyond the courtyard, and
there is only a square of sky if one looks upward. But if not quite
as Schubert saw it, it is very like; and to the imaginative visitor a
sense of the real period and the real background to Schubert's
life may be caught more readily than in the Birthplace-Museum.
And it is here, not there, that the genius began to bud, and where
we stand, looking down into the unkempt yard, the strains of
Gretchen am Spinnrade were first hummed over. Opposite, on

the other side of the Nussdorfer street, is the stone stairway down which Schubert, with his family, stepped to reach the Liechtental Church.

It is only fair to mention that the picture of a stern, industrious, all-work-and-no-play schoolmaster, so frequently drawn of Schubert's father, is only one facet of the truth. In the years of struggle, with hardly sufficient money for the needs of his own large family, he continually gave shelter and generous assistance to his own and to his wife's brothers and sisters, whose individual stories were not only those of penury and hardship, but frequently of tragedy. Music, too, obviously meant far more to Schubert's father than a subject in his school time-table. In a small book on Schubert, Ralph Bates, possibly a little guilty of the prevailing trend for the 'de-bunking' type of biography, concentrated on Franz Theodor's sexual capacities, drawing attention to his large family, his overhasty re-marriage, and the continuing succession of children in that second union.[1] If we are to draw conclusions about the sexual precosity of men from the philoprogenitiveness of the nineteenth century, few would 'scape whipping. It may be permissible to draw such conclusions, of course. But Franz Theodor's possibly oversexed nature is interesting only in so far as it illuminates Schubert. If there is a connection between it and a precosity of creative energy on the part of his gifted son, then the line of research must be followed far on, if it is to be of any help: this Ralph Bates does not do.

After the move into the Säulengasse schoolhouse, matters gradually improved until, in 1814, when his youngest son Franz was enrolled as his least considerable assistant, taking the 'Taferl' class ('Taferl' = a little slate on which the children learnt their ABC), he had six assistant teachers. There were then over 300 boys in the school.

The Liechtental parish where the Schuberts lived and worshipped is situated in north-west Vienna. The real heart of the city lay inside old, fortified walls surrounded by a sloping stretch of grass called the Glacis. During the last century the walls were

[1] 'Franz Schubert', Ralph Bates, London, 1934, p. 15, and elsewhere.

pulled down, and today they are covered by the noble boulevards of the Ringstrasse. A fifth of the population, some 50,000 people, lived in the Inner City, where, needless to say, the true life of the capital was concentrated. The streets were narrow and ran between high buildings. Here were the shops, the cafés, the theatres, the publishing houses, the University buildings, the palaces and grounds of the aristocracy, the convents and green copper domed churches, chief amongst them the towering spire of St. Stefan's Cathedral. And, surprisingly enough, open parks and gardens which gave grace and delicacy to the picturesque huddle of rooftops and towers in the City, so that foreign visitors said, in Schubert's day, that the view of Vienna from St. Stefan's tower was more beautiful than that of Paris from Montmartre, or Rome from Pincio.

The early years of the century in Vienna were clouded by the devastation and hunger caused by the Napoleonic campaigns and successive occupations. Like most occupations, Napoleon's brought nothing to Vienna of permanent value, but a great deal of temporary misery. When the phase passed a different Vienna emerged. What the overhanging threat of Napoleon had meant we can see in Beethoven's case. In the abiding good humour of Schubert's music we see what his Vienna craved—peace, and entertainment; pathos, the tears quickly dried, was not unwelcome, but nothing harrowing, no more tragedy.

We can, of course, seek too much in the background of Vienna to elucidate and illuminate the music of the Schubert who loved her so abidingly. It is not necessary to fill in that background with too many enriching details, otherwise his figure is detracted from rather than added to. There was that in him which responded to the spirit of Vienna; and that spirit, as we have suggested, was in revolt against tragedy and excitement. The 'Biedermeier' period, as it is conveniently called, cultivated the secure, the domesticated, arts and there was a great deal of sentimental verse-writing, of diaries and albums and journals, of charades and impromptu plays at home, of friendly associations in cafés, of music-making and dancing. The reaction in the arts against the epic, classical forms, its strength in the 'Storm and Stress' movement temporarily spent, gathered its forces in this strange little backwater of silver-lace borders and vignettes, before it sailed on down the broad waters of the 'Romantic' movement. The pathos, so fashionable a foil to the everywhere desired security and contentment, was exemplified in the figure of the youth who wandered the earth in a frustrated and unhappy quest for some ideal, or in that of the hopeless lover, or, occasionally, in a figure who combined the two —the man of Schubert's and Müller's 'Winterreise', for instance.

Apart from music Vienna offered to the cultivated taste little that was indigenous in the arts. It is incomprehensible that anyone should consider it a period of universal artistic achievement. Its architecture was undergoing a hygienic cleansing from the final orgies of the rococo period, and that does not make for greatness. Its painting was humble and decadent—of the 'illustration' *genre* and Schubert's friend Moritz von Schwind became its greatest exponent. Its theatres, undoubtedly fettered by the rigid censorship of the Chancellor, Prince Metternich, were given up to German dramatists, Goethe, Schiller, or Lessing, and foreigners like Shakespeare and Racine; or they were frivolously engaged in presenting farces by Bauernfeld and Castelli, fairy-tale plays by Raimund, and sentimental comedies by Kotzebue and Heinrich von Collin. The native dramatist, Grillparzer, is an isolated figure. Opera was frenziedly popular if it were Italian, and the lighter French operettas, like Hérold's 'La Clochette' and 'Marie' were well liked. The poetry of the day, in Austria, was almost negligible until many years after the death of Schubert. It was a time in which the happy-go-lucky, the *gemütlich*, the slippered, arts of Vienna might have disgusted a more tasteful and sensitive composer than Schubert and forced him into scornful silence. Instead, with his simplicity, his warm-hearted and friendly nature, his ready cheerfulness and ready tears, he *responded*; and he poured out his music in response to these various stimuli with a fecundity which never fails to amaze, and which is his unique possession. Happy such an artist: who can combine that spontaneous response with the assured technical facility to give it utterance.

The intensive cultivation of music in the houses of the middle-class Viennese families has been mentioned. Secular music was no longer the product and solace of the aristocratic patron; the prince and priest of the eighteenth century, whose establishments contained bands of musical servants hired to perform chamber and orchestral music, with a composer-servant at their head to provide that music—they were passing. Instead, the wealthy middle-classes were paying the piper, and they called the tune. The publishing houses were pouring out the songs and dance-music and pianoforte pieces which they loved and asked for. The piano was the centre of this music making, and in the large and comfortable houses of the merchants and lawyers and civil servants were held these musical evenings, often weekly, to which numbers of guests were invited, and at which part-songs and cantatas, songs, chamber-music, pianoforte duets and so forth were performed. Two aspects of this domestic music making must be stressed because of their influence on Schubert, although in fact nothing has been mentioned in the foregoing pages which has not its influence on the personality of the composer and his music: they are, the part-songs of the male-voice choirs, and the everlasting dancing. They danced the waltz, the Ländler, the galop, the cotillon, the écossaise. Of the Congress of Vienna in those days De Ligne wrote: 'Le Congrès danse, mais il ne marche pas!' It would be difficult to say which of the two forms of music, part-song or dance, was the more popular. To both the Viennese were as addicts, and Schubert no less than they. If we look at the composer against this background and try to see how it pervaded his thought and creative processes and what the music was which he poured out in response to its stimulus, the first thing that strikes one is this: he redeemed its triviality. He lent the inarticulate moods and desires of Vienna a voice—and through him they speak enduring things. When we read of the elderly Schwind returning at last to Vienna, seeking the lamplit alleyways, and the haunts of his youth, we feel that he sought, not a real city, but to recapture almost vanished impressions: the music of his friend's playing and old Vogl singing; the gatherings of the Schubertians in the drawing-rooms of Spaun and Bruchmann and Hönig to hear that music and those songs.

Although Vienna's tastes were mainly for the more entertaining side of music, Gluck, Haydn and Mozart of the immediate past, and Beethoven of the immediate present, were by no means neglected figures in her musical life. Schubert composed perforce, and published, a large amount of music in popular forms— waltzes and marches and variations—but he was also able to publish the more serious side of his work: three Pianoforte Sonatas, Opp. 42, 53 and 78, a String Quartet, Op. 29 and a Pianoforte Trio, Op. 100. The songs published in his lifetime were not only those in a lighter vein, *Die Forelle*, *Heidenröslein*, *Der Alpenjäger*, but also the ones by which his later fame grew, the profound, the dramatic, or the poignantly expressed ones such as *Gretchen am Spinnrade*, *Gruppe aus dem Tartarus*, *An Schwager Kronos*, the Harper's songs from Goethe's 'Wilhelm Meister'. Italian opera did indeed sweep Vienna off her feet, and the Rossini fever of 1816-1817 knew no reasonable bounds, but in addition the city gave a welcome to the German operas of men like Gyrowetz, Mosel, Hummel and Josef Weigl; it had known 'Fidelio', it was on the eve of witnessing the epoch-making 'Der Freischütz', and it was, in a not too distant future, to know 'Lohengrin'. If, it has been said, there is in Schubert a conflict between Rossini and Beethoven, it is because that conflict was part of the Viennese character. It was made more acute in Schubert because, in spite of his Viennese environment, it must not be forgotten that he was the child of peasants in whom was a strong Puritanical bent. We see the trait markedly in Schubert's brother Ferdinand, and in his sister, Maria Theresa. In Schubert it is the more earnest side of his nature, the side which responded to Beethoven and Goethe and produced those repeated declarations in his letters, and to his friends, that he was 'thenceforth dedicated to opera and symphony' and so forth. But the easy going and re-laxed side of that nature would re-assert itself and duet-fantasias and songs and dances came readily once again from his pen.

II·I

In October 1808, the lad Schubert won a place in the choir of
the Imperial Court Chapel. Candidates were examined in singing
and other subjects. His education had been the responsibility of
his father, his brother Ignaz, and the organist of the Liechtental
Church, Michael Holzer, who had given him lessons in organ-
playing, singing and composition, and who is reported to have
said of Schubert that whatever he came to teach him, he knew
already: a veritable legend-making remark. The fact that vacancies
in this Imperial Choir were publicy advertised in a capital city
such as Vienna and that the eleven-year-old Schubert obtained one
in a competitive examination proves that these men had given
him a grounding which was sufficiently thorough. His voice, and
his musical abilities, were part of his natural endowment; but
those alone, it is clear from the records of the event, would not
have been enough. The advantage to the boy of this place in the
choir was that it admitted him to the *kaiserlich-königliches Stadtkonvikt* (Imperial and Royal City Seminary: called so to distinguish it from a similar school in the Josefstadt suburb of Vienna,
for the sons of the nobility), the principal boarding school of
Vienna, where the choristers were given a general education,
with systematic training in musical subjects. It is doubtful
whether Schubert, not being of wealthy or noble parentage, could
have had a finer education anywhere in Vienna than he obtained
at this school. The lecturers were clerics, strict Piarists; the
material comforts of the boarders were not studied; classrooms
were very cold in winter, food was scanty, teaching hours were
long. But the opportunities for a boy of Schubert's gifts were
phenomenal. The elderly principal, Dr. Franz Innocenz Lang,
was an ardent music lover and encouraged the practice of music
amongst all the students (it was not an obligatory subject for the
non-choristers). Under the leadership of a twenty-year-old law
student, Josef von Spaun, an orchestra was formed among the
seminarists. So excellent were their performances of overtures and
symphonies that members of the public gathered thickly in the
square outside the building on fine evenings to listen to them;

and many Viennese came to think of the school as a 'Conservatoire' devoted solely to the cultivation of musical studies. From
the reminiscenses of his friends and the records of the *Stadtkonvikt* in the Vienna City archives, we can assemble these facts: the
orchestra in Schubert's day consisted of 6 first and 6 second
violins, 2 violas, 2 'cellos and 2 basses. There were 2 of each of the
woodwind, flute, oboe, clarinet, and bassoon; and horns, trum-
pets, and drums in unspecified numbers. Amongst his fellow
pupils at the *Konvikt*, who later on became his friends, or whose
names we shall meet again, are Josef von Spaun, who played
second violin and whose friendship with Schubert is one of the
brightest and most attractive things which the composer's
biographer finds in his material, Anton Holzapfel, 'cello, and
amongst the first violins, Anton Hauer and Leopold Ebner, the
second of whom made many copies of Schubert songs, which
later on proved invaluable when the originals were lost. The
musician, Benedikt Randhartinger, of whom we shall speak later,
did not join the *Stadtkonvikt* until after Schubert had left. Three
other fellow pupils who became his friends, musical, but not
members of the orchestra, are Josef Kenner, Johann Senn, the
poet, and Albert Stadler, a man of fine character, who lived at
Linz, in Upper Austria, and who became a collector of Schubert
manuscripts and copies, and a reliable source of information on
the composer.

From a humble place in the second violins Schubert quickly
showed his mettle and in a short while he was leading the orchestra; in the absence of the music master, Wenzel Ruczicka, he
became its conductor. Schubert's musical studies were in the
hands of this industrious, thorough and skilful man. Ruczicka
(1758–1823), a Hungarian by birth, had come to Vienna in 1772
and was appointed Court Organist in 1793. He was also a violist
at the Burg Theatre, and a modest composer. At some time
after 1811, when Schubert finished his studies with Ruczicka, he
began work with Anton Salieri, the famous Italian composer and
teacher. It is more than possible that Salieri's interest was aroused
by the composing activities of Schubert. It was probably not an

everyday occurrence to find one of the choirboys so outstandingly gifted in music and able to show the scores of overtures for orchestra (performed by the students under his conductorship), string quartets and substantial songs. Some of these boyhood works have survived, and the song *Hagars Klage* of March 1811 is actually named by a few of his friends as the work which aroused the Italian's interest. On several of Schubert's manuscripts, that of the String Quartet in B flat (D. 36), which he began in 1812, and on the manuscript of the String Quartet in D (D. 74) of 1813, we find Salieri's handwriting. The title page of the second of these quartets, in D major, did not see the light until 1928, when it was found in Vienna among the family papers of a descendant of Spaun's. Against Schubert's writing of his master's name Salieri added: 'premier Maitre de Chapelle de la Cour Imp. et Royale de Vienne.' There is sufficient evidence that he looked over the young composer's work. We can discount both extremes in the memoirs of Schubert's friends and acquaintances when they record the association between Schubert and Salieri: the latter was not Schubert's master in any close, systematic or continuous sense of the word, but neither was his instruction so casual or so carelessly received as would seem from some accounts, that of Anton Schindler, for example: he wrote '. . . we know for certain that Salieri never gave regular lessons in composition. If Schubert had undergone the required studies with Salieri it would have been quite unnecessary for him to have taken lessons in counterpoint with Sechter. Salieri only gave him advice on the treatment of voices'. Schindler is an untrustworthy witness. The example quoted above of the two string quartets shows that he was mis-informed over the extent of Salieri's instruction. There is a large number of 3-part canons and settings of Metastasio by Schubert, dated on various occasions in 1813, all clearly pupil's work. The lessons extended beyond *Konvikt* days and continued till 1816.

Schubert took part in daily music making—songs, pianoforte duets, chamber music—in the practice rooms of the *Konvikt* with his fellows. In his own home during the long vacation of the

school year, which came in the autumn, he played viola in a
family string quartet. His father played the 'cello, his brothers,
Ignaz and Ferdinand, the violins. In the theatres of Vienna, particularly in the Kärntnertor theatre (now the wonderful Staatsoper
of modern Vienna) and in the Theater an der Wien, he could
hear the finest opera in Europe; his first visit was probably with
his friend Spaun to hear Josef Weigl's 'Die Schweizerfamilie' on
8 July 1811. If we step back a little and review the musical influences and pressures on this sensitive, gifted boy during the
five years 1808–1813, in which he was a pupil at the *Konvikt*, it
must be admitted that few other composers in their early teens
have had such a rich and varied nurture. Between them, Vienna
and the *Konvikt* poured out for him a profusion of music—from
the richest masterpieces of Mozart and Beethoven downwards;
this music, and his work in the school, not only awakened and
stimulated his genius, but gave that genius the technical equipment by which it could express itself. What are we to say to the
ill-informed criticism which attacks that technical equipment with
head-shaking remarks such as that 'he was deficient in counterpoint' (Grove), 'the most completely lacking of all the great
composers in the purely cerebral power which is the necessary
concomitant of the highest artistic achievement' (Cecil Gray),
'a more exasperatingly brainless composition was never put on
paper' (Bernard Shaw on the great C major Symphony), 'his
pianoforte sonatas cannot, either by their comprehension or intellectual grasp, be placed by the side of Beethoven's' (Kreissle).
These critics, and others like them, confuse academic techniques,
such as the use of invertible counterpoint, fugal expositions,
augmentation, and so forth, with true intellectual processes in
music (unanalysable, and therefore unnameable), and hold good
workmanship to consist in the avoidance of consecutive fifths and
hidden octaves. They consider that counterpoint is only displayed if it is manipulative and self-conscious. All of them have
left one essential factor out of the count; if genius, the imponderable, is present, then the other factors count for nothing. The
question must be held in reserve for fuller consideration later.
Meanwhile a word could be added here on the use of the fugato,

the canon, the solemn 'chorale-tune' and other academically admired devices of the 'Romantic' composers. They were introduced when inspiration ran dry; they have been most cogently dubbed, by Paul Henry Lang, 'musical buoys'.[1] Even Beethoven, on occasion, keeps the progress of a musical finale going with a fugato 'buoy', not because *he* would have sunk without it, but because he momentarily stepped aside into contemporary practice. Schubert, never at a loss for ideas, felt no need to use these *dei ex machina*, fugato and the rest, to help his plots along. But the glory of the counterpoint which is there—unteachable, unacademic, intangible—should silence criticism:

If genius, however, is lacking, of what use is cerebral power, and faultless workmanship, and the rest? Writing of some lesser contemporaries of Beethoven and Schubert, Lang, in the article mentioned, wrote: 'The assuredness of (their) refined and orderly

[1] *Musical Quarterly*, New York, April 1953, p. 237.

craftsmanship led to playfulness and, in the end, to academicism.'
If Schubert's fecund outpourings break through the prim barriers
of classical form, it is an indication of the greatness of his genius:
only the man of small talent is always in full control of his creations.

Assertions that Schubert neglected his other subjects in the
Konvikt in order to devote himself mainly to composition are
belied by the facts: his school reports are still preserved, and in
them we can read Dr. Lang's comments on his studies. Making
allowances for the limited vocabularly of schoolmasters when
they pronounce on their pupils' progress, it is easy to see that the
boy Schubert maintained a satisfactory standard in his general
studies. But more than that, the music surviving from those years,
carefully preserved by his father, is small in bulk. Schubert had
not achieved that rapidity of composition so remarkable later on,
nor was he able to devote himself for undisturbed hours to his
music. His careful dating of some early chamber music proves
this. On the one-movement Trio in B flat, oddly entitled 'Sonata'
(D. 28), we read: '27 July–28 August 1812'; a string quartet in the
same key (D. 36) occupied him from 19 November 1812 to 21
February 1813.

The music which he composed during his last three years at
the *Konvikt* is a miscellaneous assortment, an experimental phase;
even a fragmentary opera, 'Der Spiegelritter' ('The Looking-glass
Knight') survives. There are three long PF. Duet Fantasias and an
'Overture' for string quintet, in all of which Mozart's chromaticism has almost obsessed the boy; each one of these works uses
the basic phrases:

or sections of them, in a rather mechanically worked fashion.
The prelude of his first extant song, *Hagars Klage*, is based on

the first of these ready-made themes. Several pieces for PF. solo
are still unpublished; amongst them is another Fantasia, in C
minor, where the presence of Mozart is so obvious that one
might call the work 'Schubert's Fantasia on Mozart's Fantasia in
C minor, K. 475'. Here, as an instance, is the *Andantino* section of
Schubert's fantasia:

A few items of Church music are negligible. It will be necessary
to make this rather slighting comment on the composer's settings
of liturgical texts at several points in his career. The tale of his
works is littered with numerous, short anthems, motets, offertories and the like, which are largely *ad hoc* compositions. His
words in a letter to his father '... I have never forced myself to
devotion, and, unless I become overwhelmed by it involuntarily,
have never composed such hymns or prayers (as the *Ave Maria*),
and then it is usually the right and true devotion' are somewhat
piously unreal, for they are discounted by dozens of perfunctory
examples of devotional music which he turned out, and which
clearly only touched the surface of his mind.

The titles of the few songs which survive—*Hagars Klage,
Des Mädchens Klage, Klagelied,* etc., show that the morbid appeal
of tearful poetry affected Schubert as it does most adolescents.
The one attractive song is a setting of Pope's *The Dying Christian*

to his Soul (*Vital spark of heav'nly flame*), translated by Herder as *Verklärung* (*Transfiguration*). For the first time we see Schubert beginning to achieve variety without losing the sense of the song as a unit.

The most interesting group of works is the set of five string quartets (1) in C major (D. 32) of September 1812, (2) in B flat major (D. 36) composed between 19 November 1812 and 21 February 1813, (3) in C major (D. 46) of March 1813, with an extremely able finale, (4) in B flat major (D. 68) of June and August 1813, from which the slow movement and scherzo are missing, but which has a first movement of superb quality, and (5) in D major (D. 74) composed between 22 August and September 1813. The score of this fifth quartet bears in the composer's hand 'Trois Quatours . . . composés par Francois Schubert . . .'; the other two quartets of this proposed group were probably the one in E flat of the following November, and that in B flat of a year later (Op. 168). These quartets are excellent examples of early Schubert which, with all their faults of exuberance, occasional weak organisation, and imitations of Haydn and Mozart, are alive from first to last. The history of the first one is similar to the history of many of Schubert's early works in four movements. During the years of obscurity it lay on publishers' shelves. By the end of the nineteenth century it had disintegrated; the slow movement and the first part of the finale were mislaid. The 'Gesamtausgabe' included it in the 1890 volume of String Quartets as a *two* movement work. The present writer identified the slow movement and the missing part of the finale among the autograph collection of Konsul Otto Taussig, Malmö, Sweden, in September 1950.[1]

The *Andante* of the early String Quartet in B flat (D. 36) is a pure Schubertian idyll: one of the most attractive little movements in the work of his 'prentice years and a model of ternary structure. The central section in C flat major (the tonic key is B

---

[1] The Quartet was published by Breitkopf & Härtel, Wiesbaden; Parts, March 1955; Score, September 1956. It was first performed by the Element Quartet in a broadcast concert on 23 December 1955.

FIRST PAGE OF THE SLOW MOVEMENT FROM STRING QUARTET NO. 2,
IN C MAJOR.   SEPTEMBER 1812

Herr Otto Taussig

Published 1955

flat) is a remarkable anticipation of his future fondness for the so-
called 'Neapolitan' relationship (see p. 222). He made several
attempts at a theme for this movement before he was satisfied.
His manuscript shows these rejected efforts:

Ex.4

The second one (*b*) is not a new idea. He had already used it as
the basis of an *Andante* in C major for the first String Quartet,
mentioned above, and rejected it altogether; he then arranged the
movement as a short, pianoforte solo (D. 29). Why he should re-
consider it here is a mystery. To some of the music in the fifth
string quartet, in D major, we shall return later.

IV

In October 1813 Schubert was offered a further period of
study at the *Stadtkonvikt* by means of a grant from an endowment
fund (the 'Meerfeld' endowment) if he would improve his
mathematics. But he refused the offer and left the school. This
was probably in part due to his father's persuasion, in part the
outcome of his own self-realisation. He now lived at home in the
schoolhouse of the Säulengasse and by December was attending
daily the St. Anna 'Normal-Hauptschule', a kind of Training
College for primary teachers. We encounter two legends at this
point of his life, both of which can be discounted. The first is that
he ran away from the *Konvikt*. This story derives from a Viennese
writer named L. A. Frankl, who was visited in 1868 by Schubert's
friend Franz von Schober. After the visit Frankl wrote a memo-

randum of their conversation in which Schober is supposed to
have told him of Schubert's action. Apart from its inherent
doubtfulness, and the fact that Schober's story relates to a supposed event of over fifty years before, the report was strongly
denied by Albert Stadler, who was, after all, at school with Schubert; Schober did not meet Schubert till two years after the supposed incident. The other legend, which is found in most
biographies of the composer, is that he decided to become a
schoolmaster to evade conscription. The period of conscription
was seven years, and although there were many loopholes, no
exception was made for schoolmasters. This alone disposes of the
allegation. But the truth is that Schubert was too short. The
minimum height for such military service was 1.58 metres (=5
Austrian feet); Schubert's height was 1.567 metres (=4.9
Austrian feet).[1]

During the month or so between his leaving school and starting work at the St. Anna Training College, he finished his first
symphony, in D major. (Strictly speaking it is no. 2, since there
is a partly completed score of the first movement of an earlier one
in the same key. This was composed c. 1812.) It is said to be dedicated to Dr. Innocenz Lang, and intended for performance on his
name-day, i.e. the day of his patron saint, St. Francis. Neither
statement is correct. The name-day of Dr. Lang was 4 October
(the same as Schubert's); the symphony was not completed until
28 October 1813. It is his second symphony, in B flat, which
Schubert dedicated to his old principal. The first symphony is the
culmination of the schoolboy compositions, an astonishing creation for a lad of sixteen. Absolutely in the idiom of its day, it is
therefore reminiscent of Haydn and Mozart and early Beethoven,
but only in the sense that each of these composers reminds us at
times of the other two. Schubert's symphony is completely individual in content. In the slow movement particularly, tender,
intimate, full of musical fancy, we hear his voice alone. It was

[1] The Austrian foot is slightly longer than the English foot, but this does
not affect the issue. In English measure Schubert was 5 ft. 1½ in.

probably performed by the students' orchestra in the *Stadtkon-vikt*; otherwise the first public performance took place in 1881, sixty-seven years after its composition, when August Manns gave it (complete) at the Crystal Palace Concerts.

Immediately his symphony was completed, Schubert began work on his first opera, 'Des Teufels Lustschloss' ('The Devil's Castle'), which occupied him intermittently for the next year. The words are by August von Kotzebue, the dramatist already mentioned. Kotzebue was enormously popular all over Europe. He was widely travelled, sophisticated and egotistical, a tasteless purveyor of fashionable dramas. In 1819 he was assassinated in Berlin on suspicion of being a Russian spy, an event whose more distant ripples were later to affect Schubert. Although his play is fifth-rate and calls for enormous mechanical resources on the stage, it was a 'stock' libretto; many settings of it had been made before Schubert took it up, so that we can hardly blame him for not seeing its unsuitability when many older and more experienced composers had accepted it. He finished his first act on 11 January 1814, the second on 16 March, and the work was completed by 14 May. He then took it to Salieri for advice. What his master said led him to revise the first and third acts. The second version of Act I was finished on 3 September, that of Act III on 22 October 1814 almost exactly a year after the beginning of his work. All these manuscripts are extant. It is an ambitious opera, with plenty of admirable music in it. It can best be discussed, however, with the later operatic work in Chapter III.

The work on this opera was, it has been said, intermittent. It was interrupted on many occasions, and during those interruptions Schubert produced works more congenial to the music lover. His String Quartet in E flat (D. 87) was the first of them, composed in November 1813. It was not published until after Schubert's death and the manuscript, a fragment, did not come to light until during the first World War. One of the oddest mis-datings of a work by Schubert is the attribution of '1824' to this early quartet. Reasons for the mistake will be discussed later, but it persisted right through the nineteenth century. The work is a delightful one, with one of the best finales which Schubert penned this side 1819, but how could Schubertians, from Kreissle to Grove, and on into the 1900's, be deceived into grouping the boy's work with the man's—into grouping this E flat Quartet with the great one in A minor, Op. 29? Schubert did not himself publish the E flat Quartet and the placing of the Scherzo as a second movement is the publisher's arrangement (Czerny, Op. 125: no. 1); the composer was unfailingly orthodox over the order of the four-movement scheme. By the time the String Quartets were published in the 'Gesamtausgabe' (1890) doubts had arisen about the date '1824', and the quartet was given the tentative dating 'c. 1817', which was certainly more plausible. The autograph manuscript, when it eventually re-appeared, was found to be dated 'November 1813'. A word might be added here on Schubert's meticulous dating of his manuscripts. In early works they are sometimes very detailed, the date appearing at the end as well as at the beginning (even when, in one case, it was the same day). Occasionally the time a work took him is triumphantly added: 'Done in 4½ hours' is written at the end of the first movement of the String Quartet in B flat, Op. 168. These accurate dates make the task of arranging his works chronologically a straightforward and congenial one. Grove has surmised that it was his father's methodical training which brought about the habit, but in actual fact the very early works are not so carefully dated as those which originated under the teaching of Salieri. It was probably the dating of these exercises written under supervision which induced the habit. In later years only the month and year were given; but the excellent practice persisted right up to the last work he wrote.

During his eight months training for teaching (December 1813 to August 1814) he wrote a number of songs much more attractive than the rather grim and long-drawn ballads of former years; Schubert's song volumes begin with a veritable iron age. The 1814 songs, however, include *Adelaide*, *Andenken* and *Geisternähe* (April), and *Der Abend* (July). The last song, a setting of words by Matthisson, is worth more than passing mention;

it is a rewarding example of secondary Schubert. The advent of *Gretchen am Spinnrade* three months later, so dramatic and epoch-making, eclipses the earlier songs of 1814. This is not quite fair to the graceful, serious little song of a doomed lover with its skilfully introduced *recitative* and the nocturnal atmosphere invoked so simply. At least these few songs do something to prepare us for *Gretchen*, as they certainly prepared Schubert.

A work which occupied him during February 1814 has become notorious. It is his so-called 'Guitar Quartet'. Actually it is Schubert's arrangement, with additional 'cello part, of a Trio for flute, viola and guitar by Wenzel Thomas Matiegka. Matiegka (1773–1830), resurrected from oblivion by this mis-attribution, was born at Chotzen in Bohemia. He studied music with the Abbé Gelinsk at Prague, went to Vienna in the early years of the century and worked there till his death. His Trio, entitled 'Noturno' (*sic*), was published as his Op. 21 by Artaria, Vienna, in 1807; it was, strange to note, dedicated by Matiegka to Count Johannes Esterházy, Schubert's future employer. Schubert's manuscript arrangement was discovered in 1918, and published eight years later in Munich under the editorship of Georg Kinsky, as an original work of the composer's. In the 'Zeitschrift für Musikwissenschaft', October 1928, O. E. Deutsch suggested that the work was spurious, and would prove to be an arrangement of someone else's Trio. His words were dramatically fulfilled. Three years later a well-known Danish guitar virtuoso, Thorwald Rischel, discovered an original edition of Matiegka's Op. 21 and realised that it was identical with Schubert's work. Rischel's is the only extant copy. Kinsky admitted the error, and Deutsch's acumen, in the 'Zeitschrift' of August 1932. It is surprising that anyone could accept the work as by Schubert, but many people did. The second Trio-section in the Menuetto is Schubert's own composition, and in the last movement—a set of variations—he has altered the order in the original, and turned Matiegka's Var. V into the major key, placing it first.

The genuine quartets of the year are for strings only: no. 7, in

D major, which is a slight work, and no. 8, in B flat major. This was published in 1863 as Op. 168. It was commenced as a String Trio, but Schubert changed his mind after a few lines were written. His interest in the string trio as a medium suggests that a trio of performers was readily available during these years, for we find two more examples later on, of excellent quality (both, incidentally, in B flat major again, a very favourite key). The String Quartet, Op. 168, shows his gradual emancipation from the 'mosaic' form typical of young men's work. The slow movement (*Andante sostenuto*) concludes with a remarkable 'Neapolitan' cadence—very prophetic of future uses, and the finale is an even more remarkable pointer to the future, suggesting in embryo the Scherzo of the great C major Symphony.

The summer months of 1814 were devoted to the composition of a Mass, his first completed setting, in F major. It was performed on 16 October at the Liechtental Church, and this was a great occasion for the young composer. His family and friends were there in force, and there is a well-known anecdote in which Salieri greeted Schubert after the performance with the words: 'You are my pupil, Franz, and will do me much honour.' Unfortunately a small doubt arises when we find that, by a strange coincidence, there is an entry in the diary of Wenzel Tomašcek for this very day. Tomašcek, a famous pianist-composer of that day, whose work will be mentioned later in this book since he was a forerunner of Schubert in the short, lyrical PF. piece, wrote in his diary that a Mass by Salieri was performed in the Court Chapel on that 16 October 1814. Salieri would almost certainly have been present in the Chapel for the occasion. The music of Schubert's first Mass occupied him from 17 May to 22 July. It is melodious, modest in conception and extremely competently written; it shows the influence of Haydn—there are distinct echoes of 'The Seasons' in it—and also the influence of those unnumbered and unnamed men who wrote the music for the services in the Imperial Court Chapel where Schubert had recently sung as a choirboy. That is to say, it is of its period, light, formal and devoid of any profundity and soul searching, as we should expect in a seventeen year old boy's work. It has the same easy-going, intimate style that is found in his music for the offices of the Church, which led to their brief dismissal a few pages back.

The soprano solos in the Mass in F were sung by a young woman of Schubert's acquaintance named Therese Grob. Her ancestors were Swiss, and the family lived near the Schubert home, managing a small silk factory. They were cultured, fairly well-to-do people. The mother was a widow and both her children, Therese and Heinrich, were musical. Schubert was a constant visitor to their home. His eldest brother, Ignaz, was married to an aunt of Therese's, and he was said to be in love with the plain faced, but tender hearted Therese herself. For Heinrich, who was a 'cellist, Schubert composed a few instrumental works; for Therese, a number of sacred solos including a fine *Salve Regina* (1815), and possibly many Lieder, were written. Her voice was high, a pure lyric soprano. The love affair between her and Schubert came to an end, it is said, because of his uncertain financial position and the unlikelihood of his ever being a reliable breadwinner. Therese made sure of her daily bread; she passes from the Schubert story on 21 November 1820 when she married Johann Bergmann, a master baker. The descendants of Heinrich, a family named Meangya, of Mödling, Vienna, possess a small collection of Schubert songs in a volume called 'Therese Grob's Album'; amongst them are three still unpublished songs which the family refuse to release. They are:

   i. *Am ersten Maimorgen (The first of May)*, words by Claudius, composed in 1816;
   ii. *Mailied (May Song)*, words by Hölty, composed in 1816;
   iii. *Klage (Lament)* anonymous, composed 1817.

All three are charming examples of lesser Schubert songs, and the prohibition of the Meangya family is incomprehensible.

A second performance of the Mass may have followed ten days

later at the Augustinian 'Hofkirche' (Court Church), in the Inner City; it would be, therefore, a more important occasion, but accounts of this event differ. Therese Grob said in after years that she could not remember there being a second performance, and the anecdotes grow more and more confused and unsatisfactory. But more important in the history of Schubert's creative achievement than the composition and performance of this Mass, is the appearance on 19 October of his first masterpiece in song, that is, the appearance in music of the first great German song in the sense understood today: *Gretchen am Spinnrade* from Goethe's 'Faust'. It was Schubert's first encounter with the work of the poet and the impact was tremendous. Never before in music had a poem so deeply and sincerely felt been matched with music as deep and sincere. *Gretchen* may claim to be the first song in which the music presents and explains the words in a fashion that the poet-dramatist could not, even though that poet be Goethe. The way in which the monotonous figure in the pianoforte accompaniment, which is a musical symbol of the spinning-wheel, stops at the climax of the song, when the girl's transport robs her of the power of physical movement, is unforgettable; but so, too, is the broken, sobbing resumption of that figure on the piano, for Schubert gives us here not only the spasmodic starting of the spinning-wheel, but the painful return of everyday sensation after the tranced numbness of the girl's body:

> *Oh, dreadful is the check—intense the agony—*
> *When the ear begins to hear, and the eye begins to see;*
> *When the pulse begins to throb, the brain to think again;*
> *The soul to feel the flesh, and the flesh to feel the chain.*

Yet the musical form of the song, bound to a beautiful unity by the soft, whirring accompaniment, if looked at coldly, can bear microscopic examination. It has a three-fold structure, each section terminated by Gretchen's cry 'Meine Ruh' ist hin, mein Herz ist schwer' ('My peace is gone, my heart is heavy'). This structure was imposed on Goethe by Schubert; he repeats the refrain at the end to achieve it. But there is one quality in the song

which Goethe imposed on Schubert, and which has been overlooked in the commentaries: it is the sense of rapid heartbeats,
almost of excitement, in the lines which Gretchen speaks. One
could imagine an actress uttering them breathlessly. In the middle
section of the song Schubert writes the powerful emotional and
musical climax, but each of the other two sections has a similar
rise and relaxation. But the wonder of the song, and it comes
from his greatest gift, is its melodic development. He is unrivalled in this ability to evolve a continuously significant, yet
closely inter-related, melodic line from an initial melodic fragment. In *Gretchen* the first phrase is this:

Other melodies in the song, from first to last, in all their variety
and passion, evolve from (*a*) or (*b*). It has been said that Salieri
could not teach Schubert how to decide whether a play would
make a suitably theatrical libretto; how to reject and alter and add
until a promising libretto was certain of success on the boards.
But this power of melodic evolution and development is something which neither Salieri nor anyone else could teach; it was
part of Schubert's powerful endowment and no one could have
given it to him by tuition. The tiny 'Menuetto' movement from
the String Quartet in D major, mentioned a few pages back,
shows how Schubert, in these minor and unconsidered instrumental works, had prepared his pen for these transports of his
genius. Here is quoted the opening of the melody from the first
violin part, and part of its later development:

Before the close of the year Schubert set five other poems
from Goethe including a further extract from 'Faust'—the *Scene
in the Cathedral*. The best of the five, and a song which became
quite popular a few years later, is the *Schäfers Klagelied* (*Shepherd's Lament*). Again the musical form is flawless, and Goethe's
rather stilted words (he was imitating, parodying almost, the
words of a well-known folk-song) are given music beyond their
worth.

Schubert was established as an assistant teacher in his father's
school. The 'shades of the prison-house' may have been closing
upon him, but he had, in good measure, one famous characteristic of the Viennese, the capacity to create a 'dream world' into
which the individual may slip to escape the unpleasant—or uncongenial, at least—realities of life around him. With many Viennese the world is the world of music. It was so with Schubert. That
he escaped from the realities of his uncongenial duties into a world

of composition is only too evident from the overwhelming list of works which originated in the first two years which he spent behind the schoolmaster's desk. Perhaps he knew that escape from the *Stadtkonvikt* would release him for his desired task. Perhaps it was an unrealised urge which drove him. But the results, from whatever cause, have no parallel elsewhere in music.

II

1815-1817

I

His friendship with the staunch Josef von Spaun brought
Schubert rich rewards. Not in the material sense, unless we
accept that rather charming but improbable story that Spaun supplied him with desperately needed music-paper; as Brahms has
pointed out, Schubert's extravagance with music-paper as shown
in his *Konvikt* scores, does not suggest any shortage of it. But in
propaganda, in introductions to new friends, in artistic encouragement, Spaun was tireless. He was a student of law, and at this
period was studying with Heinrich Watteroth, a professor at the
University of Vienna. Amongst Spaun's friends and acquaintances, fellow students of his in law, were Johann Mayrhofer,
Franz von Schober and Josef Witteczek. All these men were
sooner or later introduced to his friend, the young composer. In
December 1814 Spaun had given Schubert a poem *Am See*, which
had been set to music there and then. A day or so later Spaun took
the poet, Mayrhofer, to the Säulengasse house and introduced
him to Schubert using the song as an excellent reason for doing
so. (It is a pity that this first song from so fruitful a partnership is
not more endearing: after a promising start it becomes entirely
uninteresting.) Mayrhofer was a sensitive, introspective man, in-
curably realistic, and hence a pessimist. 'Morbid' is a word frequently used to describe his philosophy as we see it in his poetry.
It was an outlook due in part to chronic ill-health. He and Schubert became more and more friendly during the two years following their meeting.

A more dramatic encounter was with Franz von Schober.
This young man was the same age as Schubert but his origin and
upbringing were as different as could be imagined. His father was

born in Saxony of Swedish parents, his mother was a Viennese woman, Katharina Derffel. Shortly after their marriage, Schober senior returned to Sweden with his young wife. Schober was born in Torup Castle, near Malmö, where his father was the estate manager. The ties between Axel Stiernblad, the owner of the Castle, and the Schobers must have been fairly close; they named their eldest son Axel in his honour, and when he died, Katharina von Schober, then a widow, inherited his money. She returned to Austria and enjoyed a period of wealthy retirement. Axel von Schober chose a career in the army, while Franz, his younger brother, attended the convent school of Kremsmünster, and then went to Vienna in the autumn of 1815 to study law. Here he met Spaun and heard of Schubert. Spaun denied in after years the statement in Kreissle's biography of Schubert that Schober had learnt to know Schubert's songs at Linz in 1813, and he is obviously right. There were only a few songs in existence then, and certainly not the kind that would spread Schubert's fame.

Schober did not wait for an introduction. He sought Schubert out in the Säulengasse schoolhouse, coming upon him actually in the schoolroom, teaching small children and surrounded by piles of manuscripts. So we read in Schober's reminiscences. But even if we ignore any details of their meeting the substance remains. To Schober's remonstrances, enthusiasms and encouragements, Schubert could not remain indifferent. Half-prepared already to abandon teaching and throw the reins to his genius, Schubert was won over, and from that meeting with Schober his days as a schoolteacher were numbered. For this we owe Schober a debt of gratitude. There are others. This must be said because Schober's influence on Schubert in after years did not always tend towards the fulfilment of his genius. Schober himself was a dilettante: with no necessity to consider ways and means he tried one thing after another, law, acting, writing, publishing and so on. Schubert was fonder of him than of any other of his friends. Another of the things for which we must also be grateful to Schober was his introduction of Schubert to the elderly singer Vogl.

In the spring of 1816, Schubert tried to obtain a post as music

master at a training college—the 'Normal-Hauptschule'—at
Laibach, now Ljubljana in Jugoslavia, an establishment similar
to the college in the Annagasse, that is, one for the training of
teachers for primary schools. His application was undoubtedly
inspired by Schober's visit; it may have been equally due to his
desire to improve his material prospects in order to be in a position to marry Therese Grob. The post was advertised in February.
He received a testimonial from Salieri and in April applied for the
situation. Four months later, in September 1816, he heard of his
ill-success (the leisurely tempo of these transactions will be encountered again: it was not by any means exceptional).

The songs which Schubert had composed in 1814 and 1815,
particularly the Goethe songs *Gretchen am Spinnrade* and *Erlking*,
were by now becoming familiar and very popular with his friends.
In April Spaun wrote a letter to Goethe at Weimar and with it
sent a volume of songs (the texts all by Goethe) written out in
fair copy by Schubert. The letter, so obsequious in tone that only
a man whose head had been turned by praise would fail to be
nauseated by it, is dated 17 April 1816. This approach to Goethe
arose from an attempt by his friends in that year, to bring out a
series of books containing the songs arranged according to the
poets of the texts. The first two were to be of texts by Goethe, and
comprised these songs:

BOOK I

Gretchen am Spinnrade	*Wanderers Nachtlied* ('*Du der*
Schäfers Klagelied	*von dem Himmel bist*')
Rastlose Liebe	*Erster Verlust*
Geistes-Gruss	*Die Spinnerin*
An Mignon	*Heidenröslein*
Nähe des Geliebten	*Wonne der Wehmut*
Meeresstille	*Erlkönig*
Der Fischer	*Der König in Thule*

Jägers Abendlied

Schubert's manuscript of these fair copies, dated March 1816, is
in the Prussian State Library, Berlin. It may not be quite com-

plete; there is a possibility that one or even more songs are missing from the book. Book II contained these songs:

BOOK II

Nachtgesang	*Der Sänger*
Der Gott und die Bajadere	*Der Rattenfänger*
Sehnsucht ('Was zieht mir das	*An den Mond* (I)
Herz so?')	*Bundeslied*
Mignon	*Wer kauft Liebesgötter?*
Trost in Tränen	*Tischlied*

The manuscript of Book II, also fair copies by Schubert and dated May 1816, is partly in the Paris 'Conservatoire' Library and partly in the Vienna City Library.

Commenting on Spaun's action, Richard Capell has these unforgettable words:

> The songs were sent as offerings to the altar at Weimar, where the ageing Goethe was (while still falling in love) living half-deified. They were not acknowledged; and none of the throng of inspiring genies that wheeled invisible about the incomparable sage and bard whispered to him that through this Viennese bohemian's music and not otherwise would his poetry reach masses of the earth's population for whom without it Goethe would be nothing but a name. ('Schubert's Songs', 1928, p. 9.)

Goethe did return the books of songs to Spaun.

In May, Spaun, with his friend and fellow student Josef Witteczek, moved into lodgings in the house of Professor Watteroth in the Erdberggasse. Witteczek was courting Wilhelmine, Watteroth's daughter. Spaun introduced him to Schubert, and in later years he became an ardent Schubertian and amassed a superb collection of Schubertiana: first editions, manuscript copies of songs and instrumental works, newspaper cuttings, programmes, portraits. For a short while—possibly for a holiday only—Schubert lived there with them. According to Kreissle the manuscript of some dances of that period bore the words 'Composed while confined to my room at Erdberg, May 1816'; this was apparently a record of the rather worn practical joke of locking a composer in a room and keeping him there until he has written something. There is another example of Schubert having been subjected to this jest: it is in connection with the Overture in F for PF. Duet, and the story then was told by Josef Hütten-brenner. Neither manuscript, however, survives with Schubert's words to confirm the anecdote.

We do possess a few pages from a diary which he was keeping that year. They are dated 'June' and 'September'. The diary was rescued from oblivion by the famous collector Alois Fuchs, who recorded that he found it being sold piecemeal by a second-hand bookseller. Later the leaves became a possession of Gustav Petter, also a collector, chiefly of Schubert manuscripts, and today they belong partly to the Vienna *Gesellschaft der Musikfreunde*, partly to the Vienna City Library. The pages are not very interesting. The composer had returned to teaching and was living again in the Säulengasse house. On the page dated 13 June 1816 we read:

> I played variations by Beethoven, sang Goethe's *Rastlose Liebe* and Schiller's *Amalia*. Unanimous applause for the first, less for the second. Although I myself consider my *Rastlose Liebe* more success-ful than *Amalia* it can't be denied that Goethe's genius for lyric poetry contributed much to the applause.

This extract, familiar from being often quoted, gains a little from a discovery made only a few years ago in a library of the Austrian town of Linz. This was of the original manuscript of *Rastlose Liebe* with its definite date '19 May 1815'. The song had always been ascribed vaguely to the year 1815. We now know that it was actually composed on the same day as *Amalia*, whose date of composition has always been accurately known. So Schubert, on that June day of 1816, may have sung the two songs from an album which contained the batch of songs he wrote in mid-May 1815.

The accounts of the composition of two cantatas this summer seem to occupy more room in the Schubertian biographies than they merit. The first was Schubert's musical contribution to the celebrations attending the fiftieth anniversary of Salieri's advent in Vienna. His pupils organised a concert of original music for

TITLE-PAGE OF THE 'NOTURNO', OP. 21, BY MATIEGKA
THE BASIS OF SCHUBERT'S SO-CALLED 'GUITAR' QUARTET
Mr. Thorwald Rischel

the day (evidently Schubert was considered, publicly and privately, his pupil). There are two versions, both extant, of the music which Schubert devised, but the cantata had only occasional value: little of it now strikes one as worthy of its author. The other cantata was likewise for the celebration of a teacher— for the name-day of Professor Watteroth.[1] His law students organised the affair and one of them, Phillip Dräxler, wrote the poem. It was called 'Prometheus' and contained delicate comparisons between the semi-divine craftsman and the professor himself. (It should be remembered here and later that in Schubert's day Prometheus was looked upon as a confident creator and craftsman, rather than as Shelley's bound and tortured Titan, hurling imprecations at Zeus.) Schubert obtained £4 from the students for his music and entered the fact—rather shyly—in his diary. The music consisted of solos, choruses and recitatives, and must have been of finer quality than the Salieri example, since it created a deep impression. We have no means of judging since the score was lost at the time of Schubert's death. Two law students who sang in the chorus made Schubert's acquaintance on the occasion. One was the poet Franz von Schlechta, an old student of the *Konvikt*, but who had attended after Schubert's time there. The other was Leopold von Sonnleithner, the son of a noted Viennese barrister, Ignaz; both father and son were ardent music lovers and in Ignaz Sonnleithner's house in the 'Gundelhof' weekly concerts of music were held to which large numbers of guests were invited. The name Sonnleithner is a familiar one in musical biography since the elder brother of Ignaz, Josef von Sonnleithner, was at one time a music publisher, and as Court Secretary had had a hand in the libretto of Beethoven's 'Fidelio'. Repeated efforts were made in the middle of the nineteenth century to find the lost 'Prometheus', until finally Leopold von Sonnleithner wrote a full account of the work, as he remembered it, told the story of its unhappy disappearance, appealed to the musical public for information, and even offered a reward for its recovery. There was no result. His account was published in

---

[1] This was apparently a Protestant name-day. Details are given in O. E. Deutsch's 'Documentary Biography', p. 67.

Fellners Blätter für Theater, Musik u. bildende Kunst, 5 March 1867. He wrote there that the cantata should have been performed on 12 July 1816 in the garden of the Erdberggasse house, but owing to bad weather the performance was actually given on 24 July. The score and parts were then sent to Johann Baptist Gänsbacher, the conductor of a Music Union at Innsbruck; many years later the work was retrieved from the Göttweih Monastery (*c.* 1825). It remained in Sonnleithner's possession until 1828, when Schubert himself took it back. The composer's death occurred a few months afterwards, and the work vanished without trace. It is clear that Schubert lent it to a professional acquaintance, and it is an ironical thought that it may have masqueraded in print under another name, ignored because that name was obscure, and then lost a second time!

Schubert may have been flattered by the appearance that year of two poems in his honour. The first was by Schlechta, written after the performance of 'Prometheus'; the other, more adulatory, was by his new friend Mayrhofer, entitled *Geheimnis: an Franz Schubert.* It begins

> *Say who taught thee songs*
> *So caressing, so sweet?*

Schubert, with no compunction, set the verses to music—a charming song this time.

Schober had been to Sweden during the summer to attend to family concerns connected with his mother's inheritance. He returned in the late autumn, and settled down in residence with his mother, in a house in the Landskrongasse. In December 1816 Schubert joined him, and this time it was not for a short holiday but for many months. It was the first step to freedom after two years of servitude.

II

But those two years had produced, in spite of the duties of training and teaching, such a bulk of work that the mind is almost stupefied in contemplating it. Hard work will not explain it; a thirst, a rapacity for composition, is suggested.[1] Some idea of how Schubert worked can be obtained if we devise a kind of calendar for one of the most productive months, that is, July 1815. There are several of these 'productive months' in the composer's career—December 1820 is another one, and June 1824. But none of them can compare with the July of 1815 as these details show:

July 1815

2nd. 'Lieb Minna' (Stadler).

5th. 'Salve Regina' in F, Op. 47, for soprano, orchestra and organ continuo.

Wandrers Nachtlied (I) (Goethe).

Der Fischer (Goethe).

Erster Verlust (Goethe).

7th. *Idens Nachtgesang* (Kosegarten).

Von Ida (Kosegarten).

Die Erscheinung (Kosegarten).

Die Täuschung (Kosegarten).

8th. *Das Sehnen* (Kosegarten).

9th. 'Fernando' (Stadler), one act operetta completed (it had been started on 22 June).

11th. 'Hymne an den Unendlichen' (Schiller) for accompanied S.A.T.B. Op. 112: no. 3.

First movement of Symphony no. 3, in D, resumed (it had been started on 24 May.)

12th. First movement of symphony finished.

15th. *Geist der Liebe* (Kosegarten).

Der Abend (Kosegarten).

Tischlied (Goethe).

Second movement of Symphony no. 3 commenced

19th. The whole symphony completed.

22nd. *Sehnsucht der Liebe* (Körner), revision of a song first composed in April 1813.

24th. *Abends unter der Linde* (Kosegarten)—first setting.

25th. *Abends unter der Linde* (Kosegarten)—second setting.

Die Mondnacht (Kosegarten).

Das Abendrot, vocal trio with PF. acc. (Kosegarten).

[1] The years 1815–1816 occupy 165 pages in O. E. Deutsch's 'Thematic Catalogue', that is, just over one-third of the book. 382 works are there listed.

26th.   'Claudine von Villa Bella' (Goethe). Three act operetta
      commenced.
27th.   *Huldigung* (Kosegarten)
      Alles um Liebe (Kosegarten).

Eighteen songs, it will be seen, were composed in this month
alone. Although it is higher than the average monthly output,
yet that year, 1815, saw the creation of a hundred and fifty songs;
the next year there were over a hundred more, and the poets
range from Goethe to Schubert's own versifying friends, and
obscure scribblers like Schmidt, of Lübeck, who wrote the words
of *Der Wanderer.*

The gibe that Schubert could set a bill of fare to music arose
because it seems, at first glance, that he set uncritically any text
that came his way. The over-abundant music appeared to be
poured out over any verse, of whatever quality, provided that it
treated of themes which appealed to him, of Nature in its burgeon-
ing Springtime, the human heart and its cries. If sometimes the
verses which we encounter in his songs seem pallid and pointless
it is because German poetry in those days simply had not the
wherewithal to supply the ardent young genius of Schubert. He
had to make do with the second-rate for there was not enough of
the first-rate to satisfy his needs. And those needs were clear cut
in his own mind; there is every evidence that from the poetic
almanachs and anthologies and collected 'Gedichte' available in
Vienna, he made a careful and discriminating selection. He was
well aware of what he wanted in a poem, second-rate or not, and
nearly all his masterpieces, large and small, were born of poems
which gave him what he wanted: a definite sentiment, a definite
scene, and, if possible, a telling last verse—or even last *line.* It is
not in his minor verse that these qualities are missing, but frequently in his choice of texts from the major poets—in the high-
flown and rhetorical work of Schiller for instance. Amongst the
1815 Schiller songs is an attractive lyric *Lied: Es ist so angenehm,
so süss,* and it is an ironical fact that Schiller's authorship is disputed. The words are probably by Karoline von Wolzogen, an
early friend and patron of the poet.

In considering Schubert's choice of poetry, with its ap-

preciable amount of indifferent verse, we are faced with two
questions. The first is whether great poetry serves the ends of
music at all well. Has it not such self-sufficiency, such verbal
music of its own, that added music is apt to slow down the swift
thought and nullify the melody of the words? Shelley's 'Music,
when soft voices die' has attracted many composers, big and
small, since it was penned. Its verse is so melodious, its thought of
the essence of lyrical poetry. Is that not precisely why all its composers have failed in their settings? Take as an example from
Schubert, Goethe's text *An den Mond*. This is a fine and famous
poem, most deep in feeling and musically expressed. Schubert's
first setting, of 19 August 1815, is a plain, strophic song, quite
unenterprising. His second setting, written shortly afterwards, is
'onrunning', and ambitiously sets out to match Goethe. The
music is certainly an evocation of the serene moonlight—soft,
melancholy, and richly harmonised. Every care is lavished in the
workmanship, especially in the 'river' stanza. But the song fails to
reach the heart of the poem. Goethe's blended moods of content
and unrest, and the expression of them, are beyond any music.
Schubert catches the broad indication, but cannot possibly present the poet's detailed music.

The second question is this: is it not being wise after the event
to condemn Schubert for a lack of discrimination in setting
verses by his contemporary poets? Who of today could be certain,
however sure his taste and judgement, of discriminating amongst
modern poetry in a way that critics a hundred years hence would
applaud? The young composer of today who sets to music the
verses of Dylan Thomas and Robert Graves and Ezra Pound
cannot be sure what the critics of A.D. 2058 will say of his taste in
these matters. And if he, from time to time, should set to music
those poems by relatively obscure people which he finds in the
literary periodicals of today, he can be even less sure. But *we*
should probably commend his taste. The music critics of Schubert's own day commended his choice of poetic texts, if they
touched on the subject at all. As to Schubert's readiness to compose for any text which came his way—there is definite evidence
to the contrary. He refused, almost obstinately, to set to music

some half-a-dozen poems which were urged upon him by interested people, and not lightly urged. Two were poets: Johann Friedrich Rochlitz (1769–1842), the author of 'Der erste Ton', and Johann von Zedlitz (1790–1862), the author of the famous Napoleonic ballad 'Die nächtliche Heerschau'. Schubert refused both poems. The third of these persons was the singer Anna Milder-Hauptmann, who asked him, in her letters of 1825, to set Leitner's poem 'Der Nachtschmetterling' and if that did not please him, Goethe's 'Verschiedene Empfindungen an einem Platz'. But he ignored both her suggestions. Finally, an acquaintance, Albert Schellmann, an accomplished pianist, asked him to set his love poem 'Das Sternchen' to music so that it could serve as a valentine. But Schubert declined the request.[1]

German lyric poetry during the eighteenth century is represented in Schubert by widely diverse figures: Herder (1744–1803), Klopstock (1724–1803) and Johann Peter Uz (1720–1796). A consideration of Herder's supreme position can be left until Schubert's songs of later years. The young composer's settings of Klopstock and Uz are dutiful rather than inspired. *An Sie* and the engrossing *Die frühen Gräber* by Klopstock are two small songs of great charm: they contain workmanship so delicate that it goes unnoticed. *Die Sommernacht* is an unknown song because of its continuing exclusion from anthologies of the composer's songs. It needs an intelligent singer, for the episodic music requires skilful presentation; but the song is a lesser masterpiece. *Das Rosenband* (1815) and *Edone* (1816) are also rarely sung, but both, especially the second, are satisfying examples of his lyric forms—tuneful, with touches of poetry in the accompaniments. J. P. Uz wrote polished verses in the fashionable Anacreontic vogue of the day; unfortunately the best of Schubert's settings of six of his poems is the mutilated *An Chloen* (1816). Settings of Johann Georg Jacobi (1740–1814), like Uz an Anacreontic stylist, but more lyrical, are over-shadowed by the supreme and celebrated

---

[1] Since the above was written a lost letter from Schubert to the poet J. G. Seidl has come to light: 4 August 1828. Schubert declines a poem offered to him by Seidl since he could not discover in it anything at all which was suitable for music. ('Music & Letters', ed. by Eric Blom, October 1956.)

Litany for All Souls' Day (1816), but this is not perhaps fair to the delightfully fresh song *Die Perle*, a modest example of Schubert's thematic development, by which the whole song, accompaniment and melody, arises from the first two bars of the voice part.

A group of minor German poets, who were of the generation previous to Schubert, provided him in those years with some hundred poems, and they were clothed with a varied music which at no point touches sublimity, but is at all points charming, melodious and full of gentle poetry. L. C. Hölty (1748–1776) died even younger than Schubert; his small scale, fluent verses have none of the fire and strangeness of the 'Romantic' movement, yet foretell unmistakably that pathos and melancholy which were so fashionable in Schubert's Vienna after the upheavals of the Napoleonic wars. *Die Mainacht* is a strophic song in D minor, in which Schubert writes a characteristic, sad-sweet tune to match the poet's fluting nightingale; *Seligkeit* is a merry Ländler dance, which does not quite, perhaps, hit off Hölty's kind of bliss, but which gives one of its own—more intense and earthy. Two masterpieces are *An den Mond: Geuss, Lieber Mond* written on the same day as the previous song, 17 May 1815, and *Klage an den Mond* of almost exactly a year later. (Hölty's obsession with the moon as a poetic symbol is a psychological indication of much interest.) Each of these moon-poems is a good example of Schubert's 'modified-strophic' song, in which the endless changes he makes defy classification: one can only give instances. *An den Mond* has four verses; the first and last are set to a brooding tune in F minor (12/8), the second and third to a contrasting one in F major (4/4). *Klage an den Mond* is more refined; the 6/8 tune in F major for the first verse—the happy past— is differently, more poignantly, harmonised for the second verse —the regretful present; the third verse, which foretells the poet's early death, is newly composed but its melody has affinities with the former one. The music redeems the almost morbid sentiments.

Ludwig Kosegarten (1758–1818), a country priest in Rügen, North Germany, wrote of homely themes but with a somewhat pretentious style. Schubert was enthusiastically absorbed with his work during the summer and autumn months of 1815. On one

day, October 19, he set seven of this poet's works to music, and
in the 'calendar' for July, given above, we can see his engross-
ment. Two of the seven October songs are to the poet's lady,
Rosa; *An Rosa*, I and II, are both short, and altogether overlooked. But they are melodious and warmly harmonised, and they
lie in hand and voice so comfortably that a singer and a pianist
would find them an excellent change in a Schubert programme.
A third song from the incredible day is *Luisens Antwort*, which
deserves a mention, since, apart from its own small merit, it has
an outside interest. The poem was written by Kosegarten as an
'answer' to one by Klamer Schmidt called *Lied der Trennung*.
Schmidt's pathetic poem is the heart-broken farewell of a lover to
his Luise, certain that she will forget him. Kosegarten makes the
girl answer with eternal vows of devotion. The interest lies in the
fact that Mozart set the first to music in Vienna, on 23 May 1787,
and Schubert set the pendant to music twenty-eight years later:
Schubert answering Mozart. *Das Sehnen* is a more characteristic
and passionate song, and in *Die Mondnacht* we have the best of
the series, with touches of Schubertian harmonic piquancies and
poetic fancy. The last song, the only Kosegarten setting in 1816,
An die untergehende Sonne is rather cloying and too long drawn
to challenge comparison with *Die Mondnacht*.

   Friedrich von Matthisson (1761–1831), a native of Saxony,
theologian turned poet, who earned his living as a Professor of
Economics, had been praised by Schiller: perhaps a dubious recommendation where Schubert is concerned. He wrote Nature
poetry, not leading to gentle melancholy and introspection like
Hölty, but purely descriptive and eventually monotonous. He is
the author of twenty of Schubert's texts. Oddly enough, the settings of 1814 are more interesting, on the whole, than the later
ones of 1815 and 1816. The group is less attractive than those of
Hölty and Kosegarten. The best of the Matthisson songs are the
pure, nobly conceived *Entzückung* (1816) and the *Todtenkranz
für ein Kind* with its very original harmonies (1815). He is the
author of a number of Schubert's part-songs.

   The last of this group of poets is Johann von Salis-Seewis
(1762–1834), a Swiss poet; Schubert's settings of his poems are

very slight, but there is solemnity in the music he wrote for the famous poem *Lied: in's stille Land*, and *Der Herbstabend* is beautifully written for the voice. Both songs are of March 1816. There was a last setting of Salis, five years later, *Der Jüngling an der Quelle*, which is wholly Schubertian and irresistable.

Goethe's advent in German literature can be compared with his advent in Schubert's cognisance. Just as Goethe's stature dwarfs the poets before him, so do Schubert's Goethe songs dwarf his previous efforts. Not that Schubert works always on the scale of *Gretchen am Spinnrade* and the *Erlking*. The song *Rastlose Liebe* of May 1815 is one of the great Goethe songs, as are the 'Harper' songs (from the novel *Wilhelm Meister*) and *An Schwager Kronos* of 1816; but there are smaller love songs and lyric moods which show equally his excited genius. *Am Flusse* of February 1815, in his stormy-melancholy key, D minor, is of the true Schubertian gold, but its patch-work construction makes it inferior to the second, serene setting of 1822 (see page 203). The D minor song is almost a miniature *Gretchen*, with a similar climax of emotional transport (at 'meiner Treue Hohn'). A more successful song on the same theme of regret for past love, less passionate, but flawlessly constructed, is the lovely *Erster Verlust* of July 1815. The lightly melodious *Heidenröslein* and *Die Spinnerin* of August, the two settings of *Meeresstille* of 20 and 21 June, are such perfect translations of the poems into musical images, and so in keeping with the poet's own pronouncements on the function of music in song, that one can only conclude that Goethe never looked at the volume which Spaun sent to him, nor sought anyone else's judgement in the matter.

At the other end of the scale there is a handful of Goethe songs which are entirely lacking in appeal. Such songs as *Der Rattenfänger*, *Der Gott und die Bajadere* and *Bundeslied* are frankly tedious.

In the September or early October of 1815 comes the most familiar incident in the Schubertian biography, the composition of the *Erlking*. Most familiar: because the *Erlking*, for a hundred years after its composition, was considered to be his supreme effort in song; and the grisly subject, a perfect example of 'Romantic' scare-mongering, perfectly written by Goethe, gave it a popularity over and above its music; and so his friends vied with each other in recording the incidentals of its composition. Unhappily, it is impossible, unless one shrinks from challenging them and allows oneself to be lulled into uncritical acceptance, to believe that they remembered and chronicled accurately. Genius, we know, is incalculable; but Schubert's fingers were not. How long would it take even him to write out the song—'to whelm it on to paper', 'to get it on to paper as quickly as he could write'? Remembering that copying a song may take longer than composing it—when the composer is Schubert—even so the act of writing out the *Erlking* would surely take three hours or so? He composed the song *Amphiaros* in March 1815, and on the manuscript he wrote 'in 5 hours'; *Erlking* is about three-quarters the length of *Amphiaros*. Let the reader experiment with a few bars. This makes Spaun's story (the chief source) at once improbable. He wrote that he and Mayrhofer called on Schubert one afternoon to find him pacing up and down a room excitedly ('glühend') reading the ballad; he then sat down and in the shortest time, as quickly as he could write, the magnificent song was on paper. Then the three hurried to the *Stadtkonvikt* (a matter of nearly an hour's walk), for Schubert, Spaun tells us, had no piano, and there the song was first sung, and Ruczicka explained and praised the famous dissonance between the semitones in voice and pianoforte at the boy's cry 'Mein Vater!'. Spaun wished, and quite understandably, to convey a sense of urgency in his story of the incident, as if to correlate the rush of the rider through the midnight forest with Schubert's whelming the song on to paper. It was not a sheet of memoranda, it should be noticed, which would make the anecdote credible, for Ruczicka also played the song from the manuscript. But cold facts are against the story; we cannot imagine Spaun and Mayrhofer waiting for three hours while the song was written out, or if we can the interest evaporates. And could even Schubert achieve the perfect balance and artful workmanship in quite so impromptu a fashion? We know his almost unvarying practice (well established by 1815) of preliminary sketches: why should he abandon it for this important song? The truth is probably that we have in the records a telescoping of two or even more incidents: Schubert was pacing the room in the final stages of writing out the composition when the friends called, or else he 'whelmed' down some sketches for the song, and Ruczicka's playing came later on in the year.

The song was instantly popular in the Schubert circle; and after its publication (see page 104) continued to grow in popularity and esteem. Today perhaps we feel that Goethe's and Schubert's genius were both devoted in the ballad to elevating a fundamentally trivial idea. The assiduous attention given by later song writers to reality and psychological truth in the choice of song-texts increases our feeling that the *Erlking* is merely an artificial folk-ballad and its only emotion that of mock-horror (see how this modern tendency, however, gives greater lustre to *Gretchen am Spinnrade*). Schubert's harmonic boldness, his fresh and dramatic modulation, the vital melody in the *Erlking*—these are not one whit tarnished by our changed attitude to the text.

The exceeding difficulty of the accompaniment, graphic though it may be in conveying the horror of the ride, has contributed something to the fame of the song. Gustav Barth, a conductor of the Viennese Male-voice Choir Association ('Männergesang-verein'), told Friedländer in the 1880's that Schubert, when accompanying his father (Josef Barth), always played the right hand octaves as quavers, not triplets; Schubert said to Barth that others could play the triplets if they wished—they were too difficult for *him*. The story is vouched for by the existence of an autograph MS. in which the octaves are so written. It was probably Schubert's own copy which he used in accompanying singers of the ballad. As a contrast to this simplification of the composer's, it is on record that Liszt, whenever he accompanied the great French singer Adolphe Nourrit in the song, played the left hand runs in *octaves*.

In the two years 1815 and 1816 Schubert set most of the familiar 'Wilhelm Meister' songs. Mignon's pathetic and well loved song *Nur wer die Sehnsucht kennt* was composed three times, the first setting, of 1815, in F major is the best. *Kennst du das Land?* was also written in 1815; it remains an unloved setting of a much loved lyric. The third of Mignon's songs *So lasst mir*

scheinen, from September 1816, is fragmentary. The three songs
of the Harper were all written in that September. *An die Türen* was
Schubert's first and only setting of the text, and was published as
Op. 12: no. 3. But *Wer sich der Einsamkeit ergibt*, already attempted in 1815, is set again, this time magnificently. It is the
well-known song, Op. 12: no. 1. Schubert's favourite of the
three poems, whose words he must surely have applied to his
own circumstances, is *Wer nie sein Brod mit Thränen ass*. He set
this poem to music three times; all three settings, obviously
evolving from each other, were written in the September of 1816,
but he probably revised the third one in 1822 when it was published as Op. 12: no. 2. The first two settings are eclipsed by the
third and this is a pity, for the second is a masterpiece equally as
great as the third, although more rugged, perhaps, and un-
restrained. Its tonality is unbelievable for its period. Compare
this passage, for example, with anything by Beethoven from 1816
(his Sonata in A, Op. 101, would serve the purpose):

Ex.7

nie sein Brot mit Thrä ——· nen   ass

The criticism is sometimes made that Schubert did not fully understand Goethe. It would never have been made if it were not for the later, more elaborate, one could almost say, more obsequious, treatments of Goethe's texts. Schubert seeks always to evoke with his music a mood as close to the poet's as he can accomplish, as he did in *Gretchen am Spinnrade*, and in the song just considered. The evocation can occasionally convey the more vivid impression: in *Rastlose Liebe* the tempestuous beat of the music tells us more clearly what is in the poet's mind than his words dare do.

There remains the small group of songs which, in 1815 and 1816, Schubert composed on texts written by the friends of his own circle, chief among them Mayrhofer and Schober. The latter merely 'tried his hand' at poetry and had no serious vocational purpose like Mayrhofer. The first song in the tuneful series of Schober settings is the evergreen *Am Bach im Frühling* (1816). The great Mayrhofer songs were not written till 1817; the two outstanding ones of 1816 are the *Lied: an die Dioskuren* and the *Fragment aus dem Aeschylus*. The subjects of these two poems show Mayrhofer exploiting the short 'classical' revival which followed the *Storm and Stress* movement in Germany. Schubert used his dark, nocturnal key of A flat for both the songs; his noble and sombre style creates the mood of the two poems.

The song *Der Wanderer*, whose fame during the nineteenth century was exceeded only by the *Erlking*, was written in October 1816. On his early manuscripts Schubert gave the poet's name, wrongly, as Zacharias Werner, which is as it appeared in the anthology where he found the poem. It was an anthology of poems for public recitation, published in Vienna, 1815. In 1821, when the song was first published by Cappi & Diabelli, the poet's name was correctly given as Schmidt of Lübeck. There are two versions of the song, the earlier differing very slightly from the later one; it is called, however, *Der Unglückliche*. The poet altered the title later on to *Der Fremdling*. Schubert also altered the title, and called the second version of his song *Der Wanderer*. When he transposed the song into B minor for his employer, Count Esterházy, in 1818, he humorously added on the title-page:

> *Der Wanderer:* or
> *Der Fremdling:* or
> *Der Unglückliche.*

He was never to know that it was introduced into France in 1835, by a baritone from the Opéra, as *The Wandering Jew*. The popularity of *Der Wanderer* in the nineteenth century was excessive; today it is abandoned. It is the same with *Ave Maria, Serenade* (words by Rellstab) and *Hark! hark! the Lark!*, whose worth remains as high as ever but whose appeal has, for today's listener, temporarily faded.

III

Four symphonies were composed during these two years of schoolmastering. They are:

no. 2, in B flat: 10 December 1814–24 March 1815,
no. 3, in D: 24 May–19 July 1815,
no. 4, in C minor: Spring 1816–completed 27 April 1816,
no. 5, in B flat: September–3 October 1816.

In all probability they were performed after composition by an amateur orchestral group which had grown out of the Schubert family string quartet. This orchestral society met first in the house of a merchant named Franz Frischling, who lived in the Dorotheergasse; the house was in the Inner City quite near the Augustinian Church. In the autumn of 1815, requiring more space, the orchestra moved to the residence of one Otto Hatwig, in the Schottenhof. Hatwig was a violinist at the Burg theatre and for two years or so he conducted the society. Schubert undoubtedly played the viola in this orchestra,[1] and two of the woodwind players, Josef Doppler (clarinet) and Ferdinand Bogner (flute) became his friends and we meet their names again in his story.

These early symphonies of Schubert, like the string quartets of the *Konvikt* years, are unmistakably the work of an original artist, using the familiar idiom of his day; they are not immature, and are not imitative of Haydn or Mozart or Beethoven (save possibly the first movement of the fourth, in C minor), and they are only separated from the later symphonies in B minor and C major, because they are the work of a young genius, who like all other young artists, grew, and enriched his resources, and deepened his thought. The vital melodic charm of these four works, their varied harmony and their orchestral fancy, give them an appeal which is often lacking in the mature symphonies of other composers. Schubert's stature grows when the true worth of these symphonic movements is admitted. When Dvořák was in America he wrote an article in 'The Century Magazine' deploring the neglect of these early symphonies of Schubert, and proudly stating the number of times he had conducted them at various concerts.[2]

The symphonies in B flat major (a key in which he can hardly go wrong) no. 2 and no. 5, are the best of the four. The variations of the earlier one, innocently happy, and transparently scored, and the ardent melodies of the *Andante con moto* in no. 5, provide the best music. The excellent development of his thematic material, especially in the finale of no. 2, and the first movement of no. 5, heralds the powerful work of the 1820's. His magnificent gifts in this sphere have been mentioned in connection with the

[1] Full details of the history of the orchestra were given by Leopold Sonn-leithner in his memoirs; these were published in 1861–1863 in the 'Rezension und Mitteilungen über Theatre und Musik', Vienna. The issue for 15 June 1862 contains the orchestra's story.

[2] 'The Century Magazine', Vol. 48, no. 3, July 1894.

voice part of his songs; in instrumental work his full achievement is not so well known. Nineteenth-century judgements on it
seem almost perverse; he prefers to repeat his themes, we are told,
rather than attempting to develop them. Perhaps this book, by
quotation and reference, may do something to modify that
opinion.

The D major Symphony, no. 3, is a slighter, but charming
work, and its finale is a madcap affair—one of the first of his
orchestral movements to captivate an audience. The fourth symphony was given the title 'Tragic' by Schubert himself, but that
was some time after its composition. It is the only symphony,
apart from the 'Unfinished', whose first movement proper is in a
minor key. The title, of course, goes appropriately enough with
'C minor' as an abstraction, but most inappropriately with Schubert's light-footed dance in the opening *Allegro Vivace*. This
movement imitates certain procedures in the corresponding movement of Mozart's G minor Symphony, but not in a very assured
fashion. But there is a superb slow movement. The expressive
and shapely melody of this *Andante*, the *ostinato* accompaniment
figure, which suddenly takes on a glorious life of its own, the contrasting section in F minor, and later, in B flat minor, all contribute to Schubert's greatest symphonic movement before 1822
brought the 'Unfinished' Symphony to birth. The contrasting
section mentioned starts with a *staccato* theme in the first violins:

which is treated in imitation between the violins and 'cellos. An
'echo' phrase, very much in the manner of his songs, then appears,
and suddenly his full lyrical and poetic powers take control. The
phrase *b* of Ex. 8 above, 'echoed' between strings and woodwind,
evolves into this cadence:

Ex.8(b)   Clar.

pp

An air of contentment seems to settle over the orchestra, and the woodwind are given a long-drawn melody based on the cadential phrase quoted. The accompaniment derives from the phrase *a* in Ex. 8. It is a thoroughly Schubertian, thoroughly delightful, movement. The coda breaks away from pattering semiquaver figures into a slower, triplet rhythm in exactly the same way as the *Andante con moto* of the great C major Symphony. The last two movements fall below this standard.

Amongst the numerous dances—waltz, Ländler, écossaise—which he wrote for the piano during 1815 and 1816 there is the famous dance in A flat called by Schubert a 'Waltz' in one manuscript, a 'Deutscher', i.e. a 'Deutscher Tanz' ('German dance') in a second, and a 'Ländler' in a third, which became extremely popular in his own day. It was first published as no. 2 of the thirty-six dances in his Op. 9 in 1821, entitled by Diabelli, its publisher, the 'Trauerwalzer' ('Mourning Waltz'); this foolish name much amused the composer. It was re-printed several times, supplied with words, and even ascribed to Beethoven. Schubert had given his friend Anselm Hüttenbrenner a copy on 14 March 1818 and the dance in this version, combined with a waltz by Hummel, was published in 1826 by Schott's Sons, Mainz, as 'Sehnsucht' Waltz—by Beethoven! The error was quickly pointed out both by Anton Schindler, Beethoven's friend, and by an anonymous writer in the Leipzig 'Allgemeine Musikzeitung'. The waltz, still popular today, and known to the vast public of non-Schubertians by its use in the bastard 'Lilac Time' ('And she shall wear on her bosom, the fair lilac blossom'), is said to resemble an 'Arietta' in Henneburg's opera 'Der Jurist und der Bauer'.[1]

---

[1] This alleged resemblance was discussed in the Vienna 'Musik Zeitschrift' for February 1957. The quotation there of the 'Arietta' completely absolves Schubert of any plagiarisation.

It is a graceful example of his style in waltz-writing; but only in later years, with waltzes such as the delightful one in C sharp minor (Op. 50: no. 13), does he fully reveal how his melody could elevate and refine this homely form.

IV

1817 opens with Schubert installed in Schober's home in the Inner City. The house was called 'Zum Winter' and stood in the Tuchlauben. He hoped, doubtless, to earn his living by the sale of his compositions, by taking music pupils, by a success in the theatre. Schober, it is clear, provided him with lodging for which payments could be made whenever Schubert was in funds. It is not true that he gave Schubert room and board free; the debt to Schober of 190 florins (£19) which appears in Schubert's posthumous records, settled from the sale of his compositions within a year, was due for food and lodging. But at least the composer was free of the schoolroom routine, and his days were unhampered. He was doing what he wanted to do. If to his father and brothers his action seemed precipitate and fraught with uncertainty, and taken against all their advice and warning, it is because they were up against genius, and not talent. Talent compromises; but genius will get its own way. It tears the constraining bands; there may be agony in the doing, and the resulting wounds may profusely bleed, but nevertheless it tears them. We can only guess at Schubert's mental conflict in this rupture; his father's was more understandable. To Franz Theodor music in Vienna was not merely a precarious livelihood; it also meant that his youngest son would mix with a society of men whose moral laxity and standards of living were anathema to the strict Catholic that he was. It is fortunate that he was unable to foresee how his anxiety would be tragically realised.

In the early part of 1817, probably in March, Vogl and Schubert met. Schober's brother-in-law, Giuseppe Siboni, was an actor at the Kärntnertor Theater and through him Schober had made the acquaintance of the Court Opera singer Johann Michael Vogl. Vogl was nearing the end of a long, arduous and successful career on the boards. He was a cultured, dignified man, but in his earnestness there was, according to contemporary witness, a taint of charlatanism. Schober prevailed upon him to come to his home and meet Schubert and hear some of the young composer's songs. There are various records of the meeting. Schubert, who had as a boy venerated the singer, was discomfited by his rather stately presence. Vogl was on his guard. So many young composers had shown him their work; it did not do to encourage them too warmly when he could do so little to further their ambitions. But something happened as the two men talked and then tried over the songs. How could it not? Vogl was a composer himself, and of songs, and of quite interesting ones. He sang *Augenlied, Schäfers Klagelied,* and the just-composed *Ganymed;* he was impressed. He left Schubert with words of advice about not squandering ideas; he said the composer was 'zu wenig Comödiant, zu wenig Charlatan'—'too little of an actor, too little of a charlatan'! But soon after this first meeting, there were others, and now Vogl was seeking Schubert and exploring that treasury of songs. One career was over; the career by which he was to immortalise his name was about to begin.

Spaun wrote of Schubert in those days in his pamphlet 'Einige Bemerkungen' ('Some Observations'). His remarks were a kind of protest against the preliminary biographical sketch of the composer written by Heinrich von Kreissle and published in 1861. Spaun objected to the description of Schubert in Kreissle's work: he is there spoken of as having 'negroid' features, being a spendthrift and a contractor of debts, and an indulgent eater and drinker. The last accusation lingers on into modern biographies. Spaun's protests are convincing. He says Schubert was neither ugly, nor were his features 'negroid'. On the contrary, when he smiled or was talking ardently about subjects which interested him, his face glowed, his eyes lit up and he became almost handsome. Nor was he fat and paunchy: no sign of it, no talk of it, says Spaun. (In this connection we might wonder whether Schubert's later nickname of 'Schwammerl', which means a small mushroom, might not have referred to his diminutive stature as much as to his corpulence, as is usually assumed.) Spaun also asserts vigorously that he was moderate both in eating and drinking; they

supped together daily for years, and only once during that time—
a hot summer's day in the nearby village of Grinzing—did Spaun
ever know Schubert to be the worse for drink. His nature was
loyal and affectionate; and if his worst enemy had composed
something beautiful he would have been delighted with it. These
reminiscences of Spaun are full of interest and important as a
source; they were written in 1864, but the manuscript was not
recovered until May 1935, which accounts for their having no
effect on nineteenth century biographies of the composer.

Schubert, according to Spaun, possessed no piano while he
lived in the family house in the Säulengasse. Did access to an excellent instrument in the Schober's home lead to the series of
pianoforte sonatas in the year 1817? We have no certain means of
knowing but it seems very probable. There is also the fact that
although the stream of *Lieder* still flows, it is obvious that even
Schubert has exhausted for the time being his urge to song-
writing. Another medium proved at once a powerful attraction.
Up to this time Schubert had written very little sustained work
for the piano. There are two fragmentary sonatas from 1815.
The first, in E major, has no finale. There exists a sketch for the
first movement, which was published in the supplementary volume
of the 'Gesamtausgabe', in 1897; it is interesting to see from the
sketch that Schubert actually toned down some of his first,
startling modulatory ideas when he came to compose the final
draft of the movement.

The second sonata, in C major, followed in September. It is an
inferior work and it, too, lacks a finale, although the autograph
manuscript suggests that there may have been a fourth movement,
subsequently lost. When, in 1927, Walter Rehberg completed
and published the sonata, he used an undated *Allegretto* in C
major by Schubert (D. 346) as material for his finale. This *Allegretto* is a fragment, but it surely belongs to a later date than 1815.
As a matter of fact, a fragment of the missing finale is almost certainly to be found on a rough draft of the 1815 setting of 'Nur
wer die Sehnsucht kennt'. It is part of a 'Rondo' in C major,
2/4, for the pianoforte, dated 'October 1815'; the date is fairly
convincing. A set of vigorous and characteristic variations known

as the 'Ten Variations in F major' was another work of 1815 (February).

In August 1816 Schubert composed his third sonata, in E major. He was evidently not satisfied with the first scherzo, and so wrote a second for the work. Its five movements were published posthumously, and known for a very long time, as 'Fünf Klavier-stücke' ('Five Piano-pieces'). Then, in 1930, a part of the auto-graph manuscript came to light, and was found to be entitled 'Sonata: August 1816'. The conjectural date previously given to the work was 1817. Ferdinand includes the sonata in the list of his brother's compositions (the key misprinted as F major), so that the manuscript was in his hands in 1839. By 1843 he had sold it to the Leipzig publisher, C. A. Klemm, who dropped the un-fashionable title 'Sonata', and included *both* scherzos. Alois Fuchs also listed the work in his unpublished thematic catalogue of Schubert's compositions (prepared about 1842), but described it there as a fragment, consisting of first movement and part of an 'Allegro' (this would be the first scherzo). This is how the manu-script survives in America today, with a part of the finale in the Vienna City Library. If, in view of these fragments, and Fuchs' entry, we try to conjecture what, exactly, Ferdinand sent to Klemm at Leipzig, a mystery grows, for which there is no solution.

Why is the sonata ignored by pianists? The Schubert critic, Ludwig Scheibler, has protested that the composer's early piano-forte music (1815–1819) is largely neglected by pianists and piano-teachers. This Sonata in E major has a perfectly written first movement, intimate in tone, and richly inventive; the slow movement is a 'Nocturne', pathetic rather than passionate, and the finale is a most original movement called by Schubert 'pate-tico'. He never used the term but this once: he was probably using it, if we judge by the style of the music itself, as an equivalent of the German 'pathetisch', which means 'with pomp', 'oratorically', and not 'pathetic'. As for the scherzos: either is a worthy move-ment, and a player need not include both in a performance. Perhaps the first is the better of the two—an early masterpiece of Schubert's for the keyboard.

One other fragmentary piece was written during 1816, or possibly early 1817, although the manuscript is not dated. It is the start of a PF. Sonata in E minor. It has never been published and is quoted here complete for the first time:

Ex.9 *Allegro*   Sonata in E minor **(1816-7)**

The manuscript of this promising movement is in the Vienna
City Library.

In 1817 Schubert obviously set out to explore the possibilities
of the sonata as a form and the pianoforte as a medium. His
newly won freedom, the brief respite from daily and uncongenial
toil, produced a spate of compositions for the piano which are

full of imaginative resource and variety, records of adventures into unexplored realms of music. There are, altogether, six PF. Sonatas of 1817. One is incomplete, having no minuet or scherzo, and another is fragmentary. Their composition extends from March till November. A great deal of research and scholastic sifting of evidence went on during the two Wars in connection with these six works, for in them reside nearly all the chronological problems and difficulties of the ordering of Schubert's sonatas. It is necessary to see the Schubert sonatas chronologically. 'Whoever follows Schubert by way of the sonatas in the order in which they were composed will assuredly see his life under a new aspect. For such a series of compositions is carved, as it were, from the master's very life—indeed a master's works *are* his true biography. They are the everlasting, into which the transitory is commuted.'[1]

His first sonata of the year, composed in March, is in A minor; it was not published until thirty-six years later, as Op. 164. Because the nineteenth century knew only Ferdinand's year-date —1817—it was placed at the end of the series of six sonatas and erroneous conclusions were drawn about its style and construction. The manuscript, in the Paris 'Conservatoire' Library, leaves no doubt as to the date of composition. The work is a typical example of early Schubert and forms an apt prologue to the subsequent five other sonatas, for its technical aspects, and its rather timid attempts at development and ornamentation, were all richly amplified in the following months. The first movement, for example, contains a device for building development sections, which in various forms may be found throughout his work: the repeated sequence of a basic idea that achieves harmonic, not melodic, shape by its repetitions:

Ex.10

---

[1] Professor Erwin Ratz, 'Schweizerische Musikzeitung', January 1949.

This is repeated in G major, then in F major, and leads to another sequential pattern. The detail is quoted to show that Schubert's exploration of harmonic colour in those days, led him to ignore the jolt to the ear of his chord juxtapositions. Thus, after the E major chord at the close of the phrase given above comes the dominant ninth in G major, i.e. a chord of D/F♯/A/E. This is the kind of brusque behaviour which we never find in Mozart, or Mendelssohn. But it leads to miracles of emotional and intellectual discovery. The theme of the slow movement, *Allegretto quasi Andantino* bears an interesting, but accidental, resemblance to the opening of the finale of one of Schubert's last three sonatas —in A major (Op. posth.)

The next two sonatas, dating from May, and June, are curiosities: the first because of its intrinsic music, the second for its extraordinary history. The Sonata in A flat, of May, is very slight in substance, but it has a finale in *E flat major*—an unprecedented departure from the classical tonal scheme. The work is in three movements and the minuet is probably lost; but that these three movements are an entity and not a haphazard assembly is proved by the existence of a very old copy made by, or for, Josef Witteczek in which they are also grouped under the heading 'Sonata'. Schubert's autograph copy is dated May 1817, but was not available when the work was first published, that is, in the 'Gesamtausgabe' volume of 1888. The copy is preserved in Vienna, in the Library of the *Gesellschaft der Musikfreunde*.

The fate of the next sonata, a work in a favourite key, E minor, is almost incredible. Schubert drafted a four movement work as follows:

    i. *Moderato*, in E minor,
    ii. *Allegretto*, in E major,
    iii. *Scherzo and Trio*, in A flat and D flat major,
    iv. *Rondo*, in E major.

His manuscript is dated June 1817. In this same month he started to revise the whole work, but after finishing the first movement he gave up the task. There were accordingly *two* autograph copies of the first movement. The work was not published by him and the batch of manuscripts came into the possession of his brother Ferdinand. The last movement was evidently detached from the rest, and Ferdinand did not suspect that it belonged to the other three movements. He sold it to Diabelli, who published it as Op. 145 in 1847; Diabelli prefaced the 'Rondo' with an 'Adagio', another Schubert sonata-movement. This was originally in D flat; it was cruelly, but not unskilfully, shortened and transposed into E major for the purpose of a prelude to the 'Rondo'. The story of the 'Adagio' movement can be told later (see page 68). In 1847 the conjunction of 'Adagio' and 'Rondo' was a highly fashionable pairing as can be seen from the contemporary publishers' catalogues and advertisements: Schubert's movements were butchered for the purpose of a ready sale. Meanwhile Ferdinand had sold the other three movements to the Leipzig publisher, F. Whistling, on 12 July 1842. A short while afterwards he sold the single copy of the revised first movement to Ludwig Landsberg, a well known collector of autographs. Whistling (he bought at the same time the score of the Fifth Symphony, in B flat) decided not to publish the truncated sonata and the manuscript disappeared for a time; in fact, no one knew that it existed. When, in 1888, the 'Gesamtausgabe' volume of the sonatas was printed, Landsberg's single movement was engraved, and so this Sonata in E minor appeared as a one movement work! But in 1907, in a manner by now not unfamiliar to the reader, Schubert's manuscript was unearthed from the Whistling archives; it was purchased by Professor Emil Preiger of Bonn. In May of that year Breitkopf & Härtel published the second movement, the E major *Allegretto*. Twenty-one years elapsed. In the Berlin periodical, 'Die Musik' of October 1928, as a Schubert Centenary Supplement, the third and remaining movement was published. If, to sum up, we now repeat Schubert's original scheme, with the dates of publication given beside his movements, we find this:

i. *Moderato:* published 1888,
ii. *Allegretto:* published May 1907,

iii. *Scherzo and Trio:* published October 1928,
iv. *Rondo:* published 1847.

This is surely a unique example in the history of music publication. The four movements were published as a whole, and for the
first time, in 1948 by the British & Continental Music Agencies,
London, edited by Kathleen Dale. It has been assumed throughout
the recounting of this strange story of publication, that the
'Rondo' is, in actual fact, the finale of this Sonata in E minor. It
will be recalled that the manuscript was detached. The evidence
for the assumption is, first, that a copy of the movement in the
Witteczek collection is headed—'Sonata: Rondo', and, second,
that a short sketch for the Rondo exists on the back of a song,
Lebenslied, dated December 1816. We know from these two
facts that the movement is the finale of a Sonata, and that it was
written after December 1816. The only one of Schubert's six
works which could claim such a finale is the one in E minor.

The month of June also saw the composition of the fourth
sonata of the year. It was his most ambitious effort. The key is D
flat major, and the work opens with a soaring theme based—it is
a feature of these 1817 sonata themes—on the notes of the
common chord. He sketched the movement, revised it, composed a
slow movement, almost finished the finale and then abandoned
the work. Shortly after he transposed the sonata into E flat major,
making a few changes of detail, and in this new key he finished
the finale. A third movement, Minuet and Trio, in E flat, completed the scheme. The slow movement, *Andante molto,* first
sketched in D minor, then transposed into C sharp minor for the
first conception of the work, was left unchanged in detail; it was
finally written in G minor for the second version of the sonata.
The differences between the two versions of the first movement
were examined by Hans Költzsch in his exhaustive study of Schubert's sonatas, 'Franz Schubert in seinen Klaviersonaten', published in 1928.[1] The E flat Sonata was published by Pennauer of

[1] There is a further examination by Harold Truscott, who was apparently unaware of Költzsch's work, in the 'Music Review', Cambridge,
May 1953.

Vienna two years after Schubert's death, as Op. 122. It has been stated sometimes that the publisher transposed the work into E flat to help its sales, but this is not so. Schubert himself had completed the transposition at least by November 1817; we find the trio of the third movement also used in a 'Scherzo in D flat', clearly intended for the earlier version of this sonata but then discarded; the scherzo was dated November 1817. This dating has survived by mere chance, but since it has survived, it indicates when the transposition was finished. The sonata is the best known, and on the whole the best, of the six 1817 sonatas. It is a masterly little work, full of Schubertian melodies and of the sincerest feeling. If we consider the year of its composition, it is extraordinary to find it so free of the influence of Beethoven; or if not of influence, of imitation. We can admire the young genius, who lived in the brilliance of his great contemporary, and could yet emit his own light, and while so greatly loving and admiring the music of Beethoven (he called himself Beethoven's 'admirer and worshipper'), still be himself. If a critic occasionally gives the impression that he cannot accept Schubert's ability to fill a form called 'Sonata', so hallowed by Beethoven, with so completely different a music, he has not read Capell's cogent words—'How great our loss would be if Schubert, out of piety towards Beethoven, had felt himself restricted to composing Impromptus and Moments Musicaux!' Nineteenth-century Schubertians expressed regret that the composer transposed this sonata from D flat to E flat; but it is a 'Romantic' viewpoint. The music gains, if anything, a brightness and vivacity by being removed from the richer, darker key which was so beloved by the pianist-composers of the last century.

The fifth sonata, of July, is fragmentary; it consists only of an unfinished first movement, *Allegro moderato*, in F sharp minor. The key was not a favourite one of Schubert's. Apart from this sonata movement there is only one other instrumental movement in F sharp minor, the *Andantino* of the 1828 Sonata in A major. This may be the reason why Schubert's interest in the work failed before he completed it. It is a pity, because not only is the first movement so unlike the other five sonatas of the year, it is also uniquely different from the whole field of sonata-writing in the early nineteenth century. How stiffly imitative of Mozart and Haydn, and of each other, seem the sonatas of Hummel, Kuhlau, Dussek, Clementi and the rest, when we compare their talented efforts with the original work of this young genius; his is full of faults, it stumbles, it digresses, it is of little use for finger-practice. But it is alive, spontaneous, convincing:

For the last fifty years or so, the opinion has been held by Schubert scholars that two other short piano pieces by the composer belong to this sonata. They are the Scherzo and Trio, *Allegro vivace*, in D major and B minor, and an *Allegro* in F sharp minor (unfinished); both were published in the Supplement to the 'Gesamtausgabe', 1897. The suggestion was first made by the excellent Ludwig Scheibler,[1] and Walter Rehberg actually used the two pieces when he published a completed version of the sonata in 1928. Recently I examined for the first time Schubert's manuscript of these two pieces in the Vienna City Library, and at first it seemed as though the theory were untenable. The scherzo and finale are both written on the same folded sheet of music paper, and embedded between them is this cancelled fragment of a song:

[1] 'Die Rheinlande', Düsseldorf, 1905, p. 271.

Ex.12

ge-gen das Thor

Sie lauscht zum brau-sen-de wind

[sic]

Eventually I identified these bars as the continuation of the unfinished song *Lorma* (D. 327), composed on 28 November 1815.
It seemed impossible to reconcile the co-existence of this 1815
song-fragment composed when Schubert was living at home,
with two sonata movements written when he was lodging in
Schober's house in 1817. But in an extraordinary fashion, this apparent contradiction is a strong support for the theory. The first
movement itself, dated 'July 1817', was also written on manuscript paper containing music from 1815! This was part of the
Mass in B flat of November 1815, the same *month* as *Lorma*.
Schubert evidently economised at that period by using up half-
empty sheets of music paper from the previous years. Such
a practice keeps the Schubertian cataloguer intrigued—and
wisely non-committal about dates and styles if there is any
doubt.

The last work of the year in this form was composed, or at
least sketched, in August. It is the Sonata in B major, published
by Diabelli in 1843 as Op. 147. The manuscript sketch is in the

possession of the *Gesellschaft der Musikfreunde*, Vienna, and is dated August 1817. It is possible that the sonata was not completed till the following year, since a copy made by Albert Stadler for a young woman named Josefine von Koller, an excellent pianist living, like Stadler, in Steyr, is dated 'August 1818'. Second only to the E flat Sonata in accomplishment and in the attractiveness of its melody, it exceeds even that in the poetry and fancy of its music. It is an epilogue, as fitting in its way as the A minor Sonata of March was for prologue, to the 1817 series of sonatas.

Of all Schubert's early compositions, these sonatas form the most distinguished group and show most clearly what he was to achieve in his maturity. They are, of course, the products of a young, still growing artist; but it is only in imagination and perception that we are conscious of his youth; in style, in structure, and in originality of material, he is already mature.

Before the sonatas of his maturity were written, those wonderful 'nine' commencing with the A minor Sonata, Op. 143, there are a few unfinished sonatas, tentative essays which failed to interest him very deeply; and there is one substantial fragment in F minor, composed at Zseliz in September 1818, which may be glanced at here. It is a wild, stormy affair, with tender episodes— Schubert's 'Sonata appassionata'. The first movement is of great promise, but breaks off at the point of recapitulation; it begins with this theme, pregnant with Beethovenian possibilities, but which, characteristically, produces instead a thoroughly original development section:

There is a magnificent scherzo, in E major, and the finale resumes
the headlong rush of the first movement. A point of remarkable
interest in connection with this sonata is the fate of its slow movement, an *Adagio* in D flat. This was possibly written later on
when Schubert returned to Vienna (in November) and was used
by Diabelli as the basis for the *Adagio* prelude for Op. 145; this
work has already been discussed. The original form of the movement, before Diabelli's hack got to work on it, can be seen in the
appropriate section of the 'Revisionsbericht' of the 'Gesamtausgabe', where it is printed in full. Schubert's original manuscript is
lost, but a copy existed in the invaluable Witteczek collection and
from this the printed version was made. We can deduce the fact
that this *Adagio* in D flat *is* the slow movement of the F minor
Sonata for this reason. An old manuscript catalogue of compositions by Schubert for the piano, and for piano and violin,
compiled by Ferdinand for the publisher Diabelli, was still extant
in 1930, and in the possession of Kreissle's descendants. In this
catalogue the F minor Sonata is listed, and the *incipits* of four
movements are quoted. That of the second movement is given
thus (R. H. only):

but even with that error of copying the work is recognisable. It
has never been included with the F minor Sonata; the editors of
the 'Gesamtausgabe' did not know of Diabelli's catalogue, and
although they did reprint the *Adagio*, they had no suspicion that
it was actually part of the 1818 Sonata in F minor. But a future
edition of Schubert's sonatas, in complete sequence, should restore the *Adagio* to its rightful place. It can be seen, too, how the
key of D flat naturally links the key of the first movement, F
minor, with the rather dramatic choice, for the scherzo, of the key
of E major.

There is one final specimen in his early manner, the Sonata in
A major, Op. 120. This short, sparkling and graceful work, the

most popular perhaps of all his sonatas, cannot be dated exactly. For many years it was assigned to 1825, through a misinterpretation of early catalogues. As with similar misdatings of other works of his, no suspicions seemed to have been aroused until in 1906, Ludwig Scheibler challenged the date as absurd, and brought forward evidence that suggested an earlier one—1819.[1] He quoted a letter from Albert Stadler to Ferdinand Luib, written on 17 January 1858, in which we learn that Schubert wrote a sonata for Josefine von Koller while he was staying at Steyr. Vogl, visiting Steyr in later years, collected the manuscript sonata and took it back to Schubert in Vienna. Schubert stayed at Steyr in 1819, 1823 and 1825. Scheibler suggested that the sonata in question was probably that in A major, Op. 120, and further that 1819 was the most likely year. This date is now generally accepted, and is more reasonable than 1825. But the whole question is not a simple one. Stadler went on to say in his letter that he did not know what became of the sonata; this is a rather surprising statement since it was published in 1829, and by 1858, when Stadler wrote his letter, had become fairly well known. This raises the point—was he possibly writing about the B major Sonata, Op. 147, and not the Sonata, Op. 120? His memory may have been at fault, and the fact that he copied out the sonata in B major for Josefine von Koller may have become, after the lapse of forty years, the idea that Schubert actually composed it for her. This work in B major was also published by the time that Stadler wrote to Luib, but in the year of its publication, 1845, he moved from Linz to Salzburg, and was probably too occupied with his own affairs to take note of the publication. But whatever its date, the A major Sonata remains a gem amongst the Schubert sonatas, a fulfilment of the 1817 works, and one holding out the promise of future achievement which the last nine, in their turn, amply fulfilled.

V

A more obscure field explored by the composer in 1817, obscure, that is, in comparison with the sonatas, is that of the overture. It is an odd category; the form is a fluid one and most of

[1] 'Zeitschrift der Internationalen Musik Gesellschaft', Leipzig, pp. 485–487.

Schubert's work in it is not memorable. Throughout his life he wrote twelve unattached overtures: ten are for orchestra, and two for PF. Duet. The first to show any individuality, in B flat major, had been written in September 1816 for the small orchestral society already mentioned. Characteristics of the Schubert Overture can be found in it: the *Adagio* introduction, the use of 'Sonata-form' procedures for the *Allegro* section, and the shortened development section which becomes a kind of rondo-episode. The work in B flat imitates Beethoven but is not unattractive. There is a manuscript sketch for part of this overture (bars 87–118) which, having no title, remained unidentified. O. E. Deutsch erroneously lists it in his 'Thematic Catalogue' as part of a string quartet (D. 601).[1] From this sketch we are enabled to date the '*Andante* in A' for PF. Solo (D. 604), which is written on the back of the same paper, and thus belongs apparently to the autumn of 1816. It might, possibly, be another attempt at a slow movement for the Sonata in E major of that period.

In 1817 there were three overtures for orchestra, substantial works, and as good in their way as any of the symphonic finales which he wrote at the time. The first two are both in D major, the third in C major, and all three show quite strongly the influence of Rossini, whose popularity in Vienna had, by 1817, reached almost frenzied heights, although later on, in the 1822–1823 seasons, when Rossini himself came to the capital, the frantic enthusiasm passed all reasonable limits. We read in various documents and memoirs that Schubert liked 'Il Barbiere' and 'Tancredi', and that the last act of 'Otello' delighted him. The second and third of his 1817 overtures, in D and C, have in fact been nicknamed 'in the Italian style', but not by Schubert himself; that is, he has not so entitled them on his MSS., which is the impression one receives from printed editions, programmes and catalogues. The nickname was bestowed by Ferdinand. The 'Italian style' is, of course, unmistakable, and was remarked upon at once when the overtures were performed. One of the two, the

[1] There was a correction in Deutsch's article: 'Some additions and corrections to the Schubert Catalogue', Music & Letters, London, January 1953, p. 26.

key is not given in the programme, was performed in public at
the Hall of the 'Roman Emperor ('Römische Kaiser'), Vienna,
on 1 March 1818. It was a success, and was reported, very
favourably, in newspapers of Vienna, and Dresden. In the Vienna
'Allgemeine Musikalische Zeitung' of 6 June 1818 the notice has
the words '. . . it is fashioned in the Italian style'. All three of the
1817 overtures, no. 1 in D (May), nos. 2 and 3 (November) have
an *Adagio* or *Maestoso* introduction, and after the main *Allegro*
section, in sonata-form, they conclude with a *più mosso* coda. It
would need extensive quotation to demonstrate how thoroughly
the three are thematically and technically interlinked, but one
obvious melodic connection can be quoted:

The *Adagio* introduction, and the *Vivace* coda of no. 2, in D
major, were taken over and modified for use in a later overture,
in C major, the one which Schubert wrote in 1820 for his incidental music to the play 'Die Zauberharfe'. This overture,
although it was never played in Schubert's life-time under such a
title, is now universally known as the 'Rosamunde' overture.
This is because it was published in 1827 as part of Op. 26, which
had been reserved for the items of music from 'Rosamunde'; it
was then actually called 'Overture to "Rosamunde" '. Schubert
also used the essence of the *Vivace* coda from the 'Italian' overture in D major, distilled by his mature genius, in the finale of the
D minor String Quartet (1824) and in the first movement of the
great C major Symphony (1828):

Soon after the composition of the two 'Italian' Overtures, he arranged them for PF. Duet, and these two arrangements at last found their way into print in 1872. The three 1817 overtures are strange works: productions of a genius, greater than the one he parodied; and yet, because of their immaturity, they cannot really vie with Rossini's mature and sparkling efforts.

Besides the sonatas and overtures of 1817 there are several fine pieces of chamber music for strings, and for pianoforte and violin. Altogether the three years from 1815 to 1817 were not rich in the production of chamber works, but those of 1817 form, in logical fashion, a culmination of the period. For strings alone Schubert composed the String Quartet in G minor (25 March–1 April 1815), the String Quartet in E major (probably, but not certainly, 1816), and two String Trios, both in B flat major, of which the first is unfinished (September 1816 and September 1817). The confusion in catalogues caused by the similarities between the last two works, in key, medium and dates, can be imagined.

The quartets are closely unified in style and musical content. The main theme of each first movement is a couplet: a bold, arresting figure, based on the notes of the common chord ('con brio' in G minor, 'con fuoco' in E major) is followed by a gentle, contrasting theme. The development of these elements shows a characteristic wayward quality, but it is excellently brought off, and in the E major Quartet, the instrumental colour, particularly the brilliant, wiry use of high chords on the upper strings, is admirable. The slow movements open with quiet, lyrical sections in 2/4 time, but a more dramatic interlude follows the subdued start. In the course of both slow movements there is a notable use of a technique which is to have very fruitful results in his later work for strings. The second violin and viola maintain a rhythmical accompaniment, while the 'cello and first violin sing a 'conversational' duet:

The first movements of the two String Trios are similarly alike: delicately written, lyrical from first to last, and within their slight compass, expressive of a wide range of emotion. The first String Trio (1816), contemporary with the Overture in the same key, B flat, gives an instance of Schubert's more exalted manner in a more exalted form. Both the String Trio and the Overture commence with very similar 'Allegro' subject themes, but the Trio is much more elevated in style. A few bars of the slow movement were written but the work was never finished. The second String Trio (1817) is complete. The slow movement, apart from a passage strongly imitative of Mozart, is highly original. It contains the first appearance of that passionate, stormily-lyrical interlude, which grew out of the dramatic, contrasting episodes in his early slow movements, and which Schubert loved to introduce into his mature slow movements for chamber music combinations, i.e. the *Andante con moto* of the PF. Trio in E flat (Op. 100), or the *Adagio* of the String Quintet. The finale of the String Trio starts cheerfully enough, but deepens as it goes on, and at the close there are two features of such interest that they call for mention. There is a climax built on rushing scale-passages in triplets, passed upwards from 'cello to viola, and viola to first violin, which we find repeatedly used in future string quartets; and there is a spontaneous episode clearly prompted when his mind was suddenly charmed by a chance cadential idea.

String Trio in B♭ (1817)

It is this uncalculated seizing of stray ideas, and their immediate, spontaneous expansion into poetical and emotionally wrought episodes, that proclaim the creative genius and give Schubert his charm, his enduring appeal. In this finale, the violin figure quoted above, with that slight 'differentness' in the rhythm at *a*, produces an extraordinarily fascinating sequence of ideas, and they lead to a second tense, but pianissimo, climax. This trio is the most important of the chamber works before the *Trout* Quintet.

Finally, there are four violin sonatas, and all, by the whim of publishers, were debased in their mis-namings:

1. Sonata in D major (March 1816),
2. Sonata in A minor (March 1816),
3. Sonata in G minor (April 1816),
4. Sonata in A major (August 1817).

The first three were published by Diabelli in 1836 as Op. 137, and called 'Sonatinas'; the last was published by the same firm in 1856, and called 'Duo'. In Schubert's autographs they are all entitled by him 'Sonatas', and this title should be restored. Only the first of the four is in three movements (there is no Minuet); all the rest are full scale works. It is, strangely, in the slow movements of the three 1816 sonatas that Schubert is least himself. The tentative quality of his work, which has been described, is here very apparent, and Mozart, again, is a dominating influence. The third sonata, in Schubert's most 'masculine' key—G minor—is a sturdy work, and the most popular of the three.

But the fourth sonata, in A major, Op. 162, is a different matter. It came at the end of a year which had been full of experiments with sonata-form, and together with the contemporary String Trio, it reflects the added technical assurance of its composer. The *Andantino* is a sad-sweet movement, brimming with alternate Schubertian ardour and pathos. The finale contains a theme which is a quotation from his *Cotillon* in E flat; it would justify a date of 1817 for the dance-piece.

It was said earlier in the chapter that although Schubert was more attracted to instrumental composition in 1817, nevertheless the stream of *Lieder* flowed unchecked. There were fifty or so songs that year, the largest group being eight songs on poems of Mayrhofer. These are nearly all on classical subjects, since Mayrhofer also dabbled in the fashionable practice of re-creating the ancient Greek and Roman myths, but naturally with none of Goethe's inspired psychological penetration. The 'Fahrt zum Hades' of January is a favourite piece of the Schubertian, unknown almost in the traffic of the concert-room. In March there followed six superb songs.[1] *Philoktet, Antigon und Oedip* and *Orest auf dem Tauris* exemplify his growing powers of comment in the pianoforte accompaniment and the fusion of dramatic recitative with pure melodic line in the voice part. These are more powerful still in *Der entsühnte Orest* and *Memnon* (although Memnon is a statue in Egypt, the name of the demi-god, and his legend, are Greek). The finest of the six songs is the neglected *Freiwilliges Versinken*, an address to Helios, the sun-god, in which Schubert's declamation—half song, half recitative—is magnificent. The accompaniment is a picturesque evocation of fading sunset and the rising moon.

But the best of the 1817 Mayrhofer songs is not based on a

---

[1] Two of these songs have hitherto been ascribed to September 1820 (*Der entsühnte Orest* and *Freiwilliges Versinken*). That date is of Schubert's *copies* of the songs, made later on.

Greek legend at all; it is much nearer home, much nearer Schubert's heart—*Auf der Donau*—*On the Danube*—of April. The poet's reverie on the passing of time as symbolised by the passing waters of the Danube, touched Schubert's sensitive mind deeply; a familiar sentiment, a familiar scene and the composer's response is in his best vein, a wholly admirable blending of PF. figuration and vocal melody into an indivisible whole.

To texts by Goethe there were numerous trifling songs, but also two excellent beginnings which were, unhappily, not carried through: *Gretchens Bitte* and *Mahomets Gesang*. Then there was the masterpiece of the year *Ganymed*, the song which won Vogl's allegiance, and we can understand that well enough. Goethe fashions the myth of Zeus seizing Ganymede to the Olympian heights into an image of the beauty of a summer morning catching the poet's heart to heaven. Schubert's song, in which a profusion of melodic ideas crowds the pages, suffers if it be given a finicking interpretation; singer and pianist must paint the picture in broad, generous strokes.

Another great song of the year is Schiller's *Gruppe aus dem Tartarus*. Schubert had tried his hand at the song the previous year; a fragment of his attempt is extant and reveals music of first-rate quality. But the 1817 song is yet finer. It is an almost terrifying picture—restless, chromatic, harsh—of the spirits of the damned. 'Eternity', with the image of the broken scythe of Time, is sung in C major, and the song dies away on to the muttered notes which we heard at the start, conveying the suggestion that the music circles on for ever and ever.

But the famous songs of the year are not these huge masterpieces; they are settings of minor poets like Schubart and Claudius. There is the remarkable song *An den Tod*, a setting of Schubart, but his name is perpetuated in the immortal, ever-fresh *Die Forelle* (*The Trout*). No fewer than five copies of this song, in Schubert's hand, are known (and more, we can be certain, are lost), showing its immediate popularity. Only in the last of the five copies by Schubert, in October 1821, is the 5-bar prelude of the PF. part to be found.

It is the same with two of Schober's poems which Schubert

set during March 1817. The first, *Trost im Liede*, is a serious and musicianly piece of writing, but it is *An die Musik* which immortalises the partnership of the two friends in song. The melody of this beloved address to music is as truly Schubertian as anything he wrote—intimate, ardent, and with that indefinable touch of pathos which goes to the heart. And yet, as Charles Stanford showed in a well-known piece of analysis, the constructional details of the masterpiece reward the searcher for them.[1] There are numerous autograph copies of this song also, and one of them, in the Paris 'Conservatoire' Library, written by the composer for an unknown friend, is enclosed in a small envelope inscribed—rather charmingly—'Manuscrit, très precieux'.

The third song in a trinity of popular favourites is *Der Tod und das Mädchen* (*Death and the Maiden*) to words by Claudius, composed by Schubert in February. This also deeply impressed its first hearers, and the fact that Schubert later on used the themes of *Der Tod und das Mädchen* and *Die Forelle* for variations indicates the continuing, widespread popularity of the two songs in the circle of his friends. The manuscript of *Der Tod und das Mädchen* was later on scissored into portions by his halfbrother Andreas, and the relics distributed amongst friends as mementos. It was this person who cut away the opening of the early setting of J. P. Uz—*An Chloen* (p. 42)—leaving it as a fragment.

In August 1817 news that Schober's elder brother, Axel, was returning from France reached the family; Schubert's room was required and he was obliged to abandon his temporary refuge. The touching poem *Farewell* which he wrote, and set to music in Schober's 'Album', is dated '24 August 1817', but the 'distant land' to which friend Schober is said to be travelling was merely the French border; there he was to meet his brother. Schubert returned to his home in the Säulengasse, and resumed his classroom duties. One of the most depressing and frustrating periods of his life now began. The burden must have seemed doubly onerous after the months of freedom amongst those who were his own kind, in which his genius could command untrammelled days for its productions.

[1] 'Musical Composition', London, 1911.

III

1818-1819

I

Writing to his friends about the months which he passed in the Säulengasse house, once again bound to a routine, and excluded from easy contacts with the musicians and art-loving friends of the Spaun and Schober circles, Schubert spoke of himself as a 'frustrated musician'. At first the impetus of his creative work carried him on; the 'Italian' overtures were composed, the Sonata in E flat finally arranged to his satisfaction, a handful of songs to Schiller poems, including the *Gruppe aus dem Tartarus*, were written. There were two Mayrhofer songs, *Atys* and the charming *Am Erlafsee*. The second was printed as a supplement to a Viennese periodical devoted to poetry, music and painting, on 6 February 1818; it was Schubert's first appearance in print. But the creative fire began to die low. His sixth symphony was started in October 1817, but was not completed until the following February. It shows a great advance, in technical matters, on the previous five. The use of the orchestra is masterly, the movements are expertly organised to the point of glibness, all is crisp and competent. But there is no heart in the work; it is all externals. The expert craftsmanship is used on unattractive, trivial material, as a glance at the themes of each movement will show. A Sonata in C major, dated April 1818, remains unfinished. But for its date in Schubert's own hand one might consider it as belonging to his earliest days. The *Adagio* in E major, composed in the same month, April, is possibly the slow movement of the sonata. It was published separately in 1869 by a firm in Winterthur, and so became detached from the other two movements. The quality of the symphony and the sonata indicates the growing discontent and unhappiness of the composer in

these early months of 1818. A seventh symphony, in D, was commenced in May. Schubert's sketches for the work are in PF. score
and although none of his work on them was brought to a finished
state, the pages of this 'sketch-book' are of tremendous interest
and value. They show in an indescribable manner his methods of
work, the imagination obsessed by a scrap of melody, or a rhythm,
or a harmonic figure, evolving page after page from the impetic
and generative theme. They also reveal the methods of genius,
which does not wait for 'inspiration', nor waste its energies with
the imposing, attention-catching, opening flourish, but *starts to
work*: starts with anything that comes, confident that greatness
will attend in its own time. Schubert's sketches in these early
years show how from such ordinary and humble beginnings, his
imagination worked on until 'inspiration' followed his efforts.
The symphony sketches are very bulky, and contain twenty-five
pages of closely written score. There are eight sketched movements, all related in key to the first, and from these the requisite
four were to be chosen. The sketches were, of course, composed
as the whim took him, but they are sorted out below and grouped
into a standard four-movement scheme for the convenience of
the reader:

   I. FIRST MOVEMENT:
       Adagio, D minor, 2/2, followed by *Allegro moderato*, D
       major, 2/2.
  II. SLOW MOVEMENTS:
       1. D major, 2/4.
       2. *Andante*, B minor, 3/8.
       3. A major, 2/4.
 III. SCHERZO: D major, 3/4 and TRIO, G major, 3/4.
 IV. FINALE-MOVEMENTS:
       1. Variant (*a*) D major, 4/4.
          Variant (*b*) *Maestoso*, D major, 4/4.
          Variant (*c*) D major, 4/4.
       2. Variant (*a*) D major, 2/4, first draft.
          Variant (*a*) D major, 2/4, later revision.
          Variant (*b*) D major, 2/4.
       3. D major, 2/4.

Only the *Andante* in B minor, an admirable, deeply serious move-ment which sounds the note of the 'Unfinished' Symphony, and the Scherzo, are anything like complete. The state of mind which would reject this mass of work can easily be deduced.

His friendship with Anselm Hüttenbrenner, a fellow-pupil with Salieri, deepened that year. For his friend he wrote a set of variations based on a theme from Hüttenbrenner's own String Quartet, No. 1, in E major, Op. 3. The variations are gracefully written but largely negligible. He also facetiously inscribed a copy of his so-called 'Trauerwalzer' for his 'wine-and-punch-brother, Anselm Hüttenbrenner, world-famous composer' on 14 March 1818. It seems ironical to us that Hüttenbrenner's vapid compositions should so readily find publishers in Vienna, whereas Schubert was then, and for years to come, quite unable to secure publication for any of his work.

Anselm's younger brother, Josef, also made Schubert's ac-quaintance during the spring. The composer sent him a copy of *Die Forelle* (*The Trout*) written at midnight on 21 February 1818. It is the famous autograph over which the sleepy Schubert shook the ink-bottle instead of the drying-sand. The manuscript was reproduced in facsimile in 1870 and then, incredibly, lost: a typically Hüttenbrennerish catastrophe as we shall see later on.

At the same period he composed and almost completed a *Rondo* in D major for PF. Duet, the first original work in this medium since his juvenile efforts of 1810-1813. His manuscript bears the simple indication '*Rondo* for 4 hands, 1818' (there is no month). Diabelli published an arrangement of the work in 1835 as Op. 138, calling it 'Notre amitié est invariable'. Until 1897, when the autograph was discovered, Op. 138 was taken to be an entirely original work of Schubert's. Diabelli had given the manuscript, together with a number of other Schubert and Beethoven MSS., to his son-in-law, Josef Greipel, who became *Kapellmeister* of the Peterskirche, Vienna, in 1847. Greipel remained in this posi-tion for fifty years, and as an old man with failing powers had no realisation of the value of his autograph possessions. These were all purchased at his death by the Nationalbibliothek, Vienna, but even then they remained obscure, and unexamined. Accordingly biographers and cataloguers, right down to the Deutsch Catalogue of 1951, have given the Rondo of 1818 as a complete Schubert work. O. E. Deutsch does label the MS. as a 'sketch', but even that is an inexact description. It is an incomplete fair copy, probably intended to be a playing copy for Schubert and a partner; although possibly not quite good enough for a publisher's engraver, it is certainly no first, rough draft. Schubert's *Rondo* is in the form A B A : *codetta*: A C A: *coda*. The 'C' section is not quite finished, but a few empty leaves in the manuscript show that Schubert intended to finish it. Diabelli's hack simply cut away the 'A C' portion and published the rest. The excised part was published as a supplement to an article on the Rondo by Leopold Nowak.[1] The fictitious title has been explained as an indication that the Rondo was Schubert's offering to his new friend, the pianist Josef von Gahy. He had recently been introduced to Gahy, who was a friend and colleague of Spaun, and he delighted to play PF. Duets with this new friend. At the close of the Rondo the players' hands cross, and this is supposed to be Schubert's gesture of friendship. Unfortunately, an examination of the manuscript shows that the hand-crossing is due to the rearrangement by Diabelli; there is no justification for it in the original, and it could not have been a gesture of Schubert's at all. But one of his scribbled notes about the work has a certain interest in this connection. He sent Spaun a rough copy of his song *Lob der Tränen* and on the bottom margin he has pencilled the words: 'Spaun! don't forget Gahy and the Rondeau'.[2] He was referring to this duet and perhaps Spaun was going to hear its first performance by the composer and his friend Gahy. The work is quite attractive; Ludwig Scheibler wrote of it as a 'Polonaise alla Rondo' which is a more congenial title than Diabelli's. It heralds a series of PF. Duets that year. They were the result of a new position which the composer took up in the following July.

This was the appointment, as music master, to the establish-

---

[1] 'Oesterreichische Musikzeitschrift', Vienna, November 1953.
[2] The song manuscript is in the Vienna *Stadtbibliothek*.

ment of Count Johann Karl Esterházy. The Count, his wife
Rosine, and their children, Albert, Karoline and Marie, passed
the winter months in their town residence in Penzing, just to
the north of the Schönbrunn estate. In the summer months the
family moved to their Schloss at Zseliz, on the river Gran, in
Hungary. To that quiet retreat, in July 1818, the composer went
to take up his duties. These were many and varied and not precisely defined: he gave Marie (born 1802) and Karoline (born
1805) lessons in pianoforte playing and some kind of instruction
in musical theory, he wrote vocal exercises for the daughters and
their mother, the Countess, who sang contralto, and he accompanied the Count's bass voice in various songs, including
his (Schubert's) own. He composed PF. Duets for Marie and
Karoline to play, and also, on occasion, partsongs for impromptu
musical evenings. Although there are no records of such it cannot
be doubted that he also improvised dance music for the modest
balls and 'routs' that were held on summer evenings in the
Zseliz Schloss.

Schubert, in a bounding reaction from his winter of discontent,
wrote to his friends in Vienna that he lived and composed like a
god; that he was without a care; that he lived at last, and it was
high time, otherwise he would have become nothing but a frustrated (*verdorbener*) musician. To his father, who had at last
received recognition from the City Authorities, having been
promoted to a larger school in the nearby Rossau district, he
wrote cordially and affectionately. Letters to and from his family
and friends give a vivid quality to the year 1818, which is unusual
in the composer's story. Since he lived always in Vienna, surrounded by his friends and relatives and business acquaintances,
long letters were unnecessary, and this means a certain scrappiness
in the personal documents of Schubert. The four years, 1818,
1819, 1824 and 1825, during which he lived for many months
away from the capital, have a wealth of documentation which is
welcome.

From his friend Josef Doppler he received the following letter
giving various items of news—welcome and unwelcome—from
Vienna. It is here published for the first time in English, since it

was recovered only recently after many years of obscurity.[1] Doppler's punctuation is retained.

                                        Vienna, 8 *October* 1818.

Friend of my heart,

I ought really to quarrel with you and to revile you, since you forget, for such a time, one of your best and devoted friends, but you need not fear although you are so neglectful that I can be like that too. Oh no! I am always working for you, and in order to give you a proof of it I announce to you at once, under the same cover, that since the Overture to Claudine Villa Bella cannot be produced at Herr Jaell's concert on account of its too great difficulties—that is to say, it must be because of the oboe and bassoon passages in it, which those fellows in Baden could not execute—it will now, however, be produced by an Imperial Court Chapel Orchestra surely with acclaim, accordingly I gave it to Herr Schneidel, conductor of the said orchestra, who will give it one of these days as the first overture at a concert which he will give for his benefit in the N. Austrian 'Landständischen' Hall, and is already posted up on the placards, and is being read by the eyes of all the world; a letter from me will report to you further particulars of it.

Herr v. Blahetka, whom you will presumably have heard of, or will know about through the playing of his small daughter, begs you earnestly to compose for his daughter a 'Rondo brillant', or whatever it is, which the aforesaid young lady could practise this winter and produce at a concert, that is to say, for the pianoforte with orchestral accompaniment. You may introduce difficulties, pranks, runs or anything that the devil inspires, as you like, only leave out the octave stretches, or such like, anything which is impossible for the shape of her hands.

Hr. v. Blahetka, who is now very famous as a poet, and produces many beautiful poems in the 'Theaterzeitung', is working on a grand oratorio of which two parts are already finished. The material is biblical history, and as I hear from many who have

[1] O. E. Deutsch, 'Wiener Zeitung', Vienna, 5 April 1953.

already read parts of it, very affecting and edifying and very well
written for music since he himself is a good musician, I will transmit to you the whole of the poem since the end of the oratorio
will soon be reached, so that you might set it to music, now what
a first-rate thing that would be for you, if something by you
should come to the light of day, I trust so, don't delay with the
concerto for his daughter and apply yourself as soon as possible
to the work, but transmit to me at once the completely finished
score by post wagon. I will defray the expenses.

And now since the important commissions are all seen to, let
us go on to secondary matters. Are you well? contented, happy?
Are you busy composing worthwhile things? I must know all
about what you have done, for given the opportunity these things
might be produced. Answer all my questions and very soon; I
hope that you will have a deep enough regard for my friendship
not to put this letter aside without answering it.

As this was your name-day, I send my greetings, and wish you
heartily all the good things which only friends can wish. I remain
your loyal friend

Josef Doppler.

P.S.   Our Orchestral Society has recently re-formed and is now
on the point of becoming the best of its kind. . . . We are shortly
going to do all your Masses since we have sufficient singers.
More of this soon.

Nothing came of any of Doppler's invitations or promises in
this letter. The overture was not performed then or at any subsequent time, nor did Schubert accept—on such airy invitation—
the two Blahetka proposals. Doppler's words 'Are you well? . . .
Are you busy composing things' chime in oddly with Schubert's
remark that he was 'living and composing like a god'. But after a
while the quiet, humdrum life in Zseliz, cut off from the stimulating music and society of Vienna, began to pall. 'My longing for
Vienna grows daily' he wrote to his family. In November the return came, and Schubert took lodgings in the Wipplingerstrasse,
sharing rooms with his friend Mayrhofer. He continued to give

lessons to the Esterházy daughters throughout the winter. He lived cheaply and was able to make the payments from these lessons (and probably others) and the moderate fees from his summer duties suffice for his needs. But he was seriously contemplating music for the theatre as a means of livelihood, and he set to work immediately after settling down in his new lodgings on a one-act operetta 'Die Zwillingsbrüder' ('The Twin Brothers'). The play was based on a French original and written by Georg von Hoffmann. With the aid of Vogl's influence it was considered by the Kärntnertor Theater and later performed, but as we shall see it had no lasting success.

The 1814 song *Schäfers Klagelied* received some public performances in the spring of 1819 during the same series of concerts mentioned in connection with the 'Italian' Overtures. It was sung by Fritz Jäger, a tenor from the Theater an der Wien, the most imposing, but not the most important, theatre in Vienna; and it had a warm welcome. Schubert's name was becoming more widely known amongst private circles in Vienna. References to him, and to his songs are very frequent at that time in the friends' letters. Feeling, perhaps, that his presence in the capital during that period of rising interest was vitally necessary he resigned his position with the Esterházys and they left for Zseliz in the summer of 1819 without him. But his operetta was not, after all, given that season and he took a short holiday during July and August with Vogl, who always returned to his native town of Steyr in the summer months. Schubert delighted in the beauty of the countryside and wrote of it in enthusiastic letters to his brother Ferdinand and to Mayrhofer. He made the acquaintance of several musicians in Steyr, the clever young pianist Josefine von Koller, who may have inspired the Sonata in A major, Op. 120, and Sylvester Paumgartner, who was certainly responsible for Schubert's composing the PF. Quintet containing variations on the song *Die Forelle*, which song Paumgartner greatly esteemed. A short visit to Linz in August enabled Schubert to become more closely acquainted with Spaun's family, but a projected visit to Salzburg with Vogl did not take place. In September he and Vogl were back in Vienna, the singer to resume work with the Court Opera, the composer to his lodgings in the Wipplingerstrasse and to his dreams of conquering that Opera.

II

If we associate the years 1815 and 1816 with the composition of songs, and 1817 with sonatas, then 1818 and 1819 could be called the Pianoforte Duet years. A number of works for this medium were written, the first fruits of a rich production of PF. Duets composed during the next six years or so. It was a sociable medium one might say—and a substitute one. Schubert could play his duets with Gahy, or another friend, Franz Lachner, a Bavarian musician who came to Vienna in the autumn of 1822, or Johann Baptist Jenger, for the mutual pleasure of himself and his partner, or for the enjoyment of a circle of friends; a substitute medium, because it so conveniently adapts itself to orchestral arrangements. Nearly all of Schubert's overtures and symphonies were arranged by himself or his friends for PF. Duet, and he, like all other musicians, came to know intimately the symphonies of his predecessors, great and small, in a similar fashion. Some critics and other writers have even tried to enlarge the process and they hold that Schubert's original PF. Duets are orchestral works in disguise; a view with no evidence to support it and which can only be taken seriously because of the hold it has gained amongst music-lovers in general.

A few of the PF. Duets are known to have originated at Zseliz, and it is obvious why they did so. They formed teaching material for Marie and Karoline Esterházy. The first is a set of eight variations on a French Air in E minor. The 'Air' was a song *Le bon Chevalier* (*Der treue Reiter*), supposedly by Queen Hortense of Holland. It is a setting of words beginning

> *Reposez-vous, bon Chevalier!*
> *Laissez-là votre armure. . . .*

and in substance very like Sir Walter Scott's poem 'Soldier rest! thy warfare's o'er', which Schubert set at a later date. The variations are the finest of the early sets, with some notable modulations and vigorous writing in the final two or three. They were published in April 1822 as his Op. 10, dedicated to Beethoven by his 'admirer and worshipper, Franz Schubert'. Another less famous, and less worthy, set of variations for PF. Duet, which are almost certainly of that period, although possibly a little earlier than 1818, are those in B flat, published posthumously as part of his Op. 82. It is again in the last variation and the finale of the set that the individual Schubert is to be found. The *Rondo* in D major has been mentioned; its musical style and piquant rhythms are very like those in the 'Four Polonaises' for PF. Duet, published as the composer's Op. 75. Only of very recent years has it been possible to date these Polonaises, and to realise that they were written at Zseliz; a manuscript sketch for nos. 2 and 4, and the Trio of no. 3, turned up in the posthumous papers of the violinist Otto Dresdel, a friend of the composer Robert Franz. The sketch bore the date 'July 1818'. The Polonaises are charming dances, full of varied melodies and poetic fancies; their marked rhythms *alla polacca* give them strength and drive, and the graceful, fluid piano writing recalls Chopin. Why are they so neglected? In the sketch mentioned there is a fragmentary tune marked by Schubert 'Des' (= D flat). It runs as follows:

It evolved into the 'Trio' section of the third Polonaise, where it appears in this form:

But it also generated a second melody, more familiar to the reader, probably, than the Polonaise tune:

This is from the 'Trio' of the sixth piece in the 'Moments Musicaux', Op. 94, the *Allegretto* in A flat. It means that the date of composition of the *Allegretto* is round about 1818 and it is, therefore, the earliest of the 'Moments Musicaux'.

The first Duet Sonata, in B flat, Op. 30, was composed that year; the date '1824' is erroneous, and given because this early Sonata was associated with the second Duet Sonata, the more famous 'Grand Duo', in C major. Schindler gave the more acceptable date for the Sonata in B flat in his 'Catalogue of Schubert's Works' of 1857. The B flat Sonata for PF. Duet was published in 1823 by the Viennese firm of Sauer and Leidesdorf, and dedicated to County Pálffy, owner and director of the Theater an der Wien. The work is in three movements, there is no scherzo, and its shortness should recommend it to players. Again one asks: why is this sonata neglected? It starts with a Mozartean theme, it is true, but Schubert soon forgets his assumed accent and speaks in his own voice. The first movement has a *codetta* and a development section of great interest and imagination. The work teems with Schubertian melody, and the touches of unusual harmony, the original modulations, the imitations of thematic figures between the players, especially in the finale, should place the work occasionally in concert programmes. Instead of perhaps one more orchestration of the 'Grand Duo' Sonata, the bringing to light of this earlier one by two pianists would be a more rewarding effort.

The first of Schubert's many sets of 'Marches Militaires' for PF. Duet, was composed at that time and published in 1824 as Op. 27; the music of the three marches, in D, C and D, is a little obvious, but entertaining, and in the 'Trio' sections there is a quieter and more lyrical note. Like the overtures, the marches are all written to a pattern. But a fixed form is never a confining matter for Schubert, and his episodic departures from it usually produce music of great individuality. In later work in 'March' style there is music as thoroughly Schubertian as anything in the chamber music of the period.

The last two PF. Duets of the group are the Overtures in G minor and F major. The former work, composed in October 1819, was unknown to the nineteenth century. It came to light in 1896 in the posthumous papers of a friend of Ferdinand Schubert from whom he must have received the piece. The manuscript is a neatly written copy, and it has been suggested that the Overture was originally written for the orchestra. The PF. Duet may therefore be an arrangement. It was published in the supplementary volume of the 'Gesamtausgabe' (volume XXI). It is in the standard tripartite form: *Adagio* introduction, a main section in modified sonata-form, *Allegretto*, and an *Allegro vivace* coda. The Allegretto is a masterly piece of work having much in common with the Duet Sonata in B flat. It also shows a feature of Schubert's style in those years: a favourite harmonic clash between the diatonic seventh of a minor scale (F natural in the key of G minor) and the sharpened leading note (F sharp). Both Sonata and Overture derive tonal contrasts from the clash of F natural and F sharp—giving linkages between the keys D major/D minor/B flat major, and similar sets of keys. The second overture, in F major (with an *Adagio* introduction in F minor), was composed in November 1819 and published in 1825 as Op. 34. It is an extraordinary example of the inability of the individual to judge the merit of his own work that Schubert should have chosen to publish this markedly inferior composition rather than the previous Overture in G minor.[1] There is a legend, which originated with the untrustworthy Josef Hüttenbrenner, that Schubert composed the Overture in F in his (Hüttenbrenner's) lodgings in the Bürgerspital in three hours! This information, he said, was actually written by Schubert on his manuscript. Needless to say Josef was not able to produce the manuscript as evidence of his anecdote: it was lost. He even added that Schubert wrote the words '. . . and dinner missed in consequence'. The reader may judge for himself whether this overture, occupying a dozen pages of print, could have been so composed.

The two overtures, written for the piano in the autumn of 1819, had had a predecessor in February of that year, but it was an

---

[1] It is possible, however, that in 1825 he may no longer have had the manuscipt of the G minor Overture to hand. Friends, it is evident, borrowed the work, and it may have been temporarily mislaid.

Overture composed for orchestra. It is the last of Schubert's independent orchestral overtures: a work which, by reason of its being
composed for orchestra, stands midway between his early compositions in that medium and the later work which begins,
modestly enough, with the incompleted Symphony in E minor
and major. The overture is in E minor. It received one or two performances in Schubert's lifetime, and then disappeared until it
was published in the 'Gesamtausgabe', 1886. Alfred Einstein
looks on the work as the true forerunner of the composer's
maturity. It is a splendid composition, full of Schubert's powers
of thematic development, original and telling harmonic effects,
and significant melody. There are examples of those violent orchestral contrasts—full orchestral *fortissimos* sandwiching lightly
accompanied solo passages, which Schubert inherited from
Mozart and which are such a notable feature of his later work.
The touches of poetical fancy are most moving:

But—and the unwilling modification must be added—too much of its magnificence evaporates when it leaves the paper for actual performance. Or perhaps it is when it leaves the piano for the orchestra. Schubert in these apprentice years failed to realise that kaleidoscopic harmonies so effective on the keyboard lose their colour in an orchestral version. The varied timbres of the orchestra, the notes of strings and wind, nothing if not sustained, seem to militate against quickly changing *fortissimo* harmonies. The 'Romantic' composers abandoned them at an early stage and substituted the far more effective device of contrasting orchestral sonorities. But the experiments of Schubert and Beethoven in harmonic contrasts enabled later composers to avoid what was ineffective, and to succeed with the contrasts of orchestral timbre. For all its weaknesses, the E minor Overture remains a peak in Schubert's early work and deserves more attention than it gets. In England, at least, it has never yet been given a carefully nurtured performance by a first-class orchestra under a pre-eminent conductor. Only under such conditions is a true judgement possible.

In the letter which Schubert wrote on 3 August 1818 from Zseliz, telling his friends that he was living and composing 'like a god', he mentioned that a song *Einsamkeit*, to words by Mayrhofer, was finished. He added that he believed it to be the best song he had written. This is another example of his inability to estimate fully the merits of his own work, for this song, an extremely long one, is an unequal piece of writing with 'two grains of corn hid in two bushels of chaff'. There are only half-a-dozen Mayrhofer settings in 1818 and 1819 and none of them has won and retained a hold on the interest of music lovers. *An die Freunde* has pages of excellent Schubert, and *Nachtstück* opens characteristically, but neither of them has the power or lyrical charm of the great 1817 group. Two 'nocturne' songs, *An den Mond in einer Herbstnacht*, composed during the unhappy spring of 1818, and *Abendbilder*, of February 1819, are both a shade too long to have attracted singers. But the Schubertian holds them dear. The first page of the address to the autumnal moon is from the heart of Schubert; the soft but stately march of the accompaniment is suggested by Alois Schreiber's line: 'Leis' sind deine Tritte durch des Aethers Wüste' ('Soft are your footfalls through the ethereal desert'). The other song, a reverie at dusk by Johann Peter Silbert, has further examples of Schubert's decorative accompaniments, musical imagery evoked by the bird-song, the evening bell, the moonlight on the church roof. From a group of songs to Schiller's poems, one—*Die Götter Griechenlands*—has won a fame which its own beauty could not bring it. This is because its opening bars contain a phrase in A minor which resembles the opening of the 'Menuetto' in the A minor String Quartet, Op. 29. As a result the popular quartet sheds some of its renown on the song; the point will be taken up again in connection with the chamber work. The song is melodious, and its pathetic tone reflects the poet's sigh for the golden age of the Grecian glory 'Fair World, where are you?'

There were only two settings of Goethe, both very different, but both entirely characteristic. *Die Liebende schreibt* is a sonnet in which the distant lover is begged for a love-token. It is a tender, moving song with a touch of colour in the tonality (B flat to G flat), a touch of the picturesque in the accompaniment for the tears that come and dry without falling. But it is eclipsed by its companion song, the wonderful *Prometheus*. The form of *Prometheus* is the *scena*, that is, a series of connected movements in varying tempos and keys, suggested by the various moods of the stanzas. Schubert's vocal line is a fusion of his dramatic melody and recitative, a true forerunner of Wagner's middle-period styles. The harmonic range and the freedom of modulation, however, are far in advance of anything in Wagner earlier than *Tristan und Isolde*. The Prometheus of Schubert and Goethe is rather the defiant creator of mankind than the tortured figure of Aeschylus: the point was made earlier. The only setting to challenge Schubert's is Hugo Wolf's (1889) and it is Wolf who has suggested the comparison for he considered that Schubert had misunderstood Goethe and wrote his song to show the correct interpretation.[1]

---

[1] The topic has been presented and explored by Gerard Mackworth-Young, 'Proceedings of the Royal Musical Association,' 1 March 1952.

One sphere in which Schubert was a prolific creator throughout his life is that of the part-song for male voices. It was an extremely popular medium in the early nineteenth century, but as a movement its strength dissipated itself, as the century passed, in the multitudinous associations of the 'glee club', and in the 'Liedertafel' of Germany and Austria, until the sheer bulk of mediocrity in production and performance alike smothered it. The beginnings of the movement appeared in the second half of the eighteenth century in Germany, Austria and Switzerland. It was a mutually fertilising growth in the three countries, although the prime impulse was not the same in each one. The 'Liederschule' of Berlin were offsprings of a union between the motets in the Church service and the choruses for male voices in opera: under the guidance of composers such as Johann Friedrich Reichardt and Johann Abraham Schultz they were responsible for the popularity of the male voice choir in Germany. The term 'Liedertafel' for these associations of male singers was used for the first time *c.* 1805 (see Zelter's letter of 26 December 1808 to Goethe). In Switzerland and South Germany the choirs and their music were inspired by the choral songs of the Reformation. The composer Hans Georg Nägeli, coming rather late on the scene, supported the singing of the male voice choirs so ardently that he brought about a revival of enthusiasm at a time when it was rapidly waning. We shall meet his name again later in Schubert's life, for he was a publisher as well as a composer. In Austria the earliest part-songs seem to have been arrangements of solo songs; an early manuscript in the Vienna City Library has arrangements by one Franz Schraub of some of Mozart's *Lieder*: *Das Veilchen*, *Abendempfindungen*, etc. The part-singing was taken up eagerly in Vienna. At the time when Schubert left the *Stadtkonvikt* the publishers were pouring out an enormous number of male voice part-songs. The lists can be seen in Whistling's 'Handbuch der musikalischen Literatur' (1787–1817). Josef and Michael Haydn, Mozart and Beethoven, particularly with the well known 'Canons' of various types, had fed the river of compositions, and Schubert exceeded them all. He composed close on a hundred part-songs for male voices. There are many 'Canons' in 1813, chiefly contrapuntal exercises for Salieri; in 1815 and 1816 his part-songs are strophic in form, but from 1817 onwards he uses the 'onrunning' form as well as the strophic, and in both styles he writes masterpieces quite worthy of being put alongside the best of his songs of the period. Most of them are unaccompanied, but there are several with pianoforte accompaniment, and a few with solo voices as well. His style in these part-songs is largely homophonic and he keeps the music going by bold changes of key and extraordinary harmonic strokes. Early work shows how keenly he responded to the grisly 'Romantic' theme: *Totengräberlied* of 1813 (Hölty) and *Der Geistertanz* of 1816 (Matthisson). This *Dance of Death* poem fascinated the boy Schubert; it is made tolerable only by the closing lines in which the capering dead explain the reason for their joy: that their hearts, being dead, no longer ache. Schubert tried his hand at three solo settings, one of them completed, as well as composing the vocal quartet. The part-songs of 1817 include a first setting of Goethe's great poem *Gesang der Geister über den Wassern*, another poem with a great attraction for Schubert. His quartet *Das Dörfchen* (words by Bürger) is very typical of the easy-going, sociable Schubert part-song and consequently very popular in his day; it was later revised and published as his Op. 11: no. 1 in 1822. He also published, in Op. 17, four quartets to texts by different poets; they are all secondary part-songs, but much worthier than the humble *Das Dörfchen*. The best two are the settings of Schiller's *Liebe* and an unknown poet's *Die Nacht*; both poems mention the murmur of streams at night and Schubert's sensitive music, his attempts with voices alone to depict the purling, shadowed waters, produce a charming pair of songs. The part-songs of Op. 17 are all quite short and would make an excellently varied concert item. Finally, in April 1819, Schubert composed the fourth setting of his beloved Goethe poem *Nur wer die Sehnsucht kennt* for men's voices. It is the greatest of his part-songs, a masterly setting of the words, warm in tone, varied in 'orchestration', and full of extravagant touches of colour, of harmonic adventure, of climax and repose. The main key is E major; the first section ends in a fortissimo F major and his clash of semitonal keys inspires the modulation throughout. It is Schubert's portrait in music of the hapless girl who is 'alone and cut off from all joys'.

III

One of the last works he composed in this period is the popular and famous *Trout* Quintet; the music is for piano and a quartet of strings (violin, viola, 'cello and double-bass). Albert Stadler, his schoolfellow and friend of those days, wrote many years after Schubert's death a letter to Ferdinand Luib in which he said that the work was commissioned by Sylvester Paumgartner, an enthusiastic 'cellist and one of the leading lights in the musical life of Steyr. Paumgartner, a wealthy bachelor, lived in a large house with a music room on the first floor where private musical parties were held, and a large music *salon* on the second floor, in which midday concerts and other musical activities took place under the stimulus of this benevolent patron. He also owned a well stocked music library. Apparently he required of Schubert a composition in the style of Hummel's PF. Quintet in E flat, Op. 87. He also admired the song *Die Forelle* and suggested the variations which form a favourite movement in the quintet. Schubert sketched some of his composition at Steyr, but the music was not completed until after his return to Vienna. Hummel's Quintet, which served Schubert as a prototype, is a short, straightforward work in four movements; the Menuetto is placed second, and the third movement, *Largo*, is only a page long and serves more as an introduction to the finale. It is excessively imitative of early Beethoven, or perhaps it would be truer to say that Hummel used the same idiom as Beethoven in an oppressively lifeless manner. It is sufficient merely to glance through the works of contemporaries such as Dussek and Hummel, to see Schubert's vitality and, although clearly influenced by Beethoven, his independent style. Very occasionally one sees a trait in Hummel's instrumentation which certainly appealed to Schubert: the piano is given a chance to sing, or it will enter effectively after silence to clinch a cadence.

Ex. 22 *Allegro agitato*   Hummel, Op. 87

But that is all there is in the meagre stretches of the work. Schubert's *Trout* Quintet, on the contrary, overflows with an abundance of musical-poetic fancies. Its melodies, their presentation
and development, the instrumentation of the work, its irrepressible
good spirits and sociability—not only have these qualities made
it a greatly beloved work, but they stamp it as a universal masterpiece, the first of Schubert's chamber-works to claim the tributes
not of Schubertians alone, but of all musicians. The great qualities
of the early string quartets and trios, of the 'Duo' Sonata for PF.
and violin, of the 1817 PF. Sonatas, may perhaps have their
strongest appeal only to the Schubert lover; that is to say, their
appeal is limited. But this is not the case with the PF. Quintet,
whose appeal is for all. Even so, this first acknowledged masterpiece is not quite the whole Schubert, nor the fully mature composer. There is no point in over-praising it, nor in praising it for
qualities which it has in small measure—the serious, dramatic
power of the composer for instance. Its key is indeed a key to the

work, for A major is Schubert's key of contentment; it always introduces a mood of expansive, friendly good-humour. A German critic has suggested that the countryside of Steyr, which Schubert himself called 'über allen Begriff schön'—'inconceivably beautiful'—is a 'secret collaborator' in the quintet.[1] Certainly Schubert's happiness that year may be responsible for the overflowing ideas of the work, but the thought of Paumgartner and four other players sociably enjoying his music is quite as acceptable a 'collaborator'.

'Those happy strains of wandering and roaming—the finale of the *Trout* Quintet is a good instance—do not suggest remote and solitary landscapes; there is always a feeling of town sociability behind them.' (Eric Blom.)

Technically the finest points of the quintet are the notable development of his main ideas in the first movement, the original rhythmic patterns of his slow movement, and the colourful modulations and counterpoints in the variations. The first of these points, the development of the main melodies in the opening *Allegro vivace*, could be examined more closely because Schubert's skill is so spontaneously charming that it goes—as it should of course—unnoticed. The violin states the first theme:

Ex.23

and a long passage based entirely upon it and the preliminary flourish of the pianoforte then follows. The quoted melody grows as a plant grows, throwing out subsidiary ideas and changing and adding to its own form, until finally the piano announces this version of it, played against a rhythmic accompaniment which derives from his early experiments with the medium of the string quartet:

Ex.24

[1] 'Schubert' (Willi Kahl), Cobbett's 'Cyclopedia of Chamber Music', Oxford, 1929.

The development section of this movement then builds up its powerful climaxes on the thematic ideas of Ex. 24, used thus against a throbbing background of the upper strings:

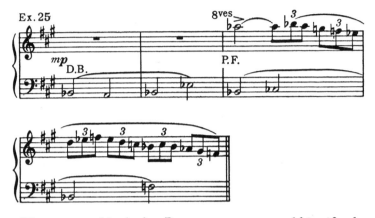

Ex. 25

We are not told whether Paumgartner approved his gift when the parts were sent to him at the end of 1819—only that he made a very moderate showing at the 'cello part. The composition completely disappeared and no more was heard of it until ten years later. It was then sold by Schubert's brother Ferdinand to the publisher Josef Czerny, Vienna, and appeared in May 1829 as Op. 114. The auditors of the resurrected work, and they were not members of the Schubert circle, had the grace to realise its qualities. In an advertising notice of 21 May 1829 Czerny announced:

> This Quintet, having already been performed in several circles at the publisher's instigation, and declared to be a masterpiece by the musical connoisseurs present, we deem it our duty to draw the musical public's attention to this latest work by the unforgettable composer. . . .

But by that time Schubert was beyond all such adulation and the recognition of this early and beloved masterpiece came too late.

IV

1820-1823

I

The four years from 1820 to the close of 1823 were the critical
ones in Schubert's artistic career and, for it does not follow,
in his life also. At the commencement he was a young composer,
unknown to Vienna at large, but appreciated by a circle of staunch
and admiring friends. Amongst those friends were far-seeing and
not uninfluential musicians such as Vogl and the Sonnleithners,
father and son. Although he had experienced a number of set-
backs, his life had brought him the satisfaction of achievement,
recognition in a limited sense, and, at the start of 1820, several
opportunities for the further advancement of his genius and its
public acknowledgement. As the four years passed his name became more and more widely known in Vienna; two of his operettas were performed in its leading theatres; his songs were sung in
public and created a profound impression; amateur and professional quartets repeatedly sang his male-voice part-songs and they
were enthusiastically applauded; and finally the publication of his
works started with the firm of Cappi & Diabelli: first of all songs
on a subscription basis, then dances, then part-songs. His fame
was spreading to Linz, Graz, the more distant parts of Austria,
the provincial capitals of Germany; and patrons in distinguished
walks of life were having their interest awakened in the young
composer. Schubert's prospects were very favourable, and his
head was slightly turned. His father and brothers became almost
strangers, and friends of his boyhood, in so far as they were not
part of the artistic circle in which he moved, were treated coolly.
And then the event occurred from which, unless one deliberately
underwrites it, the dramatic quality is difficult to remove. He
became seriously ill at the end of 1822, and, as the tide of his

affairs rose and success promised on all sides, he was obliged to withdraw from Viennese society, and in his wretched physical state watch opportunity after opportunity fail to materialise. 'They greatly praise Schubert' wrote Karl Beethoven in his uncle's conversation-book during August 1823, 'but it is said that he hides himself.' The close of the period saw one burst of effort, one meteoric blaze, as 'Rosamunde' was put on the boards. The play failed dismally, and the light is extinguished. At the beginning of 1824 Schubert was himself again; the days of aping the sophisticated man about town, and the brusque artist, were passed; affectionate relations with his father and brothers were resumed, his friendships regained their old warmth, the Viennese public quietly prepared to forget the young, disturbing theatre composer. One thing remained, and grew, until it reached an almost surfeiting climax: the publication in Vienna of his songs and, occasionally, instrumental works. But after 1823 the pattern of his life resumes the shapes and colours of the years and experiences before 1820, and we meet old names and old friends again in his story.

A rather startling event in the spring of 1820 was Schubert's arrest by the police under suspicion of subversive activities. The murder of Kotzbue the previous year, as a suspected Russian spy, had been carried out by a Berlin student, and from then onwards all Student Associations, first in Germany, and then in Austria, had been looked upon with suspicion by the police. Schubert's friend, Johann Senn, the Tyrolese poet, was arrested after resisting a police investigation into his papers, and Schubert, being present in Senn's lodgings during the affair, was arrested too. But it is clear that he was soon released. At the time of this unfortunate event he was engaged on the composition of a cantata for solo voices, mixed chorus and orchestra—an ambitious work. This was 'Lazarus, or the Festival of Resurrection', a static religious drama of a kind popular in eighteenth-century Germany, by August Hermann Niemeyer, a professor of theology at Halle University (died 1828). The drama is spoken by the characters Lazarus, Mary and Martha, the daughter of Jairus, Nathaniel, a priest, and Simon, a Sadducee. It was in three acts, of which Schubert probably composed the whole of the first two. Not all of the music has survived, but there remains a substantial fragment comprising Act I (complete) and most of Act II. The music was recovered during the middle of the nineteenth century from various owners by Alexander Thayer, the American Consul in Trieste, and author of a well known biography of Beethoven. The drama, 'Lazarus', is a meditation on Death, presented through the various emotions of the characters as they watch Lazarus die: despair and doubt (Martha), hope (Mary and Jairus' daughter), sceptism and fear (Simon), faith (Nathaniel). The poem is not without merit, but its gloominess cannot be redeemed even by the wonder of Schubert's music. And wonderful it is, the most intriguing of all his earlier choral works. The fusion of melody and recitative so remarkable in the song *Prometheus* is a feature of the vocal line of 'Lazarus' and it is supported by a most poetical and decorative style of writing in the orchestral accompaniment which suggests again and again the Wagnerian procedures in 'Die Walküre' and the first part of 'Siegfried'. The harmonic range is very wide. There are pages in 'Lazarus' which are akin to Schubert's operatic writing: the use of *recitativo* supported, not by chords, or decorated chords, as in all contemporary opera, but by a fluid use of short figures, almost *Leitmotive* in their cumulative effect. It is possible that we owe the noncompletion of this interesting work to the advent of police and politics into Schubert's otherwise uneventful life; and that his arrest broke the continuity of his work on the cantata.

The operetta 'Die Zwillingsbrüder' was performed, eventually, on 14 June 1820. It was given in the Kärntnertor Theater, with Vogl doubling the parts of the twin brothers Fritz and Franz. The operetta was extensively reported, and on the whole well received. It was given a number of times throughout the summer, and then was never revived again. But as a result of its moderate success, Schubert was commissioned to compose the incidental music to another play, based on a similar French model, to be written by the same author: it was 'Die Zauberharfe' ('The Magic Harp'). The play—little more than a pantomime, as the word is understood today, with the same kind of scenic effects—was to be

given in the rival theatre, the Theater an der Wien. The first performance took place on 19 August 1820, and although, again,
Schubert's music pleased, the stupid libretto doomed the work to
failure. Frankly, it bored the theatre-goers, and what chance had
Schubert to alleviate that boredom with his occasional numbers?
In October a last performance was given and the work heard no
more. The Overture in C major, using, as has been said, material
from the 'Italian' Overture in D major, is now known as the
Overture to 'Rosamunde', and is as popular as any orchestral
work of Schubert. It has, actually, nothing whatever to do with
the play 'Rosamunde' of December 1823.

Between these two first performances of his operettas, in July
1820, Schubert spent a few days at Atzenbrugg, which lies some
twenty miles north-west of Vienna. An uncle of Schober's
managed estates in the neighbourhood, and to his house every
summer between 1817 and 1824 Schober brought a band of young
men and women, kindred spirits, for a country holiday; there
were excursions into the neighbourhood, games in the adjoining
fields and meadows, and charades and dancing in those rooms of
the small castle at the disposal of the visitors. 1820 is the first year
in which Schubert was a guest.

Two more of his songs were printed in December as supplements: the first was the 1819 song *Widerschein*, which appeared in
an almanach called 'Taschenbuch zum geselligen Vergnügen'
('Pocketbook for Sociable Pleasures') from the firm of Göschen
in Leipzig; the second was *The Trout*, given as a supplement to
the Vienna 'Zeitschrift für Kunst', of 9 December 1820. Both
songs were later on re-published by Diabelli: *The Trout* as Op. 32
in 1828, *Widerschein* as part of the 'Nachgelassene' songs in 1832.
This second publication of *Widerschein* gave the song in B flat
instead of the original D major, but this was the only alteration
in the music (there is a slight change in the opening line of the
words); the second publication is wrongly given as a second *version* in the Deutsch 'Thematic Catalogue'; the date 'May 1828' of
this autograph is that of Schubert's copying of the song, possibly
for the publisher.

The year closes with some outstanding work. The month of

December would be graced by the presence of the String Quartet Movement in C minor (the 'Quartett-Satz') alone, but there were, in addition, the superb motet 'Psalm XXIII' for S.S.A.A., written for a new friend, Anna Fröhlich, the extended solo cantata *Waldesnacht* (or *Im Walde*) for tenor and pianoforte, and two attempts, for male voices, of the Goethe poem *Gesang der Geister über den Wassern*. Both choral sketches are of excellent quality. The first of them, in C minor, with accompaniment for violas and 'cellos, was brought to a conclusion the following February. If only the same fortunate completion could have been the lot of the String Quartet! This quartet movement, in C minor, is the only movement in Schubert's instrumental work, prior to the 'Unfinished' Symphony, which prepares us for the greatness which bursts forth in that symphony. It was intended to be the first movement of a fully executed string quartet, and in its music Schubert at last combines his lyrical effusion, of which the *Trout* Quintet is so notable an example, with the darker, dramatic, and passionate qualities of his greater *Lieder*. The 'cello, for the first time in Schubert, is as free, as adventurous, as 'virtuoso' in technique, as the other three string parts; it seems to show that the work was not intended for performance by the Schubert family quartet, and the composer was no longer bound by the limited abilities of his father's cello-playing. The slow movement, an *Andante* in A flat, is full of promising ideas, but they never take wing, as it were, and after forty-four bars Schubert threw up his task.

The setting of Psalm XXIII, *The Lord is my Shepherd*, is fairly well known in England. It has that indefinable quality of greatness although the scope is small; and although, too, Schubert is using the secular idiom of his song-writing in composing this sacred work, the expression is so sincere, so delicate, that it creates an atmosphere of spiritual exaltation at the climax and an unearthly tranquillity at the close. The text is a translation into German by Moses Mendelssohn.

When the work was first performed in England, with English text, the 'Musical Transcript' of 2 September 1854 dismissed it with these words:

... the elevation of feeling, and the deep sanctity of the devotional spirit is absent. It is more operatic than sacerdotal, and its length is too protracted for the due expression of the sentiment. The restlessness of the accompaniment also damages the proposed effect.

Anna Fröhlich taught singing at the 'Conservatoire' of the *Gesellschaft der Musikfreunde,* an association of music lovers in Austria, which we shall meet with increasing frequency in Schubert's story. The Vienna branch of the association was housed in those days in the Tuchlauben, one of the larger streets in the heart of the Inner City. Psalm XXIII was composed for Anna's female singing-class there. She was one of four gifted sisters, the others being Barbara, Katharina (beloved by the poet Grillparzer, and through whom he met Schubert) and Josefine. At an evening concert in the home of Ignaz Sonnleithner, held on 1 December 1820, Anna Fröhlich accompanied the singer August von Gymnich in the *Erlking*; during January 1821 both singer and pianist again performed the song in a semi-public concert given by the *Gesellschaft*. The song was creating a deep impression. Ignaz von Mosel and Count Moritz Dietrichstein, two officials of the Imperial Court and both influential men, as well as the brothers Sonnleithner, were becoming interested in the young composer. A few weeks later, on 7 March 1821, at a public concert given by a 'Society of Ladies of the Nobility' for charitable purposes, Vogl sang the *Erlking* to Anselm Hüttenbrenner's accompaniment, with overwhelming success.

II

Schubert's own efforts to get the *Erlking* published had been unsuccessful. The Viennese firms were adamant about the difficulties of the accompaniment. The outcome of Spaun's efforts in the spring of 1817 to interest Breitkopf & Härtel of Leipzig in the song, was first told by Max Friedlaender in the Berlin journal 'Vierteljahresschrift für Musikwissenschaft' of July 1893. According to this, the Leipzig firm, doubtful of the authenticity of the composition, sent it for confirmation to the only Franz Schubert they knew, a composer in the service of the Dresden Court. This is the relevant part of his reply:

> ... about ten days ago I received from you an esteemed letter in which you sent me a manuscript of Goethe's 'Erlking' supposed to be mine; with the greatest astonishment I inform you that this cantata was never composed by me; I shall retain the same in my keeping in order to find out who has sent you the rubbish in so rude a manner, and also to discover the fellow who thus misuses my name. ...

But Leopold Sonnleithner, Josef Hüttenbrenner and a few others had determined that the song should be published, and had not only collected the money for its engraving, but, on offering it at one of the Sonnleithner musical evenings, a hundred copies were subscribed for. This meant money enough to have *Gretchen* also engraved. The success of Vogl's performance of the *Erlking* on the eve of the song's publication must have been very gratifying to the promoters of the venture. The firm of Cappi & Diabelli (the forerunners of Diabelli's firm) acted as agents, and Schubert's Op. 1 appeared on 31 March 1821. It was dedicated to Count Dietrichstein. About six hundred copies of the song were sold immediately. *Gretchen am Spinnrade*, Op. 2, dedicated to Moritz von Fries, appeared a month later, on 30 April 1821. This song had also had several successful performances at private and semi-public gatherings that spring. Nearly as many copies of *Gretchen* (between five and six hundred) were quickly sold. In a similar way Schubert published a number of songs in 1821 and 1822 comprising altogether seven opus-numbers. Amongst these twenty songs a few may cause mild surprise: in view of the masterpieces available it is hard to understand why such very minor works as *Morgenlied*, *Der König in Thule*, *Der Schäfer und der Reiter* and others, were chosen. But most of the greater Geothe settings were there, and *Der Tod und das Mädchen* was also included. We, naturally, are wise after the event.

The success of the first seven opus-numbers led Cappi & Diabelli to accept, on their own responsibility, publication of Opp. 8, 9, 10 and 11. Of these the first contains songs; the rest are '36 Waltzes' (Op. 9), 'Variations on a French Air' (Op. 10) and three

part-songs (Op. 11). In December 1822 Schubert published three
more sets of songs on his own initiative. These were Opp. 12, 13
and 14 containing the Harper's songs from 'Wilhelm Meister',
and 'Suleika's First Song'. Cappi & Diabelli's venture with Opp.
8 to 11 was a modest enough beginning from Schubert's point of
view, but it was, at least, a beginning. From then onwards publication proceeded regularly, but spasmodically, until by the time
of his death, he had published works up to Op. 100. During
April 1821, just before the appearance of *Gretchen*, he started to
compose a duet for soprano and tenor to words by an unknown
poet, *Linde Lüfte wehen*. It is sad that a duet of such charming
promise should remain uncompleted. Since it has not been published in England, and never in an easily accessible form, it is
quoted here:

Von Jas-min ge - sträuss-chen, und von Veil-chen

au'n ____ und von Veil-chen

Another invitation reached him in the spring of 1821 to compose music for the theatre. Two additional numbers were required for the Vienna *première* of Hérold's comic operetta 'La Clochette' ('Das Zauberglöckchen'), first produced in Paris in 1817. The two items were: a tenor aria for Azolin (*Der Tag entflieht, der Abend glüht*) and a so-called *Comic Duet* for tenor (Bedur) and bass (Zedir) (*Nein, das ist zu viel*). These were composed at once and performed on 20 June 1821. They were rather inappropriately exalted in style and prolonged in structure for the light and tuneful operetta which they supplemented, and made no mark at all.

The visit to Atzenbrugg soon afterwards assumes greater importance in the Schubert records than the preceding one of 1820, or the following one in 1822. A few German dances were composed there (Op. 9: nos. 1–3, and Op. 18: nos. 29–31) called the 'Atzenbrügger Deutsche', and incidents of the holiday are enshrined in drawings and paintings by Leopold Kupelwieser, a friend of Spaun's originally, but soon becoming an intimate of Schober and Schubert. There are two excellent watercolours, one depicting an excursion by coach through pastoral surroundings to nearby Aumühle, the other, an indoor scene, showing the party acting a charade. Schubert appears in both. There is also a pencil sketch of Schubert by Kupelwieser, not a favourite portrait but evidently an extremely good likeness. It was not discovered until Kupelwieser died in 1862 when it turned up amongst his posthumous papers, together with other sketches of members of the Atzenbrugg party, including Schober. They were published by Karl Kupelwieser (Leopold's son) in 1912. The two important watercolours, familiar now through frequent reproduction, were commissioned from Kupelwieser by Schober and remained in his possession until his death (1882). They were then purchased by that eminent Schubert collector and admirable Schubertian, Nikolaus Dumba, and on his death (23 March 1900) went to the City of Vienna. The equally well known, but inferior, landscape with figures, showing Schubert seated on the ground puffing a pipe, and entitled 'Playing ball at Atzenbrugg' is a composite affair: Schober, Schwind and the artist Ludwig Mohn, all had a hand in its production and this took place years after the event.

The private concerts at the Sonnleithners' residence, the 'Gundelhof', held every Friday evening in the early days of their organisation, were duplicated in middle-class residences all over the city. During the early 1820's a remarkable development of them occurred; by popular choice the whole of the music of the evening—songs, dances, pianoforte pieces and so on—was by Schubert. The concerts devised in this way were called 'Schubertiads'. The songs, naturally, were the chief part of the concert and Vogl's voice a powerful attraction; many of the songs of the 1820's were first performed at these 'Schubertiads'. They were held at the residence of the Bruchmann family, at Spaun's, and at two other friends' homes, Karl Hönig and Johann Umlauff (all these people were practising or studying or connected with law) and at many more houses too numerous to specify. Schubert was acquainted with the Bruchmann family because of his friendship with Franz Bruchmann, a young man of character who in after years abandoned law for Holy Orders and became an austere and forbidding cleric. His sister, Justina, was in those days secretly courted by Schober. Their father was a wealthy merchant, and besides their town house the family owned an attractive residence in the countrified suburbs of Vienna called 'The Caprice'.

The Hönig family lived near St. Stefan's Cathedral. Schubert was a friend of Karl Hönig, whose sister Anna (Nanette) was ardently courted by a young painter, Moritz von Schwind. Schubert had met Schwind through their mutual friend Josef Kenner, an old *Konvikt* pupil, and they quickly became intimate. The young painter, seven years younger than Schubert, idolised the composer, and their friendship was to prove a happy and fruitful one. Johann Umlauff, a law student, was another friend of the composer's, first meeting him in 1818. He it is who is responsible for the story of Schubert's composing in the morning, in bed. A guitarist of some accomplishment, he used to sing Schubert's songs to him, accompanying himself on the guitar. The legends which arose from such imperfectly remembered events are (1) that Schubert slept in his spectacles so as to waste no time looking for them in the morning, (2) that Schubert played the guitar and himself arranged the accompaniments of his songs for that instrument. The first of these legends is surely the silliest of all anecdotes invented about a great artist. How could it ever have been taken seriously? And yet it gave rise to one of the foulest gibes ever delivered against Schubert (page 345). Umlauff is also said to have disputed with Schubert the correct emphasis of the questioning line of *Der Wanderer*—'O Land, wo bist du? ('O Land, where art thou?'). He asserted that 'du' should be stressed and come on the first beat of the bar. Schubert, rightly, of course, held to his own stressing of 'bist'.

In the August of 1821, soon after his return to Vienna from Atzenbrugg, Schubert composed the Symphony in E minor and major; it is incomplete, and unperformable except in arrangements. The manuscript is a strange specimen of his methods of impromptu work, not frequently resorted to, and, as can be seen

in this symphony, not successful. The *Adagio* introduction, in E
minor, is fully scored; there follows the first movement proper,
an *Allegro* in E major, which is scored fully up to the entry of
the second subject in G major. This is at the end of a page. From
there onwards, Schubert 'threads' the symphony right to the end.
The score is left blank for subsequent filling in; the melody is indicated throughout, in Violin I, or Flute I, as a rule; the climaxes
are sometimes more fully scored, sometimes indicated merely by
a very high note (*sforzando*) in the first violin part. Too much
remains for the 'arranger' to fill in, and the two best known com-
pletions, those of John Francis Barnett (performed at the Crystal
Palace, 5 May 1883) and Felix Weingartner (performed at Vienna
on 9 December 1934) are both failures. The music is in his early
symphonic style, and there are few, if any, hints of the 'Unfinished' Symphony (which is only a year and two months ahead,
as it were) but plenty of links with the Sixth Symphony, in C
major, of 1818. The themes are still light-hearted to the point of
triviality, and the 'Trio' of the third movement is very inferior.
It is odd how the last three symphonic scherzos of Schubert,
which have some degree of completion, are all in C major with a
'Trio' in A major (1818, 1821 and 1828) and that the transitional
link between the 'Trio' and the recapitulated scherzo is, in all
three cases, achieved by a sustained or repeated E natural. The
slow movement, *Andante*, in A major, is an attractive movement,
but short and slight. There is nothing in it to compare with the
sketched *Andante* in B minor of the 1818 Symphony in D. Schubert was the least self-critical of composers, but he must nevertheless have felt that the score of his symphony was not worth
completing: nor, frankly, is it. The development section of the
first movement contains, as is often the way with other early, unfinished work, the best music in the symphony.

The manuscript was given to Mendelssohn by Ferdinand
Schubert in March 1845. The first preformance of his brother's
great C major Symphony at Leipzig in March 1839 had been due
to Mendelssohn's enthusiasm for the work; Mendelssohn had also
tried to secure performances in London and Paris. Ferdinand
presented the score of the Symphony in E as a gesture of grateful

acknowledgement. On 22 March 1845 Mendelssohn wrote a letter to Ferdinand, which has never been reproduced since it was first published in the Vienna 'Allgemeine Musikzeitung' of January 1848. Here is an English translation of it:

Dear Professor,

Yesterday I received through Doctor *Haertel* the symphony sketch by your brother, of which you have made me the possessor. What pleasure you give me through so fine, so precious a gift, how deeply grateful I am to you for this remembrance of the deceased master, how honoured I feel that you present so significant a specimen of his posthumous remains directly to me—all this you can surely put into words for yourself better than I, but I feel it necessary, although in few words, to express my gratitude to you for your gift. Believe me that I know how to esteem the magnificent gift at its true value, that you could have given it to no one who would have greater joy in it, who would be more sincerely grateful to you for it. In truth, it seems to me as if, through the very incompleteness of the work, the scattered, half-finished indications, that I became at once personally acquainted with your brother more closely and more intimately than I should have done through a completed piece. It seems as if I saw him there working in his room, and this joy I owe to your unexpectedly great kindness and generosity. Let me hope for an opportunity to meet you in the flesh, be it in Vienna or in this place here, and to make your personal acquaintance and then repeat to you by word of mouth, once again, all my thanks.

> With respects
> Yours faithfully,
> Felix Mendelssohn-Bartholdy.

Frankfurt-am-Main,
22 *March* 1845.

On Mendelssohn's death, the manuscript passed into the ownership of his brother Paul. When, after many years, Paul Mendelssohn learned of Sir George Grove's interest in his brother's music, and of Grove's intention to write the lives of Schubert and Mendelssohn in his forthcoming 'Dictionary', he

sent the manuscript as a gift to Grove. Grove received it in
August 1868 and tells of his surprise at the reception of so bulky
a manuscript in an appendix to Arthur Coleridge's English translation of Kreissle's 'Schubert' (London, 1869). The description of
the music manuscript as it is given in that appendix, and in the
'Dictionary' itself, was written for Grove by William Rockstro.
Grove's pronouncement on the symphony: '. . . it is probable
that it did not occupy him more than a few hours' is incredibly
silly, but his judgement of the *quality* of the work is, as always
when he assesses Schubert, absolutely sound. He says: '. . . it is a
work of the old school.' When Brahms learned that Paul Mendelssohn was sending the Schubert MS. to England he became
alarmed, and begged Joachim to see that no 'Unzucht' (=lewd-
ness, mischief) would result—referring to expected arrangements,
constituting violation, by those inferior English musicians! (Letter of December 1868). Brahms himself had toyed with the idea
of finishing the work, but realising the difficulties he abandoned
the project; he may have heard in the meantime of Sullivan's
intention of doing so. In the end a musician inferior to any of
these men completed it. Barnett's account of his difficulties in
filling up Schubert's blank score is set out in his paper to the
Musical Association of 9 June 1891. There also he tells of the
extraordinary occurrence whereby the MS. of the Symphony
was nearly lost for ever. Apparently Rockstro brought the MS.
back to Grove on a personal visit. He was met at the station and
the two friends walked back to Grove's house together, discovering on arrival there that the score had been left in the train.
Next morning it was discovered and returned to Grove. On his
death the relic was acquired by the Royal College of Music, and is
now housed in the British Museum.

III

In September 1821 Schubert left Vienna in the company of
Schober to spend a few weeks at St. Pölten. The Bishop of St.
Pölten was a relative of Schober's mother and he owned the
neighbouring castle of Ochsenburg. The two friends, as far as is
known, did not actually lodge in the Bishop's residence in St.

Pölten, although Schober's mother and sister were frequently guests there. But they certainly stayed for a while in the castle of Ochsenburg. Their purpose in seeking the retreat was to work together at an opera. This was 'Alfonso und Estrella', a grand opera in the full sense of the term as far as externals are concerned. It is the only one which Schubert wrote, since both 'Des Teufels Lustschloss' and 'Fierrabras' have spoken dialogue. Schubert has dated his first act '20 September 1821'. It was finished on 16 October and the second act started on 18 October. But after the month at St. Pölten the two friends returned to Vienna, and the music of Act II was finished there on 2 November. That day Schubert wrote a letter to Spaun and informed him with relish that his dedications on the early song publications had 'done their work'. That is to say, the gratified patrons had sent him sums of money as well as grateful acknowledgements. In an added page or two to this letter Schober told Spaun of their month in the 'half-town, half-country' district of St. Pölten and how the opera had come to be written, both friends, apparently, working in a communal study, Schober passing pieces of the libretto as he finished them across to Schubert for composing! Schober's letter also told of three 'Schubertiads' held during the month, one of them attended—so he wrote—by a princess, two countesses and three baronesses. The third act of 'Alfonso und Estrella' was finished on 27 February 1822; the overture was composed later than this, in February 1823. This was probably a first draft, and the manuscript is now lost.

Early in 1821 Schubert had moved from his lodgings with Mayrhofer to a nearby house in the same street. After the return from St. Pölten he lodged once again with the Schober family in the 'Göttweigerhof', situated in the street known today as the Spiegelgasse. The move may have been to continue the work on the opera, but he continued to live there some months after its completion.

Eduard Bauernfeld, a student of philosophy, a future playwright and satirist, and a noted translator of Shakespeare, met Schubert during January 1822. Schwind, the young painter, introduced them at a Schubertiad in the house of Vincentius

Weintridt. Both Bauernfeld and Schwind were great admirers of Weintridt, a noted freethinker of his day, and Schubert, too, evidently, found Weintridt's philosophy to his taste. The meeting between Schubert and Bauernfeld, ardently desired by the latter, was the start of a close and rewarding friendship.

The summer of 1822 is poor in compositions, an understandable reaction from the intensive work on the opera. The popular 'Military Marches', Op. 51, for pianoforte duet, were probably composed at that time; the first of the three, in D major, is one of the most attractive, melodically, of his works in the form, with a delicately modulated 'Trio' section. But if compositions were lacking, performances of his songs and the part-songs of Op. 11, were very numerous during the year in Vienna, and in other, provincial, towns. The three part-songs, *Das Dörfchen, Die Nachtigall* and *Geist der Liebe* seem to us today insipid to a degree, but their appeal for Schubert's generation was extraordinarily strong. They were repeatedly performed during his lifetime.

A document of Schubert's survives from the July of 1822 to which Ferdinand gave the title *My Dream*. It is a fanciful account in a rather elevated style of writing of a quarrel between the writer and his father. Reconciliation follows the mother's death, but the quarrel is renewed. Then a gentle maiden dies and after her burial there is a further, and one gathers, a final reconciliation. It struck the nineteenth century as a queer production—but nothing more than that. Then, following upon a suggestion by Schubert's half-brother Anton, the Schubertian Alois Fellner, and after him, Walter Dahms in his biography of Schubert (1912), treated the allegory as a chapter of autobiography. The document suddenly leapt into importance. For a quarter of a century all Schubert biographies and biographical essays developed the theme that Schubert and his father had quarrelled because of the young composer's absorption in music to the neglect of other studies at the *Konvikt*. Reconciliation came with the death of Schubert's mother. The further quarrel was when Schubert finally abandoned his tasks as a teacher and left for Hungary in 1818. There was a wild disregard of dates and facts to make these theories fit the tale *My Dream*. Schubert's mother died in

1812 during his years at the *Stadtkonvikt* before he had shown
any sign of neglecting his general studies. After Schubert left the
Rossau schoolhouse in 1818 his letters to his family show no sign
whatever of estrangement—on the contrary. Nowadays the reaction against the autobiographical interpretation of the document
is complete. Inspired by O. E. Deutsch's scorn of any such interpretation, modern biographers of the composer refuse to allow
My Dream any basis in fact.

In all probability both extremes are equally at fault. Without
fully subscribing to an autobiographical interpretation one might
feel that there is something in the document of truth. Spaun, for
example, in some notes on his relationship with Schubert, 'Ueber
Franz Schubert', said:

> He told me that he often wanted to compose his thoughts in
> music, but his father mustn't know about it, for he didn't want his
> son to dedicate himself to music.

In manuscript recollections of Mayrhofer's we read:

> I often had to console Schubert's worthy father about his son's
> future, and I dared to prophesy that Franz would surely win through,
> nay that a later world would give him his due, slowly though it
> came to him at first.

Both Spaun and Mayrhofer wrote those remarks long before any
autobiographical theories were spun about *My Dream*.

What are the origins of the allegory? It has been suggested
that Novalis's flowery style, and contemporary German 'Romantic' tales are responsible. This is probably the case, and I have
suggested elsewhere that, in particular, the work of Wilhelm
Heinrich Wackenroder, which Schubert may have read at the
Stadtkonvikt, is being closely imitated. Without wishing to add
yet one more theory to those which already exist about *My Dream*,
it has occurred to me that this production of Schubert's pen may
have been the outcome of some exploit of the friends during the
Atzenbrugg holidays. Its date 3 July 1822 lends some support to
the idea, and so does the fact that a copy of the 'Dream' exists in

Schober's handwriting. They indulged in all kinds of 'pen-and-paper' games at Atzenbrugg castle; making poems on given words was one of them, making melodies from dots on a piece of paper was another. Possibly Schubert's *My Dream* was the best of the efforts during some similar, forgotten *jeu d'esprit* of the party, and Schober considered it worth preserving.

Schubert's pen was idle during the summer of 1822, but the astonishing burst of composition in the autumn gives the year outstanding importance. In September he took up the half-finished Mass in A flat which he had commenced in November 1819. It has always been assumed that he also abandoned the work in that November, but recently a pencil sketch of the song *Die gefangenen Sänger* dated January 1821 has come to light and on it there are also sketches of the 'Credo' for the Mass; the probability is that Schubert worked spasmodically on the Mass during the three years. At least he completed it in the September of 1822. Soon afterwards it was performed in the old Lerchenfeld Church, situated in east Vienna. In October he sketched, in PF. score, three movements of a Symphony in B minor. These sketches lay in obscurity amongst the mass of MSS. which passed into the possession of Ferdinand when Schubert died. They went on Ferdinand's death to one of his sons, Karl, together with a few other unfinished compositions of no saleable value, including the fragmentary duet 'Linde Lüfte wehen'. These manuscripts were discovered in Karl Schubert's possession by Max Friedlaender, in October 1883, and two years later the symphony sketches were purchased by Nikolaus Dumba. The sketches passed, on Dumba's death, into the Library of the *Gesellschaft der Musikfreunde*. The reason for recounting in detail this passing from hand to hand of the manuscript sketches will be justified later. Schubert began to score the work on 30 October. He completed two movements, but only the first page of the 'Scherzo' (not actually so called by Schubert) is written. Sometime in November 1822 the work was set aside and he never returned to it. This unfinished symphony, which was, after the lapse of half a century, to become the 'Unfinished' Symphony, so that to the whole musical world a peculiar evocative quality attached itself to the word 'unfinished', joined the other two unfinished works, in D and E, of previous years.

The subsequent history of Schubert's orchestral score of the 'Unfinished' Symphony is, as with many other works of his, almost unbelievable. In the following April (1823) the Styrian Music Society, whose headquarters were at Graz, elected Schubert as an honorary member, sending him a 'Diploma of Honour'. This honour was due to the activities of Johann Baptist Jenger, the secretary of the Society, a friend and admirer of the composer. The election and diploma were handed to Anselm Hüttenbrenner (an active musician in those days at Graz and, naturally, a member of the Society) for transference via Josef Hüttenbrenner, then in Vienna, to Schubert. The diploma was handed over to the composer in September 1823 on his return from a short holiday in Steyr and he at once acknowledged it and promised to send 'one of his symphonies in full score'. Josef stated in a letter written many years afterwards to his younger brother Andreas that Schubert handed him the score of the 'Unfinished' Symphony at the Schottentor (one of the gates leading through the walls of the Inner City: it is the one through which Schubert would naturally pass to and from his father's house and the Inner City) whence it eventually reached Anselm at Graz. This was probably in the October. From then onwards, for many years, the work disappeared from view. Schubert obviously thought no more about it; when he required one of his early symphonies he fell back on the 1818 work, in C major. Anselm Hüttenbrenner never bothered to get it performed at Graz, but perhaps this is understandable in view of its incomplete state. One might question, at this stage, Anselm Hüttenbrenner's action in appropriating a symphony score which had been sent as a gift to him, not as an individual, but as an official of a Society. After Schubert's death the Hüttenbrenners did not bother overmuch to let people know of the existence of this major work, although they themselves were only too well aware of its stature. In 1853 Anselm made a PF. Duet arrangement of the first two movements which he played with his brother. The manuscript of the Symphony was mentioned in the catalogue of Schubert manuscripts in his posses-

I B.S.

sion, which he made for Liszt in 1854. A few years later the work was referred to by Josef when he wrote to Johann Herbeck, the conductor of the Vienna 'Männergesangverein' and a director of the *Gesellschaft*. This letter of Josef's is dated 8 March 1860 and contains the words:

> (Anselm) possesses a treasure in Schubert's B minor Symphony, which we rank with his great C major Symphony, his instrumental swansong, and with all the symphonies of Beethoven—only it is unfinished. Schubert gave it to me for Anselm to thank him for having sent the diploma of the Graz Music Society through me. . . .

Before the score was finally obtained from Anselm, and obtained in a way which almost suggests a wresting of it from his possession, there were two more references to the symphony The first was in Wurzbach's great biographical dictionary of the Austrian Empire in the section devoted to Anselm Hüttenbrenner; the second was the famous paragraph in Kreissle's biography (1865):

> There is an orchestral symphony in B minor, which Schubert presented, in a half-finished state, to the Musikverein at Graz, in return for the compliment paid to him of being elected an honorary member of that Society. Josef Hüttenbrenner is my authority for saying that the first and second movements are entirely finished, and the third partly. The fragment, in the possession of Herr Anselm Hüttenbrenner of Graz, is said, the first movement particularly, to to be of great beauty. If this be so, Schubert's intimate friend would do well to emancipate the still unknown work of the master he so highly honours, and introduce the symphony to Schubert's admirers.

As a result, when Herbeck visited Graz that same year (1865) Anselm was probably half prepared to yield up the work. Herbeck ingratiated himself by promising to perform a composition of Anselm's at Vienna during the coming winter season of concerts, and on mentioning, innocently, Schubert's name, the score of the 'Unfinished' was produced. Herbeck's account of the incident makes interesting reading. Preserving an air of disinterested calm he turned over the pages of the manuscript and gradually realised the beauty of the symphony. With a casual remark to the effect that it would be quite suitable for inclusion in the concert programmes he asked if he might have the score copied. 'Oh! take the manuscript back with you—take it!' said Anselm. Herbeck bore it off in triumph, and the opening two movements of the symphony were heard for the first time in Vienna on 17 December 1865.

Why was the Symphony in B minor never finished? It is one of the great enigmas in music, and there are three suggested answers to the question, each of which must be considered. The first is easily disposed of since it arose in the years immediately following the production of the work and was based on ignorance of the facts, namely, that Schubert intended the work to be a two-movement symphony, on the lines of, say, Beethoven's Sonata in F sharp major, Op. 78. The existence of an almost fully sketched 'Scherzo'-movement disposes of the argument.

The second theory, held widely in the early years of this century, suggests that self-criticism withheld the addition of a Scherzo and Finale: that the composer could not bring himself to add an unworthy pair of concluding movements to the two supreme ones he had already written. This is a sentimental view. It invests Schubert with emotions congenial to the observer, not with those which he could actually have felt. Schubert probably had no complete idea of the greatness and originality of the two symphonic movements he had just written; his cavalier treatment of them does not support the notion. Moreover, such a feeling did not prevent him, in the years following the 'Unfinished' Symphony, from occasionally adding an inferior Finale to first-rate preceding movements, in the PF. Trio in E flat, Op. 100, or in the G major PF. Sonata, Op. 78, to give two examples which spring to mind.

The third answer to the question is a more formidable, because a more acceptable one. It is that Schubert *did* finish the symphony and that Anselm Hüttenbrenner lost the MS. folios at the back of the unbound score: folios containing the end of the Scherzo and the Finale. This theory was expounded by Dr. T. C. L. Pritchard in the Music Review, Cambridge, February 1942. There are three factual pieces of evidence which, at first sight, lend support to the theory. The fully scored opening bars of the Scherzo end abruptly at the bottom of a page, and from the oboe part a 'tie' extends outwards and this suggests that another page of the score, at least, must have followed; the four blank pages at the end of the 'Unfinished' score suggest that a whole sheaf of papers has fallen out; and finally there is the well-known Hüttenbrenner fatality where MSS. are concerned. Dr. Pritchard points out the unlikelihood of Schubert handing over an unfinished work to the Graz Music Society, and goes on to say that Anselm kept quiet about the work for over forty years because he had lost the last part of it. Now one fact is missing from the above argument which makes a whole heap of difference when it is remembered. It is the existence of the preliminary sketches. These were never in the possession of the Hüttenbrenners and their history was recounted to show that they were never out of the hands of careful owners, from the time that Schubert died to the time they entered the Library of the *Gesellschaft*. There is no hint of a sketched finale in them; there is, on the contrary, an incompletely sketched third movement. The very fact that these sketches were preserved by Schubert suggests that he was intending to resume work on them. The three pieces of factual evidence may be answered as follows. The extending of a 'tie' or 'slur' was a mannerism of Schubert's handwriting. Any student of his manuscripts soon becomes aware of this fact. The signs are often so mechanical as to have no meaning: it was almost a mark of continuity in his composition. The fair copy of his 'Scherzo' was being made, after all, from a pre-existing sketch and Schubert was aware of the necessity for the tied note in the oboe part. Next, the sheaf of papers might have been removed by Hüttenbrenner simply because they were blank! This is more likely. But even if we allow that some of the Scherzo-movement has been lost it is doubtful whether a fully scored finale of Schubertian dimensions could possibly have disappeared from the score without trace. Thirdly, in the matter of losing and ill-treating manuscripts, Josef, not Anselm, was the offender. A piece of evidence which suggest that the Hüttenbrenners told the truth when they said that the work was unfinished is the visit of Schubert to Graz in 1827. Why was the symphony never mentioned between the friends, or the possibility of a performance discussed? We might suggest that it was because it was a fragment which Schubert had forgotten about, or could not take very seriously.

In considering the music of the symphony it is essential to examine the PF. sketches for the work which, unlike the sketches for all his other finished orchestral movements, have survived. Without explaining the mystery of genius they do exemplify the *multum in parvo* which is so noticeable in the first, tentative ideas which visit genius. This is especially remarkable with Schubert who, as was mentioned in connection with his PF. sketches of the 1818 symphony, hastily wrote down and uncritically accepted his ideas for fear that the others teeming in his brain should obliterate them. The ideas for the B minor Symphony are frequently raw and unpolished, but they are unmistakably the visitations of genius, and, in the final form of the two movements, reach perfection. There is a new quality in the sketches for the 'Unfinished' Symphony—it is difficult to define. It has something of assurance, something of authority. This is particularly evident with the *codetta* music in the first movement (bars 73–83). Two examples might be quoted from these sketches to show Schubert at work. In the first movement his original but very abrupt transition to G major for the second subject, achieved by the long sustained note on the horns and bassoons, has often been commented on: a *coup de théâtre* it has been called. Here is Schubert's original idea for this transition (from the recapitulation):

Ex. 27

It is surely undeniable that this gradual and careful preparation is tedious compared with the arresting form it eventually took. The second quotation shows the development of an idea which

Schubert rejected from the final draft. It comes from the slow movement and is a treatment of the descending *pizzicato* scale of the opening two bars:

Ex. 28

etc.

This foreshadowing of Brahmsian practices was not congenial, evidently, and it does, as one can readily see, strike a false note in the unselfconscious outpouring of tenderness and sadness in the incomparable movement.

Mention of Brahms brings to mind that one gross misprint recopied again and again in the multiple scores of this symphony has been attributed to his editing. It occurs in bar 109 of the first movement, where the horns continue to play a B natural against a chord of the dominant seventh on strings and woodwind. The discord was too much for the ears of the 1860's and the first editor—if not Brahms, someone else—altered the note to C sharp. This is how it was printed by Spina in 1866 and how it appears in all subsequent editions. The text and its editions have been described thoroughly of recent years both in England and on the continent.[1]

The intimate tone and the strongly subjective emotions of his symphony were new in symphonic music, and the symmetry and formal beauty which enshrines this personal feeling cannot be too highly praised. Alfred Einstein has written:

> Not even Beethoven himself achieved anything more striking or more terse than the volcanic climax of the first movement of the 'Unfinished' Symphony. . . .

The excessive popularity of the symphony rests like a smear upon it; what are we to say, for instance, of a programme in which it is

[1] Ernst Hess: 'Zur Urtextfrage von Schuberts *Unvollendeten*', 'Schweizerische Musikzeitung', 1 March 1947. Adam Carse: 'Editing Schubert's Unfinished Symphony', 'Musical Times', March 1954.

sandwiched between Sullivan's 'Di Ballo' Overture and 'Tales from the Vienna Woods' of Johann Strauss? One feels that the manifold wonders of the symphony, whose music speaks so directly to the heart, have not received their full historical and scholastic acclaim. At first it seemed as if no acclaim at all was to be given to the work. One imagines that it must have leapt into instant popularity—but this is not quite so. A year elapsed before it was published. The Vienna music critic Hanslick asked whether the two movements were intended as a kind of background music for scenic effects in the theatre. Seven years later we find August Reissmann, in general a sound Schubertian, asking if these two movements should not be considered as part of the ballet music for a stage play—like that in B minor in the 'Rosamunde' music? How our estimation has changed! To quote Einstein once again: 'The "Unfinished" Symphony . . . that incomparable song of sorrow which we wrong every time we call it "Unfinished".' Strangely enough, in view of Reissmann's words, a composition by Schubert which has sometimes been used as a finale in performances of the symphony, and which is occasionally considered by critics and writers on music as a possibly unidentified finale to the work, is the 'Entr'acte in B minor' from the incidental music which Schubert wrote for the play 'Rosamunde'. There is much to commend the theory. The 'Entr'acte' is a true masterpiece, and would be a worthy companion to the other two movements. It was performed (on Grove's suggestion) at the Crystal Palace Concert of 19 March 1881 to serve as a finale to the symphony. It has been suggested that since Schubert was in such a hurry to complete the 'Rosamunde' music, he removed the finale of his symphony for use as an entr'acte. But the theory cannot be maintained against the facts. The manuscript paper of both scores has been minutely examined as a result of the theory, and the watermarks of both sheafs of paper are different. Although in itself this is not sufficient to disprove the suggestion, taken in conjunction with other contradicting statements it does so. For the symphony score was certainly in Graz at the time the 'Rosamunde' music was composed. Moreover, the heading of the music of the B minor Entr'acte, in Schubert's own hand, is 'No. 1:

Entre-Act nach dem 1. Aufz.' and it was certainly not an extracted finale movement that he headed so.

One actual fact which accounts for the setting aside of the symphony is his composition in November 1822 of the Pianoforte Fantasia in C major, Op. 15. It is a massively planned work in four sections corresponding to the four movements of a sonata, and universally known as the 'Wanderer Fantasia' although the name was not given to it by Schubert, nor ever used by him. The work is in C major—Schubert's 'epic' key—and we have evidence of the composer's love of what one might call 'Neapolitan' relationships in the choice of his keys. The 'Neapolitan' chord is built on the note a semitone above the key-note; in C major, for instance, C sharp (or D flat) is the basis of the chord, so that this note stands to C major in a 'Neapolitan' relationship. The *Adagio* of the Fantasia is in C sharp minor. The composer dedicated the work to Emmanuel, Edler von Liebenberg de Zsettin, a pupil of Hummel's and a wealthy landowner; it was published shortly after its composition by Cappi & Diabelli, in February 1823.

New, ornate, powerful pianoforte techniques were introduced by Schubert into this composition. The final movement, a rugged fugue, is almost *un*pianistic. Writing of the first movement Schumann said on 13 August 1828—that is, while Schubert was still alive:

> Schubert would like, in this work, to condense the whole orchestra into two hands, and the enthusiastic beginning is a seraphic hymn to the Godhead; you see the angels pray; the *Adagio* is a gentle meditation on life and takes the veil from off it; then fugues thunder forth a song of endless humanity and music.

The excessive ornamentation of the variations in the slow movement becomes almost guilty of display, but Schubert redeems it by anticipating in the baroque detail the theme of the next movement, the *Presto* Scherzo. The variations are written on an extract—much modified for the composer's purpose—from the song of 1816, the famous 'Der Wanderer', hence the name of the

Fantasia. Some critics have sought to interpret Schubert's Fantasia as a morbid exposition of the *words* of the extract, which are the despairing cry of the wandering exile, that life is empty and he is everywhere an outcast. But such an interpretation is itself morbid: it ignores the vigour and exuberance of Schubert's springtime music. The dramatic, yet broad, progress of the work belies its nickname, 'Wanderer'; from the start it knows where it is going and does not stray nor hesitate on its dynamic path. Sir Donald Tovey has said of this work that in its alternation of stormy development with quiet lyricism, and in its leisurely approach to climaxes, it looks back to the concertos of Bach (which Schubert, of course, did not know) and in its dexterous handling of the remotest possible key-relationships it looks forward to Wagner. The powerful climaxes of the work are helped and given sonority by Liszt's celebrated arrangement for Pianoforte and Orchestra; this alone would justify the later composer's version of what, to use his own words, he called: 'Schubert's splendid "Wanderer-Dithyramb".'

IV

1822 is the crisis of Schubert's life. It is during that year that we feel the real man is being buried beneath an assumed pose of the experienced, blasé man-about-town, and the off-hand, self-important artist. It was suggested at the beginning of the chapter that his head was slightly turned by the limited successes of that year and the previous one: the appearance of his work in the Viennese theatres, the publication of his songs and piano pieces, the adulation of the Schubertiads. Testimony to the state of affairs is not lacking, as the letters quoted below will show.

His friend of *Konvikt* days, Anton Holzapfel, wrote on 22 February 1822 to Albert Stadler:

… Schubert, as they say, made *bruit*, and he will likewise, as they say, make his *sort*. I rarely see him, nor do we hit it off very well, his world being a very different one, as it should be. His somewhat gruff manner stands him in very good stead and will make a strong man and a ripe artist of him; he will be worthy of art. … Schubert is working at an opera, the words of which are by Schober, a work at which they are said to have both laboured together in mutual understanding.

The 'gruff manner' is significant—how ill it goes with our picture of the gentle, goodnatured Schubert. But more telling is Spaun's heartfelt cry to Schober in a letter of 5 March 1822:

> ... Winter has gone by since then, and much that is of interest must have happened among you all, of which you should not deprive your far-off and dear friend. I am so very anxious to know all that the poetical-musical-painting triumvirate has produced. It cuts me to the soul that Schubert has ceased to sound for me. . . .

A third letter is from Spaun's brother, Anton, to his wife. Anton was staying at Steyr during the summer of 1822 and had met Vogl there. He wrote home to Linz, on 20 July 1822:

> ... To me Vogl is extremely pleasing. He told me his whole relationship to Schubert with the utmost frankness, and unfortunately I am quite unable to excuse the latter. Vogl is very much embittered against Schober, for whose sake Schubert behaved most ungratefully towards Vogl and who makes the fullest use of Schubert in order to extricate himself from financial embarrassments and to defray the expenditure which has already exhausted the greater part of his mother's fortune. I wish very much that somebody were here who would defend Schubert at least in the matter of the most glaring reproaches. Vogl also says Schober's opera is bad and a total failure and that altogether Schubert is quite on the wrong road.

This is outspoken enough, and prepares us somewhat for the tragedy of the autumn. Schober's influence, not only on Schubert, but on all the members of his circle, was no secret. It is pretty clearly stated by many of these men in the letters they later on wrote to each other, and to biographers of Schubert, such as Ferdinand Luib and Liszt. Josef Kenner, in a letter to Luib of 1858, wrote of an episode in Schubert's life 'which only too probably caused his early death, and certainly accelerated it'. The episode is the contracting of venereal disease during the late autumn of 1822. O. E. Deutsch points out in the Schubert 'Documents' (page 287) that the disease was probably syphilis, although a clear distinction between various venereal diseases was not understood in Schubert's day. Certainly the course of the illness suggests that Schubert was suffering from it. The conventions of the nineteenth-century forbade any reference to the disease in the biographies of the composer; the complete absence of contemporary references, although the trouble was known to all his friends, suggests that documents, letters and so on, have been destroyed. Schubert's illness is mentioned, if at all, as a passing indisposition. Its effects on the composer, immediate and eventual, were deep and disturbing. The shock restored him to himself—the artificialities and assumptions of 1822 vanish like smoke. The six years till his death show bursts of abounding spirits, health and creative energy, but they alternate with periods of black depression, illness and stagnation.

The onset of this disease led to his leaving Schober's house. He returned in December to the schoolhouse in the Rossau district, and lived there for the next year. He sought his family, his brother Ferdinand; and he wrote a long, warm letter to Spaun telling him of his compositions, the PF. Fantasia, the Mass in A flat, the new Goethe songs. Two letters, both undated, but which from internal evidence belong to 1823, show the beginning of a withdrawal, almost of an indifference; the first is to Leopold Sonnleithner declining an offer to compose for the *Gesellschaft* concerts, the second to the music director of the St. Anna College declining to submit an orchestral overture for performance there.

His friendship with Josef Hüttenbrenner was closer than ever, in fact, Hüttenbrenner seemed to act as a kind of unofficial, and naturally unpaid, secretary and agent to Schubert. He kept the composer's accounts, wrote to publishers, and even made attempts to secure performances of Schubert's operas, including the juvenile 'Des Teufels Lustschloss'. Schubert himself was still sanguine about the chances of 'Alfonso und Estrella'. Weber at Dresden had expressed an interest in the work, and Schubert hoped that Ignaz von Mosel might propose the opera to him. In a letter to Mosel on 28 February 1823, Schubert wrote that he had completed the overture to 'Alfonso und Estrella' and asked if his opera might be personally recommended to Weber. At the Kärntnertor theatre, during 1822, the management had been taken over by Domenico Barbaja. He was not interested overmuch in German opera, and certainly not in the hazardous business of putting on the latest works of obscure composers. Schubert's hopes in his new opera were doomed.

His health grew worse, and the need for money became so urgent that in the early part of the year he sold outright to Diabelli his copyright in the early opus-numbers (Opp. 1–7). He received £32 for the transaction, and then asked Diabelli for £24 in exchange for his rights in Opp. 12–14. The publisher haggled over the sum and beat Schubert down, and this treatment, together with Schubert's suspicions of Diabelli's accounts of sales and so forth, led to a breach between them. The manuscripts which Schubert had already sold to the publisher came out as Opp. 16 and 17 (male voice quartets) and Op. 19 (songs including *An Schwager Kronos*) but there was no other connection between the composer and the publisher for several years.

In February Schubert was confined to the house and during the month of enforced rest he composed the first of his mature sonatas for PF. solo, the second in A minor, published posthumously as Op. 143. It opens with a stark, uncompromising movement in his grandest vein, and was subjected to the kind of revision which does not often occur in his work. The manuscript of the sonata, only recently emerging from obscurity, shows him going back to make alterations in the exposition of the first movement in the light of later changes in the recapitulation. The theme of the slow movement—one of his most original essays in this type of movement, and yet one praised in the nineteenth century for its 'Beethovenish' qualities!—was originally this:

Ex.29

The change in the note at ★ to A makes the melody unbelievably stronger.

Two sets of dances, sweet and lilting, were composed during this spring of wretchedness and ill-health (the capacity of the creative artist to detach himself from material circumstances is a constant surprise to the less gifted observer, and in Schubert's case the detachment is phenomenal). The dances were in the 'Deutsche' or 'Ländler' style, which is little else than a short, substantial waltz. One set appeared as Op. 33 in 1825, the second was not published until many years after his death, as Op. 171 in 1864. The sixth dance in Op. 171 might almost be a sketch for a later work, the Scherzo in the 'Death and the Maiden' String Quartet, and the third dance is a prophetic piece of writing whose fluid, chromatic harmony might easily be from the pen of Chopin:

Ex. 30

A one-act *Singspiel*, 'Die Verschworenen', was composed during March and April while he was contending with pain and depression. And yet the music of the operetta is gay and high-spirited, and so suggestive of the legendary Vienna of the musical comedy stage, that it might be thought an outpouring of Schubert in the happiest of his days. The libretto is by Ignaz Castelli, one of a group of authors who wrote comedies for the Viennese theatres in which the basic idea was to explore the comic possibilities arising when ordinary citizens were placed against a fantastic background, such as the landscape of the moon, or fairyland, or, as in this *Singspiel*, of a sham medievalism which only existed in tales and stage plays. Castelli based his play on the 'Lysistrata' of Aristophanes. A number of disgruntled wives try to force their soldiering husbands to stay at home instead of everlastingly campaigning in the Wars of the Crusades, by denying them all matrimonial rights until they promise to give up war. Castelli published his play in February 1823 as the eighth number of a series of plays called 'Dramatische Sträusschen'. It contained a preface with these words addressed to composers:

> You are always asking for good opera librettos. Here is one! Now set it to music, gentlemen, and strike a blow for German Opera.

Schubert finished his setting at the end of April. A touchy political censorship disliked the title ('The Conspirators') and insisted that it be changed: it became 'Der häusliche Krieg' ('Domestic Warfare'). But the work was never accepted for performance at the Opera, and nearly thirty years passed before it was eventually staged. This took place at Frankfurt-am-Main in August 1861. There had been a concert version in Vienna during the March of that year and the aged Castelli was present sitting beside Hanslick. He confessed himself amazed at the sparkle and charm of the music. The operetta was performed in France[1] under the title 'La Crusade des Dames', translated into French by the famous Victor Wilder, in February 1868, and Wilder's version was later used in Vienna in preference to Castelli's original German text! The music may best be discussed later.

Schubert's illness reached a critical stage in May, and he was obliged to spend a short time in the Vienna 'General Hospital'. There is no real evidence at all that he commenced work on the 'Schöne Müllerin' song-cycle in this month; this was a later surmise. There is, on the contrary, such a bulk of existing compositions actually dated 'May 1823' that it is practically impossible for the 'Müllerin' songs also to belong to the month. The stronger probability is that he started the series of songs during August at Steyr. There are several other songs of May; they include no primary example of his work, although parts of the flower-ballade by Schober, *Vergissmeinnicht*, are delicious. He was on the look-out for a full length opera libretto; there are very long sketches for an opera called 'Rüdiger' or 'Rüdigers Heimkehr', the words by an unknown author, but whose story clearly deals with Rüdiger von Bechelaren. It is an episode from the

---

[1] It is surprising to find that as early as March 1863, 'Die Verschworenen' was given in Hoboken, New Jersey, U.S.A. This was much earlier than any performance in England.

Nibelungen sagas. But, as a critic has pointed out in another connection, the hour of the 'Ring' had not yet struck. Another very bulky sheaf of sketches by Schubert is preserved in the Vienna *Stadtbibliothek* for an untitled opera, in which the heroine is named 'Sofie'. The work may be attributed to this period since among the melodies Schubert wrote for the 'Sofie' opera is this one which he afterwards retrieved for the next opera, 'Fierrabras':

Ex.31

'Fierrabras' was a three-act opera written by Josef Kupelwieser, Leopold's brother. It is a lifeless story, as all these heavily 'Romantic' stories of the Spanish aristocracy are liable to be, since they deal with people, situations and events which never were, nor ever could be. Schubert's work was written in a short space of time—but the dates on his manuscripts have with very good reason been questioned. They are:

Act I: 25 May–30 May.
Act II: finished on 5 June.

Not even Schubert could have covered the enormous first act in five or six days. Walter Dahms has suggested that the dates for the conclusions of each act should read, respectively, 30 June and 5 August. This is rather too tidy a solution, but clearly something is wrong. Act III was finished on 26 September, and the Overture commenced on 2 October.

A word might be added here about the spelling of the title. Kupelwieser and Schubert and the writers of the nineteenth century contentedly used the double 'r'. Occasionally, as in Grove's catalogues, the spelling is 'Fierabras'. In the Schubert 'Documents', O. E. Deutsch instituted the single 'r'—'Fierabras' —since in the original Spanish he found that the word was so spelt. It means in that language 'Braggart' or 'Boaster'. Now this correction would have more force if the hero of the opera were such a character; but Fierrabras is simply a proper name, and should be spelt as Kupelwieser and Schubert spelt it. There is, moreover, evidence that in the sixteenth century (*c.* 1530) the name was 'Ferrbras'. On the whole, to use the original spelling seems the most satisfactory solution, and it will be so used here. The B.B.C. recently *translated* the title and announced the overture of Schubert's opera 'The Braggart'; this is fatuous. One might as well translate 'Faust' as 'The Pugilist'.

Recuperating from his weakness and wretched physical state, Schubert travelled to Linz and Steyr during July and August. He arrived in Linz on 25 July and was introduced by Spaun to the Hartmann family. Friedrich von Hartmann, an eminent civil servant, had two sons, Franz and Fritz; they went to Vienna in 1825, and their copious diaries contain many references to the day-by-day activities of the Schubert circle.

At Steyr, on 29 August, Schubert arranged a setting of Psalm VIII, 'O Lord, our God, how excellent is Thy name in all the earth', by the Abbé Maximilian Stadler, for string orchestra and organ. The original is for voice and pianoforte (or organ). It may have been commissioned by Sylvester Paumgartner, and it was performed in the Parish Church of Steyr by Vogl, whose copy of the voice part, in his own hand, has also survived with Schubert's copy of the same part.[1] The complete score of Schubert's arrangement, an autograph manuscript, was not discovered until May 1952.

Schubert altered a number of passages in both voice part and accompaniment; it is not a simple orchestration of the piece. He was clearly attracted to it, and strange to say there are decided Schubertian traits in the work—this phrase, for example, from bars 4–6:

Ex. 32 *mf* Maximilian Stadler

Wie mächt - ig ist dein Nam' auf Erd-en

[1] Max Friedlaender commented adversely on Vogl's alterations of the vocal part (an *idée fixe* of Friedlaender's); but they are Schubert's own this time.

which Schubert altered slightly to make even more intensely his own.

During August he continued work on Act III of 'Fierrabras', and probably this month in that summery countryside he began to compose the first songs of the cycle 'Die schöne Müllerin', which embowers, in an evergreen music, an idyll of young and tragic love in a valley, remote from the dust and traffic of the town. The evidence for August as the month of their commencement is not decisive, but it does exist: it is Spaun's remark in after years that Schubert started the 'Mill' songs at *Zseliz*. This place cannot be the right one, since Schubert was not there until a year later. But Spaun clearly had in mind that Schubert was not in Vienna, but in the country somewhere, and Steyr fits in with the fact, and the year 1823. Back in Vienna (in the middle of September) he continued to work on the songs, and the fifteenth one, *Eifersucht und Stolz*, survives in manuscript and is dated October 1823. On 30 November he wrote to Schober:

> I have composed nothing else since the opera (Fierrabras) except a few 'Mill' songs. The 'Mill' song-cycle will be published in four parts with vignettes by Schwind.

Trockne Blumen, the seventeenth song in the series, was used as the theme of a set of variations (flute and pianoforte), which Schubert composed in January 1824. The variations were written for his friend Ferdinand Bogner, evidently at his request. This suggests that Bogner had heard the song recently, so that its composition might have been in December 1823. Finally we have Schwind writing on 6 March 1824 to Schober: 'Of Müller's poems he has set two very beautifully'—which probably marks the end of Schubert's work on the cycle. The five books (not four as originally intended) were published by the August of 1824. The story told by Randhartinger in his old age that Schubert had encountered the poems through him is a pure fabrication (see page 330).

Wilhelm Müller's sequence of songs was published in Dessau two years before Schubert discovered them. 'Die schöne Müllerin' was the first part of the collection 'Poems found in the

posthumous papers of a travelling horn-player' and was sub-
titled 'to be read in the winter'. It is said to have originated in a
kind of play acted by members of Müller's circle, called 'Rose, the
lovely maid of the mill'. Schubert omitted the poet's prologue
and epilogue, as well as three poems from the main sequence;
each of these comes from one of the three emotional phases of
the cycle—hope, love, jealousy.

The music society at Linz, a more modest affair than the one
at Graz, also elected Schubert as an honorary member during
August. As far as Schubert knew this was the first of the honours,
for it will be recalled that Josef Hüttenbrenner was unable to give
the composer the certificate of election to Graz until he returned
to Vienna the following month. He was still ailing, and there are
frequent references to his state in letters to and from his friends.
Schober (at Breslau) received news of his friend's serious illness
from Schwind, from Anton von Doblhoff and from Spaun. Schubert himself wrote to Schober (the letter quoted on page 133) and
of his own condition he said:

> For the rest, I hope to regain my health, and this recovered bene-
> fit will make me forget many sorrows. . . .

He also informed Schober that Weber's new opera 'Euryanthe'
turned out badly, and in his opinion deserved its poor reception.

Schubert probably ruined his chances with Weber by his outspoken criticism of 'Euryanthe'. Spaun tells in his reminiscences
that at first Weber was extraordinarily friendly, and promised
because of Mosel's recommendation to bring 'Alfonso und Estrella' to performance in Berlin. When he enquired of Schubert
how his opera had pleased him Schubert replied: 'Right well—
but 'Freischütz' had pleased him better'. There was, in his view,
too little melody in the new opera. Weber received this coldly,
and there was no more talk of a production of 'Alfonso'. Spaun
adds that he had all this from Schubert himself. But it is an exaggeration to say that Weber and Schubert quarrelled over the
judgement. Later on, when Weber heard of the failure of Schubert's 'Rosamunde' he wrote frankly to Castelli, in Vienna, and

said the fact gave him no pleasure, but only increased his embarrassment.

'Rosamunde' closes 1823 with a strange blend of success and failure, of renown and obscurity, of brilliance and darkness. The play was by Wilhelmine von Chézy, the authoress of 'Euryanthe', and it was given on 20 December. We hear nothing about it until the announcement on the day previous to its performance, but it is fairly obvious that Schubert wrote the music in a very short space of time—one account says five days.[1] Evidence is scanty, but not entirely lacking, that the music was composed without much time to spare. He used the overture he had already drafted for 'Alfonso und Estrella', writing the final score in December. Schwind, writing to Schober two days after the performance, said:

> Schubert had taken over the Overture he wrote for 'Estrella', as he thinks it too 'homespun' for 'Estella', for which he wants to write a new one.

There is the possibility, already discussed, that the entr'acte to be played after Act I was part of the 'Unfinished' Symphony; in any case one piece of ballet music was either used as the basis of this entr'acte, or was itself based on the entr'acte. In the second entr'acte, the very popular one in B flat, the interlude in B flat minor is an orchestrated version of an early song of his called *Die Leidende* (1816). A third entr'acte was based on one of the choruses in the play. The full list of Schubert's incidental music is as follows:

1. Entr'acte in B minor, after Act I.
2. Ballet music in B minor, similar to the previous entr'acte, Act II.
3. Entr'acte in D major, based on the 'Chorus of Spirits', after Act II.
4. 'Romance' for contralto, 'Der Vollmond strahlt', Act III.
5. Chorus of Spirits (Male voices), Act III.
6. Entr'acte in B flat, after Act III.

[1] Wilhelm von Chézy, son of the authoress: 'Erinnerungen', 1863.

7. Shepherd's melody in B flat for clarinets, horns and bassoons, Act IV.
8. Chorus of Shepherds (Mixed voices), Act IV.
9. Chorus of Huntsmen (Mixed voices), Act IV.
10. Ballet Music in G major, Act IV.

The actual play is lost, but a very full summary of the plot survives from contemporary records. There are some strange flowers in the rotting undergrowth of the 'Romantic' jungle-world, but nothing stranger than this play, with its secret passages, princesses brought up by fisher-folk, shipwrecks, poisoned letters, shephered princes and the rest. After two performances the play vanished from the boards. Schubert's music was fairly well received, the 'Overture'—one of his most successful overtures—was encored, and so was the Hunting Chorus. Some of the items were published soon after the performance as Op. 26, on 24 March 1824; Schubert arranged the orchestral accompaniments for the piano. The rest of the items followed at intervals and by 1867 the whole series had been published except the delightful little piece called 'Shepherd's Melody' (No. 7). The well-known anecdote of Grove and Sullivan digging in a dusty cupboard to find Schubert's 'Rosamunde' music, placed there after the second performance and undisturbed for forty-four years, needs to be modified a little. The two men were looking for, and they found, the orchestral parts for the items published as Op. 26, for which, it has been said, Schubert had arranged a piano part. The items were nos. 4, 5, 8 and 9 in the list above.

One of the most interesting aspects of the Grove and Sullivan story, and one which seems to have been overlooked, is that Edward Schneider's office, where the tied up sets of parts were discovered, was in the Tuchlauben. Now when Schubert died, the bulk of his manuscripts was in Schober's house, which was also in this same well-known street. So between 1828, when the composer died, and 1867, when the two Englishmen found the manuscripts, the music had wandered from place to place in Vienna, but had eventually found its way back to within a few yards of its original storing-place.

The two overtures, both called 'Rosamunde' Overtures, can now be seen to have no claim to the name. The earlier one, in C major, was written for the melodrama 'Die Zauberharfe', and has become associated with the play because it was published as 'Op. 26', reserved for the 'Rosamunde' items; the later one, in D minor and major, was written for 'Alfonso und Estrella', and has become associated with the play partly because it was played at the actual first performance of 'Rosamunde' in the Theater an der Wien, and partly because the editor of the Opera Volumes in the 'Gesamtausgabe', Johann Nepomuk Fuchs, printed it at the start of the incidental music for the play. Schubert never wrote an overture for the play, and he himself referred to the Overture to 'Alfonso' as 'his "Rosamunde" Overture' (see his letter to Ignaz von Seyfried, 23 November 1826).

It is not certain whether Schubert attended the first performance, but it seems from Schwind's letter dated 24 December 1823 as though he had been ill again. Written to Schober in Breslau the letter tells us:

> ... Schubert is better, and it will not be long before he goes about in his own hair again, which had to be shorn owing to the rash. He wears a very cosy wig.

V

'Rosamunde' was the last serious attempt on Schubert's part to achieve a success in the Viennese theatres. That he never gave up hope is evident from the fact that he was engaged in sketching the music for Bauernfeld's libretto 'Der Graf von Gleichen' ('The Count of Gleichen') in the last years of his life. But these are only sketches, and there is nothing for the stage in any work of Schubert's last four years. It will be possible now to consider his achievement in this field, an achievement for which he laboured with much failure and very little success for ten years.

These operas of his, numerous and varied as they are, have been ignored by the world of music. Are they the heap of failures which most biographers and critics say they are? Who is to answer the question? How many musicians have acquainted themselves intimately with 'Alfonso und Estrella', say, from the full score, in order to find out if Schubert's one grand opera deserves its complete and utter neglect?[1] As one who has made the effort I would say that the score contains as much fine and outstanding music as any other full length opera ever written, if we judge the score purely as music. Schober's libretto, moreover, silly as it is, is not quite the absurd farrago that all the other Schubert operas, except 'Die Verschworenen', prove to be on examination, although even there, amongst the variety of plot and situation and dénouement, there are degrees of stupidity. But 'Alfonso und Estrella' would need skilful production, adequate setting and—if necessary—musicianly cutting, if it were to make its full effect: precisely, in fact, what most of the operas in the repertory need.

Schubert's librettos are all the productions of people to whom the fashionable 'Romantic' story was an obsession. Gothic, or pseudo-Gothic, lore is ransacked for the plot; the landscape of the medieval artist, natural to Dürer say, but falsified and sentimentalised by the third rate poets of the day, forms the background. Spain is the country of three of the operas, 'Alfonso', 'Fierrabras' and the early work 'Don Fernando', with castles and gardens and serenades and all the other Spanish equipment of history and legend. But no poetry or imagination uplifts the trend in these librettos. 'Romantic' characterisation and situations often tend towards puppetry: at least the danger is there. It needs the genius of Scott or Victor Hugo or Schiller to give the puppets life. Then poor Schubert!—dependent upon Kotzebue and Mayrhofer and, even worse, Stadler and Kupelwieser. Their people and situations have as much life as the *tableaux* in a wax-works.

There is, in Schubert's stage music, a tendency towards the exalted and profound manner which often leads him, so to say, to fall between two stools. On the trifling and unreal plots he bestowed the light, tuneful music that the Viennese theatres pur-

[1] At this point the reader should be warned against a vocal score of this opera, published in 1882 by Schlesinger, of Berlin. It is an abominable travesty of Schubert's work perpretrated by J. N. Fuchs, the man already mentioned as being the editor of the Opera Volumes in the Schubert 'Gesamtausgabe'.

veyed. He used standard forms—march, waltz, polonaise, the 6/8 metres of the *siciliano*, the rhythms of folk-song. But he cannot keep out of it all the depths, the sublimities, which are part of his genius. Whenever, momentarily, his librettos take on a semblance of life, the scene, say, where Mauregato realises his daughter's terror at the thought of being plighted to Adolfo ('Alfonso und Estrella', Act I), his music at once glows with invention and poetry. If only, one cries again and again when reading his operatic scores, if only he had met with a libretto containing some serious, real, credible persons and situations. What would *he* have made of 'Romeo and Juliet', 'Tristan and Isolde', 'Traviata', 'La Bohême', and so on? It is an idle speculation, but a tempting one. Had he met with librettos of this sort, we should have seen the same thing happening in the tale of his operas as happened when he encountered 'Gretchen' after the thirty or so early songs.

The 1815 operettas are these: 'Der vierjährige Posten' (one act), written in twelve days in May to words by his acquaintance Theodor Körner; 'Fernando' (one act), written in June and July, the play by his school fellow, Albert Stadler; 'Die Freunde von Salamanka' (two acts), written in November and December, the words by Mayrhofer. There is a fragmentary relic of a three-act operetta on the play by Goethe 'Claudine von Villa Bella'. The work was completed in the summer of 1815, but only the first act and fragments of the second survive. This is because the manuscript of the completed work passed into the hands of Josef Hüttenbrenner and, in after years, servants in his household used the pages of Act III and part of Act II to light fires. The irresistible question thrusts at us: do servants in a musician's household use music paper to light fires on their own initiative? One hesitates to answer.

The operettas all contain characteristic and picturesque pages, mostly at Schubert's secondary levels of interest, but all showing an incredible assurance and resource. In the aria *Einsam schleich' ich durch die Zimmer* sung by Olivia in 'Die Freunde von Salamanka' we have a song of much interest and perhaps of more than secondary value. There is a lovely modification of the theme in the 'da capo' section fully worthy of the composer's powers of thematic development.

The music of 'Claudine' contains songs having the sweet, pure expression of the smaller 1815 songs. This is most attractive in the number *Liebe schwärmt auf allen Wegen*, which has often been mistaken for one of his songs ever since Max Friedlaender included an arrangement of it in his Schubert song-volumes (Peters, 1886).

Schubert's 'apprentice years' in opera, as they might be called, include two more pieces, both left unfinished for lack of any incentive to complete them. The work 'Die Bürgschaft', composed in May 1816, is based (but remotely) on Schiller's ballad of that name. The second piece is 'Adrast' (1819), the words by Mayrhofer. Both 'Adrast' and Mayrhofer's other libretto, 'Die Freunde von Salamanka', were evidently not considered worthy of preservation by the poet; they are both lost, and in consequence Schubert's operettas, with the spoken interludes lacking, can never be performed without some adaptation. 'Adrast' has many worthy pages of music, rising at times to the levels of the Mayrhofer songs of that period.

The two stage works of his 'middle period', both of which were performed in Vienna, are neither of great interest. Schubert himself was said not to have cared for either. 'Die Zwillingsbrüder' was composed in late 1818 and early 1819. It contains much light, melodious music of an attractive nature; there is some piquant and witty orchestration as in Lieschen's Aria, no. 3: 'Der Vater mag wohl immer Kind mich nennen'; and depths of feeling here and there, notably in the treatment of 'alte Freunde' ('old friends') in Friedrich's Aria, no. 6: 'Liebe, teure Muttererde', show the real Schubert. But 'Die Zauberharfe', a Melodrama (the name was used in Schubert's day for pieces of musical declamation, words recited against a musical background) in three acts, contains almost nothing of note. It is a depressing experience to turn the pages of this score, and realise the immensities of hard work which Schubert put into the production of this music—with no result whatever.

All these early operettas, and the opera 'Des Teufels Lustschloss', have charmingly written and fully scored overtures. The one introducing 'Die Zwillingsbrüder' is particularly attractive. Would they not make a welcome change from the rather overplayed 'Rosamunde' Overture in C major?

The two major works, 'Alfonso und Estrella' and 'Fierrabras', were never performed in his lifetime, and have never been performed since. Liszt's famous production of 'Alfonso' on 24 June 1854 at Weimar was a sadly mauled and manipulated affair. And 'Fierrabras', produced at Karlsruhe on 9 February 1897, was given, we read, with text revised by one, and music revised by another, and all kinds of tomfooleries, it is evident, put in to make such a truncated result tolerable to an audience. There are beauties and splendours without number in both works, and the first act of 'Fierrabras' is second to nothing in the whole field of German Romantic opera. 'Alfonso' halts; there is no doubt that Schober was determined to provide an opera text which would draw out Schubert's powers in lyrical expression. The result is not what he intended. The characters stand about and sing songs. One longs for the end of their individual and concerted efforts. Abduction, rape, murder: Schober holds his villain back from the accomplishment of each of these actions in order that he may sing about them, his victim further postponing the event by her songs and recitatives. But what songs they are! *Doch im Getümmel der Schlacht* from Act I, *Von Fels und Wald umrungen* and the Verdian *Wo ist sie?* from Act II, are the peaks of the work. The beginning of Act II contains a song which Schober had already written; he then introduced it at this point in his play. Schubert's melody is astonishing, for the student coming upon it will recognise a 'Winterreise' song there! Schubert used the melody, years later, for *Täuschung*—the words of both poems are similar, and the resemblance is, of course, pure coincidence. It was first pointed out by Max Kalbech in his review of the Vienna production in 1882 ('Wiener Opernabende', 1884, page 82).

There is more action in 'Fierrabras', but Schubert obviously tired of his task. (This is also apparent in 'Alfonso'.) Act I of 'Fierrabras' teems with poetry and imaginative detail of rhythm, melody, harmony and orchestration. But apart from Florinda's

Aria (with male chorus) *Des Jammers herbe Qualen* in Act III, the second and third acts of the opera are on a lower and homelier —but still interesting—level.

The one quality which gives these operas such a powerful interest to the student (alas, not yet to the theatre-goer) is Schubert's gifted writing in the accompanied recitatives. This is not like, for instance, Handel's decorated *recitativo*, but displays a desire to enrich and yet unify the emotional background of the sung dialogue. It is a pointer, unknown and unacknowledged, to what Wagner was to accomplish. 'Fierrabras' uses spoken interludes; but even in that opera there is, on occasion, verse dialogue, with this exalted, declamatory music. What Schubert was struggling towards, of course, and what he nearly succeeded in reaching, was the 'Leitmotiv'. With his power of thematic exploitation and his musical response to the stimulus of words— what he would have made of it is beyond conjecture.

There remains 'Die Verschworenen', Castelli's witty, and racy, exposition of a very human situation. Schubert illustrates, with music as witty and pointed, the moves and countermoves in this game of love-lorn wives and war-infatuated husbands. He uses the march, the scherzo, the 'Romance', the polonaise, with skill, variety and gusto. And, when necessary, the music has a tenderness which brings tears. In recent years the work has been revived in London and Cambridge and charmed all hearers.

VI

During these years of Schubert's pre-occupation with the theatre there are, understandably, few Church works of any importance, but among them there is a famous, and thoroughly characteristic, setting of the words of the Mass. It is his fifth work, in A flat. Schubert's six settings of the sacred Latin text are usually divided into two groups, the first comprising the four early compositions, 1814–1816, the second the last two, mature works, in A flat and E flat. But to bring together, in this way, the Mass in A flat and the great Mass in E flat of Schubert's last year means that the earlier one is quite overshadowed. In many Schubertians the Mass in E flat arouses feelings of admiration; the Mass in A flat inspires affection. It is more lyrical, perhaps more sweet, than the final setting. It is certainly more fanciful; of all the six Masses, the fifth is most richly adorned with musical imagery, motif and piquant harmonic touch. Karl Kobald goes too far in writing of the music of the A flat Mass as a 'wreath of spring flowers, woven by the hands of fair maids, round the picture of the crucified Christ' for this gives an interpretation of the music which sentimentalises and belittles it. Yet it could be said that sections of this Mass—the 'Gratias agimus' and the 'Osanna in excelsis'—resemble a musical garland. The 'Et incarnatus est' of the 'Credo' presents one of Schubert's harmonic miracles, based largely—can one explain miracles?—on the use of the Neapolitan sixth. The music of the 'Crucifixis' is the finest in the Mass, and, at the end, the turn into A flat major after the prolonged cadence in A flat minor is a most poignant use of this favourite device. Every device of choral tone colour is used: solo voices, unaccompanied choir, occasional sub-division of the choir into eight parts, antiphony. The unprecedented key-scheme of the Mass deserves a word. From the A flat of the opening we pass to a 'Gloria' in E major; from this key Schubert passes to A major and A minor. The 'Credo' is in C major, and this provides an excuse for a 'Sanctus' in F major. The whole work again gives an instance of Schubert's fondness for what we have called a 'Neapolitan' key-relationship: A flat with A major, E major with F major.

It has been suggested that Schubert worked intermittently on this Mass between the date of its commencement (November 1819) and its conclusion in September 1822. The remark on the manuscript score, 'im 7b. 822 beendet' ('finished in September 1822') is not in Schubert's hand, but can be verified from his letter to Spaun of 7 December 1822. There are numerous sketches for the Mass in existence, and it is clear that Schubert revised it after its completion. The alterations can be seen on his autograph score in the Library of the *Gesellschaft der Musikfreunde*. That these alterations were made later than 1822 is clear from Ferdinand Schubert's copy, which was written soon after the completion of the Mass. It is said that Brahms once rehearsed the work from this copy of Ferdinand's, and was dissatisfied with certain passages; when he came to examine Schubert's revised MS. he found that the composer had altered the very passages which he found unsatisfactory.[1] The Mass in A flat heralds the series of compositions for the Church Offices, of which Leopold Nowak has written:

> One can say without fear of contradiction that in Schubert, Viennese sentiment and musical genius have been most beautifully revealed, not only in secular, but also in sacred compositions.

In conclusion there are the songs of these 'middle years'. They are dominated by the 'Schöne Müllerin' series, but considered as separate songs, none from this favourite song-cycle equals the settings of Goethe in 1821 or those of Rückert in 1822 and 1823. Individual songs such as *Grenzen der Menschheit* and the two songs of Suleika by Goethe, and *Dass sie hier gewesen* by Rückert, fully reveal Schubert's genius and in them it achieved its supreme manifestations. Nor, even in their own sphere, do the 'Mill' songs exceed the pathos and sweetness of the song, *Frühlingsglaube* (1820), or depict more graphically the sparkling water of the greatly loved *Auf dem Wasser zu singen* (1823). Schubert continued to draw on the poems of his friend Mayrhofer; the favourite song of the period is *Nachtviolen* (April 1822), but there is as well a pair of majestic songs called *Heliopolis*, I and II, which deserve mention. The mysterious 'No. 12' on Schubert's manuscripts of the two 'Heliopolis' songs can be explained thus: the two texts were drawn from the *twelfth* poem in the manuscript collection of Mayrhofer's poems. This collection is now in the Vienna *Stadtbibliothek*.

Two songs of 1823 have a richly endowed accompaniment and much ingenuity in the development of theme and motif. The one, *Der Zwerg*, has had perhaps a little more attention than it deserves; the other, *Lied*, a poem by Stolberg beginning 'Des Lebens Tag ist schwer', certainly too little attention. *Der Zwerg* owes part of its fame to the account given by Randhartinger of

[1] See the article on Schubert by Grove, 'Dictionary', first edition, page 336, col. ii, footnote.

its origins; he said it was scribbled down hurriedly before the composer accompanied him on a walk. But its portrayals of emotion—grief and horror, together with the almost Wagnerian treatment of short, musical phrases in the piano part, make a wonderful study. The other song, Stolberg's *Lied*, is stately in its measured progress; the harmonies, reaching to the future in their range, and handled with an assured technical facility, support a broad, noble melody inspired by the line 'Death's kiss is light and cool'. It is a song to which one returns with eager interest, discovering afresh, each time, its greatness and beauty.

'Death's kiss is light and cool'. There is a tendency in German commentary on Schubert to dwell rather heavily on the composer's fascinated interest in 'Death' poetry. It is easy to draw doubtful conclusions from it. But now and again a fatalistic element seems obvious in his choice of such poetry, as in the poem of Stolberg—

> *Life's day is hard and sultry,*
> *Death's kiss is light and cool.*

Schubert had indeed suffered a death-blow; although the desperate stages of his disease had passed his health would never be the same again. It is a new and strange thing to read that at the New Year celebrations of the friends on 31 December 1823, Schubert arrived accompanied by J. Bernhardt—his doctor.

1824-1825

I

After the dismal failure of 'Rosamunde' in the theatre, some revulsion against opera composition must have seized Schubert. He wrote no more, in fact, for the stage, beyond the half-hearted sketches for the opera 'Der Graf von Gleichen'. This reaction against the theatre may have been made keener by his acquaintance with two new friends whom he met at the home of the Sonnleithners, both first-rate instrumentalists. They were Ferdinand, Count Troyer, a clarinettist in the musical establishment of the Archduke Rudolph, and Ignaz Schuppanzigh. The latter, famous as a friend of Beethoven, had just returned from a tour in eastern Europe. He was the leader of an unrivalled string quartet, and the excellent playing of the four men turned Schubert's thoughts from the theatre into a new field of work. We find him in January 1824 beginning a series of chamber works, and absorbing himself wholeheartedly in them as if to thrust behind him the unhappy experiences of his failures with opera. The series opens with a set of variations for flute and pianoforte which Schubert composed for Ferdinand Bogner. His friendship with the flautist dated from the days when they had played together in the amateur orchestra which met at Hatwig's house, and it was maintained by Bogner's marriage to Barbara Fröhlich in 1825. The variations were based on the melody of *Trockne Blumen* from the 'Schöne Müllerin' song-cycle. The song, incidentally, had not then been published; it was the first one of Book V and so did not appear until the following August. The variations are of little interest; if there is anything to be said in extenuation of Schubert's use of such a song, it is that the aura of pathos and tenderness which *Trockne Blumen* has gathered

over the years was not, in 1824, so obvious in its new-minted
condition. He does not even give the song's title on the manuscript, and when the composition was eventually published, in
1850, it was entitled 'Introduction et Variations sur un théme
original'. But in the three pieces of chamber music which he composed after the variations, there is such a quality of universal
greatness and appeal that we can ignore the inferiority of the
Trockne Blumen composition. These three works are the String
Quartets in A minor and D minor (the latter known as the
'Death and the Maiden' Quartet) and the Octet in F major.

Both quartets were mis-dated during the nineteenth century.
The A minor Quartet was considered to have been written in the
summer of 1824 while Schubert was staying at Zseliz, and various
'Hungarian' influences were thought to be present as a result of
this. The D minor Quartet was attributed to January 1826, a
mistake which arose since the work was performed for the first
time in that month, and Schubert may have revised it—but not
very radically. The earlier quartet was more correctly dated from
records of the first performance of it by Schuppanzigh and his
colleagues on 14 March 1824. But Schubert probably composed
it earlier than the March of that year (the date given by Deutsch
in his 'Thematic Catalogue'), perhaps as early as the end of
January. Schwind may be quoted in evidence: 'He writes quartets
and German dances and variations without number' (letter to
Schober of 13 February 1824). The date of the second quartet
was not corrected until 1901, and in the usual rather dramatic
fashion when a lost manuscript is found. The newly discovered
autograph was fragmentary, containing only the first movement
and part of the second, but the first page bore the date 'March
1824'. Sketches for it were doubtless being written earlier in the
year, and may account for Schwind's 'variations without number'.

The Octet was commissioned by Count Troyer. It was finished
on 1 March and performed at the Count's residence soon afterwards. He himself, of course, played the clarinet, and Ignaz
Schuppanzigh was first violin. Another instrumentalist in the
first performance of the Octet, who later became a notable en-
thusiast for Schubert's chamber work, was Josef Linke, a 'cellist.

The first months of 1824 contain various repercussions of the 'Rosamunde' performance. Weber, in spite of the coolness between him and Schubert, felt no elation at the news of the failure of 'Rosamunde', and the notice of the event, posted to Dresden by the editor of the Vienna 'Theaterzeitung' only embarrassed him. This adverse notice was sent to Weber for transmission to the editor of the Dresden 'Abendzeitung', Karl Winkler. Winkler wrote verse under the pen-name 'Theodor Hell' and was the author of one of Schubert's songs *Das Heimweh*, a pleasant, serious little song of July 1816; but it is hardly likely that he knew of Schubert's interest in his poem, and we cannot believe in any partisanship on Winkler's side. Nevertheless he refused to print the notice. Then the authoress of the play felt impelled to write an account of the possible reasons why it had failed to please, instancing lack of rehearsal, general frantic haste to stage the production, and new, inexperienced personnel at the theatre. One thing in Helmina von Chézy's favour must be said: she always, from the first, recognised the beauty, lyricism and power of Schubert's music for her play. In this 'Explanation' of hers, published by the Vienna 'Zeitschrift' on 13 January 1824, she referred to '... Schubert's glorious music ... a majestic stream, winding through the poem's complexities like a sweetly transfiguring mirror, grandiose, purely melodious, soulful, unspeakably touching and profound ...' and more in the same vein of flowery description, but obviously sincere beneath its flourishes. Publication of the favourite 'Romance' from the play, with Schubert's own arrangement of the accompaniment for pianoforte, took place on 24 March ('Axa's Romance', Op. 26). His publishers of those days, Sauer & Leidesdorf, promised the Overture, entr'actes and choruses shortly afterwards. In August Helmina von Chézy sent Schubert a revised copy of her play, and asked him what sum of money he would demand for the rights of the music. He asked for £10 and apparently received it, for after his death Helmina offered 'Rosamunde' and the incidental music to various theatres in South Germany, but without success.

An activity of the Schubert circle, initiated at the end of 1822, was the formation of 'reading parties' at which plays and novels

FERDINAND, COUNT TROYER

Oil by Johann Ender, 1826   *Baroness Alice Loudon*

of the day were read; it is not quite clear how the books were read, it seems as if Schober, as a rule, read the work aloud. In the early months of 1824 the parties were being held twice a week at the house of the painter Ludwig von Mohn. They became swollen in numbers by uncongenial associates and it was felt, too, that in the absence of Schober and Bruchmann, the two leading spirits, much of their attractiveness had gone. Occasional Schubertiads were held in conjunction with the readings, but Schubert's still uncertain health prevented the musical evenings from being all that they might be. The result was that the gatherings came to an end in April. The news was sent to Schober by Anton von Doblhoff, and to Kupelwieser, then in Rome studying painting, by his fiancée Johanna Lutz. She wrote:

> The reading parties have now come to an end and very quickly. It was easy enough to see it coming, for there were too many of them to last. (15 April 1824.)

The meetings were resumed when Schober returned to Vienna the following year. Their importance lies in the fact that through them Schubert encountered many authors whose verses either directly inspired his songs, or who stimulated his interest in various literary movements of the day, in Germany as well as in Austria. We certainly owe his Heine songs to the 'readings'.

The publication of Schubert's work was well under way in 1824. The earlier scheme of bringing out songs on a subscription basis seems a long way behind, and regular publication, payment and advertisement give a professional solidity to his standing in 1824 and 1825. Reviews and criticisms of his work were also appearing in music journals and Schubert, understandably enough, eagerly read these reports. He wrote to his father on 25 July:

> ... the favourable reception of 'Suleika' gave me just pleasure, although I wish I could have had a sight of the criticisms myself, in order to see if something could not be learnt from them; for however favourable a verdict may be, it may at the same time be equally laughable if the critic lacks the required understanding, which is not altogether rarely the case.

L

Franz Schubert senior, in his turn, made a point of informing his son during the following August:

> ... the announcement of your 'Gondelfahrer' and 'Schöne Müllerin appeared in the 'Wiener Zeitung' on the 12th instant. ...

As evidence of his new status, the appearance of the String Quartet in A minor might here be documented. We have been able from Schwind's letter to see the inception of the work in Schubert's mind and pen. He composed it because of his acquaintance with Schuppanzigh the violinist, and the subsequent promise of a performance. Schwind wrote again to Schober on 6 March 1824:

> A new Quartet is to be performed at Schuppanzigh's who is quite enthusiastic and is said to have rehearsed particularly well.

The performance took place on the afternoon of 14 March in the Hall of the *Gesellschaft der Musikfreunde* in the Tuchlauben. Schwind wrote a third time to Schober and said:

> Schubert's quartet has been performed, rather slowly in his opinion, but very purely and tenderly. It is on the whole very smooth, but written in such a way that the tune remains in one's mind, as with the songs, all feeling and thoroughly expressive. It got much applause, especially the *Menuetto* which is extraordinarily tender and natural. ...

The term 'natural' here in Schwind's letter, recurs frequently throughout the nineteenth-century in connection with Schubert's music. 'A natural composer' they called Schubert. The implication is 'without art', and it had its associated terms: dilettante, amateur, unschooled and so forth. It is hard to bear, in view of the truth, and one can understand Spaun's anger at its use in connection with his friend. One can forgive Schwind his spontaneous use of the word in the above letter, but consider that very 'Menuetto', with its profundity of feeling, its highly wrought craftsmanship, its perfect technical finish and balance, and see how absurd is the application 'natural' to it—and to Schubert's work in general. The artist in Schwind should have warned him that 'smoothness' is only attained by the highest achievement in technical manipulation—so high, in fact, that it can conceal the very means by which it is achieved.

The reports of the performance in the newspapers were not appreciative. The Vienna 'Allgemeine Musikalische Zeitung' of 27 April said:

> New Quartet by Schubert. This composition must be heard several times before it can be adequately judged.

And the journal of Leipzig, with a similar title, two days later printed the well-known pronouncement 'not to be despised as a first born'. The phrase 'first born' is, to present-day readers, ironic: Schubert had actually written a dozen string quartets before the one in A minor; but it was, of course, the first one to come before the public. It was published by Sauer & Leidesdorf on 7 September 1824 under the title:

Trois Quattours
pour deux Violons, deux Altos et Violoncelle
par François Schubert.
Œuv. 29: no. 1.

The 'deux Altos' is a misprint; there is, of course, only one viola; the 'Trois Quattours' implies that Schubert was going to publish three quartets in this Op. 29 (this is a similar undertaking to the production of the early quartet in D major, see page 20). The second quartet, the D minor, was already written and its later publisher, Josef Czerny of Vienna, would have been justified in calling it 'Op. 29: no. 2'. The third quartet was composed two years later; this is the work in G major of June 1826. It was not published until 1851 and then called Op. 161.

Schubert received £4 from the publishers for his Op. 29. A similar sum was paid to him for other publications that year from the same firm: Op. 28, a part-song for T.T.B.B. called *Der Gondelfahrer*, a setting of Mayrhofer's poem, which appeared on 12 August, and Op. 27, three 'Marches Heroïques' for PF. Duet, published on 18 December. The five books of the 'Schöne Müllerin' songs were all published by August, in spite of the unhappy Schubert's complaint that they were so slow in appearing.

'It's a slow business with the "Maid of the Mill" songs, too: a book comes dragging out once every three months' (letter to Ferdinand from Zseliz, August 1824). These books were not altogether an arbitrary subdivision of the twenty songs into equal amounts, but make some attempt to present the five small 'Acts' of the play: I—the arrival at the mill (1–4), II—the falling in love (5–9), III—the brief idyll of happiness (10–12), IV—the jealousy and despair (13–17), V—the resignation and death of the young miller (17–20). It is doubtful whether Schober had any grounds for writing to Schubert on 2 December 1824: '. . . and your "Maid of the Mill" songs too failed to make a sensation, did they?' His words can only refer to the immediate reception of the cycle, for no songs of Schubert have been so consistently beloved and popular as these small but thoroughly typical specimens of his lyric genius. The five books were published as Op. 25 and Schubert dedicated the work to the young Baron Schönstein, a friend of Count Esterházy and a singer with a pleasant baritone voice, sympathetic and expressive in tone, so that he was an excellent interpreter of the Schubert song.

Besides these important publications numerous small commissions came to Schubert for songs and dances and short piano pieces, which brought him in a little money or helped to make his name better known. Sauer & Leidesdorf issued an 'Album Musical' in 1824; there were two editions, and Schubert was represented in both. The first, published on New Year's Day, contained an attractive PF. Solo in F minor, called 'Air Russe'; this has become celebrated through its re-publication later on as No. 3 of the 'Moments Musicaux', Op. 94. The variation which he had composed in March 1821 on the famous Waltz by Diabelli was published, as one among fifty others by various composers, on 6 June, and the short, but tremendously effective song to Death *An den Tod*, composed in 1817, formed a supplement to the Vienna 'Allgemeine Musikalische Zeitung' on the 26th of that month. The second edition of the 'Album Musical' followed in December. It contained another piece for the piano, in A flat, called 'Plaintes d'un Troubadour', afterwards included, as No. 6, in the 'Moments Musicaux' series. This piece, it has been suggested, may have been composed in 1818. A song was also included in the 'Album', the *Erinnerung* by Kosegarten which Schubert had written in July 1815.

Performances of the composer's part-songs were as frequent and popular as ever during 1824. They were usually part of a concert given by some celebrity, designed to serve as light relief, presumably, to the virtuoso seriousness of the soloist. Thus the young pianist, Leopoldine Blahetka, mentioned in the letter from Doppler to Schubert in 1818, and afterwards beloved by Chopin when he visited Vienna in 1830, included a vocal quartet of his in her recital of 21 March, and so, later on, did the violinists Hellmesberger and Schuppanzigh. The favourite quartet of that period was 'Die Nachtigall', words by Johann Karl Unger, which Schubert had composed in April 1821, and published as Op. 11: no. 2.

Amongst the Schubert documents of 1824, was a journal of his, which he kept in the March of that year. We know of it only through Bauernfeld, for the original is lost. Since Bauernfeld did not become acquainted with Schubert, to any degree of intimacy, until 1825, the actual wording of the extracts from Schubert's journal which he reproduced posthumously, in 1829, must remain suspect. They are all somewhat 'off centre' if we place them against our knowledge of the composer's character, and his own expression in letters. The most famous of them is a misquoted version of the original. Bauernfeld actually quoted Schubert as having written:

> What I produce is due to my understanding of music and to my sorrows; that which sorrow alone has produced seems to give least pleasure to the world.

Kreissle misquoted this as 'to give *most* pleasure', and it has been consistently misquoted ever since.

But a much more important document, authentic and extant, is a letter which he wrote on 31 March 1824 to his friend Leopold Kupelwieser in Rome. This letter is one of Schubert's most famous outpourings. It is usually quoted piecemeal, for so many topics in the work and thought of the composer have relevant support in the statements of his letter, that one can hardly avoid quoting from it when those topics are discussed. And so it has been thought necessary to quote it here in its entirety, so that any subsequent discussion of it may be easily followed. It is here newly translated.

Dear Kupelwieser,

I've been wanting to write to you for some time, but was so busy I hardly knew which way to turn. But now the opportunity has come through Smirsch and at last I can pour out my feelings again to someone. You are indeed so staunch and true. You will surely forgive me many things which others would take amiss. To put it briefly, I feel myself the most unfortunate, the most miserable being in the world. Think of a man whose health will never be right again, and who from despair over the fact makes it worse instead of better, think of a man, I say, whose splendid hopes have come to naught, to whom the happiness of love and friendship offer nothing but acutest pain, whose enthusiasm (at least, the inspiring kind) for the Beautiful threatens to disappear, and ask yourself whether he isn't a miserable, unfortunate fellow?

My peace is gone, my heart is heavy,
I find it never, nevermore....

so might I sing every day, since each night when I go to sleep I hope never again to wake, and each morning merely reminds me of the misery of yesterday. So I should pass my days joyless and friendless, if it weren't for Schwind, who frequently visits me and sheds a light from those dear, departed days.

Our Society (Reading Society), as you probably know by now, being swollen with uncouth crowds for beer-swilling and sausage-eating, has committed suicide, for its dissolution takes place in 2 days, although since your departure I rarely went to it. Leides-dorf, whom I have come to know quite well, is indeed a really profound and good fellow, yet so deeply melancholy, that I am almost afraid I have profited from him in that respect more than I care to do; also, his and my affairs are going badly, so we never have any money. Your brother's opera (he did not do very well to leave the theatre) was pronounced unusable, and accordingly no claim has been made on my music. Castelli's opera, 'Die Verschworenen', has been composed in Berlin by a local composer, and received with acclamation.[1] In this way I appear to have composed, once again, two operas for nothing. I have done very little song-writing, but tried my hand at several instrumental things, for I have composed two quartets for violins, viola and 'cello, and an Octet, and want to write another string quartet, on the whole I want to prepare myself like this for grand Symphony.

The latest news in Vienna is that Beethoven is giving a Concert, at which he intends to produce his new Symphony, 3 pieces from the new Mass, and a new Overture. God willing, I also am thinking of giving a similar concert next year. Now I close, so as not to use too much paper, and kiss you a 1000 times. If you would write to me about your own enthusiasms and your life as well, nothing would more greatly please

Your

faithful friend

Frz. Schubert

My address, then, would be c/o Sauer & Leidesdorf, because I am going at the beginning of May to Hungary with Esterházy.

Farewell!   Really well!!

Schubert's dejected spirits and ill-health are obvious from his words, and these are only wrung from his reserved nature because he trusts his correspondent—'You are indeed so staunch and true . . . things which others would take amiss' and so forth. We have in the spring of this year another example of the extraordinary detachment of the artist, for otherwise it is impossible to imagine the contentment and high spirits of the Octet born from this despairing mind. There was a sequel to Schubert's remark that he had composed two quartets, and that he wanted to write a third, and so prepare for a 'grand Symphony' in that manner. The two quartets, in A minor and D minor, were, as we

---

[1] This is not strictly true. The operetta, by Georg Abraham Schneider, conductor of the Opera House at Berlin, was given twice and then no more.

have said, considered by Schubertian biographers of the nineteenth century to have been composed *after* this letter was written. Thus they explained his words by dating the two quartets of Op. 125, E flat major (1813) and E major (1816), as early 1824. Even if we bear in mind the danger of dating works on stylistic grounds, nevertheless it is incomprehensible how such a date as '1824' could have gained any credence at all for the E major work, let alone for the earlier quartet in E flat, charming as many of its moments are. But the immature development of theme, and the generally flavourless slow movements, unmistakably proclaim their juvenile origins. It was not until O. E. Deutsch, in his valuable article 'The Chronology of Schubert's String Quartets' (Music & Letters, January 1943), assembled all the known facts in concise form, that critics and biographers became generally aware of the new discoveries, the new datings.

Significant, too, is Schubert's reference to a third quartet, which he intended to compose. This was not accomplished until two years later, when the superb Quartet in G major was written. The remarkable thing is that, although two years were to pass before he actually composed his third quartet, it was, in truth, *his next chamber work of any importance.* Only pianoforte sonatas, variations, and songs intervene between the D minor Quartet and the G major Quartet; the Sonata for Arpeggione and Pianoforte in A minor (November 1824) was not considered seriously by Schubert, and thrown off hastily for Vincenz Schuster, the inventor of the new instrument. Moreover, the 'grand Symphony', which was to be the culmination of these preparations, is clearly that in C major, of early 1828. These facts militate, in my opinion at least, against the theory that Schubert composed in 1825 a 'grand Symphony' at Gmunden and Gastein. He may have had one in mind then, and even written sketches for it, but the third quartet was to be written first. There are other factors, of course, to be considered in connection with the 'Gmunden-Gastein' Symphony, but they can be left until the appropriate time.

On 25 May 1824 Schubert left Vienna for Zseliz in Hungary, having, somewhat unwillingly, undertaken to join the Esterházy family once again in their summer retreat. According to Schwind he was resolved to write a symphony; this resolution of Schubert was common knowledge among his friends. Schwind several times mentioned it in his letters to Schober, even, at one point, confusing resolution-to-do with the actual deed. Hence the rumours and legend-promoting statements on the supposedly lost symphony, which if it existed at all could hardly have got beyond a sketched condition. A more tangible piece of luggage which Schubert took with him to Zseliz was an operetta libretto based on the epic poem of Ernst Schulze called 'The Enchanted Rose'; it was the same subject that Bauernfeld used later in the libretto he devised for Schubert on the exploits of the Count of Gleichen. But Schubert, though composing prolifically at Zseliz that summer, never worked on the operetta.

We can gather from a letter which his father wrote to him that he was received in friendly fashion by the members of the Ester-házy family. They were not uninfluenced by Schubert's Viennese renown: their music master was a more considerable figure than the obscure musician of six years previous. He lived this time, not in the servants' quarters, but in a room in the castle itself. His salary was £10 per month: for those days, a generous one. On the whole he seemed fairly content. His health at last began to mend, his spirits rose. The two countesses were by this time quite accomplished performers on the piano and we owe to their abilities and enthusiasms the many compositions for PF. Duet which Schubert provided that summer. Marie, the elder sister, was about to become engaged; Karoline, now nearly twenty years old, was a child-like, delicate character, who undoubtedly inspired in Schubert a protective and affectionate regard, which may have been the beginning of love for her. But he could never have seriously entertained any idea of a love affair with her. His social position, his health, his prospects were all against it.

To his family, as usual, Schubert wrote affectionately and in-formatively. His father's replies raise a smile today, but a smile of respect and esteem as well as amusement. They are so full of typically paternal advice: he gently reminds Schubert of his duties to God, to himself, to his employers, to his patrons. He reminds his son of the honours bestowed by the Music Societies of Linz and Graz:

> If, contrary to all expectation, you should not yet have done so, let me urge you most earnestly, to thank them in a worthy manner. These noble societies show you exceptional love and respect, which may be very important for you. (14 August 1824.)

Schubert had, of course, acknowledged these distinctions by letter, but his father's 'in a worthy manner' suggests the offering of a major composition. It is odd to find that a few months after Schubert had composed two string quartets—the first completed ones for eight years—Ferdinand wrote to him to say that he had begun to perform again his brother's youthful quartets. In this letter of 3 July 1824 Ferdinand gave a list of songs which he had handed over to Ludwig von Mohn; he mentioned 'Fierrabras', the score of which he had lent to Kupelwieser, its librettist; and, in addition, he reported that he had sent off to Schubert a volume of Bach's '48 Preludes and Fugues'. These facts are mentioned because of the replies they drew from Schubert. The replies throw light on his feelings, usually so obscure, about his own compositions, and they are suggestive in connection with his development. The strong influence of Bach in the compositions of those months in Zseliz would be unaccountable had it not been for Ferdinand's chance remark. Schubert, doubtless using the preludes and fugues as teaching material for Marie and Karoline, absorbed and unconsciously expressed the techniques and textures of these keyboard masterpieces of Bach, giving them, at the same time, an unmistakably Schubertian character. The 'Eight Variations on an original Air', Op. 35, are full of this absorption in Bach. To Ferdinand's information on the early quartets, he modestly replied:

> ... it would be better if you played other quartets than mine, for there is nothing in them, except that perhaps they please you, who are pleased with anything of mine.

On the mention of the songs by his brother, Schubert had this interesting comment to make:

I comfort myself that only a few of them seem good to me, e.g. those included with 'Geheimnis'—'Wanderers Nachtlied' (II), and 'Der entsühnte Orest'. . . .

Schubert also wished to know, at once, why Kupelwieser wanted the opera score:

Did Kupelwieser not mention what he intended to do with the opera? Or where he is sending it??

But Ferdinand was unable to give the composer any answer when he next wrote.

The letters show a deepening affection between the two brothers. From boyhood they were attached to each other—the much quoted letter written by Schubert at the age of 15 to Ferdinand, begging him for a few kreuzer to buy bread and apples and so eke out the scanty food rations at the *Stadtkonvikt*, is a good indication of the brothers' mutual affection. But Schubert's severe illness and his recent sojourn in the family home had drawn the ties closer. To whom else could Schubert unburden his grief and utter dejection of soul if not to a loved brother? Ferdinand wrote in his first letter that a musical clock in the coffeehouse called the 'Hungarian Crown' played waltzes by Schubert and, he told his brother, he was so surprised and moved that '. . . I involuntarily shed—'. Schubert replied 'Was it only the pain of my absence which made you shed tears, and could you not trust yourself to write the word? . . . Or did all the tears come to your mind which you have seen me weep?' We can understand why Ferdinand, for thirty years after his younger brother's death, remained a faithful guardian and advocate of his manuscripts, moved to continual pity by the thought of that gifted brother, so tragically dying before his name was made.

To Schwind and Schober there was a letter apiece, and it is in Schwind's letter that we get the only piece of evidence from Schubert himself that could possibly be interpreted as indicating a love for Karoline Esterházy. He wrote to Schwind that he longed damnably for Vienna in spite of the 'anziehenden bewussten Sternes' ('certain attractive star'). The star may be Karoline, but the remark hardly suggests the ardour of a lover. To Schober he opened his heart more than to Schwind, more even than to Ferdinand. As in the letter to Leopold Kupelwieser earlier in the year, he proclaims his longing for the days of his youth, particularly of that time which he and Schober had spent together composing 'Alfonso und Estrella'. To his friends and to his brother he mentioned the compositions of the summer; the Sonata in C major, for PF. Duet, known by the name which Diabelli bestowed on it, 'Grand Duo', when he published it as Op. 140 in 1838; the 'Eight Variations on an Original Theme', also for PF. Duet, which was published soon after he returned to Vienna, as Op. 35. The two duets were successfully played to the Esterházy family and their Hungarian friends, but Schubert wrote to Schwind:

> As I do not wholly trust the Hungarians' taste, I leave it to you and the Viennese to decide.

A third PF. Duet was written in September; it is the long, and very unequal 'Divertissement à l'hongroise'. Only a few years ago a preliminary sketch for part of the 'Divertissement' saw the light; it is for piano solo and consists of the *Allegretto* finale. Schubert called it 'Ungerische (*sic*) Melodie'. The manuscript bears in the composer's hand 'Zseliz, September 1824', which enables us to place and date the composition with certainty. The duet was published in April 1826 by Artaria of Vienna, as Op. 54. It was widely known in the nineteenth century with results which are not too happy; in many cases, e.g. Wagner's, it was practically the only instrumental piece of Schubert's to be known, and gave a wrong impression of his stature. Schumann wrote in his diary on 9 October 1836 that Mendelssohn 'stamped his feet' impatiently over the work.

Some Marches for PF. Duet were published the following year as Op. 40. Two of them, in G minor and B minor, are charmingly lyrical: the 'Trio' section of the first one is built on a melody so absolutely characteristic of its author in rhythm, harmony and contour, that it brings a smile to the face as if one were greeting an old friend. The fifth march, *funèbre* in style, in E flat minor, reminded a later friend of Schubert, Fritz von Hartmann, of his mother. He mentioned this in his diary and so conferred on this particular march a somewhat undeserved distinction.

Release from his not too congenial duties came in October. He travelled back to Vienna in the company of Baron Schönstein, a long letter from whom, describing the journey, has been preserved. They arrived on 17 October. It is an odd coincidence that the only two letters of Schönstein which have any relevance to the Schubert records are both of this year, 1824, and that the first gives us the exact date of Schubert's leaving Vienna for Zseliz and the second the exact date of his return to the capital—both trifling pieces of information and both quite incidental to the main points of the correspondence, but, at least, factually dependable.

Schubert was delighted to be back in his old haunts, and he and Schwind resumed their former intimacy, becoming almost inseparable. Schober wrote from Breslau and hinted at his speedy return to Vienna, but this did not take place until the following August. Best of all, Spaun visited Vienna for a few weeks' holiday and he and Schubert were re-united. At the end of the year, on 22 December, a new publisher's name appears, that of Thaddäus Weigl. In a 'Musikalische Angebinde' ('Musical Dedication'), a collection of new waltzes, Weigl included as No. 29, a waltz of Schubert. It was a charming piece, in E flat major, composed for PF. Duet in the previous July at Zseliz. Schubert arranged it in November for PF. Solo especially for Weigl's collection, and so business relations between the composer and the publisher were initiated. In a year's time Schubert was selling full scale work to Weigl.

II

In February 1825 Schubert moved his lodgings to a house next door but one to that of his young friend Schwind. The long, low apartment house is to the left of the Karlskirche and in those days pleasantly situated outside the Inner City and known as the 'Frühwirthaus'. 'As far as I can' Schwind wrote to Schober, 'I share his whole life with him'—and in that same February they gathered into their association the third member, the new friend, Eduard Bauernfeld. Schubert and Spaun had strolled out to the 'Moonshine' house on the previous Christmas Eve to visit Schwind, and had there found the young writer in Schwind's company: it was Schubert's first meeting with Bauernfeld, but a meeting long desired by the younger man, who greatly admired the music, especially the part-songs, of Schubert. The association was an uneasy and forced relationship à *trois*, and held together chiefly by the admiration which each of the younger men felt for Schubert's music. Bauernfeld was a facetious and light-minded friend. Both he and Schwind achieved solid renown in the middle years of the nineteenth century: Schwind as a 'Romantic' draughts-man and illustrator of German myth and folk-tale, Bauernfeld as a satirically humorous playwright and fablist, but in these years, when we meet them in the company of Schubert, neither is a very impressive figure. There is evidence, too, that Schubert felt for them both a tolerant, but by no means unseeing affection. Yet we owe much to both of them as 'recorders' of the composer; Schwind in his unrivalled illustrations of Schubert and Schubert's background, Bauernfeld in his biographical essays and memoirs. Schwind's illustrations are called 'unrivalled' and so, in bulk, they are. But actually, at that time, in May 1825, Schubert's protrait was painted by the water colourist, Wilhelm August Rieder, and it has become the favourite contemporary portrait, the one most frequently quoted. It is, however, surpassed in popularity by the engraving based upon it which Josef Kriehuber made in 1846. This gives a more masculine, a 'squarer', cast to the portrait of Rieder, and also flatters the composer a little.

Men and women throng the pages of Schubert's life during the early months of 1825. Schubertiads were held at least weekly and Vogl sang on these evenings the latest composed songs; they attracted many new admirers to the genius of the composer. Part-songs were performed in public and private; they, and the playing of the piano duets and dance music of the golden summer at Zseliz also won fresh friends. After Bauernfeld came the two Hartmann brothers, Fritz and Franz, with whom Schubert and Schwind drank 'brotherhood' soon after their arrival in Vienna.

Karl von Enderes, a lawyer and, later on, a notable Schubertian, also met the composer in the spring of that year.

Four women, three of them renowned actresses and singers, the fourth an obscure figure, play their part in the composer's life in those days. Johanna Lutz had no fame in the artistic world, we know her through Schubert's friend Leopold Kupelwieser to whom she was engaged. But her shrewd, kindly-affectioned comments on Schubert and his circle of friends are indispensable to our picture of the composer and his background. It was she who informed Kupelwieser of the unhappy conclusion of the 'Reading parties'. When Schubert returned to Vienna from Zseliz in November 1824 she reported to her fiancé that he and Schwind were much in each other's company and added that it was a good thing —'for if they are not of much use to each other, they do each other no harm'. She wrote in March 1825 of the activities of the Schubertians, complaining with amused, yet impatient, candour of the childish quarrels and feuds of the various cliques; 'Schubert' she wrote, 'is now very busy and well behaved, which pleases me very much.' As far as composition was concerned, Schubert was busy with song-writing; some of the songs from the 'Lady of the Lake' were probably composed during March and April, among them, for certain, the *Lay of the Imprisoned Huntsman*. He used a translation of Scott's text by Adam Storck. There were also the two nocturnal songs *Nacht und Träume* and *Die junge Nonne*, in which his melodic and dramatic power were not surpassed until the very last phase, in August 1828. The latter song contains more fascinating examples of his power of theme development: both voice and piano reveal the growth of the 'germ' motif and together give an unforgettable picture of the nun in her quiet cell— a point of physical and spiritual calm at the heart of the storm. The song was sung on 3 March 1825, *at sight*, it is said, by Sophie Müller, an actress of the Burgtheater, in her home at Hietzing, a village just to the west of Vienna. She was an accomplished singer, spoke English and loved English poetry; her youthful charm, her voice and her delightful acting were greatly to the taste of the Viennese and they idolised her. In her diary she records several visits by Vogl and Schubert, or Schubert alone, to the Hietzing residence during the early months of 1825. There both old and new songs were sung by her, or Vogl.

Another woman, attracted by the magic of Schubert's songs, was the remarkable actress, Katherina von Lászny. Schwind gave an awesome picture of this dying courtesan, still queening it over her little court, with the wreck of her beauty and charm still able to captivate the young painter, so that he wrote to Schober: 'What a woman! If she were not nearly twice my age and, unhappily, always ill, I should have to leave Vienna, for it would be more than I could stand.' After this meeting with Schwind she was taken ill and spat blood. But in spite of her enfeebled condition, and with indomitable spirit she continued to give parties and hold 'Schubertiads'. Schubert dedicated some songs and the Hungarian 'Divertissement' to her, a delicate compliment for her husband was a Hungarian. Before her marriage, Katherina also had appeared on the stage at the Burgtheater, but she was not so popular an actress as Sophie Müller: her numerous love-affairs scandalised the citizens of Vienna and Schwind concluded the account of his meeting her with the words: 'So now I know what a person looks like who is in ill repute all over the city, and what she does.'

In the previous December (1824) Schubert had received a letter from a great soprano whose performances in operatic roles at the Kärntnertor Theater had won his admiration as a boy. Anna Milder had settled in Berlin where she sang at the Court Opera, but she still kept in touch with Viennese circles, maintained a friendship with Vogl—it was with him that she had made her name in the Vienna Opera, and won Schubert's regard —and occasionally visited the city. She wrote to the composer inviting him to set to music a poem called 'Der Nachtschmetterling'. This he did not do, but he sent to her the second of the two songs of Suleika (*Ach, um deine feuchten Schwingen*), and with it a full score of the opera 'Alfonso und Estrella'. She replied on 8 March dashing any hopes which he entertained that the opera might be produced in Berlin. Frau Milder's reasons for its nonacceptance strike the present day reader of them as inadequate to say the least: she stated that its libretto was not in accord with the taste of the Berliners and *that* at a time when the variety of operas being staged makes it difficult to discover quite what was the desired type. But she very much approved of 'Suleika's Song' and sang it at her next concert, in the Jagor'sche Saal, Berlin. This took place on 9 June 1825, and was a brilliant success. Even the Berlin critics, for whom 'Lied' meant a strophic song in the tradition of Zelter and Reichardt, were captivated by the *Erlking* and the *Suleika* song; it would indeed be difficult to understand any coldness, in those days, towards those two exuberant settings of Goethe. But Schubert was not given unqualified praise; it was impossible for Berlin to accept wholeheartedly the 'durchkomponiert', i.e. onrunning, song, as a typical 'Lied'. For many years the Schubert song failed to capture this stronghold, and it was greeted there with sneers and neglect. It is ironical to think that nowadays the Schubert 'durchkomponiert' song has come to be synonymous with 'German song'. Anna Milder, triumphant with her successful concert, sent the cuttings to Schubert, who was then, in June, on holiday with Vogl in Upper Austria.

After the year of work, the year of holiday. In May he had departed from Vienna with Vogl, and the two friends arrived at Steyr on 20 May. The difference in his status at Steyr during 1825 compared with that during his first visit six years before is as marked as it was at Zseliz. In 1819 Schubert was an inconspicuous young musician, a protégé of Vogl. In 1825 he was a notable composer, the author of published songs which were loved and sung in the musical centres of Upper Austria as much as in those of Vienna. Everywhere Vogl and Schubert went their welcome was overwhelming. Theresa Clodi, sister of the young Max Clodi, a law student of Vienna who knew Schubert through Spaun, wrote to her brother from Ebenzweier Castle:

> Twice I have heard Vogl sing and Schubert play: it is and remains a divine pleasure to hear those two. (22 June 1825.)

The following 'journal' of Schubert's movements, and the documents of himself, his friends and admirers, may help to bring the summer holiday into perspective.

STEYR (20 May–4 June): Schubert stayed with Vogl in the house where the singer had been born, a flat-fronted building with a rather imposing, arched entrance at the side. It is today 32 Haratzmüllerstrasse in the Ennsdorf suburb. On 24 May the two friends visited Linz and journeyed on to the nearby monasteries of St. Florian and Kremsmünster. Schubert received an enthusiastic and warm-hearted welcome, for he was visiting people who already knew and loved his music and were prepared to honour its author. His reticent nature and still disconsolate spirits opened out under this warmth.

> In Upper Austria I find my compositions everywhere, especially in the monasteries of St. Florian and Kremsmünster, where, with the help of a worthy piano player I produced my four-handed Variations and Marches with gratifying success. (Letter to his parents, 25 July 1825.)

The 'worthy piano player' was the Dean of the Monastery, Father Heinrich Hassak. Schubert also performed alone the *Andante poco moto* variation-movement from his newly completed Sonata in A minor, published at the end of the year by Pennauer, as Op. 42. Vogl sang the new songs from Scott's 'Lady of the Lake', including the *Ave Maria*, a song which, it has been said, 'suffers today from its rather overpowering popularity of yesterday.' Schubert accompanied him, and the songs too had much success according to the composer's report in the letter quoted above. He and Vogl returned to Steyr on 27 May, remaining there until 4 June.

GMUNDEN (4 June–15 July): it is a small town on the shores of Lake Traun—'the environs of which are truly heavenly and deeply moved and benefited me' wrote the composer. He and Vogl lived with a merchant named Ferdinand Traweger, who greatly esteemed Schubert as man and musician, but whose advent into Schubert's life is a mystery. Traweger was fond of singing in male voice quartets, and while staying as his guest, Schubert composed for him two part-songs: the *Nachtmusik*, a setting of a serenade by Karl Seckendorf, and the Latin drinking-song *Edit*

Nonna, edit Clerus whose words were written in the sixteenth century. This racy text kept back the publication of the quartet; the censorship was not lifted until 1848. Schubert's setting is a full-throated enjoyment of the words, and the Latin tongue probably veils, for modern audiences, any offence in the words. We have Schubert's own word that he lived very pleasantly and freely at the Gmunden home. He became attached to Traweger's small, five-year old son, Eduard, and is supposed to have been the only one capable of allaying the boy's fears when, in the fashion of the day, leeches were applied as a remedy for fever. Eduard Traweger, who lived until 1909, was then the last surviving person to have known Schubert. From Gmunden the two friends visited Florian Clodi and his daughter Therese, whose home was Ebenzweier Castle, some three miles from Gmunden, on the lake shore. Therese, a gentle, devoted daughter —her father was blind—was a connection of Spaun's, and to the Schubertians she was known as the 'Lady of the Lake'. She managed the estate. It is a romantic picture, to imagine father and daughter listening to Schubert and Vogl performing the Walter Scott songs in a room of the castle, backed by the lake and its lovely shoreline.

The strangest and most perplexing report of these six weeks at Gmunden is the suggestion that Schubert composed there a symphony—the now entitled 'Gmunden-Gastein' Symphony. (That very title has a faint hint of the confusion which surrounds the subject.) The question will be considered later, so that it can suffice to say here that it is doubtful whether Schubert did anything more than sketch the work, although it may have been a substantial enough sketch for him to have considered it as good as finished, so far as the primal, creative impulse was concerned. Scoring and final details were for him, in 1825, routine matters, at his finger tips. But to say even that is to go beyond any documentary evidence which is reliable.

An old tradition in Gmunden says that while Schubert was there he watched a gang of pile-drivers at work and listened to their singing. These Austrian craftsmen had a repertory of songs whose very rhythmic nature helped the men to deliver a united 'hammer' blow on the pile at a strategic point in the music, actually on the *second* beat of the bar. The subject is of interest and was dealt with fully by Karl M. Klier in 1952.[1] Schubert, tradition has it, was intrigued by the song he heard and used it in his *Adagio* in E flat for PF. Trio, called a 'Notturno' and published as Op. 148. Here is the melody, said to be a pile-drivers' song, from the 'Notturno', supplied with arrows on the second beat, where the men would deliver the 'Niederschlag':

Ex.33 *Adagio*

The most significant outcome of the story, if it has any truth, and its very strangeness suggests that it has, is that it gives us a chance to date the PF. Trio in B flat, Op. 99. The 'Notturno' in E flat has always been considered a rejected movement from the B flat PF. Trio, and since Schubert is not likely to have delayed using the song he heard, it is possible that the PF. Trio was begun as early as 1825. There is no other means whatever of dating it: the manuscript is lost and there are no contemporary references to it. Two dates have been deduced for its composition, 1826 and 1827. The piledrivers' song and its tradition make the earlier one, 1826, more probable.

Schubert and Vogl left Gmunden on 12 or 13 July and spent a night or two with acquaintances at Puchberg, a village near Wels.

LINZ (15 July–25 July): Schubert went on alone to Linz, his intention being to stay with Anton Ottenwalt and his wife Marie, the sister of Spaun. They were delighted to welcome him, and Ottenwalt wrote to Spaun (then at Lemberg) that Schubert looked so well and strong, so bright of appearance and genial in mood, that it was a pleasure to see him. On his arrival at Linz, however, and after a brief greeting, Schubert hurried off to Steyregg Castle, to pay his respects to the Countess Weissenwolf.

---

[1] 'Oesterreichische Pilotenschlägerlieder' in the 'Jahrbuch des österreichischen Volksliedwerkes I', Vienna, 1952. See also 'Music & Letters', April 1953, page 181.

The castle was five miles or so from Linz and Schubert spent several nights there. Sophie, Countess Weissenwolf, was a contralto and an eager Schubertian. Now she heard the 'Lady of the Lake' songs and was entranced with them. When they were published the following April they were dedicated to her—Schubert gratifying her pretty plain hint that such a dedication would be anything but disagreeable to her. He returned to the Ottenwalts on 19 July. When Vogl joined him there, three days later, he took the singer straightway on a visit to Steyregg Castle, staying there that time for two days. They were once more guests of the Ottenwalts on their return to Linz, and in a second letter to Spaun, Ottenwalt gives a very vivid account of the two friends, and describes the five solo songs to the Scott poems. The seven settings of lyrics from the 'Lady of the Lake' contain, of course, two part-songs: *Coronach* (female voices), which is an elegy foreshadowing the intensity of the 'Winterreise' songs, and *Bootgesang*, a trifling quartet for men's voices. Vogl sang all five of the solo songs, Ellen's as well. Ottenwalt wrote:

> We heard Vogl three times, and Schubert himself condescended to sing something after breakfast among ourselves, and also played his marches, two- and four-handed variations, and an overture on the pianoforte, compositions of such significance that one cannot trust oneself to discuss them.

The overture is probably that in F minor, Op. 34, for PF. Duet. An unexpected visitor to Ottenwalt's home, and one whom Schubert, without any doubt, welcomed warmly, was Albert Stadler, a friend from the *Stadtkonvikt* days.

STEYR (25 July–11 August): Schubert once again lived in Vogl's house in the Haratzmüllerstrasse and from there wrote the long and detailed letter to his father and stepmother which has already been quoted. Rainy weather kept him indoors, and one wonders whether he used the time to continue with the symphony sketches, or, more probably, to sketch the music for a new sonata, the one in D major, Op. 53. While at Steyr he received a letter from Schwind, which, apart from personal details, informed him of the arrival of Schober, back in Vienna from his travels in Breslau; of the imminent arrival of Kupelwieser, from Italy; and news of Bauernfeld, alternatively working for law examinations and at his poetry. The Schubert circle was in the process of re-forming.

A few days later Vogl and Schubert set off for Gastein, travelling there via Salzburg. For poor Vogl the visit to the Gastein spa was in the nature of a cure, and he took the waters for his painful gout; for Schubert, on the other hand, the trip was unalloyed holiday. They arrived on 14 August.

GASTEIN (14 August–4 September): a number of compositions originated at Gastein, all of them thoroughly typical of the composer in his over-abundant, rather lush vein, and, accordingly, not in the front rank of his works. The Sonata in D major was finished and written out; its autograph is dated 'Gastein. August 1825'. There are many pages of grand music in this sonata, but some which verge on the trivial. It is unusual to find Schubert using anything but conventional Italian for the expression marks of his movements, but we find the first movement bearing, in his autograph, the direction *un poco più lento e con capriccita* (bar 48). His requirement, as well as the wording of it, are both unusual. The four songs of the period are similarly luxuriant, but unequal pieces of work. Two of them are settings of poems by Johann Ladislau Pyrker, Patriarch of Venice, who was staying at Gastein that August. He and Schubert were already on a quite friendly footing, their acquaintance dated from 1821 when the composer had dedicated to Pyrker the songs of Op. 4. The Patriarch had interests at Gastein, among them a military hospital which he had founded and directed. The two songs are *Die Allmacht* and *Heimweh*, both, like the D major Sonata, full of exalted, Schubertian writing, but neither wholly successful; each in particular oversteps the limitations of the piano as an accompanying instrument. This is perhaps a cold verdict to pass on such warm, passionate art. Then let the fine words of Richard Capell (*loc. cit.*, page 213) on the song *Die Allmacht* serve as contrary opinion:

Schubert, exhilarated by his tour in the hills of Upper Austria, his thoughts . . . all set quivering by so many revelations of nature both benign and magnificent, found in this song the outlet for over-flowing feelings. The Patriarch's verses could not have been hap-pened on at a better moment. The subject, God apprehended in nature, went straight to Schubert's heart. There, with the hills round about him, he poured forth his blessing upon the health-giving air, and thanks to the Creator of life. The magnificent song is anything but a formal piece . . . it is intensely personal and rapturous. Schu-bert's temple was the hillside; and he brought all the sounds of the open-air, the torrent, the forest's murmur, the thunder-roll, into his hymn of praise. . . .

The other two songs are *Fülle der Liebe*, a setting of Friedrich von Schlegel's poem, showing remarkable affinities with the slow movement of the D major Sonata, and *Auf der Bruck*, Schubert's second setting of Ernst Schulze, a poet to whom he returned in the next two years and who inspired him with a series of deeply serious songs.

Vogl and Schubert left Gastein on 4 September, travelling via Werfen and the lakeside to Gmunden, where they again lodged with Traweger. Once settled there, Schubert began, on 12 Septem-ber, a letter to Ferdinand, describing his journeyings and the impressions they had awakened in him. The famous account of his and Vogl's performance of the songs occurs in this letter:

The way in which Vogl sings and I accompany him, as though we were one at such a moment, is something quite new and unheard-of for these people. . . .

The composer and his singer paid another visit to Ebenzweier Castle, and a few days afterwards Vogl decided to return to Steyr. From there Schubert continued his brother's letter, but the de-tailed description proved too tedious for him. He threw up the task, and Ferdinand received the incomplete letter by hand when his brother arrived back in Vienna. Vogl had decided to go to Italy and the holiday for Schubert was drawing to an end. It seems fairly clear that since the movements of the two men were apparently determined by Vogl, Schubert was largely his guest on the holiday. Apart from the lodgings with Traweger and Ottenwalt, when both Schubert and Vogl were guests, the transport, and the hotels at Salzburg, Puchberg, Gastein and so on, were evidently paid for from Vogl's purse. On 17 September they returned to Steyr ('unfortunately' wrote Schubert in his brother's letter!).

STEYR (17 September–1 October): the quiet days here, at Vogl's house, produced four more songs. Two of them are modest pieces, but in some ways more successful than the ambitious work of the previous month, particularly the fresh *Wiedersehn*. This song remained unpublished until 1843, when it appeared obscurely in a symposium entitled *Lebensbilder aus Oesterreich* (*Pictures of Austrian Life*). The other two songs form a pair, textually related, for both poems were taken from a play entitled 'Lacrimas' by Wilhelm von Schütz, which Schubert must have found in Vogl's collection of dramatic literature. The first is *Florio*, a small, likable song in E major. But the other, *Delphine*, the outpouring of an impassioned woman, is a masterpiece, fully the equal of either of the Pyrker songs, and neglected, possibly, because of the over-riding demands on voice and intelligence.

On 1 October Vogl and Schubert arrived at Linz as the guests once more of the Ottenwalts. They found Stadler there on a second visit, and since Vogl was unable, or unwilling, to go to Steyregg Castle, Schubert went without him, taking Stadler as companion, to pay a third visit to Count and Countess Weissenwolf. Stadler shared a bedroom with Schubert, and years afterwards recalled the composer's amusement over an incident which occurred before they fell asleep. Schubert sang a tune from the 'Magic Flute', but Stadler could not remember the second part to it, and so was unable to join in the 'duet'. He also related how, in the morning, Schubert flatly refused to rise early and go for a walk with him into the inviting countryside.

The last 'recital' which Schubert and Vogl gave, in which some of the new songs of August and September were sung, as well as the much admired 'Lady of the Lake' series, took place at Anton Spaun's home on 3 October. Anton was a younger brother of Josef's. After this Vogl betook himself to Italy, and now he more or less drops out of the composer's story, save for a few isolated appearances. Schubert met Josef von Gahy at Spaun's little Schubertiad and returned with him to Vienna, where they arrived on 6 October.

'Schubert is back' wrote Bauernfeld in his diary. 'Inn and coffee house gathering with friends often until two or three in the morning.' Schober, Schwind, Kupelwieser, Bauernfeld, Schubert—they were together again, and there re-commenced the round of convivial parties, concerts, Schubertiads, with the autumnal Viennese background; the summer and the holiday were over, yet the social life to which Schubert gladly abandoned himself meant an end, for a while, of work. The next compositions bear the date December 1825.

The publications of that year were again numerous and varied and four publishers accepted his work. Diabelli eventually brought out a delayed Op. 19, containing the three Goethe songs *An Schwager Kronos*, *Ganymed* and *An Mignon*, which he had purchased before the rupture with Schubert. This may have acted as a kind of peace offering for negotiations were resumed soon afterwards and Schubert sold him a whole batch of work: his early Mass in C major, two offertories, a large number of waltzes and écossaises, and the fine 'Salve Regina' in F major, composed in 1815. These works Diabelli published as Opp. 45–50. Cappi, formerly a partner of Diabelli, now in business on his own, bought two batches of manuscripts from Schubert. The earlier one contained German Dances Op. 33, and the PF. Duet Overture in F, Op. 34; the latter a group of songs published as Opp. 36, 37 and 38. Of this group the most famous is Op. 36: *Der zürnenden Diana* and *Nachtstück*, which Schubert had dedicated to Frau von Lászny. But the masterpieces, instrumental and vocal, were published by more modest houses. From Sauer & Leidesdorf there came the superb set of variations for PF. Duet in A flat, Op. 35 and the six 'Grandes Marches', Op. 40, dedicated by Schubert to his doctor J. Bernhardt. Pennauer, a recently founded publishing house, brought out the Sonata in A minor, Op. 42, with which Schubert was charming his friends during the summer months in Upper Austria, and three songs: the second *Suleika* song as Op. 31 (a delayed publication) and the well nigh incomparable pair of nocturnes, *Nacht und Träume* and *Die iunge Nonne*, as Op. 43. Pennauer's recent establishment led his manager, Franz Hüther, to write rather appealingly to Schubert on 27 July 1825:

> Kindly fix the most exact price you can ask of a beginner. . . .

The close of this sentence was translated in the nineteenth century 'as a beginner' and taken to refer to Schubert, whereat the hapless publisher was execrated for meanness. But Hüther was, of course, referring to his firm as the 'beginner', unable to pay extravagant fees.

There were a few trifling dances from Schubert's pen published in various 'Dance Albums' of the day, and hence completely lost until they were exhumed in the early years of this century. Diabelli re-issued the *Trout* (still without its opus number, 32); and *Der Einsame,* that most attractive of the fireside songs, appeared as a supplement to the *Wiener Zeitschrift* of 12 March 1825.

This was a large body of work to be published in one place by a composer in one year. The compositions are not shallow efforts designed to catch the interest of the moronic amongst the musical Viennese, such as the variations of Czerny, the dances and 'Morceaux' of Blumenthal and Weiss; they contain serious and significant works. Why, with the appearance of this music, ambitious and yet so likeable, did Schubert still fail to catch the ear of Vienna, and hence of musical Europe? One can only remind oneself, once again, of Schubert's inability to appear before the public in some executive capacity. There is no question of his obscurity. A glance through the pages of contemporary musical periodicals and publishers' announcements will show the wide international reputation of composers such as Herz and Pixis, who are not only abysmally inferior in our judgement to Schubert, but must have appeared at least moderately so to any informed music lover in their own day. But those two, or any similar composers one might select, were pianists, and the musical public knew them well in that capacity. It is possible that Schubert's very songs, which first opened the door to reputation for him, eventually proved, in his day, a drag on that reputation rather than a help to it. A song writer, however attractive his songs, is a lowly specimen in the world of music (just as an opera composer, however modest, is an important one). And although we can read in the Berlin 'Zeitung' of 11 June 1825:

> Rich enjoyment was afforded by the evening musical entertainment given by the Court Opera singer, Mme Milder, at Jagor's Hall on the 9th inst., which was numerously and brilliantly attended. . . .

and, again in the Dresden 'Abendzeitung' of 19 August 1825:

> The young, talented tone-poet Schubert, whose song compositions betoken the musical painter, continues to do excellent work in that unfortunately much neglected species. All his compositions testify to profound feeling combined with considerable musical theory. His songs find many purchasers. . . .

there is no escaping the conclusion that musicians could still agree with all this, and yet not consider Schubert seriously. The attitude persisted for decades and was held with particular obstinacy in England right up to the 1870's: merely a song-writer. In Vienna itself even song-writers, presumably, had a following of enthusiasts, outside their own circle of friends and patrons, for we find that Schubert received the mild honour of having his 'likeness' on sale in the Inner City. On 9 December 1825, Cappi announced the publication of his portrait, an engraving made by Johann Nepomuk Passini from the water colour by Rieder: it is the most famous of the contemporary Schubert portraits. 'An extremely good likeness' said the publisher's advertisement, 'of the composer of genius . . . who has so often enchanted his hearers with his vocal compositions. . . .' A *song* composer's portrait after all!

III

The music of 1824 and 1825 contains nothing for orchestra, that is if we exclude the problematical 'Gmunden-Gastein' Symphony from the sum of works. This is something very different from the years prior to 1824. Schubert's preoccupation with songs and chamber music, while undoubtedly satisfying his need for creative work and nourishing his genius, must equally have seemed to him the only way, after his abandonment of opera, to earn money. He composed what the publishers would accept, PF. Duets and Solos, songs and String Quartets, pouring into these works the highest he knew and was capable of.

The songs of the period fall into three major groups, the settings of texts by Sir Walter Scott, by Mayrhofer (the last of Schubert's songs on his old friend's poems), and by a new poet, Ernst Schulze. The Scott songs, especially those of the 'Lady of the Lake', were the most frequently performed and freely documented of all Schubert's songs in his lifetime, with the sole exception of the *Erlking*. None of them, except possibly *Coronach*, is first-rate Schubert, and all are eclipsed today. Something stilted and artificial in the Scott lyrics, which is mitigated by his picturesque word and phrase, stands exposed in the German translation without mitigation. And Schubert, dealing with the not-quite-genuine, never achieved the supreme touch.

This is made very clear when we glance at the Mayrhofer poems, which burn with sincerity however melancholy and despairing they may be. Mayrhofer, there is no doubt, was morbidly attracted to Death: the words of the song, *Der Sieg*, tell of his breaking the bondage of the flesh for the world of the spirit. The solemn chords of the opening and the passionate heart of the song (with a hint of 'Doppelgänger' technique) are in Schubert's 'grand style'; the song is a perfect vehicle for the bass singer. In the last of the four songs, *Auflösung*, the poet bids sun and springtime dissolve, for eternity's oblivion calls him. Schubert's music is an ecstatic flood—the great curves of the melody buoyed up by sweeping arpeggios on the piano. Ernst Schulze, a tragically doomed poet, is the author of five songs of 1825. *Um Mitternacht* is one of the endlessly varied nocturnes of that bright summer. It is a stylish, beautifully developed song, worked skilfully within modest limits. Schubert's finest settings of Schulze were yet to be: they came in the following year (1826).

We find Schubert several times in 1825 selecting a pair of poems from the work of various authors. After composing them it seems as if his interest in the poet was exhausted; he drew no further from his work. Pyrker's *Die Allmacht* and *Das Heimweh* are one example; the 'Two Scenes' from Schütz's *Lacrimas* are another. There are Jakob Craigher's *Die junge Nonne* and *Totengräbers Heimweh* as yet another pair of songs. *Die junge Nonne* ranks high among Schubert's great soprano songs and if its somewhat sentimental words prevent it from ranking quite so high as *Gretchen am Spinnrade*, it is easier to sing, and it is easier for the singer to stir an audience with its sentiments. Schubert's power of 'linear' development—the evolution of fresh and significant melodies from his initial 'germ-motif' is remarkably displayed in this song, and the treatment of his motif in the accompaniment is almost without peer amongst his 'onrunning' songs:

Ex.34

The obscure poet Karl Lappe is immortalised by Schubert's composition of two poems from his pen, *Der Einsame* and *Im Abendrot.* Grove has said the inevitably right word about the first, when he instances the recurrence of the group of four semi-quavers in the accompaniment as imparting 'an indescribable air of domesticity to the fireside picture'. But it must not be thought that there is anything 'domestic' in the workmanship of the song, for that is filled with touches of genius: the crickets, the fall of the embers, the relaxed limbs of the rustic, are depicted graphically in the music, and detail after detail betrays Schubert's love for his song of 'true contentment'. As for *Im Abendrot*: one could argue reasonably, that the sheer beauty of its penmanship reveals a similar love on the part of the composer for his created work. The song is a miracle, for no amount of analysis or description seems to add one iota to an explanation of how these simple chords and diatonic phrases can achieve sublimity such as exists in this song of God in the hour of sunset: a Schubertian sublimity, a quality which no other composer but he possessed. It is a re-velation of the aspiring spirit of man, which reaches its heaven through poetry alone.

In the letter to Leopold Kupelwieser quoted in full earlier, we read of Schubert's intention with regard to the two string quar-tets and the Octet of 1824: they were to be preparations for his 'grand symphony'. No one thinks of these three works as 'pre-parations' in any sense of the word; their greatness is self-evident and their function self-sufficient. The first quartet, in A minor, is a beloved work; in some ways we group it with the 'Unfinished' Symphony as giving us the heart of the composer. But with the quartet, as with the symphony, it is doing him an injustice to let the emotional directness, the poetry, the sheer beauty of the musical sound—which is ear-bewitching—prevent admiration and appreciation of his technical power: power used with masterly ease in development and formal construction. The adroit inter-play of major and minor modes in the first movement, foretold so emphatically, and yet so persuasively, in the melody of the open-ing bars, the colourful use of the 'Neapolitan' sixth, the contra-puntal tissues, all these factors must also be appreciated. His power of theme-manipulation, now richly pouring into his in-strumental forms from his song-writing techniques, gives a lyricism so elaborate and highly-developed that only the closest examination reveals the genetic relationship between the component parts. One of the more obvious examples is given here:

The slow movement is based on the Entr'acte in B flat from the 'Rosamunde' music; not merely the theme, but the whole of the first section is common to both pieces. The Entr'acte had, of course, been written only a month or so prior to the quartet movement; Schubert probably thought that he was rescuing the music from oblivion. In the third movement he dispensed with customary 'Scherzo' form, and reverted to the old-fashioned 'Menuetto', but he wrote a minuet unlike any other he had ever composed. The opening motif on the 'cello, taken up directly by the other three strings, is once again a germinating idea and it pervades the whole minuet, the 'Trio'-section as well. Is this 'cello motif taken over from his song *Die Götter Griechenlands*, an 1819 setting of Schiller's text? The point has intrigued writers on Schubert ever since it was raised by Willi Kahl in 1929.[1] It is more than possible that Schubert's mood in those days, of aching regret for the vanished days of his youth, a mood preserved for ever in the Kupelwieser letter, recalled Schiller's words to his mind:

> *Schöne Welt, wo bist du?*
> *Kehre wieder, holdes Blüthenalter der Natur.*

> *Fair world, where art thou?*
> *Come again, O golden age of Nature.*

And if the words were recalled, the music as well came to mind and pen. The song, like the 'Menuetto', veers between A minor

[1] Cobbett's 'Cyclopedia of Chamber Music'.

and major. If it is not merely fanciful to look upon A major as Schubert's key of contentment, then by association of ideas A minor is his key of yearning for lost contentment, of *Sehnsucht*. But full consideration of the Schiller song quotation will be taken up in connection with the octet.

The second quartet of that spring is the famous 'Death and the Maiden' String Quartet, in D minor. Its appellation derives from a mere song title, but as with the 'Wanderer' Fantasia of 1822, the temptation was irresistible, and unresisted, to weave fanciful interpretations and philosophies round the quartet by associating the music of *the whole work* with the subject of the poem which Schubert had set as a song in 1817. He selected the melody of the 1817 song and wrote variations on it for the slow movement of the string quartet; naturally, since the song embodies in music the mood of Death's words in the poem, these variations ring the changes on a limited range of emotions: noble, passionate, austere, sombre, and, at the end, consolatory. But the nineteenth century's incurable tendency to read meanings and fantasies and stories into all music prompted the theory that Schubert was, in the other three movements, also expounding some aspect of Death; the theory reaches absurdity in trying to account for the *siciliano* and tarantella rhythms of the finale. This, mark the word, is called a 'Dance of Death'. If Schubert, like many an artist of his day and race, was interested in the artistic possibilities of the 'Death' motif, it was always the most solemn and profound manifestations which inspired him. To imagine him extending this interest to the flippant and ghastly medievalism of the 'Dance of Death' is only possible to writers who know little of the composer's personality and outlook, and, it must be added, who ignore the *context* of the 'Death' variations. For there is much of grace, vivacity and charm in the quartet movements; much more, in fact, of a healthy artist's absorption in 'Life' than of a morbid one's portrayal of 'Death'.

All the techniques developed in his early quartet writing, perfected in the 'Quartettsatz' of 1820, show rich manifestations in the D minor Quartet. The music is urged forward with a powerful impulse by the pitting of the 'cello in its dramatic, high register, against the sonorities of chords high in the upper strings. Or if

Schubert's mood is lyrical, and the first violin is pouring out its song, he avoids a static congealing of the music's progress by remarkably buoyant figures of accompaniment in the middle strings. The finale of the quartet is perhaps overlong. But the rhythmic and metrical experiments are original to a degree, and although in discussing them similar experiments by Brahms have been mentioned there is little doubt that Schubert's spontaneous and incalculable pen produces results which bear little relationship to Brahms' somewhat deliberate, calculated rhythmic variants. The best of Schubert's experiments in this finale is too long to quote (pages 51 and 52 in the miniature Eulenberg score), but the poignant harmonies which introduce it might be quoted as revealing Schubert's deepening emotion: not pathos, nor the easily solaced sadness of *Erster Verlust*, but a savagery of grief seems to be portrayed here which was to lead to the heartbreak of the 'Winterreise' songs and of *Der Doppelgänger*:

Most musicians are agreed that the D minor String Quartet is Schubert's most successful piece of chamber music, and therefore one of the supreme accomplishments of all chamber music. Although the G major Quartet of 1826 and the C major Quintet of 1828 each contains isolated movements of greater value than the corresponding one in the D minor Quartet, neither of them is, as a whole, so sustainedly great. The finale of the quartet and the first movement of the quintet are inferior. Every single movement of the 'Death and the Maiden' Quartet is a masterpiece. The work was performed in January 1826, and then set aside, never played again, not published until after Schubert's death. What must his inward thoughts have been in considering this music and its—as far as he knew—oblivion? Is there any pain or frustration to be compared to that of the creative artist's, whose work is not so much misunderstood, as politely set aside as of not much account, and then forgotten?

Similar neglect, following upon a single performance, awaited the third piece of chamber music, the octet for clarinet, horn, bassoon, double-bass and string quartet in F major. The work may have been performed privately at Count Troyer's lodgings soon after its composition, but it received a public performance on 16 April 1827 at a concert given by Ignaz Schuppanzigh in the Hall of the 'Musikverein'. A report of the concert spoke well of the music, but grumbled rather at its duration: this is, in fact, nearly an hour. The music was then shelved and remained in obscurity for a quarter of a century, when C. A. Spina published a truncated version as Op. 166.

Schubert's scheme of movements in the octet follows its proto-type, that is, Beethoven's Septet in E flat, Op. 20, composed in 1799 when Beethoven was 29 years old. Troyer, without doubt, requested that Beethoven's septet (very popular in Vienna at that time) should be Schubert's model, just as in the case of the *Trout* Quintet, Paumgartner had proposed Hummel's Op. 87. Schubert added a second violin to Beethoven's score, but otherwise he fol-lowed the older composer's work closely. The Septet in E flat has a six-movement scheme, Beethoven including a Scherzo as well as a Minuet, a set of variations as well as the conventional slow move-ment. The Octet in F major is similar, save that the Minuet and Scherzo movements change places. Both first movements and both finales have a slow introduction; in Beethoven these are *Adagio* (18 bars) and *Andante con moto alla marcia* (16 bars), in Schubert they are *Adagio* (18 bars) and *Andante molto* (17 bars). The variation-movement of each composer is *Andante*, 2/4 and placed in the dominant key of the respective work. Besides obvious points of resemblance such as these there are others more subtle; for example, Beethoven foreshadows in his *Adagio* prelude the main theme of the first movement:

and Schubert does the same thing in his first movement:

The publication of the octet in March 1853 omitted Schubert's variations and his minuet so that the work conformed to the four-movement scheme of orthodox 'Sonata-form'. The complete work was not published until 1875. Today, performances of the octet are very frequent. The wonder is that it is performed at all, instead of being, actually, one of his most popular pieces of chamber music. It is a late, 'Romantic' example of the classical 'Cassazione' or 'Divertimento', and a forerunner of the 'Suite' as a series of instrumental pieces not necessarily in dance-forms. This midway and 'transitional' status alone could be sufficient to damn it. Then, in view of its length, and of the players it requires for its performance, one could understand that it might be a rarity in chamber music programmes. When we are inclined to grumble at the neglect of this or that piece of Schubert's, it would be well to cast a glance at the octet, and be grateful that it is not one of them. The music of the octet is as varied as can be wished in such a long work. Schubert's moods range from the light-hearted dance of some of the variations,[1] and the pastoral measure of the 'Minuet', to the passion and ardour of the *Adagio* slow movement and the Finale. In some ways the world of the octet gives us Schubert's world more truly than anything else he wrote; the 'Death and the Maiden' Quartet spiritualises his world, the C major Symphony exalts it to a sublimity and majesty which it only in part possessed. The octet gives us Schubert's everyday Vienna: his bohemianism, his sociability, his exuberance, his easy-going 'bonhomie'; glimpses of the streets and fair-grounds of the city about him; a hint of the theatre, a snatch of song from the coffeehouse and beer-garden; and all conveyed together with the sudden inspirational flash when the poetry and picturesqueness of life in Vienna burn for a moment in his music. The intensely dramatic introduction of the finale (F minor), built on *tremolo* bases like drum-rolls, has more to it than mere preluding. For one thing it re-appears in the course of the main movement with great effect and carrying all kinds of possibilities for 'programme' interpretations. For another, it makes use of the figure from the song *Die Götter Griechenlands*. At this point we may resume discussion of the use of this motif in the 'Menuetto' of the A minor String Quartet. The two motifs from the quartet and the octet are here quoted together:

If the words of the song did, as was previously suggested, articulate a mood of Schubert's in that spring of 1824, then these two motifs may have been derived from the song itself:

---

[1] The theme of the variations is taken from his early operetta 'Die Freunde von Salamanka'. This was first pointed out by William Glock in his short life of the composer, 'Lives of the Great Composers', ed. A. L. Bacharach, London, 1936.

But it is also more than possible that all three ideas in the song, the quartet and the octet, derive from a common source. A source from which Schubert, while yet preserving his own unique individuality, drew again and again, sometimes consciously, but sometimes subconsciously; for to him, as to all musicians in Vienna, the source was in the heart of their musical being— Beethoven. He is a conscious factor in Schubert's creative work in the octet: is he possibly an unconscious factor too? If so, the source of these motifs is not hard to find:

This is the theme of the 'Trio'-section from Beethoven's Seventh Symphony, in A major, a work whose influence on Schubert was profound and pervasive; we find evidence of it throughout his creative life, in small songs, in large instrumental pieces. The above theme from the 'Trio' of the third movement of Beethoven's symphony was an influence as strong as that of the dactyllic rhythm of the second movement, the *Allegretto*, whose quality has been called 'positively Schubertian'.

IV

The three works, the two string quartets and the octet, form a cohesive group not only on stylistic grounds, but because they

have in common their use of melodies from the composer's past—
from 'Rosamunde', *Die Freunde von Salamanka*, *Die Götter
Griechenlands*, *Der Tod und das Mädchen*. It gives a peculiar aura,
a unity, to the trio of compositions. No other group of works by
the composer has quite that unity; there is nothing like it in the
several Pianoforte Duets which he composed in the summer of
1824 at Zseliz. They form, for all that, a very distinguished group.
A set of six marches, the second and third of them the best he ever
wrote, were published in May and September of 1825 as Op. 40
(Books I and II). The 'Eight Variations on an Original Theme in
A flat' is Schubert's masterpiece in variation-form. It has a majesty,
a warmth and a poetry which infuse every bar. The Hungarian
'Divertissement', published as Op. 54 in 1826, was fairly well-
known in the nineteenth century and on the whole did not serve
Schubert's reputation as an instrumental composer very well.
Wagner's and Mendelssohn's derogatory judgements have been
mentioned. They are not undeserved. Many of Schubert's faults
are present in the duet: triviality (Wagner's complaint about the
work), rhythmic monotony (Mendelssohn's complaint, due perhaps to the pseudo-Hungarian atmosphere), protracted repetition; but we find few of his virtues.

The group of duets is dominated by the Sonata in C major,
published as the 'Grand Duo', Op. 140, in 1838, and dedicated by
the publisher, Diabelli, to Clara Schumann. The term 'Sonata'
had ceased to be commercially profitable by 1838, and the appellation 'Grand Duo' has apparently come to stay. It is a great example of the composer's epic style (observe the key), almost the
supreme one, and each of its movements is so broadly planned
and so generously filled with music, that the proportions of the
work suggest a symphony rather than a sonata. The result is not
surprising: writers ever since it was first published have wondered
if it were a symphony in disguise. Schumann was the first one to
propose the idea. He was of the opinion that Schubert had arranged a symphony for PF. Duet until the manuscript came into
his wife's possession, a gift from Diabelli, and he saw for himself
Schubert's own title: 'Sonata für Pianoforte zu vier Händen'
('Pianoforte Sonata for four hands'). But he could not give up

the notion. 'A man who composes so much as Schubert' he wrote, 'is not too particular about the title he dashes down on his work, and it could be that he wrote SONATA at the head of his composition, whilst in his own mind he thought of it as a SYMPHONY.'[1] He then went on to talk of the 'symphonic' effects which are found in the duet, and the resemblances to Beethoven's symphonies: in particular the *Andante* of the Second Symphony, and the finale of the Seventh. His arguments ignore the facts: that Schubert was engaged in teaching two young piano pupils and providing them with material; that the manuscript of the work is beautifully written and represents Schubert's last word; that when he sketched a symphony in PF. score he did not hesitate to write at the top the word 'Symphony'; that all Schubert's big compositions for the piano, from the 'Wanderer' Fantasia at the beginning to the 'Lebensstürme' Duet at the end, teem with 'symphonic' effects, string *tremolandos*, horn and trumpet calls, drum rolls and woodwind 'solos', all of which Schumann spoke of as if they were only to be found in the one work alone. Nearer our own day Sir Donald Tovey follows Schumann. In his 'Essays in Musical Analysis', Volume I, he writes on Joachim's orchestrated version of the duet, and says: 'The GRAND DUO is unique among Schubert's four-handed works in the disconcerting nature of its orchestral style. Not even the FUNERAL MARCH FOR THE CZAR, Op. 55, is so full of the kind of orchestral things the pianoforte obviously cannot do, or so deficient in the things, pianistic or orchestral, that it can do with enjoyment.' Tovey then proceeds to enlarge on another problem altogether, which had, during the nineteenth century, become entangled with the other: whether or not the 'Grand Duo' was the lost 'Gmunden-Gastein' Symphony. Even to entertain the idea that it might be so is to ignore, or to be ignorant of, irreconcilable dates, and other uncompromising facts. Joachim orchestrated the 'Duo' in 1855; there are two other similar versions, by Anthony Collins (1939) and Karl Salomon (1946).

The most conclusive argument against the 'symphony-in-disguise' theory of the 'Duo' lies in the failure of any of these

[1] 'Neue Zeitschrift für Musik', Leipzig, June 1838.

orchestral versions to convince. In its orchestral garb the work betrays, only too obviously, its pianistic origins. Liszt's orchestral version of the 'Wanderer' Fantasia, without question conceived for the piano by Schubert, is more convincing. In so far as Schubert's organisation of a sonata differs from his organisation of a symphony, it is possible to see that the 'Duo' belongs to the former type of work. And its first movement is a close relation of the two solo sonatas, in A minor and C major, which Schubert wrote in the following spring.

All three, for example, open with a pregnant, octave phrase coupled with a few soft chords marking the cadence. They each have a bold, fanfare-like episode of clanging chords, which assumes great importance as the movement proceeds. In the opening movement of all three sonatas there is another feature which gives an underlying unity, almost persuading us that Schubert was writing in them a three-fold expression of one, prevailing, creative mood. It is the way in which the second subject is derived from the first. The two subjects could be looked upon not as contrasting themes, but as two variants of the same theme. The three pairs of themes are briefly quoted here to illustrate the point:

There was a similar evolution of the second subject in the first movement of the octet.

The Sonata in A minor not only preserves a wonderful unity between the parts of the first movement, each part evolving admirably from its predecessor so that the movement has a quality of inevitableness from the dreamy passages at the opening to the tremendous challenge of the last bars, it also possesses a unity from movement to movement. This is possibly deliberate, for the themes of the whole sonata are built on the interval of a third: minor in the first, third and last movements, major in the second movement. The variations of the second movement, the finest set from a prophetic point of view which he wrote, do not quite sound the emotional depths of those in Op. 35, but have all kinds of other advantages, being more concise, easier to play, and simpler of texture. The Scherzo is the best of all the sonata-scherzos and it presents splendid points of development, especially the way in which the rhythm of the opening is clothed with the poignant harmonies of the minor ninth (bars 29 *et seq.*), or delicate melody (bars 42–50). It is fascinating to see the influence of the fifth variation in Beethoven's 'Diabelli' set on Schubert's Scherzo:

Beethoven's 'Diabelli' Variations were re-published in early 1824 as the first part of a collection of variations on the publisher's waltz-theme. The second part contained Schubert's single variation together with the single variations of forty-nine other composers. It is not too much to suppose that Schubert had been playing Beethoven's celebrated '33 Variations' from this big publication, and that the work inspired his own interest in variation-form during these years when he wrote his best work in the form. Not only in the Scherzo of Schubert's sonata, but in the preceding variations-movement, and in the PF. Duet Variations of Op. 35, we find evidence of the deep impression made by Beethoven's 'Diabelli' set.

The companion sonata, unfortunately left incomplete by Schubert, is in C major. The manuscript, dated 'April 1825', was given by Ferdinand Schubert to Schumann on the occasion of his famous visit to Vienna in the spring of 1839. Schumann published the slow movement in his journal, the 'Neue Zeitschrift für Musik', the following December. At some later date his friend Adolf Böttger, divided the music up, and it is now scattered piecemeal over Europe. A page from the first movement (bars 71–135) is in the Fitzwilliam Museum, Cambridge, the rest of the movement is in the Vienna City Library. This Library also possesses the last part of the 'Menuetto' and the 'Trio'. But the whereabouts of the rest of the work is unknown. The last two movements are unfinished but in spite of that the sonata was published by the firm of Whistling, Leipzig in 1861 as 'Last (sic) Sonata'. It was given the title 'Reliquie', but the name has never caught on, nor has the work ever established itself in the concert room. Some writers have, with reason, advocated the performance of the first two, complete movements as an 'Unfinished' Sonata. Others consider that the remains of the 'Menuetto' and finale are too substantial to be silenced in this fashion, and attempts to launch the Sonata have been made with *ad hoc* conclusions provided by various pianist-composers; there is one, for example, by Ernst Křenek in 1921. But to no avail.

The first movement is in the composer's grandest style, and if the other movements had been on the level of this one, we should have had a sonata as eminent among its companions as the D minor String Quartet is in its particular sphere. As it is, the slow movement is rather easy-going Schubert, the 'Menuetto' is a fiery movement, with some striking, improvisatory passages in the second half, but the 'Rondo', *Allegro* in 6/8 time, is a trivial piece of writing. Schubert makes one or two noble attempts to deepen the significance of his 'Rondo' theme, and in one episode achieves with his material a sense of tranquillity and repose which proclaims the genius. But he was disheartened by the intractability of his themes and, it has been suggested, laid the work aside for good when he left Vienna for Steyr.

The two sonatas and the 'Duo' provide an excuse for a review of Schubert's pianoforte style in the middle 1820's. The bare octaves and unisons, strong but uncompromising, which he used for the first time in the Sonata in A minor of 1823, Op. 143, are more frequent in these later works, more frequent, but just as tense and unyielding. His piano techniques are simple ones and not altogether free of awkwardness. This lack of grace leads to the accusation 'unpianistic' but the point is that Schubert's techniques are entirely subservient to his material. Whereas Mozart and Beethoven would sacrifice something to shape their material to the demands of the player, Schubert sacrifices nothing. It leads to quite ungainly structures in the C major 'Reliquie' Sonata, which the reader of the music, or the private player, can ignore when lost in the contemplation of that music's grandeur, but which cannot be ignored by the professional pianist or concert audience. Schubert's fondness for broken chords, either supporting right-hand melodies, or themselves supported by striding unisons in the bass, often give a welcome grace to his musical progress especially when they fuse into a lyrically and harmonically developing pianism, grateful to the player's hands:

These extracts are both taken from the last of the three solo sonatas of 1825, the one in D major composed at Gastein in August, and published by Artaria in the following April as Op. 53. It is the least satisfactory of the eight sonatas of his maturity. The techniques mentioned, bare unisons and octaves, broken chords, fanfares of heavy chords, all embody rather second-rate material in this sonata, and Schubert's lush melody, apt to luxuriate in the summer of 1825—we have glanced at a few songs which fail because of it—runs to extravagant lengths in the slow movement and Scherzo of the work. The final Rondo contains a fragile, delicious tune, famous because of its use in the regrettable 'Lilac Time', which introduces a graceful and likeable finale hardly big enough to serve as a conclusion to the three preceding movements. It is a fault with many of his finales, not entirely redeemed in the great Sonata in G major of the following year, 1826. But before we resume Schubert's life in that year it would be profitable to survey his achievement and his powers as a creative artist at the summit of his career.

VI

THE ARTIST

To appreciate Schubert's achievement as an artist, that is, to view his work as a whole and estimate his originality, his workmanship and his range, and do so with a fresh and un-influenced mind, is today difficult to the point of impossibility. So powerfully original a genius as his produced an ardent and adoring following, impatient of criticism; but it also provoked misunderstanding, misguided interpretation, and even hostility. The years following his posthumous fame abounded in these mixed emotions and very able spokesmen voiced them. Today, the judgements of the middle and late nineteenth-century critics on Schubert are accepted by the majority of music lovers, for, preserved in books and periodicals, these judgements have deter-mined the twentieth century's approach to his music. To reach a portrait of the essential artist behind this firmly entrenched mass of mixed commentary is therefore impossible, for no one can rid his mind completely of it. But some of it must go—it genuinely obstructs a vision of the true Schubert.

It is difficult to keep out of one's words a note of protest in the clearing away of obstructions: but while, it is hoped, the protest will not grow shrill, one has to risk the accusation that a defensive note is unnecessary for Schubert's greatness, that he needs no protest. This is hardly true. No Schubert lover wishes his com-poser acclaimed for doubtful virtues or from dubious standpoints. Nor, on the other hand, can he leave ill-considered detractions unchallenged. Only from those who view his work steadily, and view it whole, can informed judgements be expected or acceptable. Otherwise distortions of the man and his music will continue to be repeated without challenge.

There is, first, the question of Schubert's 'education' or 'culture'. The point interested Vincent d'Indy and he wrote:

> Schubert must be considered as the type of genius without culture. In forms where a plan is indispensable his works are very unequal, not to say utterly defective. . . .

And to this judgement of a minor French composer may be added that of a similar English one, Hubert Parry:

> Schubert is conspicuous among great composers for the insufficiency of his musical education. His extraordinary gifts and his passion for composing were from the first allowed to luxuriate untrained. He had no great talent for self-criticism, and the least possible feeling for abstract design, and balance and order. . . .

One tries to read these passages patiently and avoid brushing them aside with a word, but they are too widely heeded to be so peremptorily dismissed. But what do d'Indy and Parry mean by 'culture', 'education' and 'training'? They were actually, whether aware of it or not, taking over the critical outlook of the previous generation, which had dubbed Schubert a 'natural' musician, 'untaught, unschool'd', who sang 'as the birds sing', and so forth, because his phenomenal genius and fertility were incomprehensible. But to believe that Schubert had no musical training, and to base arguments on it, is simply false: it ignores the facts. His education, both general and musical, was as thorough, as prolonged and as profitable as that of any of the composers whom Parry had in mind. For five years he attended the chief boarding school in Vienna, one, if not under the direct patronage of the Austrian Imperial Court, at least very closely attached to it. His music teachers were accomplished musicians and one of them, Antonio Salieri, internationally renowned. His friends were poets, painters and composers. Schubert, it is true, knew only Vienna: but what rival, in the world of music, had his city amongst the cities of Europe?

In a letter to Spaun, written during July 1825, Anton Ottenwalt has these words:

> Schubert and I sat together until not far from midnight, and I have never seen him like this, nor heard him: serious, profound, and as

though inspired. How he talked of art, of poetry, of his youth, of friends, and of other people who matter, of the relationship of ideals to life, etc. I was more and more amazed at such a mind, of which it has been said that its artistic achievement is so unconscious, hardly revealed to, and understood by himself—and so on. Yet how simple was all this! I cannot tell you of the extent and unity of his convictions—but there were glimpses of a world outlook that is not merely acquired, and the share which worthy friends may have in it by no means detracts from the individuality shown by all this.

Both Parry and d'Indy in their remarks on balance and form are voicing the views of their day, a day in which any departure from Beethoven's and Mendelssohn's methods with sonata-form was looked upon almost as heresy: a viewpoint which is to us no longer tenable. It is Schubert's chief glory that he could be contemporary with a dominating figure like Beethoven, without slavishly imitating him. To be fair to Schubert, and despite these detractors, it is easy to name many of his mature works in all of which a 'plan is indispensable' and which display that plan, and which are neither unequal, nor in any way defective: the 'Unfinished' Symphony, the String Quartet in A minor, the last Sonata, in B flat major.

But quite apart from these tentative answers to such judgements on Schubert's 'culture', there is a third, devastating one. Genius is so powerful a factor in these matters, that other factors are, by comparison, negligible. Even if it were true that Schubert is a type of 'genius-without-culture', then that state is all-conquering, and 'talent-with-culture', even if the culture be gathered from the finest flower of the world's scholarship, droops and fails. If musical genius, without plan, or the least feeling for abstract order, can produce the D minor String Quartet, or the String Quintet in C major, then d'Indy's criteria are false ones, and we, and our judgements, are wrong.

The reason why Schubert is criticised on the grounds that his movements lack an organically planned structure, lies possibly in his poetic approach to the composing of music. He wished to feel intensely, and to express to the utmost of his powers, the present moment in his music: not for its significance as a link with what

SCHUBERT
COPPERPLATE ENGRAVING BY J. H. PASSINI FROM RIEDER'S AQUARELL,
ON SALE IN VIENNA, DECEMBER 1825
Historische Museum, Vienna

has gone and what is to come, but for its momentary effect as sound, as pleasure for the listener. This is not to say for one moment that he was indifferent to the structural necessities of sonata-form, in fact, the contrary has been urged where his purely transitional passages are concerned; but drive and cohesion —the achievement of which was second nature with Mozart and Beethoven—are not Schubert's first consideration. His invention flows strongly; his themes and episodes and figuration are unified by it, they are not a succession of poetic notions, nor does he simply graft a series of intensely felt miniatures cleverly on to each other.

There are other obstacles in our way, if we wish to see the artist in Schubert clearly. There is the pronouncement, which seems so odd today, that he was deficient in counterpoint, and that this deficiency (somehow bound up with that supposed lack of education) is shown by the absence of *fugato* and *canon* and other academic piquancies in his instrumental work. The counterpoint in the slow movement of the 'Unfinished' Symphony, in the octet, in the 'Variations on an original theme in A flat', Op. 35, and in the slow movement of the great C major Symphony, is not only amply sufficient to dispose of the charge, it positively asserts that his powers as a contrapuntist are equal to those of any of the great composers, when vitality, and musical worth, are the points at issue. That *fugato* and *canon* were not congenial devices of his in composition is, actually, a tribute to his fertility and abundant creative energy. Composers of the post-polyphonic age often resort to antiquarian devices of the kind, and to *stretti*, augmentation, double counterpoint and other favourite scholastic structures, when their creative powers temporarily fail. The cogent words of P. H. Lang have already been quoted in this connection (page 17). Even Beethoven only rarely fuses his creative energy and the *fugato* device: one thinks immediately of the close of the 'Marcia funèbre' in the 'Eroica' Symphony, but parallels to that supreme example are not so common. Schubert was never so much at a loss for what to say as to be obliged to resort to these academic diversions. But he could, when his genius demanded it,

o   B.S.

use comparable contrapuntal devices to urge his music forward. A superb passage in the finale of the C major Symphony shows canonic tensions set up between trombones and violins at the climax of the development section:

Ex. 45

Certain criticisms of his constructional methods are commonly found in analytical treatments of his first movements. They are these: that he writes 'development' episodes in the exposition section; that when he reaches the development section itself he repeats his themes in various keys rather than develop them. Evidence from here and there in his compositions can be adduced to support both of these statements, but they cannot stand against a total view of his work. J. A. Westrup has urged: 'By what rule is development forbidden in an exposition section?' And how, in the light of the superb thematic treatment in work after work of his maturity can he be said to repeat, rather than to develop, his themes? Consider the first movement of the String Quartet in G major: the fusion, the contrasting, of themes, in re-mote regions of music which his questing mind reaches while he is obsessed with the congenial opening theme—this manipulation is a matter for wonder. He has no formulae, no patterns upon which to build the 'free fantasia'; for him, as for Haydn and Mozart, each development section is an adventurous setting forth, and new challenges bring entirely new responses. Usually, Schubert's main theme, and its attendant subsidiary themes, form the basis of the section, as in all three mature string quartets; but sometimes, as in the String Quintet in C, a minor episode in the exposition section does service, and in the PF. Trio in E flat, a mere idea in the *codetta* of the opening section expands and flowers in the middle of the movement and completely dominates it. His development section may be pure poetry evolving from his stated material as in the PF. Trio in B flat, or it may become a closely argued, logical piece of prose as in the A minor Sonata of 1825, and certainly in the 'Unfinished' Symphony.

And if some of his transitions are accused of being abrupt, e.g. the celebrated presentation of the second subject in the first movement of the 'Unfinished' Symphony (see page 121), others, and they in the majority, are miracles of gradualness and inevitability. Sir Donald Tovey quotes one of them, the return of the main theme in the 1828 Sonata in B flat, praising it almost extravagantly in an essay on Schubert's tonality.[1] The three sonatas of that last year, of which the one in B flat is the third, are full of examples of this masterly transition from section to section.

That Schubert was repetitive, that his rhythmic obsession sometimes produced monotonous results, that his finales are generally inferior to the high level of the preceding movements, that his lengths are not always 'heavenly'—these criticisms can be admitted when they are qualified. For example, when Schubert is accused of being repetitive is it admitted that repetition is an essential ingredient of music in the eighteenth and nineteenth centuries, and that all composers repeat passages in their work, especially if they are pleased with them? Is Schubert more repetitive than Wagner, or Chopin?

When his finales are criticised as unworthy of the rest of the work, does the critic take into account that the importance and elevation of the final movement became established only after the death of Schubert, and that *all* composers prior to, say, Schumann and Mendelssohn wrote light-hearted finales to sonata and quartet and symphony. Beethoven's Ninth Symphony is an exception to the universal trend; but even in that work who would place the

[1] 'Music & Letters', October 1928, page 362.

choral finale in any other but the lowest place if the four movements were set in order of merit? The tendency to strengthen the
character of the final symphonic movement, which reaches far
out in Brahms and Sibelius, and in composers of the twentieth
century, is, from an artistic point of view, sound theory. But in
practice it makes heavy demands on the attention of the listener.
Audiences of today are more capable, and more willing, to give
that attention than were those of the early nineteenth century. As
a point of irony it may be urged that Schubert's only mature
movement of this kind—the finale of the C major Symphony—
probably contributed as much as anything else to the rise in importance of the symphonic finale.

Schubert's exuberances, and trivialities, are occasionally attributed to a lack of 'taste'. Good taste, with no other quality to
support it, is a limp attribute. The minor composer, who never
offends with exuberances, and never reveals unexpected departures, either upwards or downwards, from a uniform level of
achievement, avoids thereby the accusation of 'bad taste'; is this
to be preferred to the adventuring, the questing, the vitality of
music which refuses *no* path of exploration? Commenting on the
music of Hummel, Kreuzer, Spohr, excellent examples of the
'minor' composer just specified, P. H. Lang, in the article already
quoted has these words:

> There are no excesses in this music, no confusion, no controversy,
> no roughness of any kind, and no haphazard gestures—nothing but
> confidence in a well ordered tonal world, in the excellence of the
> métier.

When Schubert commences the finale of a PF. Sonata like this:

Ex. 46
Allegro moderato
L.H. *p*

should 'good taste' have nudged his elbow and suggested more
sober paths? Then we should have lost the deliciously tuneful and

May-time dance which originated with those bars, and which embodies the spirit of the Viennese countryside in sunshine and spring. Again one feels that the only satisfactory answer lies in the music itself.

Schumann is responsible for the phrase 'heavenly length' used of Schubert's instrumental movements. The length of a piece of music is not measured by the minutes it takes to play, or by the number of bars in its movements, but by a more intangible quantity—its power to interest the listener; and the issue is complicated by the fact that not all composers are equally interesting to music lovers. If and when Schubert fails to interest, his movement seems long—but duration of time has little to do with it. The fifty minutes of the Octet are unalloyed delight; the forty of the PF. Trio in E flat seem longer than their duration measured by the clock.

And with the mention of that work we may have reached, perhaps, the root cause of the Schubertian mis-judgements and aversions of the nineteenth century: the PF. Trio in E flat. It was a very famous work. It had formed the 'pièce de resistance' of the only public concert which Schubert ever gave, and to which his death, following so tragically soon afterwards, lent an added fame. It was his first composition to be published outside Austria. It was a favourite of Schumann's and he devoted an article to it in his journal 'Neue Zeitschrift der Musik', which was a long and glowing tribute. Years before Schubert's sonatas, quartets or symphonies were known in Germany, this trio was well known and well established. It contains music worthy of Schubert at his greatest, and such music exacted tribute, of course, from musicians everywhere; but it also contains, in greater measure than any other work of its period, the composer's faults. It is long-drawn; it is repetitive; it is diffuse; and its trivialities, the opening of the finale, for instance, seem all the more trivial against the sombre and passionate depths of the slow movement. Its length is exceptional in Schubert's chamber music; the Octet, not very much longer, contains, after all, two extra movements. In addition, where he almost always charms, in the Trio-section of the third movement, writing enchanting melody or devising imitation patterns, this time he fails, composing for the E flat Trio the most heavy footed and enigmatic bars in all the work of his later years. When early critics began to form judgements on Schubert's power as an instrumental composer, the E flat Trio loomed large in their view, and, we now see, too large.

II

It is pleasant to turn from this negative, defensive attitude, to a positive assessment of what Schubert the artist, as craftsman and pioneer, actually achieved, and to begin with what is perhaps his most endearing mass of work—the songs. For although his work in other fields has an equal claim to greatness, it was as a song-writer that he first became known, and as a song-writer that most people immediately think of him. His choice of poems, and the questions raised by that choice, have been discussed earlier. One of his glories is that he lifted inferior verse and sentiment to the heights of his genius, and gave to mild thoughts mildly expressed a universality and power that the poet never dreamed of. 'Winterreise' is the supreme example. Müller's poems relate the grief-crazed wanderings of a jilted lover, now crying out in anguish, now numbed with the thoughts of past happiness, tossed about by stormy weather, frozen by snow and icy winds. But the light of Schubert's genius shines steadily behind Müller's puppet-play until great shadows loom on the firmament; the unhappy lover assumes the tragic aspect of man himself, the wanderings become man's bewildered progress through life, tossed by winds of emotion, frozen by grief. 'Fremd bin ich eingezogen, fremd zieh' ich wieder aus . . .' sings the lover at the start: 'A stranger I came hither, a stranger I depart. . . .' The opening words of the little verse-tragedy, in Schubert's hands, take on the import of man's advent into this world, and his departure from it: the mystery unexplained. The song *Der Lindenbaum*, in which the lover broods on past happy hours with his sweetheart, is elevated by the wonderful music until it is the very essence of man's longing for the innocence of the golden past, of Dante's *Nella miseria*— 'There is no unhappiness so great as remembering happier hours'. But 'Winterreise' has many parallels. Any handful of Schubert's masterpieces, *Die junge Nonne, Sei mir gegrüsst, Aufenthalt, Im Frühling,* all these show the miracle at work; the limited, commonplace words, the universal appeal of the song.

It is by seeing the whole corpus of his songs, composed throughout his life, from first to last, that we find the growth of his power in this direction. At first he obsequiously provided the poem with musical illustration; as time went on his composing of songs more and more resembled a process comparable to translation. He created in music the poem's literary values, and at times his music reached the poet's thought and expressed it more trenchantly than the poet himself had done. This differing approach was most tellingly and aptly displayed by Theodor W. Werner in his article on Schubert as a 'self critic'.[1] He discussed Schubert's two settings of Goethe's *Am Flusse,* the first composed in February 1815, the second in December 1822. The poem represents Goethe's emotion 'recollected in tranquillity'. Schubert's earlier setting is passionate, tortured; he gives it the direction *Wehmütig* ('Sorrowful'). The second one is serene, strophic: its equable flow is marked *Moderato.* Schubert in his mature years, it is seen, entered more fully into Goethe's mind—in Werner's phrase, he progressed from the poem to the poet.

The 1822 setting was referred to as 'strophic'. Schubert's varied forms of song are broadly classed into three groups: first, the strophic song, in which each verse is sung to the same melody, with the same accompaniment; second, the *scena* type of song, in which there are several clearly distinct sections with different key-signatures, and *tempo* indications; third, the 'on-running', or *durchkomponiert* song, in which the varying moods and ideas of the poem invoke different musical treatments, but in which a basic unity is obtained by a uniform type of accompaniment. The first group, the 'strophic', comprises also the so-called 'modified strophic' song, where Schubert, to obtain variety, departs from his repeated musical strophes so that on their return they are renewed and fresh to the listener. The well known songs of the 'Schöne Müllerin' song-cycle will serve admirably as illustrations of the various groups:

[1] 'Schubert als Selbstkritik', 'Musica', Cassel, May 1948.

i. *The simple strophic song:*
  Mit dem grünen Lautenbande
ii. *The strophic song with refrain:*
  Trockne Blumen
iii. *The strophic song with recitative:*
  Am Feierabend
iv. *The 'modified' strophic song:*
  Pause
v. *The 'scena' song:*
  Der Neugierige
vi. *The 'on-running' song:*
  Eifersucht und Stolz

It was not, however, Schubert's way to proceed from the strophic song, as an elementary form, to the 'on-running' type as the final crown, so to say, of his work. He wrote strophic songs to the very end of his life—*Am Meer* or *Die Taubenpost,* which is an admirably modified strophic song, are contemporary with *Der Doppelgänger.* It has already been suggested, too, that the strophic *Am Flusse* is a grander achievement than the earlier 'on-running' setting. There has been recently an attempt to review the strophic song, and to question whether the intensive, illustrative type of 'Lied' which was imitated from Hugo Wolf's methods, but without his genius, does not tend to an aridity and songlessness. Brahms asserted that composing the declamatory song was child's play compared with the devising of a satisfactory strophic melody for all the stanzas of the poem. Schönberg has said that he came nearer to the heart of the poem from Schubert's strophic settings than he did from a reading of the poem alone: an extravagant view perhaps, but most singers and students of the Schubert songs will have found that a musical passage has a sharpness which clarifies the poet's text, especially where it deals with deep emotions and sentiments that touch Schubert's sensitive spirit.[1] On many occasions Schubert sets to music a poem in which a repeated emotional pattern is perfectly served by a strophic setting.

---

[1] 'Das Verhältnis zum Text', in the 'Blaue Reiter', 1912, edited by Marc and Kadinsky.

In the poem 'Frühlingstraum', Müller writes two stanzas, each
with a three-fold scheme; the first stanza may be summarised thus:

I dreamed of May and its blossoms/
The cockcrow violently woke me in the icy dawn/
Who painted the frost-flowers on the window pane?

and the second stanza runs:

I dreamed of loving a maiden/
The cockcrow violently woke me from my sore musings/
When the flowers on the pane blossom, shall I hold my love again?

The form of this poem, verse for verse, perfectly fits Schubert's
strophic melody.

Because Schubert frequently used a loose, flexible organisation
in his 'on-running' songs it would not be true to consider them
planless altogether, and that he set them, as it were, piecemeal as
he ran through the poem. His method of work was not the same
in every case when he composed a song, but there are in existence
many of his sketches for songs which he never completed, and it
is possible to say that in most cases that method was invariable:
his poem first engendered a *melody*. It was not necessarily a
melody such as we find in *Die Forelle* or *Who is Sylvia?* The
broken, passionate themes in *Gruppe aus dem Tartarus* or *Der
Doppelgänger* could equally be the starting point of the song. On
the first writing down the melody and its offshoots were shared
between the voice and the right hand part of the pianoforte accompaniment, for Schubert indicated in this way the short interludes that were to fall between the vocal phrases. Bass notes were
inserted in the left hand part where a touch of Schubertian re-
moteness in the harmony must not be forgotten. This method of
work can be fully studied in the sketch for the unfinished song of
1827 called *Fröhliches Scheiden*. His many sketches also make it
clear that modulatory harmony was part of his musical thinking
and not born of improvising and exploring at the keyboard. This
is particularly clear from the rapid sketch of Karoline Pichler's
Der Unglückliche, where melody and bass only are written down
by Schubert; yet, between them, they suggest all the tonal and

harmonic colour which we have in the completed song. Schubert's extant sketches for the first part of the 'Winterreise' (nos. 1 to 12) are important; from them it is clear that the full conception of the song is present in embryo in his first writing down. It is the masterly refinement and added detail which one cannot deduce from these problematic sketches. How will he continue this? one asks. 'But it is the very essence of genius that it can, and does, solve the problems for which the rest of the world can envisage no solution.'[1] This should be remembered when judgements are passed on fragmentary sketches, e.g. those for the third movement of the 'Unfinished' Symphony; we do not know what Schubert might have done with those enigmatic pages.

Yet, when his work is finished, the problems solved, there is a simplicity and inevitability about the music that may deceive the naïve listener or student into imagining that it was all superficial and 'natural'. The very simplicity of means in Schubert's great songs enables him to bring off effects and sudden strokes which the elaborate and sophisticated techniques of later composers, particularly of the French school, miss completely. The poignancy of a climax is driven home with a steely point in a phrase of perhaps two semitones: in Gretchen's song at the words 'And ah! his kiss!' or in the 'Winterreise', when the wanderer ejaculates 'Oh! were the whole world dark!'

Ex. 47
(i) 'Gretchen am Spinnrade'

(ii) 'Einsamkeit'

[1] Winton Dean, 'Tempo', London, 1951–1952.

Harmonically, too, atmosphere can be created by a slight un-usualness in the diatonic chords, quite impossible in the rich chro-maticism of later epochs. The chord of C minor, for example, instead of an expected 6/4 on the dominant, produces in *Im Abendrot* an effect of piety and nocturnal meditation out of all proportion to the means used (A):

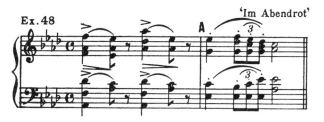

In view of the esteem and love which his songs aroused in his friends and acquaintances, and their ardent interest in his com-position of them, it is wonderful that his own integrity, and his faith in himself, should have kept his method of work inviolate. Perhaps Schober's more trivial taste prompted many of Schubert's lighter, lyrical songs, but we need not grieve over that. Spaun, however, commented on Vogl's influence over Schubert by deny-ing that it existed! Schubert's oldest friend was emphatic that no one had any influence over Schubert's compositional methods, and he was surely right. Some firm instinct, true and unerring, told Schubert that he was capable, as no man before him, of fixing in music the cry, the emotion of the human heart. He refused to be tempted away from his path.

III

His methods of work, which we have glanced at in his songs, but which are just as evident in his instrumental compositions, were not understood, and certainly not correctly presented by early biographers; as a result not very serious consideration has been given to Schubert as a craftsman. In those early biographies, Kreissle's, Grove's, Reissmann's, emphasis was laid on the more sensational aspect—his speed of working: a string quartet in a week, a symphony in less than a month, seven songs in one day, and so forth: and these are facts, of course, except that they give the extent of his fair copies of the particular compositions, and we do not know anything of preliminary work on them. But the reader is only too prone to assume that such *speed* of production must be attended by *carelessness* of production. In this connection Parry[1] can be quoted again:

> As a rule this speed of production was almost a necessary condition of Schubert's work in all branches of art. He had no taste for the patient balancing, considering, and re-writing again and again, which was characteristic of Beethoven.

More will be said later on about Schubert's re-writing again and again; here it is enough to say that, when discussing genius, no hard and fast rules can apply. We know today very much more about Schubert's procedures, and his work, than did the biographers of the nineteenth century. The new attitude began with Eusebius Mandyczewski in the 1890's, when every available song manuscript of the composer's was scrutinised and correlated and edited for the ten song-volumes of the 'Gesamtausgabe'. Mandyczewski was staggered to find how many manuscripts often went to the making of one song: two, three, even four versions were made by Schubert in his search for the ideal setting. We know of yet more of these manuscript preparations than Mandyczewski did, and it is a fairly sound surmise that Schubert sketched all his major works, and most of his minor ones, too, and did so throughout his life. Sometimes, in a burst of inspired writing, the sketch needed no radical revision, and so we have those hastily written songs like *Waldesnacht* of December 1820. But it is also obvious that other song manuscripts, for instance, *Der Leiermann* at the close of the 'Winterreise', are beautifully copied from a sketch no longer extant. For a number of Schubert's compositions we possess the finished work and the preparatory sketch, or sketches; those for the PF. Trio in E flat and the 'Unfinished' Symphony provide inexhaustible interest to a student. The sketches already mentioned for the Symphony in D, of 1818, enable us to generalise

---

[1] 'Studies of Great Composers', London, 1894, page 234.

a little on Schubert's methods with instrumental composition. As with his songs, he starts with a melody: ideas of accompaniment are sketched here and there, sometimes quite fully. Occasionally he will go back and insert the introductory bars. If he decides that, for the sake of balance or amplitude, a few bars must be inserted into music already written down, connecting signs are clearly marked over the insertion and its ultimate place in the sketch. These are 'aides-memoires' for his own benefit.

'His sketches' writes Gerald Abraham, 'are generally shorthand memoranda on a large scale, not germinal ideas to be watered with blood and tears like Beethoven's'; and while this is in the main true it must be pointed out that Beethoven's sketches do not, like Schubert's, tell the whole story: themes and transitions caused Beethoven to shed his blood and tears, but it is obvious that when these difficulties were overcome, he found large tracts of his movements rising as spontaneously and easily to his pen as ever Schubert did. Parry does not mention this fact.

When Schubert's melodic phrases begin to germinate, and ideas grow rapidly in his mind, his writing degenerates to a scribble—but never to illegibility. His mental excitement is obvious in the shaky handwriting. The difficulty which rises, when this kind of composition reaches its perfect expression in his finished work, is that of our intellectual apprehension. When he is intellectually on fire, so much arises in his mind and goes down on to paper at once, that it is impossible to apprehend the creative process: one gratefully accepts the result, but is left with a feeling that the process has elements almost of the supernatural in it. This explains why his friends attributed 'clairvoyance' to his methods, which is an explanation untenable today. In the last resort genius evades analysis, and one is thankful that it is so.

With later instrumental work Schubert's facility is astonishing and the pros and cons of what he intended to set down must have been debated and settled in his mind with hardly any delay. Even then afterthoughts refined and improved his initial ideas. In the manuscript of the Sonata in A minor of 1823 the episode immediately following the announcement of the main theme was revised and altered after its re-appearance in the recapitulation

had shown Schubert a better way with it. The alteration in the
melody of the slow movement has already been quoted. The
change he made in the subject of the *Allegro ma non troppo* of the C
major Symphony of 1828 is well known, but, for all that it is so
familiar it is an extraordinary modification; being made after the
whole movement was written it entailed literally hundreds of re-
visions of the score.

His alterations sometimes suggest a kind of subconscious cere-
bration, and certainly the progress of ideas from year to year
shows that in the non-conscious depths of his mind there was a
continual working at basic musical ideas—ideas, possibly, which
he felt were not fully exploited when he first used them. From
the string quartets the following two examples will show this process at work, although they show it at its most obvious. In the
first 'couplet', the 'cello, pitted against the upper strings, plays a
short phrase like a challenge.

The second pair of extracts form a close parallel; the poignant
theme in the first violin, played against *tremolo* strings, is shown
in its earliest, and in its latest manifestation:

From his symphonic work the following three short extracts show a favourite type of imitation, which in his mind takes on a more and more dramatic form until in the finale of the last symphony it reaches the culmination of power and excitement:

There are in his songs, also, many exemplifications of the unity of his work, the development, when his powers were mature, of embryo ideas which he could not fully use in his youth. The economy of *Der Doppelgänger* is only possible in the master whose youth flung out the extravagance of *Erlking*, and we are fortunate that Schubert encountered the Heine poem at the height of his genius, and the Goethe ballad in his inflammatory youth.

Mention of melodic ideas which re-appear in his work with deeper significance and a more defined emotion, brings the question of his melody, and its characteristics, into the discussion. Of inexhaustible variety and charm it is one of the primary factors of greatness in his music. Whether modern tendencies are really such as genuinely to set aside the basic importance of melody, or whether those tendencies are to set out in directions away from the 'vocal' melody as a basis for musical thought, it cannot be denied that only music which manifests an incomparable gift of melody survives, and that the one linking factor of all the great composers is their singular ability to charm with attractive and lovable melodies. The charm of Schubert's melody is, in the last resort, unanalysable, but certain features which are common to his melodies, in so far as they contribute to an appreciation of the artist at work, are worthy of mention. One striking feature generates a kind of tension, driving his melody onward it is this fondness for chromatic *appoggiaturas*. They have an almost anguished quality—the ear aches for the resolution, and is charmed and soothed when it comes:

The whole of this short waltz could be given as an example. There is a similar, quotable example in *Am Flusse* of 1822, where the A sharp sets up a melodic tension beautifully eased in the passing to A major on the words 'weave her hair'.

Further examples will be found in many of his dances, Op. 33: no. 10 and no. 15; Op. 18: no. 11; Op. 171: no. 3 and no. 5

P

(particularly in the last dance), and in numerous other songs of which *Letzte Hoffnung* provides excellent uses of the device.

The second subject of the Overture to 'Fierrabras' is perhaps the most rewarding example of this harmonic 'tension' which Schubert can set up in his melodies. The theme is quoted with the harmonic outline only:

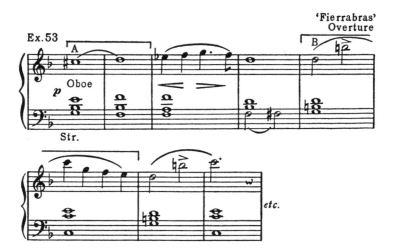

The diminished seventh at 'A', a typical 'off-key' start to a theme in B flat major, gives the melody an initial impetus, but the unexpected move of the bass from F natural to F sharp in bar 4 forces the melody to take on shapes of G major and C major. The 'tension' created at 'B' is almost painful in its urgency. But how admirable the workmanship here! The cadence in C major, using the diminished seventh of the opening passes easily and naturally back to the tonality of B flat for a repetition of the tune. How still more admirable the whole 'build' of the overture when it is realised that (1) Schubert's intention all along had been to write a melody in C major, that being the orthodox dominant key of an overture in F major: the whole of the B flat tonality is itself an 'off-key' start to the theme, and (2) the first section came to a close in the required key, C major, but it was at once set aside by the powerful intrusion of a 'German sixth' E flat/G/B flat/C sharp; this chord leads quite naturally into the progression at 'A' in the above example.

A more difficult feature to define, but one which cannot be missed when we hear his melodies, is the strongly characteristic 'finger-print' in his melodic use of the minor mode. It is compounded of a fondness for decorating the dominant of the key with semitones above and below it. Thus, in C minor, the dominant G is approached from F sharp or A flat, and as a kind of corollary, the tonic C is similarly adorned with B natural or D flat. The close of the song *An den Mond* (Hölty) not only reveals both features, it will also serve to show how completely Schubert made these semitonal features a part of his melodic style: could anything be more purely Schubertian than the melody now quoted?

Ex.54

'An den Mond' (Hölty)

It is seen that the phrase proceeds from G minor (with A flat and F sharp adorning the tonic note) to its close in D minor (the dominant A now associated with G sharp and B flat). The tendency is, naturally, closely related to his partiality for the chord known as the 'Neapolitan' sixth. This chord is based on the semitone above the key note: in C minor it is the chord of D flat major (usually in its so-called 'first inversion', i.e. with F natural as its lowest note). And we find that these chromatic notes stand out like indices of the minor scale for Schubert, for his use of them in his melodies soon pervades his instrumental textures. In the variations of the Octet, a poignant passage in variation V could be quoted as an example. The key is C minor; the theme is played by 'cello and double bass in unison; the descant-like duet for first violin and clarinet in the quotation show the D flat and B natural grace-notes for the tonic note, C, and the dominant is decorated in like fashion by A flat and G flat (= F sharp):

Ex.55   Octet: var. V

The pathetic tone of the *Andantino* in the Sonata for PF. and violin, known as the 'Duo', is exquisitely conveyed by this 'pointing' of the semitones: in key A flat major, the mediant and the dominant are flecked with chromatic colour in this way (bars 61 to 66). The possibilities of modulation with these chromatic notes seem, in Schubert's hands, inexhaustible.

The so-called 'Hungarian' influence in his melody, and the various folk-song influences which writers from time to time try to persuade us went to the formation of his melodies, can all be largely discounted. Vienna in his day was a cosmopolitan city open to many influences at high and at low levels. The Italian sources and the Italian nourishing of her artistic exploits in architecture, painting and music, the French influences then supplanting those of Italy, the German and English influences on the dramatic and poetic literature of the time, all these higher influences were obvious and acknowledged. The dance rhythms and folk-songs of the Slav and Magyar peoples, nearer than just at Vienna's doorstep, in the house itself, made themselves felt at low levels. But Schubert probably fought consciously against these extraneous tendencies and pulls. To him Mozart and Haydn and Beethoven were the models for his music and, in later life,

Bach. He refused to succumb to Salieri's persuasion over the setting of Italian texts in preference to German, and Rossini's influence quickly passed; it merely stimulated, as suggested already, elements which were part of his innate musical being. When the composer actually used Hungarian themes and idioms he was fully conscious of the presence of them and labelled his work 'Divertissement à l'hongroise'. Themes sometimes quoted by writers as displaying an unconscious Hungarian influence, for instance, the subjects of the finales to the String Quartets in A minor (1824) and G major (1826) and to the E flat Trio (the theme in C minor, marked *L'istesso tempo*), show a facet of Schubert's own style. It appears in his songs, and in his marches for PF. duet written at various periods, and is apparent in work showing no trace of Magyar influences. He was not, apparently, averse to using folk or national songs on occasion but none of these uses is documented with any degree of reliability. The pile drivers' song of Gmunden mentioned in the previous chapter is traditionally spoken of as used in his 'Notturno', Op. 148, but we do not know the name of the song, or anything certain about it. Even less reliable is the suggestion that he used a Swedish song in the slow movement of the E flat Trio. This was first stated by Leopold Sonnleithner, but he did not call it a *folk-song*. The theme, so obviously Schubert's own that it is hard to take Sonnleithner's suggestion seriously, is supposed to have been taken by Schubert from the song 'The sun is sinking' by the Swedish composer Isaak Berg. It has never been traced. To the wrongly named 'Magyar' group, belongs a type of theme which Schubert wrote in later life, a kind of sublimation of those quoted just previously, containing great charm and originality. Little trace of vocal melody remains, the themes are purely instrumental, and depend for their full effect on the inseparably associated harmonic changes which accompany them. Two examples of this wonderful type of instrumental melody are found in the 'Notturno', Op. 148 and in the 'Fantasia' for PF. and violin, Op. 159. The finest example is the attractive theme which opens the 'Fantasia' for PF. Duet which Schubert dedicated to Karoline Esterházy:

Together with this late characteristic might be mentioned an early one. That is the unusual tendency in the years between 1818 to 1822 to repeat short phrases within the melody. The famous tune which forms the second subject in the first movement of the 'Unfinished' Symphony contains an excellent example of this feature, but it is found in many related works of the period:

Sequences, used freely but not obviously by Schubert, have as a rule a harmonic basis. In other words the repeated phrase does not always proceed up or down scalewise, but moves from one harmonic progression to another according to the scheme in Schubert's mind. The song *Who is Sylvia?* illustrates the point well, and here is another, less familiar one, from Estrella's aria *Von Fels und Wald umschlossen* in Act II of 'Alfonso und Estrella':

And it is in the extraordinary effects which he achieved by taking his sequences, on this harmonic basis, to extravagant lengths that we find so much to admire and to marvel at. Numerous instances could be quoted but the piquancy of the scheme can be seen in these bars from *Morgengruss* in 'Die schöne Müllerin':

Even more startling juxtapositions occur in the song *Die Liebe hat gelogen* (bars 8–11), where the scheme is C minor—A flat major: C sharp minor—A major. In the song *Delphine*, of 1825, there is an extended sequence of this nature leading to astounding harmonic shifts (from the words 'Wozu auch Blumen reihen und wässern' to '. . . wie verscheinen die Kleider!'). In his instrumental work these sequences are often purely harmonic, that is, they are deficient in, if not devoid of, melodic interest; there are examples in the 'Trio' section of the Scherzo in the 'Death and the Maiden' String Quartet, and in the first movement of the G major String Quartet (bars 210–225). They lead to the association of strangely assorted chords. Quite apart from harmonic sequences, however, there is a development in his later years of this jarring juxtaposition of unrelated chords and tonalities which produce a cold, or stark, emotional effect:

IV

Schubert's harmony is fundamentally that of his own day. He is perhaps overfond of the modulations possible to the diminished seventh chord, although he can use this accommodating 'pivot' in entirely fresh and striking ways (the passage, for instance, in the song *Stimme der Liebe* on a poem by Stolberg, at the words *Tränen der Sehnsucht*, and the *Crucifixus* of the E flat Mass). The chord which displaced the diminished seventh in the affections of the later 'Romantic' composers, namely the augmented fifth, is found occasionally in Schubert also. As a 'passing' chord, the augmented fifth has always been used, of course; it was its use as an unresolved discord, notably by Wagner, that gave it its peculiar significance and colour. But although, strictly speaking, Schubert's use of it is as a 'passing' chord, he dwells upon it at such length, and gives it such emphasis, that he was obviously attracted by its—to his ear—acid quality. There are exceptional uses of it in *Gruppe aus dem Tartarus* and in the *Nachthymne*. In Op. 171, the fifth dance, in B minor, has already been instanced as containing examples of the 'tensions' set up by chromatic discordances between melody and harmony; the same dance also contains a holding of the augmented fifth chord which is suggestive:

Ex. 61   Op. 171: no. 5

An even more emphasised lingering is found in the unfinished Sonata in F minor of 1818 (first movement):

Ex. 62   Allegro   Sonata in F minor (1818)

And its repeated occurrences in the 'Sonnett III' of Petrarch (1818) give passing touches of weirdness to the music:

Ex. 63   Voice   Pf.   'Sonnett III'

These harmonic resources are enriched by various chords of the sixth, the so-called 'French' and 'German' sixths, and the 'Neapolitan' sixth, mentioned previously, for all of which Schubert showed a marked fondness, especially for the third of these chords. In his young days Schubert's love of these colourful chords was an obsession; the secondary songs of 1815 and 1816, especially the longer ballads, use the progressions based on these sixths almost *ad nauseam*. In later life his use was more sparing, and more telling:

But of the chord of the 'Neapolitan' sixth—which is a *common* chord on the semitone above the key-note, he never tired. His uses of this chord, as a melodic 'spicing', as a cadence, as a harmonic progression, as a basis for modulation, are so numerous that one must put it at the head of all that is implied by Schubertian device and characteristic. One instance can be given here, his loveliest use of it, perhaps the most exquisite bars he ever wrote. They come from the first movement of the C major Symphony, in the recapitulation of the second subject. This is, with typical unorthodoxy, in C minor, and the return to the orthodox key of A minor is managed by this use of the 'Neapolitan' chord:

The music then moves at once into G minor, and the above bars are treated sequentially, so that G minor proceeds to A minor.

The most familiar of his practices, the shift from minor to major, and *vice versa*, and the drop to a key a third below his tonic key, have been so fully discussed, annotated and quoted by scholars, that a mere mention of them here is all that is necessary; they are so much a part of his musical thinking, and consequently so much a part of his musical heritage, that numerous references have, in any case, been made to them already. But another, less familiar feature, may be noted in connection with these shifts, and that is his frequent practice of starting outside his main key, and then swinging into it with a charming effect that may have a variety of emotional reactions. There may be surprise, as in the finale of the 'posthumous' Sonata in B flat, since the key seems to be established as C minor; there may be a darkening, tragic effect, as when the placid D flat harmonies which open the song *Memnon* unexpectedly drop into B flat minor; there may be a freshness, a vivacity, as in the Waltz, Op. 9: no. 29; or there may be a feeling of satisfaction, of homecoming, as in the 3rd Ländler of Op. 171, which has already been quoted on page 129. *Memnon* was quoted from the songs: there are many more similar uses there. In *Auf dem Wasser zu singen* the key of A flat minor at the start is held right through the song for the pure joy of a flood of bright tone-colour when the key of A flat major is reached, and the watery scene of the poem is bathed in sunset radiance. Depths of meaning and significance are achieved if he delays the main key because the poet's words suggest a refined use of the procedure. Both Tovey and Capell dwell affectionately, in this connection, on the wonderful way in which the main key of C major is held back in the song *Dass sie hier gewesen*, so that the preliminary remarks of the poet are given ambiguous harmonies, and the diatonic C major is not used until at length the words 'I know that she has been here' are sung. The chords at the start of the song—they have been called 'ambiguous' only in the sense that they are non-committal in the key of the song—form one example of Schubert's fondness for the occasional, inexplicable chord: others can be found in the coda of the first movement of the 'Death and the Maiden' String Quartet, and in the slow movement of the Sonata in A minor, Op. 143. They give his music a momentary darkness, a crudity, from which it emerges into his more usual sunny and equable moods with a renewed charm.

One feature of his harmony has no convenient label, except the vague one of 'chromatic'; yet once seized upon, and understood, it can exercise by its surprising originality and skill, a fascination which is like a spell. It is his supreme ability to sense the possibility of chromatic progressions, which are not obvious or implied, in the course of the diatonic notes in his melody. So skilful and delicate are these harmonic processes that it is not easy to discuss them in words. A simple example must be given, more obvious than most, to make the point plain. The melody which is quoted in the next example is simple and familiar: it is the close of the song *Hark! hark! the lark!*:

Ex.66   *decresc.*   A   'Hark! Hark! the Lark!'

At 'A', Schubert's harmonies produce a modulation to D minor. Granted that many composers would avoid the tonic chord of C major at this point, it is doubtful whether anyone but Schubert would have avoided it in such an unusual way, but a way which, once discovered, seems inevitable. A song which will yield rich rewards in this field is the lightly regarded *Ungeduld* from the 'Schöne Müllerin' cycle, and an even more astonishing feat of unusual harmonic progression is brought off in the almost unknown *Totenkranz für ein Kind*. It would be a fascinating experiment to give this melody to a score of composers and see whether any one of them would hit upon Schubert's incredible cadences, drawn from the note progressions.

V

Schubert's piano techniques were briefly discussed in the previous chapter. They are not unassailable, and if it were possible to consider them apart from the material they embody, we might agree that he shows in them a 'half-mastery' of the keyboard, as it has been called. But in his orchestral and chamber-music techniques, he is a master among masters. The opportunities of his schooldays in the *Stadtkonvikt*, when intimate acquaintance with orchestras and chamber ensembles was an everyday experience for him, have been discussed. It is clear, right from the start, that such techniques were acquired easily and thoroughly from first-hand sources. Naturally, as his music gained individuality and depth with the passing years those techniques served a richer personality, but the first symphony and the first quartet are perfectly written for their respective mediums. These two mediums, the orchestral and the quartet, are chosen because by general agreement they represent the peak of a composer's technical achievement, and, in Schubert's case, his quartet techniques appear also in other chamber-music combinations. An individual feature of his orchestral writing is his partiality for violent contrasts, either of dynamics, or of instrumentation. This feature was one which he derived from Mozart. One of the most moving examples is the bar or two of quiet oboe melody which interrupt the progress of a *fortissimo* orchestral passage in the *Andante* of the 'Unfinished' Symphony, but equally effective contrasts between such solo and *tutti* passages add thrilling moments to the 'Alfonso und Estrella' Overture. His 'conversational' solos between the woodwind instruments are renowned, but they are a feature of his more mature works, first appearing markedly in the sketched Symphony in E, of 1821. The use, though, of three trombones, which did not appear in the Beethoven orchestra until the fifth Symphony, in C minor (1805), was Schubert's habit in the earliest orchestral works. It is in the advanced treatment of these instruments that his chief contribution to orchestral technique lies. They are not merely brought in to re-inforce climaxes, but are used with much expressiveness, often *pianissimo*, and the third trombone is frequently used as a bass for flutes and clarinets. Their solo entries in the first movement of the great C major Symphony are of the essence of epic poetry. He is fond of scoring his melodies for violins and bassoons in octaves, which gives a certain 'difference' to the *timbre* of his music, and the combination of horns and bassoons for dark, 'middle register' chords was a happy and original stroke; this tone colour opens the slow movement of the 'Unfinished' Symphony and, with the *pizzicato* bass strings, announces a different symphonic world from those of Mozart and Beethoven. Various individual points of orchestration are famous in his two mature symphonies. The 'call' phrases of the horn, in both the symphonic slow movements, in the episode leading to the recapitulation, are of the highest poetry and Schumann wrote a well-known and enthusiastic page on the second of them, likening the horn to a visitant from another world as it softly sounds among the even softer strings. There is an equally beautiful 'call' phrase given to the horn in the 'Kyrie' of the E flat Mass, at the same formal point.

Several references to his string quartet writing have been made in earler chapters. As a contrast to the bold use of the 'cello in his later string quartets, we could instance his conventional and timid treatment of the viola. The emergence of the viola as the solo instrument of the string quartet is a feature of late nineteenth-century techniques: to Schubert (who himself played the viola), it was, in general, a filling-in instrument. One feature of his quartet writing, which persisted right to the very last, was his addiction to the use of *tremolo* bowing. This is usually not considered very good form in quartet technique, suggesting orchestral colour and procedure. But it depends on the quality of the music so scored: Schubert's parts are lively and complex; they are as frequently *pianissimo* as otherwise; the melodies so accompanied are elaborately phrased and divided between the instruments. It is a legitimate device if used, as he used it, powerfully, and no one would deny its attractive quality both to players and listeners. In the String Quintet of 1828, there is an interesting development of his quartet techniques. The device of the 'duet' for two stringed instruments is also a prominent characteristic of the Quintet. It is played by the two violins, or the two 'cellos, accompanied by the other three instruments. Alternatively, in the *Adagio*, the three 'middle' instruments play the theme and the 'outer' instruments first violin and second 'cello, embroider and decorate. His Quintet, in other words, resolves itself into a violin duet, or a 'cello duet, or a trio with violin and 'cello *obbligato*. In all three cases the viola is, if not negligible, subordinate. It is now of interest to contrast this technique with that of Mozart, who, in his String

Quintets uses an antiphony of two string trios; his two violins and first viola are contrasted with the two violas and 'cello. Mozart's first viola is now the bass of the first 'Trio', now the treble of the second 'Trio'.

Perhaps the most notable feature of Schubert's technical handling of the pianoforte in chamber ensembles is his treatment of it as a purely melodic instrument. This was mentioned in connection with the *Trout* Quintet, but further examples are to be found in profusion in the two PF. Trios, in B flat and E flat.

The criticism of his pianoforte style applies chiefly to his sonatas. A more lyrical pianism is used in the Impromptus, Moments Musicaux, and in the shorter, isolated pieces which he may have intended to publish as similar essays, such as the 'Drei Klavierstücke' of 1828. In these short pieces Schubert is famous as an innovator; he is looked upon as the forerunner of the 'Romantic' school, in which composers like Schumann and Chopin were able, through his example, to throw off the shackles of 'Sonata-form'. It is, of course, a greatly simplified view, and takes no account of the fact that minor composers such as John Field, Václav Tomašek and Johann Worzischek, had already established the short, piano piece in the early years of the century. Tomašek in particular is a forerunner of Schubert in this sphere, and his influence on the composer is much more certain than Schubert's, say, on Chopin. The very frequent use by Schubert of broken chords whose top notes coincide with the notes of his melody is a pure Tomašekian procedure, and even the lesser man's melodies contributed something to Schubert's. Here is the theme of Tomašek's 'Eclogue', Op. 51: no. 6, written in 1815:

Ex. 67

Tomašek

We have only to think of the prelude to Schubert's song *Pause*, or the 'Trio' section of the Scherzo in the D minor String Quartet, to feel that the lesser composer's work had no inconsiderable effect on Schubert's development. But although, apart from his songs and lyrical pieces for the pianoforte, Schubert was not, from the point of view of 'Form', a pioneer, as far as harmonic and tonal range, and emotional content, are concerned, he is one of music's foremost innovators. The 'Romantic' movement in the arts sprang from the literary 'Storm and Stress' movement of the eighteenth century; it was held in check by the little reactionary movements which followed that tumult, and during which Schubert lived. But he is an initiator in emotional content, and in the 'atmosphere' which he evoked by his chromatic warmth and richness. When he wrote the theme of the 'Quartettsatz' in 1820, he produced a typical 'Romantic' theme whose echoes resound throughout the nineteenth century.

The shifting, melting chromaticism of his melody and harmony were to lead to the slow movement of Schumann's PF. Trio in D minor, Op. 63, and that, in turn, to the Prelude to 'Tristan und Isolde'.

It is not the formal changes in the 'Romantic' period which are so remarkable, but the re-orientation of musical thought, the different aims of composers in using their *materia musica*, and this is the sense in which Schubert is a pioneer. In matters of form, however much he may have distorted structures, he remains the last of the classical composers. He could not, living in the Vienna that had been the scene of Mozart's and Haydn's productions, which was even then witnessing the work of Beethoven, ignore his immediate past and escape from the pressure of his present. In matters of content, he may be perhaps the first of the 'Romantic' composers. But while his music cannot be looked upon simply as an Indian summer of the great Viennese classical period, nor can it be thought of simply as the precursor of the 'Romantic' school; both elements are present, the former the more strongly. There is in his work, as Alfred Einstein wrote, 'a lost paradise of purity, spontaneity and innocence.' And this suggests the 'Classical' master rather than the 'Romantic'. Whatever the 'Romantic' school was, it was not 'innocent'.

A word must be spared for one department of his music which, although not entirely neglected in performance, is strangely left out of account in consideration of his work as a whole, that is, the dance music. This vast mass of work, chiefly for the pianoforte, and extending from his very earliest years almost to the end of his life, is even yet not properly catalogued and identified. O. E. Deutsch, in his 'Thematic Catalogue', makes a brave effort, but leaving, as he does, the numerous dances in their haphazard assemblies as Opus-numbers, merely ignores the problem. Nor has the influence of these dances on his other work been adequately traced. For to Schubert, his short dance-pieces were the equivalent of the 'journals', the 'diaries', the 'note-books' of his fellow authors in the literary and artistic worlds. In them he jotted down ideas, he tried out pianoforte techniques, he sketched instrumental movements; and in them he embodied the moods and

Q

emotions of his passing days when larger work did not suit him. Much of his dance music was, we have it recorded by his friends, the fruit of hours of improvisation at the piano, while those friends danced. With a relaxed, but active mind, and busy fingers, and with the stimulus of an *ostinato* dance rhythm, the music welled up, and was embodied in the piano dances. It is fascinating to read through these 'journals', and to try to decipher them. One example of a sketched instrumental movement may be quoted. Here is the sixth dance of Op. 171, written in 1823; the continuation further on, in bar 7, is even more suggestive of the Scherzo in the D minor Quartet which it shortly became:

Ex.69

The quality of the music in these few bars indicates how far Schubert was prepared to take the simple music of the Ländler, in key, in style, and in thematic importance.

VI

The contrast between the pianistic style of writing shown in Schubert's sonatas and that in the Impromptus and dances is fundamental. To him the PF. sonata was, like the symphony and string quartet, an exalted form calling for more elevated and authoritative thought. The shorter pieces are more homely and intimate. It is true that one Impromptu, Op. 90: no. 1, opens in a manner suggesting a sonata, but the impression passes as the piece gets under way. No amount of taking thought would, of course, enable a minor composer to achieve the 'grand style', by which phrase Matthew Arnold designated the style of Shakespeare and Dante and Goethe. But Schubert shares with the other great composers of his race the supreme power of this 'grand style' of utterance by natural endowment. It is the non-Viennese quality in his physical and mental inheritance. He can, like Beethoven and Mozart, lay it aside temporarily, but it, and not the homelier, Viennese ways of speech, is his natural voice, and the more modest pieces and songs may at any moment swing up and out into music composed in this universal and timeless style of his. When Schubert wrote in his more unassuming vein, it was chiefly because he was being sociable, that is, he was accommodating his music to largely unmusical people, to those who danced, or worshipped, or wept and languished to his songs. For them he adopted the immediate idiom of his day, or even of his yesterday. He produced work without the true Schubertian fire, though unmistakably his. For with him art was never self-conscious. His technique was at his finger-tips, acquired and then forgotten. Dr. Walter Ford writing on these matters in connection with Schubert, states that 'self-consciousness fosters exaggerated sensibility and a limited outlook . . . idiosyncrasies of style [lapse] in the end into mannerisms and weaknesses'.[1]

Schubert's utter self-devotion to his genius made him abandon all regular methods of earning a living; it was not to spend his days in Bohemian idleness or conviviality, but to devote himself solely to the hard work of learning his craft as a composer. His decision makes the charge of 'dilettante', sometimes levelled at him, a preposterous accusation. This is how such an accusation was worded in the 'Edinburgh Review' of October 1883:

> His attitude towards the art was throughout his life that of a very gifted amateur, who wants art just as far as he can get enjoyment out of it, and turns away at the point where hard work begins. . . .

It is hard to refute this with patience. Josef Hüttenbrenner was probably telling the truth when he reported that the easy way of earning money by giving lessons was refused by Schubert who said that he would rather eat dry bread than do so, for lessons would interrupt the tireless application to his musical work, and deflect his energies. He never swerved from his high ideals; even though he was not entirely aware of the greatness and force of his own genius, he never, in order to earn a living, descended to the

[1] 'Music & Letters', London, October 1928.

easy production of inferior, catch-penny work, nor to the undertaking of regular hack-work, for that would have prevented the total dedication to his art. Anything less like the amateur, the dilettante, or the idling Bohemian of the arts can hardly be imagined. He was, and made himself so by hard work, the professional composer *par excellence*.

It might perhaps be a fitting conclusion to this chapter on Schubert's art, to consider in a brief paragraph what not to look for in Schubert. The very elements which many music lovers find most congenial are either absent altogether in his music, or only briefly encountered: wit, understatement, sophistication, picturesqueness, delicacy, bravura. These attractive qualities must be sought elsewhere, in the songs and piano pieces and orchestral suites of other men. Schubert's song-texts are neither erotic nor cynical. His expression is full-blooded, personal, extravagant, and the nearest he gets to humour, as Richard Capell has said, is good-humour; but it is not an urbane expression, nor an introverted one, and it is the power already spoken of, by which his music achieves sublimity, and radiates a 'light that never was on sea or land', that raises him above the level of the lesser composers, who are otherwise almost his equals in melodic charm and the affectionate spirit.

VII

1826-1827

I

A restless searching for a means of livelihood: that is the impression one gets from the records of these two years in Schubert's life; a means of livelihood which would leave him with leisure enough for his composing, and one which would not make such excessive demands on his powers as teaching had done. His words to Josef Hüttenbrenner, already quoted, were: 'I would rather eat dry bread than teach.' And we cannot wonder at this decision when we read Hüttenbrenner's further information that in his father's school, Schubert taught for nine hours a day. But neither would he now accept the kind of teaching post that had he done in 1824, as a music master to the Esterházy household. Instead he applied for positions as music director (Kapellmeister), sought a favourable play for an opera libretto, and wrote to publishing firms in Germany, offering them various compositions. In Vienna itself his work was being published at a rate which could not last: in 1826, twenty works were engraved and published, in 1827, twenty-two. Not that he was unable to keep up this rate of supply; he could easily have done so, but the public was surfeited, and the publishers grew cautious. Writing in those days from Vienna to a Leipzig music periodical, a journalist said of Schubert and his songs:

> He works almost too much at this species, and earlier excellent things are scarcely to be surpassed by the good ones which follow.

And yet the efforts to find a post, to establish himself in opera, or to make a name in Germany, misfired, and not altogether by an unlucky combination of circumstances; partly it was by reason of complex elements in his own character. The initial impulse was dissipated, and the slightest discouragement acted like a snub. Not for him the fighting persistence of Beethoven or Wagner, the dogged perseverance of Brahms. A factor which emerges from the reminiscences and memoirs of his friends and acquaintances, recorded years after his death, is that he was reluctant to invite them to his paternal home, and avoided, if possible, their calling on him there. His origins were of the humblest; there was in Vienna no social standing in the calling of a schoolmaster, and Franz Schubert senior was, in addition, desperately poor. The son, finding that his music opened doors into social circles far above him, did what many other artists have done before him, and since: without allowing it to change his affection for, or loyalty towards, the members of his family, he concealed those humble origins. But such concealment, and the sensitive pride which engenders it, are bound to take their toll of self-confidence. His shyness, remarked upon by strangers who met him, may well have been an involuntary defence against any advances which might penetrate his reserve in these matters. His modesty was, perhaps, the outcome of a conflict between two opposing emotions: unwilling shame over his lowly birth and upbringing and supremely confident belief in his own ability, and in the greatness of his own musical endowment. So the drive forward was made with initial confidence, and after a while the impetus was lost. Schubert, the musical giant, was time and again unable to put aside the insignificance attaching to the youngest son of a humble and penurious schoolmaster.

Actually, in the February of 1826, that humble schoolmaster received an overdue recognition of his tireless and unremitting work in Vienna's schools. As the conclusion of his forty-five years of teaching drew near, neighbours and fellow citizens in the Rossau district petitioned the Court that he be awarded the freedom of the City of Vienna. On 23 February 1826, Franz Theodor took the burgess's oath. But no word on the event from his son is extant.

Schubert's compositions of December 1825 and January 1826 were some half a dozen settings of poems by Ernst Schulze. They were written in his lodgings near the Karlskirche. Like the Säulengasse house, this dwelling place of Schubert's is still standing in Vienna, decayed but picturesque, and having an authentic suggestion of old Vienna in its ungroomed, unaltered antiquity. In addition to composing the Schulze songs there, he was that winter revising—it is not known how thoroughly—the D minor String Quartet. He had written of it, in 1824, as finished, and it is doubtful whether the revision was very extensive. The date 'January 1826' still attaches itself to the work because of this possible retouching. Schubert had only to lift his eyes from the pages of his manuscript to glimpse through his window the symbolical sculpture at the approaches to the Karlskirche. The 'Death' symbol of his quartet is precisely of the same kind as the huge skull which he could see amongst that sculpture. The trappings of Death were part of baroque decoration; to Schubert, in literature, they were the same. Neither in January 1826, nor at any other time, was he morbidly attracted to 'Death' poetry, nor 'Death' imagery.

The quartet was rehearsed on 29 and 30 January by a group of friends, the first violin being Josef Hauer, who later on related that at this rehearsal Schubert corrected the freshly written parts, and also cut out sections of the work. These were, of course, temporary cuts for the forthcoming performance; the score, the source of the work, was not in any way abridged. The work was first performed at the house of the lawyer Josef Barth, a friend of Spaun and of Schubert. He was an amateur musician and singer. For him, it will be recalled, Schubert played a simplified version of the accompaniment to the *Erlking*, and he also dedicated to Barth the part-songs of Op. 11. A second performance followed later on, in February, at the residence of Franz Lachner. The work remained in manuscript until Czerny of Vienna published it, posthumously, in July 1831.

The young comedienne and singer, Sophie Müller, entertained Schubert and Vogl several times during the course of the year at her villa in Hietzing; it is easily reached from the Karlskirche district and lies to the north of Schönbrunn.[1] Schubert took his songs to these social evenings and Sophie or Vogl sang them. Songs such as *Die junge Nonne* (which Sophie is said to have sung

[1] It is today the Hietzing suburb of the city.

at sight), *Die Rose*, Annot Lyle's and Ellen's songs from the Scott romances, were well suited to her voice and Anselm Hütten-brenner wrote that she sang them 'most touchingly'. She died, tragically young, a year or so after Schubert's death.

In April Schubert applied for the post of assistant music director (*Vice-Hofkapellmeister*) to the Court Chapel. The vacancy was caused by the promotion of Josef Eybler to the principal Director-ship, a position never filled by the Emperor since Salieri had left it in 1824. The fact of Schubert's application has always been known, but the actual document, in his hand, was not discovered until 1895. It was then found among papers in the possession of descendants of Maria Theresa, Schubert's younger sister, and pub-lished for the first time. It is couched in the usual obsequious terms which are used to ruling princes and their Court officials. The only points of interest in the list of facts provided by Schu-bert as evidences of his suitability for the post are (1) he claims that by his vocal and instrumental compositions his name has become known in the whole of Germany as well as in Vienna and (2) he states that he has to hand five Masses, all of which have already been performed in various Vienna churches. Usually he is so indifferent to the past works of his youth that to have these Masses correctly remembered and numbered is unique. That all had been performed is very likely; but there are no records in the case of the second and third (G major and B flat major). That his name was so widely known is an understandable exaggeration of the facts, but it does suggest that Schubert may have received, and read, the reports and reviews on his work which were being printed in various German periodicals. His application is dated 7 April 1826. Since the post had been vacant for two years without any serious dislocation of the music performances in the Court Chapel it is no surprise to find that the business of filling the post was taken at a pace even more leisurely than usual. On 19 Decem-ber the final list of applicants was prepared for the Court Chamber-lain, Prince Ferdinand Trauttmansdorff, the same man, inciden-tally, who had sanctioned Schubert's boyhood appointment to the choir of the Court Chapel. There were seven applicants besides Schubert and, with one obscure exception, all the names are familiar to readers of musical biography. But the eight men were passed over, and the candidate named for approval by the Court was Josef Weigl, the principal conductor of the Court theatres. A month later the appointment of Weigl was confirmed, and Schubert informed of his failure on 27 January 1827. Both Spaun and Bauernfeld mentioned the appointment in their memoirs, but in both records there is possibly more of their individual reaction to the affair, than an accurate memory of Schubert's own.

The coming of Franz and Fritz von Hartmann with their friend Ferdinand Walcher into the Schubert circle coincided with Spaun's re-appearance in Vienna. He returned on 20 April and was continually with Schubert. The composer had regained an old friend, but he lost a new one for Bauernfeld had left Vienna on 15 April for several months in Carinthia. Bauernfeld was not without a certain shrewd power of assessing a man's worth—his comments on Schober, Schwind and Schubert, written at various times in his journal, are apt and revealing; but he was volatile, satirical and facetious. He became famous in middle life as a writer of comedies, and even produced a mild, nineteenth-century equivalent of 'Animal Farm', in which the politics of his day were satirised in the form of a fable. As a youth, in Schubert's company, he was rather the self-appointed 'life-and-soul-of-the-party' and no friend, in the sense that Spaun was. Sometimes his suggestions and decisions showed a complete lack of wisdom, so that Schubert withdrew: there was the suggestion, for example, that he, Schwind and Schubert should live together and pool expenses. This they never did, and it was Schubert who discouraged the idea.

Bauernfeld's Carinthian tour was a prelude to his undertaking a position in a government department concerned with affairs in Lower Austria, so that it was partly business, partly pleasure. He had promised Schubert to write an opera libretto, and the composer's ardent interest in the progress of the work shows his eager grasping of this renewed opportunity to establish himself. But Bauernfeld's lack of wisdom is evident in the story he decided upon —'Der Graf von Gleichen'. The plot hinges on a bigamous marriage and would never have been passed by the censor of the day. Yet, half-knowing this, he persisted in his writing. Apart from

its subject, it will be seen from the poet's journal what a dreary repetition of stock material he would present to the unlucky composer:

> ... I thought of the libretto for Schubert and set to work on 'Der
> Graf von Gleichen'. Dramatic and musical contrasts; orient and oc-
> cident, janissaries and knighthood, romantic wooing and wedded
> love etc.—in short, a Turkish-Christian outline. The verses flow
> pretty easily for me.

After Schubert had sent in his application for the Court *Kapellmeister* position, it is possible that he may have tried to obtain a
post as assistant conductor in the Kärntnertor theatre. The story
was first related by Anton Schindler in 1857. According to this
account Schubert composed a portion of an opera-libretto, and
the music was then put into rehearsal. The ageing soprano,
Nanette Schechner, broke down owing to the difficulty of his
music and to the fact that her powers were failing. Schubert became obstinately angry, refused to alter anything, and left the
theatre in a fury of disgust. Most of this is pure invention. In May
1826 Nanette Schechner was twenty years old and had just made
her first appearance in Vienna. A letter of Schubert's was written
that very month: it gives in an extraordinary fashion the *coup de
grâce* to Schindler's inventions; he wrote to Bauernfeld in Villach
that 'Mlle. Schechner has appeared here in "Die Schweizer
Familie" and pleased enormously. As she looks very like Milder,
she might be good enough for us'. Schober also wrote a month
later to Bauernfeld and said: 'In matters theatrical I inform you
only that Mlle. Schechner revolutionises the town by her wonderful singing in *German*. Since Milder it is said that no such voice
has set the air vibrating, and she is still youthful, pretty and viva-
cious into the bargain. Schubert has heard her and chimes into the
hymn of praise.' And it is this voice that we are asked to believe
was unable, through age and incapacity, to perform some vocal
music by Schubert. It is hardly necessary to add that Schindler
was unaware of the existence of these two letters. We might also
ask: if Schubert were applying for the post of an assistant *conductor*, why was he required to *compose* music? The obvious
course would have been to ask him to conduct Mlle. Schechner
in an aria of her own choice—say from *Die Schweizer Familie.*

And this suggests what is probably the truth of the matter, if there is anything in it at all. It was Schubert's conducting, not his composing, which failed to please the authorities, and it is quite possible that a singer could not accommodate her voice to arbitrary tempo or dynamics. The touch of obstinacy in Schindler's anecdote has an authentic ring, and if Schubert refused to slow down or to quieten his accompaniment, then the *prima donna* might very well break down.

II

Schubert tried no more for positions of the kind. An operatic success, publication of work, gifts from patrons, and perhaps a concert of his own music, these were now his aims. The last idea loomed larger in his mind as the time passed, and both Schwind and Bauernfeld urged the matter of a concert devoted solely to his compositions. As for publication, the stream rose steadily; in the first four months of 1826 five publishers were issuing his compositions. Pennauer brought out the Sonata in A minor, Op. 42; Matthias Artaria the Sonata in D major, Op. 53, and the seven Walter Scott settings as Op. 52; Cappi the 'Marche funèbre on the death of Alexander I' for PF. Duet, Op. 55; Thaddeus Weigl (brother of Josef, the yet to be successful candidate for the Court *Kapellmeister* position) the songs of Opp. 57 and 58; and Sauer & Leidesdorf the Overture to 'Alfonso und Estrella', arranged by Schubert for PF. Duet, Op. 69. This overture was overlooked and not re-published when the 'Gesamtausgabe' of Schubert's works was organised by Breitkopf & Härtel; it remains inaccessible. It was dedicated to Anna Hönig, sister of Karl Hönig, Schubert's lawyer friend. Schwind was her constant wooer, but her intensely religious views were leading to a slight friction between them. The reader of the Schubert 'Documents' will find a misleading description of the overture on page 510, where it is said to draw on themes from the opera. It suggests that here is a second overture, different from the earlier, well-known work. This is not the case. The duet is merely an arrangement of the familiar overture in D minor/major, in which none of the material is taken from the opera itself.

At the close of June, Schubert, whose pen had been idle for
months, composed his last string quartet, in G major. It is a
supreme work, flawed only in its over-facile finale; but the three
preceding movements are of an unsurpassed greatness. Without
the humanity of its predecessors, in A minor and D minor, and
hence without their popular appeal, it has a grandeur and breadth
of conception which their more modest dimensions could not
compass. It was performed privately in Vienna, possibly by a
quartet led by Josef Slavík, but the only recorded public performance was in Schubert's concert of March 1828, provided that
the item in the programme called a 'New' String Quartet, meant
the one in G major. As with the Octet, and the String Quintet in
C, the score of the quartet lay undisturbed on Diabelli's shelves
for over twenty years, until, following a performance in Vienna,
it was published by Diabelli's successor, C. A. Spina, in 1851.
The manuscript is still extant, and in the possession of the Vienna
Nationalbibliothek. The quartet occupied Schubert ten days (20 to 30
June), days of absorbed and concentrated work. While he was so engaged, on 26 June, Vogl married. We learn the fact, not from Schubert or his friends, but from Sophie Müller, who wrote in her diary:

26 June 1826. Vogl, the singer, marries Rosa.

Vogl had returned from Italy, presumably restored in health,
and after his marriage took his bride Kunigunde, the daughter
of a painter Josef Rosa, to Steyr.

The Schubertiads of that year grew more frequent, and more
numerously attended. They were held at the houses of Schubert's
friends, Spaun, Witteczek and Enderes. Anton von Spaun, the
younger brother, was passing through Vienna during June and
wrote to his wife: 'A Schubertiad at Enderes, to which more than
20 people have been invited.' The new songs that were sung were
to more poems of Schulze, and included the fascinating *Ueber
Wildemann*, and the perfectly expressed music of *Im Frühling*, one
of Schubert's masterpieces of song, in which the poet's mood of
tender, but not harrowing, regret for the spring, and the love of
youth, is ideally matched. Some four-handed marches for the
pianoforte were also performed, but which ones they were is not
known: O. E. Deutsch's surmise, that they were the two 'Charac-

teristic Marches' of Op. 121 seems not to be likely. They were more probably the recently published 'Funeral' and 'Coronation' marches of Op. 55 and Op. 66. Schober mentioned these duet marches—but not naming them—in his letter to Bauernfeld of June 1826, written from a house in the village of Währing, where he and his mother were staying. It is to the north-west of Vienna, actually not very far from Schubert's birthplace. Schober had written in this letter the words already quoted about Mlle. Schechner. He then continued:

> If only Schubert would write an opera for her; perhaps yours would be suitable. If only he were not such a naïve barbarian. When I asked him recently why he had not come to see me during the whole of my illness, he answered innocently: 'But you are never to be found at home'. . . . Today Schubert is to come out here; I hope he will keep his word.

Schubert, with Schwind, visited the Schober house at Währing during the summer, and may even have slept there a night or two. But there was no prolonged stay as is evident from the fact that Schubert wrote letters from Vienna during June and July; he was, moreover, bored at Währing, according to Bauernfeld. But three or four songs were composed there in July, and two of them are as famous, in England, as anything he wrote: the settings of Shakespeare's *Hark! hark! the lark!* (from Act II of 'Cymbeline') and *Who is Silvia?* (from Act IV of 'The Two Gentlemen of Verona'). There is a third, more obscure, setting of a Shakespearian text from the same period, the drinking-song *Come! thou Monarch of the Vine* from Act II of 'Antony and Cleopatra'. It is of interest to watch the evolution of legend where the first, most popular, song is concerned. It became known amongst the friends that Schober's garden abutted on that of an inn 'Zum Biersack', where the noise of games and music frequently disturbed the Schobers and their guests. Hence the song was written, they presumed, with a background of noises from an inn garden. It was an easy step, as time passed, to place the writing of it actually *in* the inn garden, instead of beside it. Now Schubert's autograph of the three Shakespeare songs is in a small, rather 'home-made' booklet of plain paper, with music staves ruled in pencil. Enough! The story takes shape: Schubert's inspiration was so sudden that lines were hurriedly pencilled on a piece of paper to accommodate his muse, and what piece of paper more likely, in an inn garden (especially a Viennese inn, where every waiter is plentifully supplied with little plain-backed chits), than a bill of fare? The legend, in its final form, was told to Kreissle in all solemnity by Schubert's friend Josef Doppler, and faithfully reproduced in most subsequent biographies.

Schober, in those days, was managing a small lithography business in Vienna, and wrote to Bauernfeld that it was prospering pretty well. Bauernfeld was kept very well informed from Vienna during his Carinthian tour, and as a result we also are kept supplied with news in that plentifully-documented year. Schubert wrote again to him on 10 July warning him that a projected holiday with Spaun to Linz or Gmunden was impossible since he had no money. In view of his numerous publications in 1826 this does not suggest over-generous payment by the publishers. He informed Bauernfeld of Vogl's marriage, of Schwind's difficulties with the rigidly devout Anna Hönig, and of Schober's prospering business. There was also a renewed plea for the 'Graf von Gleichen' libretto, by which he hoped to make money, if not reputation. At the end of the month Bauernfeld returned to Vienna and handed over the book of the opera to Schubert. The composer never completed work on the music, but his sketches for it are very bulky, consisting of thirty-six large, and fifty-two small pages. In October 1826 the censor refused to license the play, but by then the composition of it had begun, and Schubert, rather pointlessly it seems, continued to work occasionally on it.

The publication of the Sonata in A minor as Op. 42 had brought some recognition of his powers as a composer for the pianoforte. In particular it had aroused the interest of Hans Nägeli, the Swiss composer, theorist and music publisher. On 18 June, in fact, Nägeli had written to his agent in Vienna, Karl Czerny, suggesting that Schubert might contribute to a series of pianoforte compositions to be published under the general title 'Musikalische Ehrenpforte' ('Musical Portal of Honour'). Czerny did so, and Schubert himself wrote on 4 July to Nägeli, expressing his willingness to comply with the commission, and offering a sonata for £12 in advance. Whether this modest demand was too much for the Zürich publisher, or for some other reason, the project hung fire. But doubtless we owe to it the composition soon afterwards of the Sonata in G major.

In August Schubert was ill and penniless. With a desperate effort to do something to improve his position he wrote to two Leipzig publishing firms on 12 August, to H. A. Probst and to Breitkopf & Härtel; the letters are very similar and Schubert expressed in both the wish to further his name in Germany. He offered the two firms songs, piano sonatas, string quartets and PF. Duets. He also singled out for mention the Octet, which shows that Troyer's commisssion did not carry proprietary rights in the compositions. The two string quartets yet unpublished were the 'Death and the Maiden' Quartet, and the recently composed Quartet in G major. The unpublished sonatas which he offered were the A major of 1819 and the A minor of 1823. He makes no reference to any PF. Trio, so the work in B flat major, Op. 99, may not have been completed. The replies from both firms arrived quite promptly. Probst evidently knew Schubert's work, and was a little afraid of it. But he did suggest that songs and pianoforte compositions would be considered. Schubert sent him three works via Artaria, the Vienna publisher. Breitkopf & Härtel said nothing of his work. But they clearly remembered the incident of April 1817, when a song called *Erlking*, by Franz Schubert, had been sent to them, and which they had mistakenly attributed to the Franz Schubert of Dresden. Their letter was written with a veiled tone of sarcasm. They offered a number of copies of the published work instead of a fee, and they claimed to be 'wholly unacquainted'—not with Schubert's compositions, they could hardly claim to be that—but 'with the mercantile success of your compositions'. The letter was, in the same contemptible manner, addressed to 'Franz Schubert: famous composer in Vienna'. Schubert had no more dealings with them.

A general lack of finances and an undercurrent of uncertainty about the future seem to have been the lot of each of the friends that summer and it was perhaps the reason for some trivial bicker-

ing and quarrelling amongst them, from which Schubert, if not
quite immune, emerged without any serious breach. The air
cleared temporarily during September when his friend, Leopold
Kupelwieser and Johanna Lutz were married. We have read some
of Johanna's friendly and affectionate comments on Schubert in
earlier pages. He was clearly fond of both of them, and is said to
have played the pianoforte for dancing at their wedding, and to
have refused to let anyone else take his place there. An extraordinary development of this improvisation of nuptial dance
music came to light only recently during the second World War.
Richard Strauss in the course of a conversation with a lady discovered that she was a descendant of the Leopold Kupelwieser
whom Schubert knew. She was Frau Mautner-Markhof, a grand-
daughter of Paul Kupelwieser, the second son of Johanna and
Leopold. She then went on to tell Strauss of a strange family
tradition. During Schubert's improvisation, one waltz tune so
charmed the bride that she never forgot it. As the years passed
her three sons grew up quite familiar with the tune, heard from
their mother's singing and playing, and they, in turn, passed the
tune on to their sons and daughters. Eventually, in 1943, Frau
Markhof played it to Strauss. Here it is, a Schubert waltz melody
preserved by ear for over a hundred years, which we owe in the
first place to the admirable Johanna Lutz:

Ex.70

Strauss arranged it for PF. Solo: a rather luscious version of a Schubert waltz, with the melody, in G flat major, given to the 'tenor' voice, but attractively written for all that. His manuscript is now in the possession of the *Gesellschaft für Musikfreunde*.

Two very original part-songs for male voices, in Schubert's most graphic vein, are *Nachthelle* and *Grab und Mond*. The poems are by Johann Gabriel Seidl, a young Viennese poet personally acquainted with Schubert. Both poems are nocturnal. In the first the night is starry and serene, and Schubert's light, quick chords and the high, poised tenor melody depict the scene vividly: it is a difficult piece to perform but sheer delight to the listener. The second poem describes the moon shining into a grave, and the vague symbolism—the light never returning—seems to imply that death is the final end of man, and no word comes back to deny it. Schubert's unaccompanied part-song has an unearthly, hollow effect, with startling harmonic progressions and unresolved discords: a piece of impressionistic colouring inspired by the poet's scene—'silver-blue moonlight', and his question—'Quite mute?' The two pieces were composed in September 1826, probably for performance in Vienna; the only record of such a performance is of *Nachthelle*, sung in the following January.

At the end of the month Vogl and his bride returned to Vienna from Steyr, and the singer was heard once again in the Schubertiad evenings. His failing voice was eked out with much expressive 'word-singing' and gesture. Bauernfeld noted in his journal of 17 December 1826:

> Vogl sang Schubert songs with mastery, but not without dandyism.

This 'histrionic' attitude of Vogl was uncongenial to many of the circle; Schwind on occasion was contemptuously uncivil to him. It is certain, too, that Vogl introduced embellishments and ornaments in the melodies of the songs which could not have been very patiently borne either by Schubert or the more thoughtful of his audience.

The old schoolhouse in the Säulengasse was sold during October. Franz Schubert senior received £660 for the property and a small share—£20—came to Schubert. This break with one

R   B.S.

memory of his childhood was followed at once by a link with another one, for soon after the sale of the house he moved into lodgings in the Schober's new home, and this was a mere stone's throw from the *Stadtkonvikt*. Schober and his mother were now installed in a house in the Bäckerstrasse. Schubert began work on the Sonatā in G major, probably intending it for Nägeli, or, failing him, for one of the various publishing houses in Germany should occasion arise. But whatever mercenary or 'celebrity' impulse ordered the composition of the sonata, once it was begun the impulse was primarily and purely artistic. The noble, exalted music of this great movement reveals the Schubert Sonata at its finest; the corresponding movement of the B flat Sonata of 1828 is exactly similar in style and treatment, and equally admired. The manuscript of the G major Sonata is a proud possession of the British Museum, and the sketches for the slow movement, remaining in Schubert's fair copy, give the autograph a more than normal interest. At bar 30 the slow movement was cancelled and restarted because the theme quoted in the next extract failed to satisfy its composer and was rejected out of hand:

Ex. 71

Further sketches for the slow movement are to be found at the back of the page containing the beginning of the 'Menuetto'.

One morning, just as Schubert was nearing the end of his work on the first movement of this sonata, Spaun called to see him. He made nothing of the interruption to his work, persuaded Spaun to sit down, and then he played the almost finished movement through to his friend. Spaun praised it highly and Schubert said: 'Since you like the sonata, you shall have it, for I like to do something to please you, when I can.' And eventually he placed the published work, dedicated to Spaun, in his old friend's hands. This incident was told by Spaun himself.

Several visits to Sophie Müller by Vogl and Schubert are recorded during October, and Jenger was also a visitor. No songs are actually named in the diary which Sophie kept, but doubtless the new Shakespeare songs were sung, and since Op. 59, containing the three wonderful Rückert songs, *Du bist die Ruh'*, *Lachen und Weinen* and *Dass sie hier gewesen*, had just been published, these songs would surely form part of the programme. In fact, not only does Sophie record buying some songs which were probably those of Op. 59, but one feels that she would find *Lachen und Weinen* irresistible, and that her singing of it would be wholly delightful. Another popular and cultured actress of the Burgtheater was Antonie Adamsberger, also, like Sophie, lost to the Viennese public through retirement. Although not in close touch with Schubert, she introduced Bauernfeld, from the Schubert circle, to Grillparzer, and during the October of 1826 she sang to the dramatist several songs by Schubert, including the Harper's song *Wer nie sein Brot mit Tränen ass* and *Ave Maria*. This was at the monastery of St. Florian. Grillparzer was returning to Vienna from a visit to Goethe at Weimar.

Many performances of Schubert's songs and part-songs had taken place at the evening concerts organised by the *Gesellschaft der Musikfreunde*, or the 'Musikverein', as it is also called. Schubert was in close touch with the association and esteemed by its officials: men such as Josef Sonnleithner and Rafael von Kiesewetter. At this period he promised to dedicate a symphony to the 'Musikverein'. In October the Committee voted Schubert 100 florins (£10) as a token of gratitude for his services to the musical activities of the Society and as an encouragement for further work. He acknowledged the gift on 20 October 1826. The series of Society minutes and the exchange of letters with Schubert have, in my view, been distorted by associating with them an undated letter of Schubert's referring to the score of a symphony which he was presenting to the Society. This association suggests that the 'Gmunden-Gastein' symphony was, by October 1826, in a finished and performable condition, a quite unjustifiable conclusion. The whole matter is considered in detail in the appendix (page 354).

III

At some time toward the end of November Schubert left the Schober family house and lived alone for a few months in lodgings near the 'Karolinentor'. This was a gate in the ancient, fortified wall leading to the Inner City, and is now demolished; it was opposite what is today the *Stadtpark* in Vienna, and not far from that section of the Ringstrasse known now as the 'Schubertring'. To get to his lodgings his friends walked on the wall, or Bastion, and they complained of 'the most frightful mud'.

He had resumed friendly relations again with the publisher Diabelli. Their renewed partnership was introduced auspiciously (or inauspiciously: it depends on the reader's point of view) by the 'Marches Militaires' of Op. 51, published in August; the first of the three marches, in D major, is Schubert's most popular, indeed, *only* popular, march. Pennauer also published some marches for PF. Duet: the ceremonial Op. 55 for the dead Tsar Alexander I, and the march, Op. 66, for the Coronation of his successor, Nicolas I. Amongst the various songs, the three Rückert settings of Op. 59, from the firm of Sauer & Leidesdorff, have been mentioned. The only other publication of interest is from Weigl, namely, the 'Divertissement in E minor, on French themes' published in June. This PF. Duet, called Op. 63: no. 1, was the first movement of a three-movement work. But its two companion movements, the 'Andantino varié' and a 'Marcia', were lost sight of for a year or so; when they were published, Weigl called them, not Op. 63: nos. 3 & 4, but by a new opus-number, 84: nos. 1 & 2. He thus effectively dissected the work for ever, for although this error has been repeatedly pointed out since the late nineteenth century, no attempt by publishers or performers has been made to assemble the scattered parts into a whole.

A young Bohemian violinist, Josef Slavík, mentioned earlier on in connection with a private performance of the String Quartet in G, had come to Vienna early in 1826 after a successful career in Prague. He hoped to make an international reputation. Schubert met him through the pianist Karl von Bocklet, and we owe to the advent of this violinist two works for violin and pianoforte, although neither is of any great moment. Slavík was a technician. He favourably impressed Paganini when the latter visited Vienna in 1828. A year later Chopin visited Vienna for the first time and he and Slavík became very friendly. Chopin wrote home that Slavík was a 'second Paganini', and added, awestruck, '36 staccato notes to a bow!' Schubert must have realised where Slavík's real achievement lay, for the two compositions he wrote for him tend to exploit the virtuoso style of violin-writing at the expense of musical values. The first was written in December 1826; it is the 'Rondeau Brillant' in B minor, planned on the usual lines for such a form: slow introduction leading to a 'Rondo allegro'. It could not, coming from Schubert at the end of 1826, be entirely without depth, but the various episodes are on the long side, and the inevitable repetitions involved in Rondo-form make it too protracted for its style and material. The same month saw the probable start of a large vocal composition which, to the Schubertian, is not a significant work, the 'German' Mass, as it is usually called. It was intended for celebrations of Low Mass in the vernacular and the words are by Johann Phillip Neumann, professor of physics at a Technical Institution in Vienna. The college is very near the Karlskirche where Schubert formerly lodged. Neumann was a cousin of Watteroth, through whom he became acquainted with Schubert. The Mass consists of eight separate religious songs to be sung by the choir and congregation during the intervals between the various stages of the Office: Introit, Gloria, Credo and so on. Schubert received £4 from Neumann for his composition.

Both text and music were published in 1827 without the authors'
names, although naturally not without their permission. The
reason why this slight and not unsentimental work has occupied
so much space is that it became immediately, and has remained to
this day in Vienna, very popular and greatly loved by the people.
There are several arrangements to be had besides Schubert's own,
and the first 'number', which begins *Wohin soll ich mich wenden?*
is known and sung by many Viennese who have not the least
idea that it is by Schubert, but who know it in numerous versions
as a popular piece of Church music.

Performances of his works, songs and instrumental compositions, in private and semi-public concerts, were from now on very
plentiful in Vienna. The December of 1826 saw three large
gatherings of his friends, at Spaun's house near the Schotten-
kirche, at Hönig's, and at Witteczek's. The first, called by Franz
von Hartmann in his diary 'a big, big Schubertiad' took place on
15 December 1826. It was a gathering of distinguished, middle-
class people, who were named in welcome detail by the diarist.
Besides the friends and acquaintances in Schubert's immediate
circle, including the newly-wedded Kupelwieser and Vogl, with
their wives, there were Grillparzer, Schlechta and many officials
of the Imperial Court. Gahy and Schubert played the six marches
of Op. 40, and Vogl sang song after song—over thirty of them.
This evening Schubertiad inspired Schwind, years afterwards, to
his very famous sepia drawing called 'Schubert evening at Spaun's'.
The picture deserves more than the brief mention it can receive
here, for it yields up much pleasure to those prepared to look
beyond mere identification of the persons in the collective 'portrait'. The scene, Schubert at the piano, Vogl singing, and the
men and women of the audience gathered about these central
figures, is not a representational portrait of the particular party of
15 December 1826. It is an imaginative reconstruction of the
many Schubertiads of the period. The original now hangs in
Schubert's birthplace in the Nussdorferstrasse, saved for the city
of Vienna by the efforts and pleas of O. E. Deutsch. There are
one or two inferior and somewhat sentimental imitations by other
painters of Schwind's noble conception.

Apart from the private parties there were the evening entertain-
ments of the 'Musikverein' at which, during the winter session of
1826–1827 numerous songs, including *Der Zwerg, Der Einsame,*
An Schwager Kronos, Die junge Nonne, and Psalm XXIII for
female voices, were sung. At a concert in the Kärntnertor
Theater on 2 December the Overture to 'Alfonso und Estrella'
was revived. It received a notice in Berlin—somewhat equivocal
—and one in the London music-journal 'Harmonicon', which was
distinctly favourable: '. . . a revived overture by Schubert, full of
striking effects, and worthy of being better known.' In the early
days of 1827 Karl von Bocklet, the pianist to whom Schubert had
dedicated the Sonata in D major, Op. 53, and Josef Slavík, performed the 'Rondeau Brillant' for Domenico Artaria, the music
publisher. Schubert was present at the performance. This was a
prelude to publication and Artaria brought out the piece during
April 1827 as Op. 70.

A new friend of those days was Ferdinand Walcher, introduced to Schubert and his friends by the Hartmann brothers.
Walcher, a young law student, came from Lower Austria; he was
courting Sophie Kleyle, the daughter of a well-to-do Viennese
family who lived, during the summer months, in a country residence at Penzing. Schubert visited the Kleyle family frequently
and was a welcome and popular guest. Penzing lies to the north
of Schönbrunn, and the pretty residence and gardens of the
Kleyle's are still in existence today.

IV

During the latter months of 1826 and in the whole of 1827, the
two brothers, Fritz and Franz von Hartmann, kept full diaries of
their activities in Vienna. They were friends, in the first place, of
Spaun, but the friendship soon embraced the whole of Spaun's
circle; they encountered Schubert almost daily at the particular
Kaffeehaus in favour with the circle of friends at the moment, and
were at all the evening Schubertiads. Inevitably there are numerous
references to Schubert in their diaries and these can all be found
quoted fully in the pages of the Schubert 'Documents'. We do
not meet the name Hartmann in the nineteenth-century biographies

of the composer and it is due to O. E. Deutsch's researches that these diaries have been found, and the relevant entries published. In a few instances they correct error and supplement our information on the period. But most of the diary entries are the merest social chit-chat, and contribute very little that is vital. They do not tell us much that is new about Schubert's Vienna, being concerned almost entirely with the names of the people whom the two young men met, the *Kaffeehaus* to which they resorted in the evening, the practical jokes and jesting in which they indulged, and the time they went home. Naturally the Hartmanns were not gifted with second sight, nor were they aware how eagerly their pages would be scanned by future Schubertians. We cannot blame them for not watching Schubert more closely. He comes and goes in their pages like a ghost, he says nothing and does nothing except accompany his songs on occasion; we are not told what he looked like, how he played, what work he was engaged on, what he said about publishers, performers, concerts, plays, operas or books. Their comments on the Vienna *Kaffeehaus*, its atmosphere and its functions, are welcome. At that time the 'Grünanger' was the favourite haunt, a *Kaffeehaus* still standing today, in the district behind St. Stephen's Cathedral. The Viennese *Kaffeehaus* has no real counterpart in English life, yet an attempt must be made to understand its unique function, for it is an essential factor in the life of Schubert, as in the life of any Viennese of his day. Grove's attempt to equate it with the English 'club', to excuse Schubert's use of it, and to talk about the amount of drink consumed there, is no help at all. He based his conclusions on too scanty a supply of facts and a misinterpretation of those facts which were to hand. From the Hartmann diaries alone we can deduce that Schubert found these 'coffeehouses' simply a meeting place for congenial souls, and Grove's further statements about 'daybreak driving the friends back to their lodgings' and that 'few constitutions could stand such a racket' do not need the diaries to prove their absurdity. Distortions of this kind were to lead to preposterous misjudgements of Schubert. The coffeehouses of eighteenth-century London vanished during the next hundred years; in Vienna they survived and do so today.

When we read of these nightly gatherings, Schubertiads in private houses, discussions in the *Kaffeehaus*, the 'Musikverein' concerts, it is hard to find any relation between Schubert's outward life, which suggests a leisurely, almost lazy, progress from day to day, and the fire of creation which burned in him, the unremitting labour of composition which chained him to his desk during the day. It is this which gives his appearances in the journals and letters of his friends a ghost-like, unreal quality. He seems so quiet and controlled, almost insignificant, whereas we know all the time he is striving toward, and urging his powers to reach up to, the vision of the 'Winterreise'.

A truer picture of his moods can be found by reading a little below the surface of the comments made by his friends on his actions. Here, for example, are the allusions of the two Hartmann brothers to 4 March 1827:

> I went with Fritz to Schubert's, who had invited us, but never appeared at all. (Franz von Hartmann.)

> We went to Schober's, where we met Spaun, Schwind, Bauernfeld and Kriehuber with his wife and sister-in-law . . . because Schubert, who is Schober's lodger, had invited us to hear some new compositions of his. Everybody was assembled, but friend Schubert did not come. At last Schwind undertook to sing several of Schubert's earlier songs, which enchanted us. At half-past nine we all went to the 'Castle of Eisenstadt' where Schubert too arrived soon after us, and won all hearts by his amiable simplicity, although he had deceived our hopes by his artist's negligence. (Fritz von Hartmann.)

He was caught away from the actualities of daily life into the world of the 'Winterreise'—into *his* world, as it has been suggested, rather than Müller's. The flimsiness of social claims to keep him from his music is implied, if we read with understanding, in a further comment. This comes from a letter written to Ferdinand Walcher, then in Venice, by his fair friend Sophie Kleyle at Penzing:

> We do not lack visitors, for we have several each day; Angerer and Jenger come more often than usual, and Schubert too has given us the pleasure once already; he was most amiable and talkative, but escaped suddenly, before anyone had an inkling. . . . (1 June 1827.)

Besides the self-absorption in composition, or perhaps because of it, he had to bear both the lack of any promising situation or source of income, and wretched health. They were both, the financial outlook and his enfeebled condition, slowly growing less bearable. Schober in his old age passed on reminiscences of Schubert which were not too reliable, nor too kindly. He said of the early days of 1827 that Schubert was in love with Auguste Grünwedel, a young girl whom we find mentioned in the Hartmann diaries. Schober, one evening in the *Kaffeehaus* suggested to Schubert that he might marry her. Schubert rose angrily, made no reply, and hurried out of the place. Afterwards, in a calmer mood, he tried to answer the utterly tactless remark with a conventional parry, that he was convinced no woman would ever marry him.

Another incident of those days shows Schober in an equally vivid light. At a breakfast party on 6 January 1827 at Spaun's house, Gahy played two sonatas by Schubert and then some German dances. The dances were those of Op. 67, but we do not know which sonatas were played: it is almost certain that one of them was the work in G major, dedicated to Spaun. Schober joined the party halfway through and expressed his displeasure with the sonatas. Possibly a little jealousy embittered his remarks, for Spaun resented them, and the two men nearly quarrelled. Schober preferred Schubert's lighter, more lyrical vein. His attitude to the composer's more serious work, like the sonatas, contrasts strongly with that of Spaun. The reaction of each man tells us more about him than it does about the music which provoked the reaction. In the same way the type of music which Schubert wrote for each of his two friends, pleasing them with the kind they preferred, is revealing.

Another Schubertiad for a large gathering of people was held a few days after the 'breakfast' incident, again in Spaun's house. The Sonata for PF. Duet in C major, the 'Grand Duo', was played by Schubert and Gahy, followed by the 'Variations in A flat', Op. 35, a popular work amongst the Schubertians of that time. Vogl sang a series of songs including *Nacht und Träume* and *Im Abendroth* (which he sang twice).

A blow to Schubert's hopes came in the form of a polite rejection by Probst, the music publisher at Leipzig, of the proffered manuscripts (15 January). These were piano pieces, probably incorporated later on in the 'Moments Musicaux'. Probst claimed to be overburdened with work, since he was publishing the 'Complete Works' of Kalkbrenner! A different kind of letter came a few days afterwards from Ferdinand Walcher. He was the possessor of a pleasant, high baritone voice, and sang various Schubert songs, including *Auf dem Wasser zu singen*, with great charm. His letter enclosed two tickets for a performance of *Nachthelle* at the 'Musikverein', a part-song which, as Walcher wrote, is '. . . for a principal and damned high tenor'. The interest of his note—apart from the warm and affectionate terms expressed toward the dejected composer—lies in the opening paragraph. Walcher wrote a snatch of plainsong to the words 'Credo in unum Deum' and then continued: 'Du nicht, das weiss ich wohl, aber das wirst Du glauben . . .' and he then informed Schubert that Tietze would sing *Nachthelle* and so forth. Is there any point in hedging over this plain statement of Walcher's to Schubert? It means, in effect: ' "I believe in One God"—you do not, that I know well, but you will believe this. . . .' Schubert's unorthodox beliefs were known to his family and friends from quite early years, and his continuing association with like-minded professors and students in Vienna had, if anything, intensified them. It may be this unorthodoxy which vitiates his sacred music, and prevents it taking the last, clinching grip on the listener's admiration and attention. Walcher's 'Unum Deum' is the God of the Christian Church; Schubert was no sceptic where 'Gott in der Natur' was concerned. In that hymn to Nature's God, *Die Allmacht*, Schubert pours out a paean of praise from the depths of his soul. But there is no sacred music, or very little, of the same intensity in his Masses, or other settings of liturgical texts. It has been stressed that there was no conscious revolt in Schubert's attitude: one cannot imagine his being so positive as to adopt a belligerent unorthodoxy, and his position was partly subconscious, partly unapprehended. How, otherwise, can we account for his quite sincere words to his father:

... they also wondered greatly at my piety, which I expressed in a hymn to the Holy Virgin and which, it appears, grips every soul and turns it to devotion. I think this is due to the fact that I have never forced devotion in myself and never compose hymns or prayers of that kind unless it overcomes me unawares; but then it is usually the right and true devotion. ...

The hymn to which he refers here is, it is significant to note, the purely secular poem of Scott's *Ave Maria*, not the words of the angel's salutation to Mary. But for all Schubert's sincerity and simplicity, he is devoid of the implicit faith of Bach and Beethoven, and certainly of Bruckner, and hence incapable of the unarguable, unanswerable sublimity of assertion in their sacred music.

Walcher left for Venice in the spring of 1827 and as a farewell offering Schubert wrote in his album the delightfully fresh and original piece for piano known as the 'Allegretto in C minor' (D. 915) and inscribed it 'To my dear friend Walcher for remembrance, 27 April 1827'.

v

The manuscript of the first twelve songs of 'Winterreise' is dated 'February 1827', indicating the time at which Schubert started writing the fair copy of the first of them, *Gute Nacht*. He found these twelve poems (entitled 'Die Winterreise') in an almanach called 'Urania', published in Leipzig in 1823. The eagerness with which he started composing these songs, and the exhausted state in which their composition left him, show how congenial to his taste and to his gifts, were the straightforward and limpid verses of Müller. He was overjoyed to find another series of songs by the poet of the 'Schöne Müllerin' and he did not spare himself as poem after poem stimulated the creative power within him and—one might almost say—extorted musical scene after musical scene from his imagination, those incomparable scenes of despair and heartbreak, violence and numbness, in a landscape of snow and ice and bitter wind. In the late summer of 1827, after the first twelve songs were finished, Schubert encountered Müller's complete and final version of the cycle. This was included in a book entitled 'Poems from the posthumous papers of a travelling horn-player': 'Die Winterreise' was the second of the three parts in the book. It then contained twenty-four poems, but the new ones were not supplementary to the original twelve: they were inserted in various places. The book was dedicated by Müller to the 'Master of German Song, Karl Maria von Weber, as a pledge of his friendship and admiration'; he died in 1827 before Schubert's setting was published. When Schubert found Müller's final version he set to music the extra twelve poems, taking them as they came and placing them all together at the end of the twelve settings he had made in the spring of 1827. It has been said many times that Schubert *altered* the order of Müller's poems, but he did not do so deliberately as the above account makes clear.

Schubert's two manuscripts, with the whole series of twenty-four songs, has survived. The first one consists mostly of rough drafts, and is so full of alterations and additions that the publisher's engraver found it unreadable. Thereupon a fair copy was made and submitted to Schubert who not only corrected it, but radically altered it in a few places.[1] Since this copy, from which the first edition was printed, disappeared for many years, and since Schubert's 'foul papers' survived, several commentators, Max Friedlaender (1884), Mandyczewski (1894), Erwin Scheffer (1938) and others, have drawn attention to what they have deemed errors in the first edition. But Schubert himself made the changes. The copy made for the engraver is now in the *Stadtbibliothek* of Vienna. The manuscript containing the next twelve songs, from *Die Post* to *Der Leiermann*, Schubert's (not Müller's) Part II, is in fair copy; it is dated 'October 1827'. Only a fragmentary sketch exists for one of these songs, for no. 23, *Die Nebensonnen*.

Two of Schubert's friends mention these months in his life, and the composition of 'Winterreise'. Mayrhofer's paragraph is rather sentimental; his words that Schubert's winter had come upon him, hence the creation of 'Winterreise', take no account of the incredible detachment of the artist. How, otherwise, one

[1] The biggest change is in the second song, *Die Wetterfahne*, at bars 15–18.

might ask, if the winter were upon him, did Schubert come to write the ebullient, springtime music of 1828—the great C major Symphony, the String Quintet in C, the last three sonatas? Spaun's reminiscences of the 'Winterreise' period are more realistic. After relating the occasion when Schubert called the friends together, and sang the 'Winterreise' to them, he added:

> We who were near and dear to him knew how much the creatures of his mind took out of him, and in what anguish they were born. No one who ever saw him at his morning's work, glowing, and with his eyes aflame, yes, and positively with a changed speech, ... will ever forget it ... I hold it beyond question that the excitement in which he composed his finest songs, in particular the 'Winterreise', brought about his untimely death.

The music of the song-cycle heralds a new phase in his work, one which he did not live long enough to redeem from mere promise: a new power of intellectual depth in his treatment of thematic ideas, a new tranquillity, a richer imagery.

*   *   *   *

In the way which we have noticed before, the 'fashionable' song of that period was *Der zürnenden Diana*; it was sung on several occasions in Vienna. Later on it was *Norman's Song* from the settings of the 'Lady of the Lake' lyrics. Another performance of Psalm XXIII was given by the singing pupils of the 'Conservatoire' on 18 March; it took place in the *Gesellschaft* concert-hall, a building situated in the Tuchlauben, which leads from the Graben. Schubert moved into lodgings in this same street soon afterwards, living again in the Schober household; their new residence was next door to the concert-hall. He had two rooms and a music-closet at his disposal—more comfortable quarters than he had ever enjoyed before.

On an occasion during February 1827 Beethoven, confined to his sickbed, had been given a batch of Schubert songs by Anton Schindler. Most of them were in printed editions, but a few were manuscript copies of published or unpublished songs made by Schindler. Beethoven examined them with great interest and according to Schindler (not, as we have seen, an entirely reliable witness) exclaimed at their number, length and variety.[1] Occasionally he uttered the ambiguous remark: 'If I had had this poem I would have set it'; was this pleasure in the poem, or dissatisfaction with Schubert's effort? Finally he pronounced: 'Truly in Schubert is the divine spark!'—which sounds very like a poetic invention on Schindler's part. The manuscript copies made by Schindler are not lost, and today, bound in one volume, are in the possession of Otto Taussig of Malmö. They comprise twenty-six songs, and contribute a few details of interest: most notably that the prelude of four bars in early editions of the song *Augenlied* was genuine Schubert, and not, as Mandyczewski considered, an addition of the publisher's. *Augenlied*, as copied by Schindler, is so ornate compared with the published song, that it is almost certainly an embellished version by Vogl. Similar ornate variants are to be found in other songs amongst the Schindler copies, also due to Vogl's efforts.

On 18 March Schubert is said to have gone in the company of Anselm and Josef Hüttenbrenner to visit the dying Beethoven. He had never met, nor spoken to Beethoven in all the years of his musical activities in Vienna. So much he told Spaun himself, and that disposes of many anecdotes, plausible and piquant though they may be, in which Schubert and Beethoven are supposed to have associated with each other.

Beethoven died on 26 March 1827. There is an extraordinarily vivid and detailed account of the dead composer in the pages of Franz von Hartmann's diary, quoted in the Schubert 'Documents', page 621. Schubert was one of thirty-six torch bearers at the funeral. Beethoven was buried in a small, square grave-yard known as the 'Friedort' ('Place of Peace') to the left of the Währingerstrasse as it leaves the city; in those days the cemetery lay beyond the city boundaries. After the funeral ceremony Schubert, Schober and Schwind, accompanied by the younger Hartmann, Fritz, visited the *Kaffeehaus*, 'Castle of Eisenstadt', and remained there discussing the dead composer until late into the night. The grisly story of the toast to Beethoven, followed by a

[1] Schindler wrote two accounts of the incident: (*a*) 'Allgemeine Theaterzeitung', Vienna, 3 May 1831, (*b*) 'Beethoven-Biographie', Münster, 1840.

second toast to the 'next one to die'—who was, in fact, Schubert himself—is an invention.

Soon after Beethoven's death, Schubert met at the house of Katharina von Lászny the pianist and composer Hummel, with his young pupil Ferdinand Hiller. Hummel was on the point of abandoning his career as a pianist. He delighted Schubert by going to the piano after Vogl had sung *Der blinde Knabe* and improvising on the theme of the song. The incident was related many years after the event by Hiller.[1]

April was full of performances of his work, new and old. One can well understand the frustration and depression which seized him when he encountered the apparently recalcitrant attitude of German publishers to his offers of compositions; he himself, in Vienna, was surrounded by every evidence of esteem and popularity. Or do we, in reading of these performances, isolated from the musical life of the city, gain a wrong impression? In that year, it will be remembered, the English musician Edward Holmes was in Vienna, recording fully the musical life of the capital, yet saying no word of Schubert. Even so, the following list seems favourable on any count: four part-songs (6 April), vocal quartet (12 April), the Octet, first public performance (16 April), 'Nachtgesang', for male voices and horns (22 April). There were also numerous performances of solo songs, and four Schubertiads, at one of which, on 21 April, Franz von Hartmann wrote that there was 'an enormous attendance'. Two days after that another of these popular gatherings was held at Witteczek's home. Schubert paid a grateful tribute to this loyal friend; it took the form of a dedication: the three settings of Seidl's nature-poems, the impracticable, but masterly *Im Freien, Das Zügenglöcklein* and *Der Wanderer an den Mond*, were 'offered in friendship to Josef Witteczek' and published as Op. 80 in May 1827 by Tobias Haslinger. This new name amongst Viennese publishers of his work appeared for the first time the previous month. In April, Haslinger had published the G major Sonata as Op. 78, but he did Schubert a disservice by calling the work 'Fantasia, *Andante*, Menuetto and

---

[1] 'In Wien vor 52 Jahren', and 'Kunsterleben', both accounts published in 1880.

SCHOOL REPORT MADE BY SCHUBERT'S FATHER FROM ROSSAU,
MAY 1827

Herr Otto Taussig

Allegretto'. The title 'Sonata' was just beginning to lose favour, and for many years remained unfashionable, until, towards the end of the nineteenth century it re-emerged with an added *cachet* of distinction as the Viennese masters loomed larger above the wreck of the 'Romantic' movement. But Haslinger has fastened the label 'Fantasia' so firmly to this pure sonata-movement of Schubert's that it will remain there for all time. Diabelli published Op. 62, four settings of poems from Goethe's 'Wilhelm Meister', including the superb duet *Mignon und der Harfner*, which, since duet *Lieder* are so completely uncongenial today, is consigned to oblivion. Diabelli had also re-published the song *Auf dem Wasser ʒu singen* in March, as Op. 72: it had been a supplementary issue to the 'Wiener Zeitschrift' of December 1823.

During May and early June Schubert spent a few weeks at the village of Dornbach, which lay to the west of Vienna. He went with Schober and they lived in the inn 'Empress of Austria'. It was a charming spot, cupped by the wooded hills of the 'Wiener Wald'—the ideal place for the birth of the song *Das Lied im Grünen*, one of Schubert's most exhilarating songs of springtime. We know of no other compositions originating at Dornbach, but it is very likely that Schubert composed or sketched there some of the 'Impromptus' purchased during the late autumn by Haslinger and published as Op. 90. There would be money, in modest amounts, from Haslinger and Diabelli. The first published three sets of songs in May: *Die Allemacht* and *Das Heimweh* as Op. 79, *Im Freien* included in Op. 80, and the three songs to texts by Rochlitz, one of them the delicious little serenade *An die Laute*, as Op. 81. Diabelli re-published some supplements, *Der Wachtelschlag* as Op. 68, and *Die Rose* as Op. 73. This last publication is noteworthy as containing the very first list ever made of Schubert's published works, Opp. 1–74, thus including publications by firms other than Diabelli's. The last opus in the list, 74, is one of the Schubertian mysteries (Op. 82: no. 2 is another). Op. 74 is an arrangement made by the composer of a comic trio called 'Die Advokaten'; the music is by one Anton Fischer and Schubert's arrangement of it was made in 1812—when he was a boy of fifteen. It must therefore have been published without his knowledge, for he is hardly likely to have sold the trifling composition of another composer, when he had so much unpublished work of his own; but how Diabelli obtained the manuscript is almost incomprehensible. We must suppose that it was taken to the composer by one of the men on the fringe of his circle, Lachner, perhaps, or Schindler. There is no word from Schubert himself about the publication—no denial, no refutation.

Two short, but very typical songs, were given as supplements to the 'Wiener Zeitschrift' of 23 June 1827. *Wanderers Nachtlied* (the celebrated poem by Goethe beginning 'Ueber allen Gipfeln ist Ruh') and *Trost im Liede*. The first was re-published in Schubert's lifetime, but the second, a finer composition, was re-published by Probst, together with two other 'Zeitschrift' supplements, as a spurious Op. 101, in December 1828, just after Schubert's death.

On his return to Vienna in early June 1827, he was honoured by being elected a 'representative' of the *Gesellschaft der Musikfreunde*. It was a further acknowledgement of the regard in which his work was held by the Society; there were no duties required of him. But the distinction thus conferred may have spurred him on to the completion of the symphony sketched at Gmunden.

VI

The various threads which connect people living in social communities, and which, in Schubert's Vienna, weave an ever shifting web, now tightening, now breaking, now fastening again, suddenly form a pretty pattern during 1827, centring round the young and charming figure of Louise Gosmar. She was introduced to Fritz von Hartmann at a ball held in the residence of a wealthy merchant, a friend of her father's. Fritz and Louise discovered a mutual love for Schubert's music and talked of it while they danced. At that time Louise was a singing pupil in Anna Fröhlich's class at the 'Conservatoire', and soon found that Anna was a friend of Schubert's. Anna, knowing that Louise's parents wanted to give her a surprise for her birthday, went to Grillparzer and begged him to write a short birthday-ode in honour of the event. Grillparzer, in love with Katharina, Anna's younger sister, willingly complied with her request. Anna took the poem to Schubert, asking him if he would set it to music, and explaining why she wanted it.

The outcome is a well-known story in the Schubert records. He did compose the poem, a delightful serenade for a loved child, for contralto solo and chorus, just as Anna had asked him. But the chorus was for *men's* voices, and Anna wanted it, of course, for her female singing class. Schubert rectified his mistake at once, with a good-humoured acknowledgement of his foolish blunder. On 11 August the young ladies of the singing class were secretly conveyed to the Gosmar's residence at Döbling, a village to the north of Vienna, on the way to Grinzing. A piano was carried into the garden, and Schubert's and Grillparzer's 'Serenade' was sung by Josefine Fröhlich and her sister's pupils. It was a lovely summer's night and the effect created was unforgettable. Schubert was not present during the performance, but he heard the piece a few months later sung in Vienna and expressed his satisfaction with it. This 'Serenade', like the Mass in F major of 1814, and the 'Prometheus' Cantata of 1816, occupies a bigger place in the Schubert story than in the affections of the Schubertian. It has some utterly delightful and very characteristic moments, but it is too long drawn out for its material. As with many of Schubert's vocal pieces in the 1825-1827 period, a figure of accompaniment, original and striking at first, is kept going for page after page, and does not escape monotony. Thus, in the 'Serenade', the piano figuration, a vivid representation of the gentle knocking on the door of the sleeper's room, is played continuously until the ear wearies of it. The original form of the part-song, contralto solo and men's chorus, is preferable to the second, since the variety of *timbre* is welcome. Louise Gosmar, soon after the 'Serenade' birthday gift, fell in love with Leopold Sonnleithner, Schubert's friend and well-wisher. They were married in the following May.

Schwind was studying during 1827 at Munich; there is a possibility that he and Schubert were not quite so closely in touch since no letters were exchanged between them during the young painter's absence. But it was only a temporary loosening of the ties. Bauernfeld, too, working in his Government office is not so frequently encountered, but Schubert still worked spasmodically at his opera-text, 'Der Graf von Gleichen'.

A new haunt, called the 'Wolf preaching to the Geese', was favoured by the friends that summer; it was an inn rather than a *Kaffeehaus*, very near Schubert's and Schober's dwelling. But the endless discussions between the members of the circle continued just as ardently as they had at the 'Grünanger' and the 'Castle of Eisenstadt'. Schubert also visited Grinzing during the season to sample there the 'Heurige', the wine pressed that year. The centre of the village still looks today as it did in Schubert's day, and can easily be recognised from Schwind's well-known drawing, with Schubert drinking the 'new' wine in the company of Bauernfeld and Lachner. On 15 August 1827 he was met there by Hoffmann von Fallersleben, a chance meeting. Fallersleben, a poet and a collector of German folksong, best known, perhaps, for his authorship of 'Deutschland über alles', was on a visit to Vienna in the company of Heinrich Panofka. Years later he wrote a significant sentence in his autobiography 'Mein Leben' (1868) about this meeting with Schubert; he said: '. . . there was nothing in his face, or in his whole being, that resembled my Schubert.' It is, as already said, impossible to reconcile the externals of Schubert's being with the internal fire of creative energy which transformed him when he worked, as Spaun has pointed out. Vogl's wife, Kunigunde, writing to her daughter in 1850, also said that Schubert was 'a little, insignificant-looking man'.

VII

Through his friendship with Johann Baptist Jenger, Schubert was able to spend a short holiday that year at Graz, then a small township in south Austria, the capital of Styria. It was known to Schubert as 'Gratz', the name being altered in 1843. The town possessed a University, two fine Gothic churches and was within easy reach of lovely countryside. His hostess was Marie Pachler, an accomplished and cultured woman, whose piano playing had charmed Beethoven. Jenger had met her while staying at Graz. The visit had been long planned, in fact Schubert had been invited in 1826 but had had no money for the journey. Karl Pachler, his host, was a man of substance, kindly and just a little shy of his distinguished guest; he combined the activities of barrister and brewer, which sounds a fascinating conjunction of occupations. Schubert had promised, in a letter to Marie Pachler of 12 June 1827, that he would come to Graz with Jenger, and the two friends left Vienna on 2 September by coach.

The days he passed at Graz were the last period of holiday leisure and sunshine which Schubert was to know. He found nothing but friendliness, consideration and warm admiration there. His old friend Anselm Hüttenbrenner, who lived at Graz, was drawn into the circle, of course, and he, Jenger and Schubert made music for their own, and the Pachler's delight. The familiar coloured drawing by Teltscher of the heads of these three musicians was made at that time when the artist also visited Graz. Schubert heard the opera 'The Captivity in Egypt' by Meyerbeer at the Graz Theater, and was said to dislike it; a concert, at which *Norman's Song* was performed, was given in his honour (for he was, it will be remembered, an honorary member of the Styrian Music Society), and a comic play was staged for home performance by the Graz natives and their visitors.

There were several excursions, one to the castle of Wildbach, which was managed by an aunt of Pachler's. This visit greatly impressed not only the visitors but their hosts also. Among the people whom Schubert met at Wildbach was the father of Johann Nepomuk Fuchs, who afterwards made such a deplorable vocal score of 'Alfonso und Estrella', and who, instead of being execrated for such work, was appointed editor of the Opera Volumes in the 'Gesamtausgabe' of Breitkopf & Härtel. On 20 September Schubert and Jenger returned to Vienna, taking four days over the coach trip and seeing the towns of Fürstenfeld and Friedberg and climbing the summit of the Eselberg, before descending the valley road to Vienna via Schleinz.

Schubert wrote a warm letter of thanks to Frau Pachler, and said during the course of it:

> Above all, I shall never forget the kindly shelter, where, with its dear hostess and the sturdy 'Pachleros' as well as little Faust, I spent the happiest days I have had for a long time. . . .

Faust was the seven-year-old son of the house, a frail-looking, delicately formed boy. Schubert wrote a march ('Kindermarsch') for PF. Duet and sent it to him during October. He wrote on the manuscript a short letter to the boy's mother in which he warned her 'I fear I shall not earn his applause, since I do not feel I am exactly made for this kind of composition'. His self-distrust is not groundless; in attempting to write down to a young musician's level of understanding, he suppresses completely his own individuality. The 'Kindermarsch' is without any point of interest. Faust and his mother performed the march on 4 November, in honour of Karl Pachler; it was his name-day, and for this worthy occasion Schubert had promised the piece. He added in his letter to Marie Pachler that his 'usual headaches' were assailing him again, an ominous touch. A very different piece of music was also sent to Graz at that time; Schubert dispatched the full score of 'Alfonso und Estrella', since the possibility of a performance of the opera at the Graz Theater had been discussed. But this never materialised, although the score was hopefully kept by Karl Pachler for many years.

While he was at Graz Schubert composed two songs; the words of the first, *Heimliches Lieben,* were given to him by Marie Pachler, but those of the second song, *Eine altschottische Ballade,* suggest that it reached Schubert in a more round-about fashion. The Scottish ballad is 'Edward', from Bishop Percy's 'Reliques of Ancient English Poetry' and was translated into German by Herder. An examination of Schubert's text suggests that he used not a literary source at all but a song, namely, Loewe's setting of the ballad, his Op. 1: no. 1, published by Schlesinger of Berlin three years previously. Textual discrepancies in Loewe's text re-appear in Schubert's, but are not to be found in any one of Herder's own version of the poem, of which there are three.[1] Schubert had also composed at Graz some dances known as the 'Grätzer Walzer' and a single 'Grätzer Galopp'; the twelve waltzes were published in January 1828 by Haslinger, as Op. 91, and he included the 'Galopp' in a series of similar dances called

[1] See 'Monthly Musical Record', London, December 1955.

'Favorit Galoppe'. On his return to Vienna Schubert set the two poems *Das Weinen* and *Vor meiner Wiege*. They were by Karl von Leitner, a young poet who was a friend of the Pachler's and greatly admired by Marie. Schubert set the poems at her request. He included with them the two others he had composed at Graz, *Heimliches Lieben* and *Eine altschottische Ballade*, and intended to publish all four as Op. 106, dedicating the edition to Marie Pachler. The songs were lithographed by the Vienna 'Lithographisches Institut' but not, at first, given an opus-number. Moreover, at the last minute, the *Ballade* was removed and *To Silvia* substituted for it. Jenger wrote to Marie about the opus of songs, promising to bring her copies to Graz himself. But this he never did, and Marie received no copies from Schubert's own hands: instead she was obliged to buy her own.

Besides the manuscripts of the opera and the children's march there was at Graz another autograph of Schubert's: this was the sketch he wrote for the song *Die Nebensonnen*, which comes near the end of the 'Winterreise' song-cycle. The page was purchased from Faust Pachler many years later by Witteczek (October 1842). The second twelve songs of 'Winterreise' are fair copies in Schubert's hand, and are dated at the start 'October 1827'. If Schubert was working on *Die Nebensonnen* in September, it seems fairly clear that sketches for Part II of the song-cycle were being composed before the Graz holiday, that is, in August. But the final drafts and fair copies were being made during October although months passed before they were in the publisher's hands. No attempt was made by Schubert, or Haslinger, to re-assemble the twenty-four songs so that they corresponded with Müller's final order. The twelve songs from February were called 'Part I' and published in January 1828 as Op. 89: nos. 1–12. The next twelve, of October, were called 'Part II' and published after Schubert's death, in December 1828, as Op. 89: nos. 13–24. There is a faint possibility that the retaining of the original twelve songs as 'Part I' may have been deliberate on Schubert's part, and that he intended the cycle to be thought of, and performed, as in two parts; to give a literary analogy, we could cite Shakespeare's 'Henry IV'. It would ease the strain on both singer and audience to have either part of the cycle, and not both, in a public performance.

Further settings of Leitner, from the book of his poems which Schubert had received from Marie Pachler, were completed in November: *Der Wallensteiner Lanzknecht, Der Kreuzzug* and *Des Fischers Liebesglück*. The Leitner songs are an undistinguished group, while at the same time containing characteristic work. The poet's ideas are of a humdrum order—Capell calls them feeble-minded!—and they induced a certain spineless kind of writing from Schubert. The best of them is the erotic *Fischers Liebesglück* with its piano imagery, which suggests the swaying boat beneath the stars, but even that develops perfunctorily.

The month is graced by the composition of the second Trio for Pianoforte, violin and 'cello, in E flat. Schubert's sketches for the work, as well as his fair copy, are extant. It has been suggested that the work loomed too large in the nineteenth century, but this is not to belittle the achievement of its creation. It is a masterpiece and contributed much to the musical developments of 1828, particularly in the new organisation of the first movement, an organisation which Schubert had tried already in the G major String Quartet. The assertion made by Leopold Sonnleithner to Ferdinand Luib, in a letter written in 1857, that the theme of the slow movement was taken from a lost song by the Swedish composer Isaak Berg cannot be dismissed out of hand. Schubert did meet Berg in 1827 and heard some of his songs. But it would need the evidence of the song put before us to be convincing, for the C minor theme said to be derived in this way seems pre-eminently the composer's own. A manuscript copy of the Trio was in the possession of Karoline Esterházy at Schubert's death. He gave her the copy since the original had gone to the Leipzig publisher Probst, during 1828, for publication as Op. 100; this has since been lost. Karoline's manuscript suggests that Schubert had come into closer touch again with the Esterházy family, probably when Marie, the older sister, was married in Vienna on 1 December 1827. The surmise gains support from the fact that the Fantasia in F minor for PF. Duet, Op. 103, composed in January 1828 and published posthumously, was dedicated to Karoline.

The publications in 1827 included works for PF. Duet: Op. 75, the set of four Polonaises, from Diabelli, and two movements belonging to the 'Divertissement in E minor', mistakenly published by Weigl as Op. 84: nos. 1 and 2. A third PF. Duet was the rather showy set of variations on a theme by Hérold, which Haslinger published in September as Op. 82. This publisher also brought out during that same month Schubert's Op. 83, three Italian songs written for the great bass singer Luigi Lablache, and dedicated to him. They are undeservedly neglected, although this is perhaps understandable since they require the highest artistry as well as a noble voice. At the close of the year Haslinger published the first two of Schubert's famous series of Impromptus. They were called (eventually) Op. 90: nos. 1 and 2, the *Allegro molto moderato* in C minor, and the skimming *Allegro* in E flat. A year later the publisher advertised all four numbers of the opus, but the third and fourth pieces did not appear until 1857. By that time Tobias Haslinger was dead, and his son Karl published them. The third piece, the *Andante* in G flat major, was transposed into G major; the fourth is the *Allegretto*, which, like the song *Auf dem Wasser zu singen* is supposedly in A flat major, but commences in the minor key and postpones the resolution into the major key for as long as possible in order to delay the sheer, sensuous satisfaction of the change.

Schubert continued the series of 'Impromptus' until there were eight in all: the last four are dated December 1827 and actually entitled 'Impromptus' by the composer. This should dispose of the theory first announced by Schumann and supported by other writers, including Einstein, that the four pieces are a sonata, broken up to be more saleable. The four pieces, an *Allegro moderato* in F minor, the *Allegretto* in A flat major, the *Theme and variations* in B flat major, and the *Allegro scherzando* in F minor, seem to have an underlying key scheme such as would befit a sonata; but the key of the third is an awkward one to square with the others, and the first piece is certainly not a 'first-movement' from any formal point of view. The variations, a popular item, are based on a variant of Schubert's favourite theme from the 'Rosamunde' entr'acte in the same key. The four pieces were published complete by Diabelli, in two books, as Op. 142, in 1838. The influence of Schubert's 'Impromptus' on novel trends in pianoforte composition during the nineteenth century has been unduly stressed. Until 1838, it will be seen, only two of them had been published, and although they are not, in fact, movements from sonatas, there is little to distinguish them from Schubert's smaller sonata movements, that is to say, from his lighter slow movements, minuets and finales. The ironical fact, in my own view, is that they influenced Chopin, Schumann and Brahms, if at all, in their *sonata* writing, rather than in their shorter, lyrical pieces.

On 26 December the new PF. Trio was performed at a 'Musik-verein' concert, and was given by Karl von Bocklet, Schuppanzigh and the 'cellist, Josef Linke. This performance doubtless inspired Schubert to make the final effort to give a concert of his own, and when, in fact, he did so, the PF. Trio in E flat was the chief item. The performance in December may also have inspired him to compose what was the last work of the year: a 'Fantasie' in C major, for PF. and violin, composed for Slavík and Bocklet. It is a full scale work, containing much vituoso writing for both instruments. But like the 'Rondo brillant' it fails to reconcile the claims of such technical display with those of his own genius. All four sections promise well at the start: the emotional undertones, the poised themes, the exalted atmosphere; but all too soon the rich embroidery begins and the music grows turgid. A set of elaborately decorated variations on his song *Sei mir gegrüsst* forms the third movement. At the first performance, in January 1828, Slavík was said to be unable to cope with the difficult part, and the piece failed to please. The 'Harmonicon' representative in Vienna was, for all that, again kind in his judgement: '. . . a new Fantasia for PF. and violin, from the pen of Franz Schubert possesses merit far above the common order.'

Reviews of this kind were frequent in the press of provincial Germany also, during 1826 and 1827. Before glancing at the four major works of the period, we might perhaps look at what Schubert's contemporary critics said about the music being published. The man who treated his work with the greatest seriousness wrote in the Leipzig 'Allgemeine Musikalische Zeitung'. He was

Gottfried Wilhelm Fink, a composer and writer on music, who had evidently taken a fancy to Schubert's Op. 21 (songs, including *Auf der Donau*) in 1824, and although not wholly approving, yet realised the young composer's gifts and appreciated the master touch in his music. Each successive work which reached his journal, Op. 42, Op. 39, Op. 59, was given the same serious regard, and the pages on Op. 42, the Sonata in A minor, are full of admiration. Finally, on the Sonata in G major, Op. 78, published and misnamed by Haslinger, he wrote a long and comprehensive study which was sensible and approving. Did Schubert see this review we might wonder? He would have appreciated the worth of the reviewer and enjoyed the well-considered praise. But a similarly named music journal in Frankfort dismissed the Sonata in a few lines; taking Haslinger's title as an indication that there were four separate pieces for the piano, it said of them: '. . . recommended for piano practice.' This Frankfort journal also reviewed regularly the Schubert song publications. It used a rather grudging tone, being unable to give up the basic idea in Germany of that day, that 'song' meant 'strophic song' and that there was something not quite *en règle* in Schubert's dramatic and richly wrought 'on-running' songs. Berlin was even more intransigent over the strophic song; but when the reviewer in the Berlin 'Allgemeine Musikzeitung' did encounter Schubert's use of that straightforward form, as in *Die Dioskuren*, he could not speak too highly of such settings. In Weimar and Munich, music periodicals reviewed the songs and spoke of them with moderate approval.

In Vienna itself there is seldom an independent voice to give us an insight into the reception there of Schubert's work, since most of the music critics were friends or partisans of his. But his songs were obviously popular with the general public, and his dance music was heard everywhere—even on the music-box mechanism of inn clocks.

VIII

There are, it has been suggested, four major works of this period—the String Quartet in G major, the Sonata in G major, the PF. Trio in B flat, all of 1826, and the second PF. Trio in E flat of 1827 (a year spent mostly in the composition of miniatures: songs, part-songs and piano-pieces).

The String Quartet in G requires four first-rate players in performance, and like the D minor Quartet, demands absolute unanimity of phrasing and interpretation between the first and second violins. It is music of the grandest, noblest order. The first movement ranks with the first movement of the C major Symphony of 1828 as one of Schubert's most successful essays in sonata-form. His method, in the quartet, the earliest definite and conscious use of it, is to write an opening theme of great breadth and nobility, which, we are persuaded, is more in the nature of an introduction since an obvious and energetic 'first theme' follows it at once. But as the movement proceeds and his purpose unfolds, we see the noble *motif* of the introductory bars assuming a greater importance. The 'energetic' theme is developed and worked in all kinds of imaginative ways, but above it, beyond it, as it were, is the majesty and power of the primary theme, lifting and ennobling the music. We find this 'double-theme' in other works of the last years, in the PF. Trio in E flat, in the String Quintet in C, in the last symphony, and in the second of the 1828 sonatas, the one in A major. It represents one aspect of the composer's artistic growth: early works display a double presentation of the one main them, the second more elaborate than the first, *cf.* the D minor String Quartet. This device grew into the finer, more satisfactory one we now consider. The String Quartet in G major opens with a held G-major chord which swells in a quick *crescendo* and breaks into rapid, G-minor figuration. This is repeated in the dominant key, D major. Its novelty is still a striking feature even today, when our ears are shocked by nothing. The apparent 'first theme', one of Schubert's loveliest inspirations, is now played by the first violin over softly thrummed chords in the lower strings, which move down through whole tones, G major to F major, F major to E flat major, and thence to G major:

Ex. 72

Schubert's huge extension of dominant tonality (D major) for the 'second subject' section of his exposition is achieved by exploring the subsidiary keys of F sharp minor, B flat major and B minor. A lyrical theme is heard in all three keys, combined with a rising and falling *arpeggio* played with *tremolo* bowing. The development section exploits all four of these expositional ideas in writing which is coherent and well organised—but on fire. Nothing in the exposition but is transfigured and glorified in the wonderful sweep and ecstasy of these pages. Themes having no connection in the exposition are brought together to produce new situations, new emotions, just as two characters in a play might encounter and set going a tense, unexpected development of the plot:

Ex. 73

The melodic tensions which Schubert can set up by unexpected harmonic changes and re-orientations in his themes are wonderfully realised in this movement, in, for example, bars 185–189, where a C flat instead of the normal C natural gives an aching unresolution to the melody. The tone-colour contrasts of the quartet, especially the rapid *tremolo* bowing set against the organ-like sounds of the sustained chords, show that Schubert was fully aware of his medium, and delighted with that one minor aspect of it. Broad, impassioned transitional episodes link the main sections of the movement; they have been described and quoted in the remarkable article on Schubert's tonality by Sir Donald Tovey mentioned earlier in this book. The *coda* to the movement might be read as a Schubertian 'Credo', for the music proclaims with no mental reservations at all his belief in the unity of the major and minor modes.

The slow movement in E minor is elegiac in tone, but contains the famous, almost notorious, episodes where classical tonality is completely thrown aside. Even if on paper Schubert's devices can be explained, in sound they are extraordinary. No attempt is made to placate the ear; while in the bass the strings move down from E minor to C sharp minor, and thence to B flat minor, the violin and viola reiterate a *staccato* phrase in an uncompromising G minor. There is a moving *coda* in E major, a foretaste of the Schubertian tranquillity of 1828, and in the key which was to embody that unearthly mood—his key of dreams and consolation.

The Scherzo, in B minor, is full of the rhythmic energy which animates the corresponding movement in the great C major Symphony, but the finale, similar in mood, and even in theme structure, is a little too superficial. The course of events had already been told, and told well, in the finale of the D minor Quartet. This time the tale does not grip. The best part of the movement is the C sharp minor passage, the theme shared between second violin and 'cello, in bars 322–354. This is in the mood of the Ernst Schulze songs of the period, and actually recalls one of them: *Ueber Wildemann.*

The sonata in the same key, written four months later, nowhere reaches the heights of the string quartet, but nowhere becomes as shallow as the finale of the chamber work. The expansive, hovering melody of the opening movement is built on a favourite sequential plan: a phrase in the tonic key followed by an almost identical phrase in the subdominant:

Ex. 74

So natural and spontaneous are the results of this plan that it was probably a subconscious creative 'kink' of his. The unpredictable nature of Schubert's development-sections is borne out by this sonata. What would Beethoven have made out of the above theme? We can partly answer this question because a similar theme opens his G major PF. Concerto, Op. 58. He would, for the purposes of development, largely ignore it, using, if any part of it were used, only the mere opening half-bar figure. But Schubert used the whole stretch of the theme in imitative patterns, played *fortissimo* and gaining in power until they are thundered out in majestic and wide-spread chords.

Ex. 75

Twice this huge crescendo is presented, but there are a number of significant changes of detail to be found in the second occurrence, for the climax and relaxation occur in keys so chosen that Schubert can return to the soft serenity of his recapitulation through a G minor to G major change.

Although the slow movement, an *Andante* in D major, is not a 'Theme and Variations', it has a remarkable resemblance to the variation-movement in the Sonata in A minor, Op. 42; there is the same song-like theme, and the same energetic, clangorous episodes in minor keys. The composer works at a scheme of rhythmic elaboration in this movement, and both themes are subjected to it; great variety is obtained within a short movement. The following quotation gives the outline of one theme's rhythmic development and evolution:

Ex. 76

The 'Menuetto', a stately B minor movement, is marked *Allegro moderato*. To bring out the full effect of Schubert's *appoggiaturas* the *moderato* indication must be carefully observed. It seldom is in performance. The 'Trio' is a lyrical contrast in B major, derived from the close of the 'Menuetto' in a flash of genius, and

appealingly beautiful in its miniature compass: one of the most
lovable passages which Schubert ever penned. There is the same
lowering of tension in the sonata-finale as there was in the string
quartet; we have a homely, tuneful movement, completely individual in that it proclaims its composer throughout, but with few
touches of poetry to lift it above its everyday level. One of these
touches is found in the theme in C minor, which is decorated by
short scale-like passages in a way prophetic of mid-nineteenth-
century styles.

The two PF. Trios do not, in spite of the similarity of medium,
suggest a unit in the way that the two string quartets of 1824, or
the three sonatas of 1828, certainly do. If the story of the pile-
drivers' theme is sufficient grounds for giving the earlier Trio the
date '1826', then something like eighteen months separated the
two compositions; in Schubert's life that was a reasonably long
period. The style of the first movement of the B flat Trio would
confirm the date (although alone it would be insufficient evidence). The main theme, a buoyantly lyrical and strongly charac-
terised melody, is played at the outset, and followed by a complex
modulatory episode based on a fragment from it, the triplet
figure in bar 2. Then comes its second presentation, not more
elaborate this time, but differently instrumented, a famous touch
of Schubertian charm:

Ex.77 *Allegro moderato*

The use of the piano as the singer, with the strings providing a
light background, is irresistible. The development has the same
underlying plan as in the G major Sonata just considered. The

T   B.S.

melody is given *forte* in the minor key, builds up imitatively to a big climax and then yields to the second contrasting subject played in a soft, *dolce* episodic style, just as in the sonata. Towards the end of the development section of this movement, there is a remarkable 'false start' to the recapitulation; listeners with no sense of absolute pitch would be quite taken in, although the key is G flat, not the orthodox B flat. It serves the same purpose as a similar trick in the sonata—Schubert can glide from G flat into the fresh and sunny tonality of B flat for the 'real start'. And once there we realise that the G flat passage was a transposed version of the first presentation of the theme (bars 1–25).

In the E flat Trio, the opening is likewise a bold, typical theme, with the three instruments in unison, but the ground-plan of this movement belongs to his later styles of sonata-writing; the unison theme is introductory and is followed a few bars later by the 'main theme' of the movement. The two themes are quoted here in outline only:

The second subject is devoted to two vigorous themes in B minor and C minor, although the essential unity of the whole exposition is obtained—perhaps, according to strict classical procedure, wrongly—by references to themes (*a*) and (*b*) above. Then, in a remarkable way, the *codetta* is launched with a quiet little tune, harmonised with all his resource, which seems at first hearing to be an entirely new idea:

But examined, it can be seen to unite elements from the two themes of Ex. 78: the rhythm of (*a*), the melody of (*b*). The *codetta* theme is used as the basis of a long-drawn development section, a complete break with his procedures hitherto. The essential union of (*a*) and (*b*) into the *codetta* theme is clear when the introductory theme logically emerges from it, ready for the recapitulation. Lack of dramatic contrasts prevents the movement from taking a place in the front rank of Schubert's first movements, certainly it cannot compare with the first movement of the earlier Trio. But the next two movements, an *Andante con moto* in C minor, and a canonic Scherzo in E flat, are much finer than anything in the companion work. The threnodic march of the C minor movement heralds the *Andante con moto* of the last symphony. The finales of both Trios hardly deserve all the derogatory adjectives usually bestowed on them. They are, it is true, entertainingly written: dance-like metres, and heart-easing melodies produce lightweight movements. But, to begin with, the craftsmanship is admirable. Light movements, like Schubert's two finales, are not found so perfectly articulated and structurally sound, in the music of lesser men. Nor could Schubert, it has been repeatedly said in these pages, produce, in 1826 and 1827, music without moments of depth, and beauty, and passing wonder. The episodes in D flat and G flat, in the finale of Op. 99, where the pianoforte rises and falls, *pianissimo*, through three octaves, are delicious; and the introduction in the finale of Op. 100 of the C minor theme from the *Andante* movement, is a tremendously impressive passage, and one of the earliest instances in musical history of such a 'cyclic' device, a device to become so dear to the 'Romantic' period in the next thirty years.

The Trio in E flat was completed during November 1827, and, as already recorded, its first performance took place the next month. Schubert, in those days, was a sick and dispirited man. The disease contracted five years earlier was inwardly and inexorably undermining his health. To the headaches of which he had complained in the letter to Marie Pachler were added giddiness and nausea. Twice that autumn he cancelled arrangements because of ill-health. The second of these occasions was a party given by Anna Hönig. The letter he wrote to her has only recently been discovered. Its contents were known and are briefly stated in the Schubert 'Documents' (page 681). Here it is published for the first time in English:

[Outside]   To Miss Nanette v. Hönig, *personal.*
[Inside]
  I find it very difficult to have to tell you that I cannot give myself the pleasure of being at your party this evening. I am ill, and *in a way* which totally unfits me for such a gathering. With the renewed assurance that I am extremely sorry not to be able to oblige you

I remain,
Yours faithfully,
Frz. Schubert

Vienna, 15*th Oct.* 1827.

His material prospects had never been so gloomy; he seems to have lost heart where operatic composition was concerned, for can we imagine the music for 'Der Graf von Gleichen' hanging fire in the way it did if his heart had been in it—he who had set 'Fierrabras' in a few months? And the Viennese market was almost saturated with his work. We have seen that the anecdote is false, which tells of the toast he drank on the night of Beethoven's funeral. Schubert never toasted the 'next traveller' along the road of death. But a salutation as gloomy as this, and as prophetic, occurs in a poem of Bauernfeld's; he read it to the assembled friends on New Year's Day, 1828, in the house where Schober and Schubert were living. It contains this remarkable verse:

> *The spells of the poet, the pleasures of singing,*
> *They too will be gone, be they true as they may;*
> *No longer will songs in our party be ringing,*
> *For the singer too will be called away.*
> *The waters from source to the sea must throng,*
> *The singer at last will be lost in his song.*

Within the year the 'singer' was, in fact, called away, and only his songs remained to recall his image to the friends.

VIII

1828

I

Bauernfeld's prophecy bore an uncanny resemblance to the truth, but life itself outdid the poet in giving that truth an air of ordained doom. The pieces of the pattern seem to fall carefully into place as we look at the last year of Schubert's life: it has the elements of closure, and like all endings, it promises many beginnings. His friends, all of them, even the estranged Mayrhofer, were in Vienna, and in touch with him again. There was no holiday, and he remained in Vienna the whole year; he did not leave the beloved city even for a few weeks in the neighbouring countryside. The pace of composing was forced; masterpiece followed masterpiece in staggering succession. The stimulus of creating this superb music gave him life as few men know it. Then, as the year waned, his friends departed. He took up lodgings with his brother Ferdinand. It was like a homecoming, and there his last, fatal illness was to overtake him. The work of composing never ceased; the feverish power of his genius which exacted this music and drove him to such spiritual exaltation, in the end gave him death. When it came, death was like an exhausted sleep.

During January the Schubertians met at Bogner's café for their evening convivialities. Schubert was not always present, but it is clear enough that his music was the attractive force which held the men together. The friction between Spaun and Schober occasionally produced open disagreement. The two men were temperamentally poles apart, and even in their response to the music of their friend, it has been suggested, that temperamental difference was most marked. The earnest thoughfulness of Spaun was frequently at odds with Schober's mercurial spirits. But their mutual love for Schubert kept them together. 'Through him', Spaun wrote of Schubert, 'we were all brothers and friends.'

Throughout the early months of the year they met frequently —often once a week—in Schober's rooms for the 'reading-circles', now resumed after a lapse of four years. Various books of prose and poetry were read, usually by Schober, whose experience as an actor was doubtless an asset. The literature chosen was chiefly the work of minor 'Romantic' authors such as Tieck, but Kleist, Goethe and Aeschylus also figured in the readings. At one period the poems of Heine's 'Reisebilder' ('Travel Sketches') were read, and Schubert must have been present, for all six of his Heine songs are in the group so entitled. He may have sketched some of them during the spring of 1828. The two settings of Leitner, *Winterabend* and *Die Sterne*, each a different picture of the night sky, were composed in January, and Schubert also sketched during the month the 'Fantasia' in F minor, which is today gradually winning the esteem it deserves, as his greatest work for PF. Duet. Schubertiads continued to be as popular as in the previous autumn, although the composer was not always present. 'Schubert kept us waiting for him in vain' wrote one of his admirers, 'but . . . Titze sang many of his songs so touchingly and soulfully that we did not feel his absence too painfully.' The last Schubertiad to be held in Spaun's lodging's took place on 28 January, for the forty-three-year-old lawyer had at length become engaged to be married. His fiancée was Franziska Roner, whom Franz von Hartmann was delighted to describe in his diary as 'very nice, cultivated and pretty'. The Schubertiad was held in her honour. There seem to have been no songs, but the PF. Trio in B flat and the Variations in A flat, Op. 35, were played; the first by Schuppanzigh, Bocklet and Linke, the second by Schubert and Gahy. The evening ended with dancing until the small hours. Spaun and Franziska were married in the Peters-kirche on 14 April.

During February Schubert was working on the C major Symphony. The month ascribed to it, 'March,' is written at the start of the full score; there must therefore have been preliminary work of an earlier date, and that this preliminary work was in an advanced stage is obvious from Schubert's letter of 21 February 1828 to the publishers Schott's Sons of Mainz. He mentioned in it a symphony, a completed work. This was in all probability the finished PF. sketch, begun at Gmunden in 1825, completed in Vienna by February 1828, and orchestrated in March. Later, presumably, in March, when the symphony was finished, he composed the setting of Grillparzer's poem *Mirjams Siegesgesang* (*Miriam's Song of Victory*). The music is for soprano and mixed chorus, but remains on modest levels of appraisement since the accompaniment was written for piano, not orchestra. It is a noble work, conceived on broad and balanced lines, with some vigorous and exciting passages when the text describes the Red Sea overwhelming Pharaoh and his host. The fugal treatment of the opening and closing choruses has been ascribed to the influence of Handel. The publisher Haslinger may have lent Schubert some of the oratorio scores of that composer: that he did so is purely conjectural. But we know that Schubert was reading and playing Bach's fugues from the '48', and the passages in *Miriam's Song* recall Bach rather than Handel. The cantata may have been intended by Schubert as the chief adornment of an ambitious project then engaging his mind. This was the organising of a concert consisting entirely of his own compositions. It would account for the piano accompaniment to the *Miriam* cantata—a practical issue. The concert evening was an ambition which had recurred to him at intervals for the past five years, but circumstances had not been favourable. Now, in this fatal year, obstacles melt away, and the dream becomes a reality.

We read in the Schubert records his petition of 6 March to the *Gesellschaft der Musikfreunde* for the use of their concert hall in the Tuchlauben premises. This was granted, and the concert, postponed from 21 to 26 March, was advertised in the Vienna 'Theaterzeitung'. Tickets at 2/6 each were sold by Diabelli and Haslinger, although the programme was headed 'Invitation to the Private Concert which Franz Schubert will have the honour of giving. . . .' The cantata, *Miriam's Song*, it is fairly obvious, was intended for the women's singing-class of Anna Fröhlich and the male-voice choir of the *Gesellschaft*, with Josefine Fröhlich singing the soprano solo part. Presumably it was not ready in time, for another setting of Grillparzer, the 'Serenade', which Schubert had composed for Louise Gosmar, was sung, and the men's chorus gave the long-drawn and rather uninspiring *Schlacht-gesang* (*Battle Song*), to words by Klopstock. This composition, for double chorus, seems to be a grandiose expansion of a former setting dating as early as July 1816.

The instrumental items were both, from a modern point of view, dubious choices: the first movement of a string quartet (called 'new' in the programme, and presumably taken from the work in G major of 1826), and the whole of the PF. Trio in E flat. The string quartet movement ranks with his greatest work, but it is anything but 'popular' in its appeal, and the PF. Trio, with its leisurely progress, and of elegiac sadness in some of its moods, is hardly a winning item. Vogl, accompanied by Schubert, sang two groups of songs, and a new song with horn obbligato, called *Auf dem Strome*, was performed by Ludwig Titze and Josef Lewy.

A packed audience, all ardent admirers of the composer and determined to make the evening a success, applauded each item with shouts and stampings. Schubert, his fellow performers, and his close friends, were all elated by the triumphant progress of the evening.

The concert was reported briefly in Leipzig, Dresden and Berlin, but it is almost unbelievable that the Vienna papers ignored it altogether. The advent of the virtuoso violinist Paganini three days after Schubert's concert claimed their entire attention. Fate, having with one stroke cleared the way for that concert, was not concerned that the fruits of it be fortunate, and there is an ironic touch about the incidence of the concert of Paganini. One reads in a contemporary reference these astonishing words: '. . . minor stars [i.e. Schubert] paled before the radiance of this comet in the musical heavens [i.e. Paganini]'. The concert was not forgotten by the people who had attended and the editor of the Vienna journal 'Musikzeitung', Johann Schikh, wrote on behalf of a number of them, begging Schubert to repeat the occasion.

He made £32 from the concert. Unless a good deal of the sum went in settling debts, it is difficult to know why he was unable to leave Vienna as the summer approached for a much needed holiday. He pleaded lack of money when declining two invitations from the countryside. The first was from Ferdinand Traweger, the friend with whom he had stayed in Gmunden during 1825. It was a generous invitation making it clear that Schubert could stay in Traweger's house for as long as he wished, and in order not to embarrass the composer he asked a nominal sum for full board and lodging: it was 8d. a day! The second was from the Pachlers at Graz, again, a generous and accommodating offer. There were probably others, for Jenger wrote to Marie Pachler that Schubert had received several invitations from friends at Gmunden. But a short excursion into the Wiener Wald at the beginning of June, to Baden and the Heiligenkreuz Monastery, was the only break that year. Schubert was accompanied by Schikh and Lachner. At Baden, where they spent a night, Lachner organised a friendly competition, and he and Schubert each wrote a fugue for Organ Duet, which they played on the Abbey church organ the following day. Schubert's manuscript has been inscribed by some unknown friend 'Baden, 3 June 1828'. His fugue is in E minor and was published in 1844 as Op. 152; it is a mild, but not unattractive, piece.

Another 'occasional' composition, which, like the E minor fugue, is not without a certain wan charm, is the choral song *Glaube, Hoffnung und Liebe*, finished during August. Schubert wrote it for the consecration of a new bell at the 'Minorite' Church of the Holy Trinity in the Alsergrund suburb; the church was becoming famous, since Beethoven's funeral service had taken place there. It was situated in the Alser Strasse, not very far from Schubert's birthplace. The music of the processional chorus, accompanied by wind instruments, is in a slow 6/8 tempo which vividly suggests the rocking swing of a huge bell.

Glimpses of Schubert, his friends and the Viennese scene during August, like scenes through a peephole, are provided by the diaries of the Hartmann brothers and Bauernfeld. Schwind's brother was at home and the group of friends read 'Faust' at Schober's home on one evening, play-acted Kotzebue's one-act satire 'Die Unglücklichen' at Bauernfeld's on another, and, on

most evenings, seated outside a favourite alehouse, 'Die Eiche',
near St. Stefan's Cathedral, watched the moon rise over the city.
At the beginning of September they all attended the première of
Bauernfeld's comedy 'Die Brautwerber' ('The Suitors'), which
had only a moderate success, but which Schubert found 'extraordinarily pleasing'. Soon after this Bauernfeld left Vienna, and
Schwind departed for Munich the next month. Mayrhofer, after
the brief appearance during the spring of the year, lost touch
with Schubert, and the marriages of Vogl, Kupelwieser and
Spaun meant an inevitable loosening of the ties between them
and the composer. The Hartmann brothers also bade farewell to
the capital and to the Schubert circle, leaving for Linz at the end
of August.

II

These summer months spent in Vienna were devoted to composition. Schubert, instead of recuperating from his work in the
spring, drove himself harder. His desire to initiate publication in
Germany, which could only be achieved by piano or chamber
works, led him to write several pieces of this sort in the early
summer. The great 'Fantasia' in F minor was finished in April
and played to Bauernfeld by Schubert and Lachner on 9 May. It
has, in the highest degree, all those characteristic qualities of the
composer which have endeared him to generations of music
lovers, and the 'Scherzo' section is one of his finest stretches of
writing for the piano. Two other duets, one of May and one of
June, although published separately and usually considered as
independent compositions may have been designed as movements
from a third 'Sonata' for PF. Duet, designed but not completed
by the composer. The first is the *Allegro ma non troppo* in A minor,
published by Diabelli in 1840 and given the catchpenny title
'Lebensstürme' ('Life's Storms'). It is a strong, vigorous movement in sonata-form, and contains what is, in the opinion of
many Schubertians, his loveliest melody. The melodic 'tensions',
discussed in the previous chapter as being so remarkable a feature
of the Schubert melody in the 1820's, lead, in this one, to some
fascinating shifts from key to key. The second duet would have

contributed, perhaps, the finale of the sonata. It is a 'Rondo' in A major, published by Artaria as Op. 107 a month or so after the composer's death. Schubert had written it for the publisher. Again, the melodic charm of the work is irresistible; Schumann, who thought this 'Rondo' one of Schubert's best compositions, has some remarkably interesting things to say of it (in a letter to Friedrich Wieck, 6 November 1829). In the last episode of the rondo (at the change to C major) Schubert uses the sequence-structure to achieve some most admirable harmonic and tonal effects, so new and, for their day, so revolutionary, that we can understand some of the concluding sentences in Schumann's letter mentioned above:

> I remember playing that very Rondo at an evening party at Herr Probst's, but at the finish both players and listeners stared at one another, rather at a loss to know what to think, or to know what Schubert meant by it all. . . .

In the letter which Jenger wrote on 4 July to Marie Pachler, warning her that Schubert and he would probably not, after all, be able to come to Graz that year, he added that the composer was in Vienna working at a 'new Mass'. None of the composer's manuscript sketches for this Mass, nor his fair copy, is dated, but it is evident from Jenger's letter that he had begun work on the Mass in E flat after his return from Baden in June. The music is for a quartet of solo voices, mixed chorus and orchestra. Schubert intended originally to 'figure' the 'cello and bass line for organ continuo, but changed his mind and struck out the words 'e organo' from his score. It is said that he meant the Mass for performance in the 'Minorite' Church; if so, the request to write a processional chorus for the consecration of the bell may be connected with his decision. The Mass was performed for the first time in the church nearly a year after Schubert's death, on 4 October 1829.

During August he completed a batch of songs on poems by Ludwig Rellstab. These were nine in number and Schubert may have intended them to form a kind of song-cycle: *Lebensmut, Herbst, Liebesbotschaft, Kriegers Ahnung, Frühlingssehnsucht,*

Ständchen, Aufenthalt, In der Ferne and *Abschied*. Schindler, in his reminiscences of Schubert, would have us believe that he found these poems of Rellstab among the posthumous papers of Beethoven, and that he handed them over to Schubert. Rellstab, years later, added a grace-note or two to the anecdote: he said that Beethoven had *asked* Schindler to give the poems to Schubert, and to suggest that he might set them to music. Dates, apparently so unimportant to these tale-spinners, will not square with the two stories.

The first two songs, *Lebensmut* and *Herbst*, are practically unknown. They were both composed earlier than the other seven. *Lebensmut* is considered a fragment, but is it actually so? A cursory glance at the song shows that Schubert's intention was to repeat the prelude of the song as a coda, although he has not written it out. This done we have a complete song, of a lively conception and much charm. Capell suggests that Schubert broke off because Rellstab's second stanza would not fit the music of the first, and this may be so: but there is no need to sing any more than the first stanza. The song is far too good to leave in obscurity. It was not published until 1872. The second song, *Herbst*, is an even finer work. The original draft was lost, and not until the song-volumes of the 'Gesamtausgabe' were practically completed, did a copy turn up. Schubert had written it during April 1828 in the album of the violinist Heinrich Panofka. It was published in the last volume of the songs in 1895. The stormy, E minor movement of the song recalls *Die Junge Nonne*. When the remaining seven songs were actually composed we do not know; the fair copy is dated 'August 1828'. They are as famous as their companions are obscure for they were published as the first part of the song series entitled by the publisher, Haslinger, 'Schwanengesang'. This so-called 'song-cycle' contains fourteen songs altogether, nos. 8–13 being six settings of Heine: *Der Atlas, Ihr Bild, Das Fischermädchen, Die Stadt, Am Meer* and *Der Doppelgänger*. The last song of the series was composed later, in October: it is *Die Taubenpost*, a setting of a poem by Seidl. This was added by Haslinger, without the composer's authorisation, surely to avoid the number thirteen; since it is actually Schubert's last song

anoforte, it rightly belongs there, at the close of
\e Heine songs were probably sketched and re-
luring 1828, from the time when Schubert had
·ing the reading-circles. But final touches, and
th   made in August. It is also possible that Schubert .   sh an opus consisting of the six Heine songs;
Spaun wrote in his reminiscences that Schubert was then going to
dedicate the collection 'to his friends'. With one possible exception
each of these six songs is a masterpiece of the front rank. The
assembling of the fourteen songs of the 'Schwanengesang' cycle
is due to the association of Ferdinand and Haslinger, after the
composer's death. They were not given an opus number and appeared in April 1829.

At the end of August Schubert took up lodgings with Ferdinand in his brother's new home. This lies to the south of the
Inner City and was, in Schubert's day, a new suburb, the street
in which Ferdinand's house was situated not even named. The
move was recommended by Schubert's doctor, Ernst Rinna, who
thought that the change of air was desirable. Schubert's health
was dangerously impaired. He had complained for the last year of
headache and nausea: his constant overworking, together with the
haphazard conditions of living and eating, which were his daily
existence, combined to bring him dangerously low. He probably
adopted the doctor's suggestion with relief.

His brother's house still stands today. The street is now called
the Kettenbrückengasse, and is situated in a district of populous
thoroughfares, open market stalls and food shops, and dingy,
tall apartment houses. The typically Viennese structure of Ferdinand's house shows a small courtyard surrounded by tall buildings. Schubert's room was on the right of the stairway.

As soon as he was settled in his new quarters he received the
last of a long series of letters, written throughout that year from
the publishers H. A. Probst of Leipzig and Schott's Sons of
Mainz. Both men had written to him, by an almost incredible
coincidence, on the same day, 9 February, offering to publish
songs and pieces for piano solo or duet. The prolonged negotiations with Schott came to nothing. The composer refused to be

brow-beaten into accepting niggardly fees for the proffered works. The vocal quintet *Mondenschein,* with an added PF. accompaniment, was sent to Schott's and retained by the firm, despite the fact that Schubert refused their offer of £3 for it. Three years after his death they published it—for nothing.

Probst accepted the PF. Trio in E flat, which had been so successfully received in the March concert. He gave Schubert £6 for it. The information imparted by Lachner to Grove that Schubert had received only 17/6d. for the Trio was an invention. The same source provides the false statement that Haslinger paid Schubert 10d. for each of the 'Winterreise' songs. Schubert wrote to Jenger during September saying that he had handed the second part of 'Winterreise' over to Haslinger for engraving. He had evidently completed these songs also during the autumn. The date ascribed to the second part of the song cycle is October 1827; but this is written above the fair copy of the first one, *Die Post,* and we do not know exactly when the others were composed. It is interesting to think that *Der Leiermann* may be contemporary with *Der Doppelgänger* and the other dramatic, Heine songs—or even later than they.

Besides the two large German publishing firms Schubert was approached by a more modest establishment, Karl Brüggemann, of Halberstadt, who also wanted pieces for piano solo or duet. These were to appear in a monthly album (a popular publishing device of the first half of the nineteenth century) called a 'Museum for PF. Music and Song'. Schubert expressed his willingness to contribute, but as in the similar affair with Nägeli, of 1826, nothing came of it, unless, as in the previous case, we owe to Brüggemann's invitation the sonatas of September 1828.

The few publications of 1828 in Vienna were an indication of his impossible situation there. He had reached a limit where Viennese firms were concerned. The first twelve songs of the 'Winterreise' were published as Op. 89: part I, by Haslinger, in January; three songs by Sir Walter Scott, *Lied der Anne Lyle, Gesang der Norna* and *Romanze des Richard Löwenherz* (the king's song from 'Ivanhoe'), appeared as Opp. 85 and 86 in March, from Diabelli; and the three well-known songs to poems by Goethe, *Der Musensohn, Auf dem See* and *Geistes-Gruss,* Op. 92, from Leidesdorf in July. Various songs had been privately lithographed and appeared during the summer. The only instrumental work of any importance is the 'Moments Musicaux' published in the spring by Leidesdorf as Op. 94. Moreover, when Schubert died there were very few publications impending: the group of songs known as Op. 108, containing the Schulz song *Ueber Wildemann*, was possibly designed by the composer, and, of course, there were the PF. Trio with Probst and the second part of 'Winterreise' with Haslinger which had yet to make their appearance. But his dealings with the Viennese firms were obviously declining, and after his death Ferdinand fought an unceasing but losing battle with publishers for nearly thirty years to get his brother's work accepted.

It is certain that his compositions, if not accepted by firms in Germany, were being sold there, and the reviews of some of his publications in the German papers were very definitely encouraging, and, on the whole, fair in judgement. The Leipzig 'Allgemeine Musikalische Zeitung' under its editor-reviewer G. W. Finck, was generous with space and praise in 1828, as it had been in 1827. In the three issues of 23 and 30 January, and 6 February, there were sensible and readable reviews of his songs in Opp. 79, 80, 81 and 83, and the 'Marie' Variations of Op. 82. The similarly entitled periodical of Berlin was, however, grudging in its praise of the Italian songs in Op. 83, and decidely satirical over the 'Winterreise' songs of Op. 89. This was for reasons already detailed; in Berlin 'German' song meant the strophic song and Schubert's bold schemes and modifications, and richly coloured accompaniments, disturbed and antagonised the Berliners. Munich and Dresden also reviewed various song publications, and if their praise is somewhat lukewarm, at least it is praise.

Besides letters from publishers, there were letters from distant friends and acquaintances who wrote of their admiration for his work and their appreciation of it. Johann Theodor Mosewius, music lecturer at Breslau University, wrote warmly of the two Müller song cycles. In an accompanying letter to Schober, their mutual friend, he added that he kept his pupils busy singing all the songs of 'Winterreise'. Princess Charlotte Kinsky, to whom

Schubert dedicated the four songs later known as Op. 106, wrote a cordial letter to him in July and enclosed a welcome gift of money. In Schumann's diary for 1828 there are numerous admiring references to Schubert, and this admiration was expressed in a letter to the composer which for unknown reasons he did not send. The long letter of 11 October from Anton Schindler, then in Pest, showed the same warm liking and respect for the composer's work and actually urged Schubert to go to Pest and repeat there the successful concert of the previous March.

But he was, by that time, wretchedly ill, his spirit beaten and almost broken. How is it possible to enter into the bleakness of his mood? Who can doubt but that he knew of his own powers? Could he who had composed the Symphony in C major, the Heine songs, the 'Winterreise', be unaware of the greatness of his genius? The utter indifference of the Viennese public towards those gifts must have induced at times a sick anger and frustration. And publishers like Schott's Sons, who halved his modest demands of payment for compositions, might be dealing with one of their own paid hacks. On 2 October he wrote desperately to Probst, who was still delaying the publication of Op. 100, the E flat Trio (and who went on doing so until Schubert was dead, so that he never saw a copy of his first publication outside Austria). This is his letter:

> I beg to inquire when the Trio will at last make its appearance? Is it that you do not yet know the opus number? It is Op. 100. I long for its appearance. I have composed, among other things, 3 sonatas for PF. solo, which I should like to dedicate to Hummel. I have also set several songs by Heine of Hamburg, which have pleased extraordinarily here, and finally written a quintet for 2 violins, 1 viola, and 2 violoncellos. I have played the sonatas in several places with much applause, but the quintet will be tried over only in the near future. If any of these compositions would perhaps suit you, let me know. . . .

The reason why he composed a String Quintet, and particularly why he chose so unusual a combination of instruments, is a mystery. The three sonatas were marketable, and in spite of the slightly unfashionable aura beginning to gather round the term

START OF THE C MAJOR EPISODE FROM THE RONDO IN A MAJOR, OP. 107
SCHUBERT'S FIRST IDEA, ALTHOUGH CANCELLED, CAN STILL BE READ

Deutsche Staatsbibliothek

'sonata' he could have disposed of them reasonably quickly. But a big chamber work was another matter. It is, of course, little more than guesswork, but as he was then living with Ferdinand, one wonders if there may have been a revival of family quartet and quintet playing to suggest the composition of this work. His use of two cellos in the quintet had been the practice of Boccherini; but the combination had fallen into disuse in the early nineteenth century, when 'String Quintet', following the practice of Mozart and Beethoven, meant two violas and not two cellos. Schubert had played some of the sonata movements at an evening party held in the house of Dr. Ignaz Menz, on 27 September, but he is no doubt exaggerating a little in his report of their success 'in several places' for he wrote his letter only six days after the completion of the three sonatas. But the Heine songs had evidently been performed and had made their mark. Probst replied to this letter, but expressed interest only in the songs.

There is a note of tragic irony in Schubert's remark that the quintet would be tried over only in the near future. This work, of such supreme beauty and eloquence, lay unperformed for many a long day; not until 1850 was a cut version played in Vienna and not until three years after that was it published by the firm of C. A. Spina.

III

A short break in the routine of work occurred in early October, probably on the advice of his doctor. Ferdinand and Franz set off from Vienna on a walking tour of the district to the south of the city, to Unter-Waltersdorf, and then on to Eisenstadt, where Haydn's grave was their objective. They may have been accompanied on this excursion by friends, but it is not known for certain if this were so. In Schubert's weak and enfeebled condition the exercise could have had no beneficial effect.

After he returned to his lodgings he received Schindler's invitation to go to Pest, but such a venture was out of the question, and Schubert had no time even to acknowledge the letter for shortly after its arrival his last, fatal illness overtook him. His pen was not yet put aside, however, and in his last two songs, the

u   B.S.

miracle of detachment astonishes again. *Die Taubenpost* is a love-song, merry and tender and passionate by turns. *Der Hirt auf dem Felsen* he composed for Anna Milder-Hauptmann, yielding at last to her entreaties to provide her with a virtuoso vocal piece; the text is a composite affair drawn partly from Müller and partly from Wilhelmine von Chézy. The shepherd pipes to the spring, and so the song is provided with a clarinet obbligato. It is no empty showpiece, as the Victorians assumed rather too readily, declaring emphatically that *Die Taubenpost* was unquestionably Schubert's last song, as though *Der Hirt* was something to be hushed up. It has been sung a great deal during the last thirty years or so and has proved to be full of endearing Schubertian melody and sentiment; even the final coloratura raptures at the return of spring are filled with pure joy. The song was copied by Ferdinand after his brother's death and conveyed to Frau Haupt-mann in September 1829 by Vogl. The very last productions are no fewer than four church compositions. He wrote a second, choral setting of the 'Benedictus', for his only published Mass, the one in C major, Op. 46; it was requested by Diabelli, the publisher of Op. 46, to serve as an alternative to the first setting if there were no soprano soloist available. There were two offer-tories, 'Tantum ergo' in E flat for vocal quartet, chorus and orchestra, and 'Intende voci' in B flat, for tenor solo, chorus and orchestra. The publication of these pieces gives yet another fan-tastic example to add to the chronicles of Schubert's published works. The two offertories were quite unknown during the nine-teenth century. When the volume called 'Smaller Church Works' was published in the 'Gesamtausgabe' (Volume 14), in 1888, a short sketch for the first one was found and printed as a supple-ment in that volume. A little later someone discovered Fer-dinand's copies of the vocal and instrumental parts for this 'Tan-tum ergo', and also for the other, then unknown, offertory, 'Intende voci'. Full scores were made up from these parts and the two works were published in 1890 by Peters of Leipzig. Later still, both of Schubert's own manuscripts were discovered, and these were published, as authentic versions, in the supplemen-tary volume (No. 21) of the 'Gesamtausgabe', in 1897.

The fourth liturgical work was the final version, with accompaniment for woodwind and brass, of the 'Hymn to the Holy Ghost', commenced in the previous May. The text is by A. Schmidl. It was published by Diabelli in 1847 as Op. 154. All these church compositions were doubtless written with the object of strengthening his hand if ever the opportunity came of obtaining a position in the imperial or city churches of Vienna; no primary impulse, such as drove him that month to compose *Die Taubenpost*—slight though it is, dictated the composition of the four church works. The chords move in harmonic clichés, *religioso*, and the melodies are solemn and conventional. It was an indifferent epilogue to the year's work but it would hardly be possible to provide such a series of masterpieces with any epilogue at all which was not something of an anticlimax.

IV

In reviewing that series it is fitting to start with the first one of the year, the great[1] C major Symphony. The work is by general agreement the summit of his achievement in music. It might be mentioned, in passing, that the symphony seems in an almost uncanny way to have been approached by numerous tentative preparations. Right through the body of Schubert's work runs the prophetic promise of the symphony. This is not the place to consider the numerous foreshadowings but they give the symphony a strange sense of fulfilment. It is a fulfilment in other meanings of the word. The Schubertian device of the main theme which 'broods' over the movement is nowhere so marvellously exploited as in the first movement, where the *Andante* horn theme of the opening bars gradually assumes a greater and greater authority until it is played at the close of the movement with the

---

[1] 'Great' is, strictly speaking, simply a translation of the German word 'gross', used conventionally in Schubert's day for works scored for full orchestra, or otherwise using full scale musical forces. It can also be translated as 'Grand', e.g. 'Grand Opera', 'Grand Mass'. It was retained in the case of this symphony, after the general disuse of the term, to distinguish the work from Schubert's 'Little' Symphony in the same key of 1818. Nevertheless, the other connotation of the word—witness the small 'g'—is always present, for the world of music thereby pays tribute to the greatness of the symphony.

full panoply of the orchestra. Nor does any other movement of Schubert's exemplify so well his ability to bring together contrasting ideas so that they generate new emotions and new patterns, nor his equally skilful power of fusing those ideas into a unified whole. There are perhaps five separate ideas which are so blended or opposed in the first movement and the development section leads the listener through wonderfully varied experiences, from light, lyrical pleasure to highly dramatic excitation of feeling. The famous trombone entries in the *codetta* leading to the development section have always been looked upon as recalling the listener's attention to the opening theme of the work. Strings and woodwind build up a patterned background, using material from the second subject, when the three trombones enter with their stately phrases. William McNaught, however, considers that these were 'freshly minted' by the composer, and not derived from the opening horn theme.[1] It is possible, surely, for them to be both: a sudden inspiration, the wonder of which is that it threw up phrases so remarkably like the generative theme of the movement. We have evidence here that the theme was hovering in Schubert's mind as he conceived the evolutionary progress of the movement. A small point, overlooked in performance, is the importance of the oboe phrases at the start of the *Allegro ma non troppo*; they complete the violin themes and should not be allowed to disappear into the background.

Schubert's chromatic harmony and the harmonic 'tensions' set up in his melodies have frequently been mentioned, so that it is pleasant, as a contrast, to be able to draw attention to the purity

[1] 'The Symphony', ed. Ralph Hill, London, 1949, page 157.

and charm of the clear, diatonic harmony in this movement (bars 268–274, for example).

The slow movement is the whole world of Schubert: his poetry and passion, his tender response, his technical gifts of thematic development, his use of the orchestra which is without equal in the sphere of non-pictorial music, and, above all, that subjective, intensely personal approach to the listener which woos and wins his affection. An episode which deserves the highest admiration in its technical handling is the A major recapitulation of the second theme, the one first heard in F major. The novel treatment of the brass instruments, that is, as utterers of poetic ideas instead of mere reinforcers of noise, won the willing tributes of the nineteenth century, although its orchestras refused to play the work. The child who conducted the *Stadtkonvikt* orchestra was the father of a man who became an absolute master of the orchestra as a medium for his thought.

The Scherzo is written in full 'sonata-form', an unusual scheme for that time, but one which elevates this section of the symphony to an importance which is hardly warranted, since a relaxation of tension would have been a welcome thing here. But the relaxation comes with the A major Trio, for here we listen to one of Schubert's sustained melodies, sumptuously harmonised and orchestrated.

The finale has been called a 'poem of speed'. It is a volcanic outpouring of music: neither the *tarantella* rides of the quartet finales, nor the lavishly written rhythmic and melodic episodes of the PF. Sonatas, nor the varied dance measures of the Octet and PF. Trios, contributed more than a trifle to this new and colossal movement. It exploits rhythmic patterns:

Ex. 81

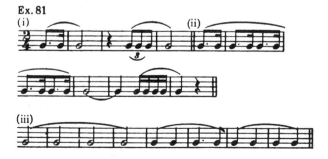

The differing lengths of these phrases will be noticed; the danger
of a monotonous, 'four-square' rhythm in the finale is avoided by
skilful uses of the irregular rhythms in the above example, and by
an overlapping of melodic phrases. Just as in the first movement
Schubert fused his melodic fragments into a new and varied
music, so in this movement he fuses his rhythmic elements.
Melodies, continually varied and modified, embody the rhythms,
and their combined counterpoints. In the development section
the use of canon and imitation between the subject themes is admirable on paper and electrifying in performance. At the close ot
this section there is the inspired, and celebrated swerve into E
flat major for the recapitulation. It is quite unorthodox, but inevitable, springing as it does from the Schubertian trick of passing to
a key a third below the tonic key, by two downward steps (G to
F, F to E flat). And the fact seems to have been missed by his
critics, that he was repeating the similar process by which he had
reached his development section (G to E flat) and achieving in
that way a remarkable tonal unity.

   Unity of another kind is obtained between the four movements
by the use in each one of a similar ascending and descending
motif, which is used in all four of them as a foil to the main theme
or themes:

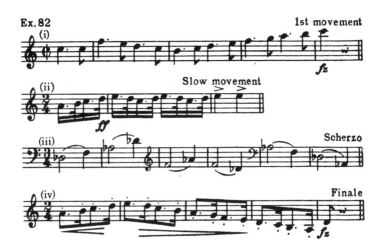

Schubert, as is well known, revised the symphony by erasures and alterations, after it was scored and completed. There was a good deal of preliminary revision too, and in nearly every case he strengthened and refined his melodic and thematic writing. He offered the score, as he had promised, to the *Gesellschaft der Musikfreunde*, and it is more than likely that he then sent the letter usually ascribed to 1826. There is no record of the work being rehearsed, but this must have been undertaken, and it was found too difficult. Schubert withdrew it and replaced it by his earlier C major Symphony. After his death it remained with Ferdinand until Schumann's historic visit to him on 1 January 1839. Then, at last, and because of Schumann's advocacy, the symphony was performed (in a considerably 'cut' version) at Leipzig on 21 March 1839 under Mendelssohn's conducting. The performance was part of the last subscription concert of the season at the famous Gewandhaus. The work was published in 1840 by Breitkopf & Härtel in parts, and in an arrangement for PF. Duet. Nine years later the score was published. The rejection of the symphony by the orchestral players of the *Gesellschaft* in the spring of 1828 was repeated in melancholy fashion again and again as time passed. In 1836, and in 1839, Viennese orchestras refused to play it. When Habaneck in Paris, in 1842, and Mendelssohn in London, in 1844, tried to rehearse the symphony, the players would not go on with it. There is no point in simply dubbing these men 'orchestral tyrants' as Grove did; there was a great deal to be said for them—ask any orchestral string player today (especially a cellist!) who has played in the symphony. The overall impression which we have of the symphony's greatness and sublimity takes no account of the sweat and boredom of string players coping with the work and obliged to play the same accompanying figure for bar after bar—running sometimes to lengths of over a hundred bars. William McNaught, in the essay already quoted, remarks with cogency: 'So the wheels go round, while we enjoy the journey. The players of 1844 could not know, as today's players know, that this was the whirring and breathing of a new creation!'

The first performance in England was a private one. It took

place at Windsor Castle in 1844 and was given at Prince Albert's instigation by his private orchestra.[1] He had obtained the MS. score and printed parts from Mendelssohn. In France the symphony was first given on 23 November 1851. Berlioz wrote of the performance: '. . . this Symphony . . . is, to my thinking, worthy of a place among the loftiest productions of our art.' Whether his compatriots agreed with him is doubtful, for the *second* performance of the symphony did not take place in France for another forty-odd years—on 17 January 1897.

Today criticism is stilled. But no other work of the period, of comparable greatness, has so divided opinion, and inspired almost malicious derogation as well as affectionate esteem.

Equally poetic uses of the orchestra, although possibly not so apt, touch the Mass in E flat with colour. This is his master work in the six settings of the Mass which he composed. The most exalted moments in the liturgical text had inspired the best music in all the earlier Schubert Masses, and did so again in the last of them: such passages as the 'Et incarnatus est' and the 'Crucifixus' in the 'Credo', the 'Sanctus', the 'Agnus Dei'; he responded to their appeal as ardently as ever, and with masterly results. In the 'Crucifixus'—a 12/8 setting in A flat minor—the trembling rhythms of the strings invoke a kind of shuddering horror at the picture of the crucified Christ, and the final cadence in A flat major after the prolonged preparation in the minor key is very moving. The 'Agnus Dei' is overpowering in its effect; orchestral and choral masses of sound are piled up into *fortissimo* climaxes which die away to a whispered 'miserere'. It is as if the burden of sin were too heavy and these 'miserere' interludes have the peace of exhaustion. The threefold 'Holy! Holy! Holy!' of the 'Sanctus' besieges the ear with the juxtaposition of key-changes: E flat major, B minor, G minor and E flat minor pass in the space of seven bars. The final 'Dona Nobis' achieves the same effect at the end of the Mass as the 'miserere' choruses of the 'Agnus Dei': it suggests the exhaustion which follows a paroxysm of grief. It will be observed that Schubert is attracted by the *humanity* of the

---

[1] There are, unfortunately, no documentary records of any kind, concerning this performance, in the Royal Archives at Windsor Castle.

words of the Mass, if that rather vague word may be permitted. The universal quality of the two great Masses of Bach and Beethoven, in which the sufferings and aspirations of man as symbolised in Christ are transcended into an act of worship is absent in Schubert's E flat Mass. Not the sin and suffering of mankind, but the Babe of Bethlehem, the dying and risen Christ, human adoration and the prayer for peace are the living images in his mind and in his music.

In considering the work of his last year it is difficult to avoid the belief that the composition of the songs of the 'Winterreise' had a profound effect on his musical sensibilities and techniques. The new, *intellectual* quality in the development sections of his movements, although there were signs of it before the composition of the song-cycle, becomes very noticeable, in the 'Lebensstürme' PF. Duet, and in the PF. Duet Fantasia in F minor, for example, as well as in the sonata-movements of the C major Symphony and the String Quintet. It derives from the styles and procedures in the 'Winterreise' songs such as *Die Wetterfahne*, *Auf dem Flusse* (this song particularly), *Irrlicht* and *Der Wegweiser*. Another feature which was born in the 'Winterreise' pervades the work of 1828: the tranquillity, the dream-like serenity of the *Lindenbaum*. It is found in the slow movement of in the Trio-section of the Quintet, in the slow movement of the Sonata in B flat, in the melodic interludes of the 'Lebensstürme'.

The use of the five stringed instruments in the Quintet has been discussed earlier. The blending of the tranquil emotion of the *Adagio* in this great piece of chamber music with the passionate outburst at the heart of the movement is achieved with a new assurance, and the 'wellnigh incredibly lovely sounds' evoked by the *pizzicato* decorative work of the first violin and cello combine to make this one of the loveliest *Adagios* in all music. 'I hold the very look on paper of this E major *Adagio* to be beautiful' wrote Richard Capell.

A word can be given here in connection with the end of the exposition of the first movement, where the double bar is reached.[1] This is what Schubert wrote:

[1] This was first discussed by Dr. Eric Blom, 'Observer', 4 May 1952.

In performances, the players often treat the dominant seventh in
the fourth bar above as if it were a 'first ending' chord, that is to
say, since they are not observing Schubert's repeat-signs, they
omit the chord altogether and pass from the G major chord in the
third bar to the diminished seventh in the fifth bar. This preserves
the soft tones of the whole passage, it is true, but Schubert obviously intended the *fz* explosion of the omitted chord to be
echoed by the *forte* chord of A major in the seventh bar of the
quotation. To leave out the chord in performance is a violation of
his intention and an arbitrary interference with his music.

The plaintive Trio-section, which foreshadows Bruckner, contains the deepest feeling in the whole work. It is of the same
essence as the 'Miserere' and 'Dona Nobis' of the E flat Mass, and
even nobler than they. It speaks vividly of the development of
Schubert's art, that this Trio, filled in previous works with the
slightest of material—air or Ländler—should be so profoundly
elegiac.

The last instrumental works of the year, and, accordingly, the
last he ever penned, were the three pianoforte sonatas, in C minor,
A major and B flat major. They are in a signally fitting manner his
last compositions, for Schubert was a pianist all his life. The very
first extant work of his that we possess is a pianoforte piece, and
before that there were variations and dances for the piano, now

lost. His friends knew him as a pianist, as a solo player, as a duettist, as an accompanist—rarely as a singer, never as a conductor. The long series of PF. Sonatas is richly epilogued in these three of September. The first, in C minor, is the most Beethovenish of his works, but in externals only, for Beethoven was always an abiding influence under the surface of his thought. This first sonata is full of 'hard sayings' especially in the chromatic episodes of the first movement. But how the thematic power of these passages gains from the harmonic 'tensions' set up in them!

Ex.84
(Outline)

The second sonata opens nobly with one of Schubert's 'gestures', and its humble beginnings are worth looking at. Sketches for all three of these sonatas are extant; considering that they are long, full-scale works, and that the sketches are ample preparations, the staggering industry of the composer seems beyond the capacity of normal beings. Here is his first idea for the A major Sonata —a *multum in parvo* passage without question:

Ex.85

The slow movement is a soothing cradle-song, but this, also, has a central episode which is chromatic and abstruse. The finales of the two sonatas are both extended movements. They teem with all manner of captivating ideas: the harmonic strokes of the C minor *Allegro* and the huge span of the music in the development section of the A major Rondo (*Allegretto*), being wholly admirable. But each concludes a sonata which is already of big dimensions, and so makes heavy demands on a listener's response. The position is not, however, made easier by well intentioned pianists who play these two finales at a breakneck speed in the hope that hereby the duration will be shortened. For the minute or two saved, most details of Schubert's thought and imagination are sacrificed.

The finale of the third sonata, in B flat major, is shorter, and although more in the composer's 'Impromptu' vein, achieves an equally acceptable music. This last sonata is a general favourite. The inspired and masterly use of tonality in the first movement, achieving an unconventionality of progression by the simplest of devices, was greatly relished by Sir Donald Tovey and led to one of his finest essays.[1] There is much in common between the first movement of the Sonata in B flat, and that of the G major Sonata, Op. 78, of 1826. Both use a broad dignified theme in the opening bars, and this is partnered by a lilting dance-tune later in the movement; and in both movements unexpectedly powerful structures are built up on these themes. But it is because the serene slow movement (in C sharp minor) and the finale rank as partners equal in greatness to the first movement, that we can award the palm to this last sonata as the finest which Schubert composed.

The 'Schwanengesang' is not, of course, a song-cycle in the accepted sense of the word. In comparing its artistic achievement with that of the 'Winterreise' a different standpoint is necessary. The whole of the 'Winterreise', it has been said, is greater than the sum of its parts, and the whole is supreme; but no individual song in the cycle approaches the two great Heine songs of the 'Schwanengesang'—those tragic vignettes, *Die Stadt* and *Der Doppelgänger*. In these fourteen songs Schubert's invention was never more vivid, more sanguine. The tragedy of the death of young genius becomes more poignant in the case of Schubert, for no other creator who died, as he did, so early in life, produced just before his death work so novel and challenging as we have in the 'Schwanengesang'.

The Rellstab songs are especially picturesque, and although, with the exception of *Aufenthalt*, none quite taps the depths in

[1] 'Music & Letters', London, October 1928.

Schubert, they are all very attractive and well known. Each one gave the composer a definite scene: a summer brook, a sleeping camp, night and the nightingale, storm-swept mountains; and a definite sentiment: contented or aspiring love, apprehension, despair; and to such verses Schubert instantly responded with songs of abiding value. The Heine poems intensify the emotion and give the scene greater reality. The sting of tears in the eyes, the salt sea-wind on the lips, the oppressive agony of frustrated love in the midnight watches—Heine creates life, not flights of literary artifice. The result is a series of firm, first-rate songs from *Der Atlas* to *Der Doppelgänger*. There is an extraordinary sense of Nature as a factor in man's tragedy—the sea as a symbol of grief and unhappy love in *Am Meer*, the mist pierced by the sun's ray as a picture of sudden self-knowledge in *Die Stadt*, the darkness of midnight, embodying the heart's loneliness, in *Der Doppelgänger*.

The titles of these Heine songs were provided by Schubert himself. It should be noted that he called the first song, not *Atlas*, but *The Atlas*; in other words, the poem is not about the mythical Titan who bore the world on his shoulders, but about a man bowed down with the burden of unrequited love. *Das Fischermädchen*, although a charmingly tuneful song, is perhaps the only one of the six not created *en un jour de largesse*. There is a deeper note of irony in the words than Schubert saw, or chose to see. This ironic, mocking tone in Heine, so appealing to English tastes, is not so well appreciated by German speaking races. In Heine the combination of Jewish descent and French sympathies is too much for the German critic. But in the last three songs Schubert catches the ironic note to perfection—the music reveals the suffering and the satire. With the incomparable *Doppelgänger* he inaugurated a new, and dangerous, way of composing songs, the 'recitative' song, in which the vocal line has the dramatic qualities of speech and in which all the genial elements of a song—melody and pulsing rhythm—are suppressed in favour of the predominating atmosphere and drama of the lyric. He should have placed a signpost on that path: 'For the genius only.' Too many indifferent composers have set forth on the path and lost themselves in unmusical morasses.

The Schubertian treasury of song begins with *Gretchen am Spinnrade* and ends with *Doppelgänger* and there is the same integrity of emotional feeling in both, and in all the span of great songs between. *Die Taubenpost*, Schubert's last song, belongs neither in body nor in spirit to either the Rellstab group or to the Heine group of songs; for all that it can inspire an affectionate response in the Schubertian. It is in the style of the 'Mill' songs and its syncopated, throbbing accompaniment represents the lover's heartbeats, not anxious as in *An mein Herz*, but keenly anticipatory. Sometimes the emotion changes and the lover pours out his confident love in a charming melody; the broken phrases, passing between voice and piano, speak of the rapt mind when he confesses that the *Carrierpigeon* of the title is *Love's yearning*, and are most imaginatively composed. The song proves, if proof were needed, that Schubert, as time passed, would have written another song whose character would be determined solely by the poem in his hands, not by the discoveries and revelations of the Heine music. But there was no more time left for him.

V

Amongst the performances of his songs and part-songs in Vienna in 1828 there was again a favourite piece: it was the setting for a quartet of female voices of Psalm XXIII. It was fatally apt; the shadow of death lay across the composer's path during that autumn. In the new district where Schubert lodged with Ferdinand, the water supply and drainage were far from satisfactory and in October Schubert contracted typhoid fever from infected water. His debilitated condition undoubtedly allowed the disease to gain so rapid a hold. The first signs that he was seriously ill appeared on 31 October when, with his brother, he visited a tavern situated near the old family home in the Säulengasse. He was nauseated by the fish he tried to eat, and from then onwards till his death he seems to have eaten almost nothing. For a day or two he worked on, and one of the most incredible events of his life must now be recorded. He arranged with the well-known theorist, Simon Sechter, to take a course of instruction in fugue, and even attended the first lesson, on 4 November, in the company of a fellow composer, Josef Lanz. What lay behind this fantastic decision? Was it the insistence of friends like Lachner, that he was a 'natural' composer, just because the overflowing abundance of his work did not fit in with their little scale of 'form'? Was it the report that his Masses did not please the Emperor, because they were not 'in the Imperial style'? Did he think to unlearn his genius, and absorb the talent for writing neat, contrapuntal fugues? Whatever the reason, he soon became too ill to continue with the studies and on 11 November took to his bed. It cannot have been easy for Ferdinand and his wife to be burdened with this sick man. Their apartment consisted of a large living-room and two small rooms, one of which was occupied by Schubert. There was also a twelve-year-old child Therese. Professional nurses were employed and Schubert's little step-sister, the thirteen-year-old Josefa, also helped to nurse him.

He wrote to Schober the well-known letter which is so moving to read, appealing for books, especially by Fenimore Cooper. It is odd for English readers to contemplate Schubert absorbed in those days of sickness with 'The Last of the Mohicans' and 'The Pilot'. Schober, perhaps remembering Schubert's behaviour to him in the days of *his* sickness, did not come near: he said it was because he feared infection. Bauernfeld, Lachner, Spaun, and possibly Josef Hüttenbrenner, visited the dying composer. With Bauernfeld Schubert discussed their projected opera, the 'Graf von Gleichen', but various incidents recorded by other writers in the nineteenth century as having occurred at this time are dubious. On 16 November two doctors, Josef von Vering and Johann Wisgrill conferred over the illness and diagnosed typhoid fever.[1] His regular doctor, Rinna, was himself ill at the time. Schubert's illness could not have been an uncomplicated business with the deep-seated trouble still present from the disease of 1822, and it is surely not a coincidence that one of the two doctors above, Vering, was a specialist in venereal diseases. One of the last tasks

[1] 'Bauchtyphus' in German, and translated erroneously by nearly all nineteenth-century biographers of Schubert in English as 'typhus fever'. The mistake would probably have persisted still had it not been for the investigations of Frank Walker into the question: see his 'Schubert's last illness', 'Monthly Musical Record', London, November 1947.

Schubert undertook was the correction of the proofs of Part II of the 'Winterreise', which was due to be published, and actually appeared a few weeks after the composer's death, on 30 December 1828.

The end was near. On 17 and 18 November Schubert became delirious and at times was restrained with difficulty in his bed. During his wandering he asked Ferdinand, 'Why do you let me lie in this black hole?' His room was dark and probably not particularly inviting during those mid-November days. At 3 o'clock in the afternoon of 19 November he died, turning to the wall with the words: 'Here, here is my end.'

The following day his father announced the death from the house in Rossau. On Saturday, 22 November, the body was taken to St. Josef's Church in the Margarete district and was there consecrated. Schober, at the request of the Schubert family, had written new and appropriate words to be sung to Schubert's melody for his poem 'Pax Vobiscum' and this was performed in the Margarete church. After the service the body was taken to the Währing suburb, and was buried in the cemetery there. Shortly before he died, Schubert, in his delirium, had whispered to Ferdinand words such as 'Beethoven does not lie here' and his family took them as meaning that he wished to be buried near Beethoven. Only two graves separated those of the two composers. The Währing District Cemetery is a small graveyard lying to the left of the Währingerstrasse as it leads out from the Schotten Ring of the Inner City. Today it is called a 'Schubert Park' and preserves still an air of peace and antiquity although the bodies of the composers have long since been removed to more honoured graves.

His family and his friends were half prepared for the tragedy of his end, but when it came the shock was great. Their emotions may be summed up in the words which Schwind wrote to Schober, when the news reached him in Munich on 24 November:

> I have wept for him as for a brother, but now I am glad for him that he has died in his greatness and has done with his sorrows. The more I realise now what he was like, the more I see what he has suffered.

And Jenger wrote to Marie Pachler at Graz:

> ... that I am still unable to conquer my sorrow over the death of my good friend Schubert, and have been feeling unwell since his death, Baron Grimschitz will likewise tell you.

The small possessions left by Schubert were valued at £6 and among them was some 'old' music. What this music actually was is not known: the designation 'old' suggests used, printed music. It was certainly not his accumulation of manuscripts, which were still at Schober's house in the Tuchlauben. His juvenilia would be in his father's house in the Rossau district, and the newly composed songs, string quintet and sonatas, of little worth in the eyes of the official evaluators, were not even inventoried. Shortly after Schubert's death, Schober transferred all the composer's manuscripts to Ferdinand's apartment in the Kettenbrückengasse.

The expenses of Schubert's illness and funeral were heavy for the pinched resources of his father and brother. From Ferdinand's detailed records we derive the fact that Schubert possessed nearly £5 at the time of his death, and the total money paid out for doctors, nurses, medicines and so forth, came to £13. The funeral and other posthumous expenses paid by his father increased this amount to £60. In seven months these debts were cancelled by the sales of his last compositions. From Haslinger, in December, Ferdinand received £15 as a first instalment for the 'Schwanengesang' songs; from Czerny he received that same month £10. Further fees followed from these two publishers, and from Diabelli, amounting to £20. In June he was able to submit an account to his father showing that he had received altogether £64 in publisher's payments. Ferdinand's biggest stroke of business was with Diabelli in 1830; this transaction must be considered in detail in the next chapter, but the sum of money involved can be mentioned here in connection with the other fees: it was £240. There was then no need for Ferdinand or Franz Theodor Schubert to have had any qualms about the funeral outlay in which they were involved. Nor was this the last of the incoming money. Ferdinand was his brother's heir by courtesy only; Schubert left no will. But his careful custody of the huge mass of manuscripts,

x

his ceaseless endeavours to publish the works, his efforts to interest editors and impresarios and conductors in the larger compositions, symphony, opera and Mass, cannot be ascribed entirely to cupidity. His love for Franz and his pity over the hapless fate of so gifted a brother, was undoubtedly the stronger urge.

There were memorial poems in Schubert's honour published in various Vienna journals, and soon the first obituary notices began to appear. A subscription fund to erect a memorial stone over his grave was opened under the direction of Schober, Jenger and Grillparzer, and a concert was organised by Anna Fröhlich to help the funds. It was held in the hall of the 'Musikverein'—where his own concert had been so successfully given a few months earlier—and amongst the items performed were *Mirjams Siegesgesang* and the PF. Trio in E flat. Sufficient money was raised to swell the subscription funds to the required amount, and the plan was put into operation. The memorial was designed by Schober and executed by the architect Christian Friedrich Förster. A bust of Schubert, perhaps based on a death-mask, was carved by Josef Alois Dialer, an acquaintance of the composer, and cast in iron; it was not bronzed over until a later date. Grillparzer wrote the much-criticised epitaph. He made one or two attempts at it, all of which show, first, that Schubert's reputation was almost entirely that of a song-writer; second, that he was a considered to have been cut off by death before he had accomplished anything of supreme value.

In July 1830 the memorial was completed, the bust—a very fine piece of work and a congenial likeness of the composer—installed, and pilgrims to the grave could read what Grillparzer had finally written of Schubert:

THE ART OF MUSIC HERE ENTOMBED A RICH POSSESSION
BUT EVEN FAR FAIRER HOPES

The Vienna journal 'Allgemeine Musikalischen Anzeiger' of 6 November, wrote of the memorial:

The tombstone is simple—as simple as his songs; but it conceals a profound soul, as they do.

And now the darkness descended. At the end of 1830 the
memorial had been erected, the vast bulk of his manuscripts was
stored on Diabelli's shelves, his operas, symphonies, and Masses
slumbered in the big iron chest which Ferdinand bought for safe
storage. His friends were scattered, and leading Viennese musicians, to whom he never meant very much, almost forgot the
humble composer who had moved amongst them. When Chopin
visited Vienna in 1829 and again in 1830, Schubert might never
have existed if we judge by what the young Pole found in the
musical life of the capital, and Karl Czerny, in the 'Reminiscences'
of his life in musical Vienna up to 1832 makes no single mention
of Schubert's name.

The slow gathering of light during the nineteenth century
until the noonday of his reputation in the twentieth, requires a
chapter to itself.

IX

HIS CENTURY AND OURS

I

When Schubert died, his unpublished manuscripts, an enormous number of them, lay in various places scattered about Vienna, Graz and Linz. His juvenile pieces, dating back to 1810, were still in the Rossau district, at the schoolhouse in the Grünetorgasse. The works of the 1820's were in the music closet of his rooms in Schober's house, in the Tuchlauben. Ferdinand in the Kettenbrückengasse apartment had the songs, the sonatas, the string quintet and the offertories, composed during the autumn just before the composer died. In a short time these three large collections were brought together and in Ferdinand's possession. It might be of interest to glance now at the whereabouts of other small collections of Schubert manuscripts in that November of 1828, of whose existence Ferdinand was probably unaware.

At Graz, the Hüttenbrenner brothers, Anselm and Josef, possessed between them a sizeable collection containing the scores of the 'Unfinished' Symphony, the operettas 'Claudine von Villa Bella', and 'Der Spiegelritter', the opera 'Des Teufels Lustschloss', the '13 Variations on a theme by Anselm Hüttenbrenner', numerous vocal trios, and several songs, including the 'blotted' copy of *Die Forelle*, and *Der zürnenden Diana*. Also at Graz were the scores of 'Alfonso und Estrella' and the 'Kindermarsch', both with the Pachlers. A second copy of 'Alfonso und Estrella' was in Berlin, in the Library of the Court Opera.

At Linz both Spaun and Stadler owned Schubert manuscripts. Stadler possessed quite a number of part-songs, including the *Ruhe, schönstes Glück der Erde* and the magnificent five-part *Nur wer die Sehnsucht kennt*. He also had the manuscripts of the early PF. Duet Fantasia in C minor (D. 48) and four solo songs, *Der*

Kampf, Thekla, Der Strom and *Das Grab*. Spaun had merely the parody called *Die Epistel* and the *IV Canzonets* said (but erroneously) to have been written for his wife.

Karoline Esterházy, at Zseliz, owned a number of Schubert manuscripts, most of them dating from 1818 and 1824, when Schubert was her music master. The instrumental pieces were the PF. Trio in E flat, several dances composed in January and October 1824, two PF. Duet Overtures, in C major and D major (the 'Italian' Overtures). She owned a few songs, *Blondel zu Marien, Abenlied, Ungeduld, Die Blumensprache, Das Abendrot* (composed for her father), and *Das Geheimnis*. Other song manuscripts were in the possession of various friends: Josef von Gahy (*Der Blumenbrief, Das Mädchen* and *Bertha's Lied*), Witteczek (the wonderful *Waldesnacht*), Schober (*Jägers Liebeslied*), Streinsberg (*Grablied für die Mütter*), and one Freiherr von Stiebar had been given by Schubert the fifth autograph copy of *Die Forelle*— the only one containing the 5-bar introduction. Two cantatas, *Gebet* and the *Deutsche Messe*, were also in private ownership: the first was with Baron von Schönstein, the second with the author of the text, J. P. Neumann. Karl Pichler, Holzer's successor at the organ of the Liechtenthal Church, had come into possession of the manuscripts of the Mass in C and the *Tantum Ergo* (D. 460). The female choruses *Gott in der Natur* and 'Psalm XXIII' were owned by Anna Fröhlich, and numerous PF. Solos, e.g. the '*Allegretto* in C minor' written for Ferdinand Walcher, were to be found in the albums of various friends of the somposer. One 'album', belonging to Therese Grob, contained several songs, among them three which have remained unpublished to this day.

It is impossible to trace the separate destinies of all these little collections. Some of the manuscripts are now lost, some are still in private possession, some are in the national libraries of London, Paris, Berlin, Vienna and Washington, others are in the hands of dealers. But the fate of Ferdinand's manuscripts, although mysterious in a few cases, can be given with some certainty. He gave several of them to his son Karl; these were unfinished fragments or sketches, which one can hardly avoid noticing were unsaleable.

The sketches for the 'Unfinished' Symphony and for the Symphony in D of 1818 were among Karl's manuscripts. A year or so after Schubert's death, in early 1830, the publisher Anton Diabelli finally accepted Ferdinand's offer of the Schubert manuscripts: it was the second time he had approached Diabelli, the first being only a few days after his brother's death. The publisher, for the sum of £240, acquired so numerous an assemblage of pieces, that publication of them went on regularly, if spasmodically, right through the nineteenth century, and on into the twentieth. Today, nearly a hundred and thirty years afterwards, publication is still incomplete: eighty pieces remain to be published.[1] As far as bulk alone is concerned, in the mere number of musical compositions, Schubert outdid all his peers, even though his life was shorter than that of any of them. Ferdinand's catalogue as he revised it for his offer to Diabelli is given here:

A. All the solo songs in his possession.
B. Pianoforte music, comprising:
    1. *Adagio* and Rondo, for PF. and String Quartet [*recte* 'Trio'],
    2. Sonata for PF. and Arpeggione,
    3. Three Sonatinas for PF. and Violin,
    4. Sonata in A, for PF. and Violin,
    5. Set of Variations,
    6. Sonata in D (composed at Gastein),
    7. Four Sonatas,
    8. Fugue in E minor, PF. or Organ Duet.
C. Chamber music, comprising:
    1. Trio for violin, viola and 'cello.
    2. Nine String Quartets,
    3. String Quintet in C,
    4. *Adagio* and Rondo in F, for PF. Quartet [identical with B. 1],
    5. Concerto in D, Violin and Orchestra,
    6. Octet, for 2 violins, viola, cello, bass, horn, clarinet, bassoon.

His concluding paragraph gives the items which were excepted from the sale: 1. the Operas, 2. the Oratorios, 3. the Cantatas

[1] See Appendix II.

with full orchestra, 4. the Part-songs, 5. the Symphonies, 6. the Overtures, 7. the Masses. The whole catalogue is not a complete record of the items which changed hands, even if allowances are made for an understandable generalisation, and Ferdinand must have reconsidered the exceptions above, for he later included the part-songs, the overtures, and some of the cantatas with orchestral accompaniment. Quite apart from the unspecified songs, there were numerous PF. Solos and pieces of chamber music not given in the catalogue. An attempt is made here to supplement the rather broad lines of the statement with a few details. The songs sold to Diabelli numbered approximately 250. They were published as follows: 137 songs in 50 sets or volumes ('Lieferungen') under the general title 'Nachgelassene musikalische Dichtungen' ('Posthumous Musical Poems') between 1830 and 1850; another 17 songs published with opus numbers between 1850 and 1867; from the rest many were sold to the firm of J. P. Gotthard in Vienna, which published another 50 or so between 1868 and 1872. A few more were purchased piecemeal by various firms up to 1894, but the bulk went to Breitkopf & Härtel for publication in the song-volumes of the 'Gesamtausgabe' (1894 and 1895).

The 'PF. Music' section mentions a set of variations and four sonatas. The variations were those of 1815, known as 'Ten Variations in F' (D. 156); the sonatas were three of 1817, in A flat, B major and A minor, and one of 1823, in A minor (D. 784). It is ironical to see Diabelli receiving, at last, this Sonata in A minor, which Schubert had withdrawn in a fit of dudgeon in the spring of 1823. Other items of pianoforte music not mentioned by Ferdinand, although they were passed on to the publisher, are these: *Adagio* in D flat, Rondo in E major, Fantasia in C minor (D. 993) and several Minuets in various keys.

Amongst the items of chamber music there are nine string quartets. These are as follows: (1) in C minor, 1812; (2) in B flat, 1813; (3) C major, 1813; (4) in B flat, 1813; (5) in D major, 1813; (6) in D major, 1814; (7) in B flat, 1814; (8) in G minor, 1815; (9) in G major, 1826. Besides these nine there were two others, unnamed by Ferdinand. They were (*a*) a quartet in C major (D. 3) and (*b*) a quartet in C minor (D. 103). When Diabelli bought these eleven quartets they were all complete. Between 1830 and 1890 three of them—all written on loose leaves—had disintegrated: the fifth of the nine above, in B flat, and the two unnamed quartets. The missing movements of the quartet in C major have been recovered, but those of the other two quartets, in B flat and C minor, were irretrievably lost.[1] All that remained of these two quartets has now been published; of the B flat Quartet there were the first movement and the finale, and these were published in the 'Gesamtausgabe' in 1890; of the C minor Quartet, only the first movement (*Grave* introduction, followed by an *Allegro*) survived and was published in Vienna in 1939.[2]

Additional unnamed pieces include several part-songs for male voices, among them the powerful setting of Goethe's 'Gesang der Geister über den Wassern' with its sombre accompaniment for bass strings; a number of liturgical works such as the offertories of October 1828, and the 'Magnificat' in C, of 1816; and numerous orchestral overtures including the two 'Italian' Overtures in D and C of 1817, the third overture of that year, in D, the overtures to 'Alfonso und Estrella' and 'Fierrabras', and the very early overture to the play 'Der Teufel als Hydraulikus'. Strangely enough, there were also in this large collection of pieces some sketches for an early overture (in D major) and the first of all his symphony sketches, based on this very overture, and dating, in all probability, from *Stadtkonvikt* days; these sketches were almost certainly included by error, for they were quite unpublishable, and of no interest to such a firm as Diabelli's. Slowly, as the century wore on, piece by piece made its appearance. At some time in the 1840's Diabelli handed over several manuscripts of compositions which had been published to his son-in-law, Josef Greipel, organist at the Peterskirche, Vienna. Greipel died in 1897 and his manuscripts were purchased by the Vienna *Nationalbibliothek*. Apart from these most of the manuscripts are still in private possession, quite a large number still in the hands of the

[1] See page 20.

[2] The manuscript of the two published movements of the String Quartet in B flat has recently seen the light after many years of obscurity. It is in the possession of J. H. Farrer, Haslemere.

Cranz brothers, the last successors to Diabelli in the publishing business.

Ferdinand was left with the scores of all his brother's operas and other stage works, all his Masses, his symphonies and his oratorios, numerous small works not considered in the sale to Diabelli, and all the duplicate copies made by Schubert. He sold the 'Reliquie' Sonata in C major and the Symphony no. 5, in B flat, to the Leipzig publisher Whistling, in July 1842. Two years later, in 1844, he was visited by the well-known collector of autographs, Ludwig Landsberg, and sold to him a number of the smaller manuscripts. These included the first movement (a duplicate manuscript) of the 1817 Sonata in E minor. Landsberg bequeathed his Schubert MSS. to the Berlin State Library. In 1859 Ferdinand died. His collection of manuscripts, the still unpublished symphonies, operas, Masses, and so forth, he left, not to his son Karl, but to his nephew, Eduard Schneider, the son of his, and Franz's, younger sister Theresa. Schneider was a lawyer whose offices were in the Tuchlauben. The Schubert autographs were stored in the roomy cupboard of his sanctum and it was there, in 1867, that Grove and Sullivan were shown them. As a custodian Schneider was conscientious, and fully aware of the value of his inheritance. There had been some talk in the city about his unsuitability as the guardian of such a treasure, and this imputation he much resented. On 10 March 1861 he wrote to Johann Herbeck, the well-known conductor of the Vienna 'Philharmonic' Orchestra;

> ... there is no cause for any art-lover to regret that Schubert's manuscripts have come into my possession.

Nor was there. In course of time, they were all purchased by Nikolaus Dumba, and after publication in the volumes of the 'Gesamtausgabe', Dumba bequeathed them, either to the Library of the *Gesellschaft der Musikfreunde*, or to the *Stadtbibliothek* (City Library) in Vienna. The sketches, given away by Ferdinand to his son Karl, were also bought by Dumba and from him they too reached the *Gesellschaft* Library.

Two other important collections of Schubert manuscripts in

Vienna must be mentioned in conclusion. They were the copies he had sent to the publishers Haslinger and Artaria, both of whom kept the music after they had published it. Other publishers, as we have noticed, destroyed it. Artaria's possessions found their way chiefly to the Berlin State Library; amongst them is the Rondo in A major for PF. Duet, Op. 107. But Haslinger's manuscripts, including the priceless 'Winterreise', and the 'Impromptus', are still, in the main, in private possession. The autograph of the Sonata in G, Op. 78, however, is in the British Museum.

II

If we view the progress of Schubertian publication, performance and scholarship during the nineteenth century, we find that there are two epochal years. The first closes the forty or so years after his death, during which time, with no external aids at all, no propagating societies, no advocating critics or performers, his music had to make its own way into the hearts of the coming generation; in 1864 the first full-length biography, that of Kreissle von Hellborn, was published in Vienna, and within a twelvemonth the 'Unfinished' Symphony was discovered and performed. The second climactic year is 1897, the centenary of his birth, when with the last volume of the 'Gesamtausgabe' his total major output was at last available in print, and it became obvious, with the close of a century's sifting and assessment, during which the perishable had vanished from music, that Schubert's reputation as a great master was expanding yearly and striking ever deeper roots.

In the first of these periods, up to 1864, his songs, naturally, kept his name alive, although the more contemporary values and idioms of the songs of Schumann, Robert Franz, Loewe, and hosts of song-composers now forgotten, left Schubert no longer unchallenged in his own field. In the few years following his death publication of his work was comparatively plentiful. As Grove had written: 'Death always brings a man, especially a young man, into notoriety, and increases public curiosity about his works.' The collection of songs called by Haslinger 'Schwanengesang' was followed by the *Trout* Quintet, Op. 114, the PF.

Sonata in A major, Op. 120, and the two PF. Duets, Fantasia in F minor, Op. 103 and Rondo in A major, Op. 107. By the end of 1829 these instrumental pieces, together with twenty-two songs, brought his published works to Op. 120. Nine works followed in 1830, including the PF. Sonata in E flat, Op. 122, the two very rousing marches for PF. Duet, Op. 121, two ill-assorted String Quartets, in E flat (1813) and E major (1816), Op. 125, and the song with clarinet obbligato, familiar in England today as *The Shepherd on the Rock*, which Schubert had composed just before his death for Anna Milder-Hauptmann. The String Quartet in D minor, and Psalm XXIII for female voices appeared in 1831. A few volumes of the 'Posthumous Musical Poems' had also been published. Public curiosity was satisfied, and publication almost ceased. The three Sonatas for PF. and Violin, called 'Sonatimas', were published as Op. 137 in 1836, and two years later the 'Grand Duo' in C major, Op. 140, the cantata of 1828, *Mirjams Sieges-gesang*, the early Mass in B flat, and the last three PF. Sonatas appeared. For the next six years or so there was nothing. Schubert had wished to dedicate the last three sonatas to Hummel, but by 1838, when they were published, that famous pianist-composer was dead. Diabelli decided, aptly enough, to dedicate them to Schumann. Soon after the honour thus paid to him, to-wards the end of 1838, Schumann visited Vienna for the first time. Quite casually, according to his memoirs, he remembered that Ferdinand Schubert was still living there, and on impulse he visited him. It was on New Year's Day, 1839. In spite of the enormous number of manuscripts which Ferdinand had sold to Diabelli, there was still the greater part in his possession, and when the lid of that iron chest was lifted Schumann must have been staggered at the quantity of music lying there. He looked at the symphonies and appreciated at a glance the value and im-portance of the great C major Symphony. Ferdinand was per-suaded to copy it and send the score and parts to Mendelssohn in Leipzig. The outcome of all this is well documented in the Schu-bert annals. Mendelssohn gave the symphony on 21 March 1839. Even in its 'cut' version the work was considered to be rather long; but its success was unquestionable. A year later Breitkopf

& Härtel published the work, in parts.[1] This was Schubert's second important publication outside Austria.

Schumann was, at that time, the editor of the Leipzig music journal 'Neue Zeitschrift für Musik', and he published in the issue for February 1839 several Schubert documents which he had received from Ferdinand: *My Dream*, the poem which Schubert wrote in September 1820 called *Der Geist der Welt*, and the pitiful cry *Mein Gebet* of May 1823. In addition four letters from Schubert were printed for the first time: one of them being the very first he wrote; it was to Ferdinand from the *Stadtkonvikt*. Schumann also persuaded Ferdinand to write a series of biographical articles on his brother; these important sources of information on Schubert's life were published in the 'Neue Zeitschrift' between 23 April and 3 May 1839. They conclude with a catalogue of compositions, arranged chronologically, containing several items which later biographers would have done well to observe, for many misdatings could then have been avoided.

Ferdinand hoped by his catalogue to draw the attention of publishers and public to the store of works still available. The occasional appearance in those years of new publications by Schubert, containing works of the magnitude of the 'Grand Duo' and the three 1828 sonatas, as well as the many small, charming songs, kept the composer's name before the public, even if that public's interest was not very active, but there was no response whatever to the catalogue, in spite of Schumann's added appeal, and his offer to act as an intermediary between owner and publisher. In 1842, the attempts made by Leopold Sonnleithner and Alois Fuchs to find the lost cantata 'Prometheus', even by advertising in the Vienna 'Musikzeitung', provoked Schumann into writing this paragraph:

> ... if only the unprinted things of Schubert, which he is known to have composed, could be brought to light! For instance, in the library at Berlin, there is a grand Opera ('Alfonso und Estrella') and in Vienna over fifty works of still greater value. These things cannot

---

[1] See 'The Discovery of Schubert's C major Symphony', by Otto Erich Deutsch. 'Musical Quarterly', New York, April 1953.

print themselves: those whose chief business it is ought to give themselves some trouble, that the world may at last come to a full and correct appreciation of the value of Schubert.

The songs published in the 'Posthumous Musical Poems' continued to appear regularly, but it was not until 1845 that two more instrumental works were published: the Sonata in B major, Op. 147 and the *pastiche Adagio* and Rondo, Op. 145. But soon after that period of silence the activities of two musical organisations in Vienna renewed general interest in his work and gave a fillip to the publication of it. To one of these organisations *Schubert* was a golden name: it was the 'Association of Male Voice Choirs' ('Männergesangverein'). His choral part-songs for male voices are not known today, but they were loved and admired then. In 1847 a congress of these choral societies was held in Vienna and a whole-hearted and enthusiastic resolution was passed by all the members to hold a Schubert Festival Concert on 19 November, the anniversary of his death. Gustav Barth, son of Schubert's friend Josef, was the conductor, and a varied programme of chamber works and part-songs was given. The second of the two organisations was a famous String Quartet team, whose leader was Josef Hellmesberger; he and his colleagues gave a session of chamber music concerts in Vienna annually, the first in 1849; the concerts continued for many subsequent years. Hellmesberger was a member of a famous Austrian musical family, and his quartet of string players achieved international renown as sensitive interpreters of the classic string quartet. From time to time he brought forward the Schubert chamber music, first the two published quartets in A minor and D minor, then also the unpublished works, the String Quintet in C, the String Quartet in G major, the Octet. Hellmesberger's efforts would not win our admiration today. He gave the Schubert compositions with heavy 'cuts', and with passages from other quartets interpolated. Nevertheless the compositions were undoubtedly successful and publication slowly followed the concert performances: the G major Quartet, Op. 161, in 1852; the Quintet, Op. 163, in 1853; the Octet, Op. 166, in 1854.

Again the stream of publication dried up, having awakened

little other than local interest. Eight years passed, with practically no publication of any importance. In 1862 the 'Reliquie' Sonata was published, a year afterwards the early String Quartet in B flat appeared as Op. 168. But the years of obscurity were past. In December 1864 Kreissle's important biography of the composer made its appearance. Its full, circumstantial detail, and the admirably complete catalogues of printed and unprinted work, classified into various sections, songs, PF. music, orchestral music, and so forth, placed the whole vague business on to a scientific and easily consultable basis. The book was not, however, entirely without preliminary studies, and we might now glance at the work of Kreissle's predecessors which led to his achievement.

III

Ferdinand's biographical essays have been mentioned. They were the first to appear after the phase of the 'obituary-biography' had passed. In the year following Schubert's death there had been four of these obituaries, by Bauernfeld, Leopold Sonnleithner, Mayrhofer and Spaun. Each year that passed produced an occasional report of performances of Schubert's compositions, or reviews of his published works, but between 1829 and Ferdinand's 'From Franz Schubert's Life' of 1839 there was nothing of substance. In 1840 Anton Schindler's biography of Beethoven was published; it contained a few anecdotes referring to Schubert, but none of them is at all reliable. A year later Wilhelm von Chézy and Franz Grillparzer both published work in which they related memories of their dead friend and his music. Two Viennese musicians, Alois Fuchs and Ludwig Neumann, were both busily collecting material for a life of Schubert and the former compiled, in connection with his projected biography, a 'Thematic Catalogue' of Schubert's works, seeking the collaboration of Ferdinand in that particular task. Neither project came to anything. The next biographical work of any size was written by Schindler and published in the 'Niederrheinische Musikzeitung' of March 1857. As biography it is valueless, containing no new facts but much dubious anecdote, for instance, the story of Schubert's application for the post of assistant conductor at the Kärntnertor

Theater. But Schindler did give in connection with his biography a long, chronologically ordered catalogue of Schubert's works. This was much fuller than Ferdinand's, since Schindler, in 1831, had had access to Diabelli's purchases of Schubert MSS., and his list is valuable and authentic. Here then was a dated catalogue which could have saved later biographers many a crass error. As late as 1907 Ludwig Scheibler drew attention to this forgotten catalogue made by Schindler (which was 'often ignored', he wrote) and pointed out that the dates given there for these three works:

1. String Quartet in E flat, Op. 125: no. 1, 1813
2. String Quartet in E major, Op. 125: no. 2, 1816
3. PF. Duet Sonata in B flat, Op. 30, 1818

were much more plausible than those attributed by the editors of the 'Gesamtausgabe' volumes, and other writers.

The biographical material gathered by Fuchs and Neumann was acquired by Ferdinand Luib, a Viennese scholar and musician, who set about the task of writing Schubert's life with exemplary thoroughness. He got into touch with all surviving friends and acquaintances of Schubert—some whose connection with the composer was very slight—and sent them short questionnaires and appeals for information. His plan never materialised, but from among the many answers he received, those of the Hütten-brenners, Stadler, Bauernfeld, Anna Fröhlich and Ebner are still preserved, although unpublished, and contain plenty of supple-mentary though hardly vital information. The 'Luib' letters are preserved in the Vienna *Stadtbibliothek*. Finally, the biography was undertaken by a man great enough to sustain the interest and labour necessary for such an enterprise, Heinrich Kreissle von Hellborn. Appropriately enough, when we realise the preponder-ance of lawyers and law-students in the Schubert circle, Kreissle was a Viennese lawyer, who held high office in the Austrian Court's Department of Finance. A fine musician, and a director of the *Gesellschaft*, he was the ideal man for the task. His biography has not been dimmed by the passing years, at least, it should not be considered as entirely set aside by subsequent work. It is still an encyclopedic mine of information. Naturally, in the course of a hundred years, much more information about the composer and his music has seen the light and Kreissle's artistic judgements were based upon imperfect knowledge and an insufficient realisation of Schubert's true stature. These deficiencies he shared with all musicians of that day. But as a source book for the lives and personalities of the men and women who surrounded Schubert, as an account of the composer's music and manuscripts, as a picture of the mid-nineteenth century and its attitude to the man and his music, it is an invaluable book. It had been preceded by a 'Sketch'; Kreissle wrote a short biography in 1861 which was published serially in the Leipzig music journal 'Die Signale für die musikalische Welt'. This sketch provoked Spaun's wonderfully intimate study of his friend entitled: 'Some Observations on the Schubert biography of Kreissle von Hellborn'. This study was not published however, and so, unfortunately, had no bearing on Kreissle's final work.

IV

In France and England we find, perhaps understandably, nothing like the interest in Schubertian performances and publication as in Austria and Germany, mild enough there. His songs made their way and won a lasting esteem in both countries. In 1831 the great dramatic soprano, Wilhelmina Schröder-Devrient sang the *Erlking* in London and it was published that year by Wessel & Co. This London firm then began a serial publication called 'Series of German Songs' and by 1839 thirty-eight of Schubert's songs had appeared in it. It was in that year that the very famous passage was printed in the 'Musical World' expressing suspicion at the number of Schubert songs pouring from the press when, it said, 'one would think his ashes were resting at peace in Vienna.' One thinks, ironically, in reading this passage today, of the vast treasures still awaiting publication when those words were penned, and of the surprise of the writer if he could have been told that *three hundred songs* were yet to appear. Wessel included in his 'Series' songs such as *Der Wanderer, Ave Maria, Die Forelle, Die junge Nonne* and so on. They were spoken highly of in contemporary journals, but the performances of them would probably bring a wry twist to the mouth today. There was always the insufferable Victorian inability to leave anything alone, if it were not immediately of the present, as we have seen in the case of the Hellmesberger Quartet performances. When Margarete Stockhausen at a London concert on 13 February 1840 sang *Gretchen am Spinnrade*, this was her text:

> *Let me weep again,*
> *My heart is sore,*
> *Since Damon hath left me*
> *For evermore. . . .*

and in the programme the words are said to be '. . . by Mr. Oliphant, imitated from Goethe'. The 'Musical World' pronounced the song to be '. . . a very pretty German melody by Schubert'. But the instrumental works made no headway at all in England. The Overture to 'Fierrabras', given in June 1844, was dubbed by the 'Musical Examiner', 'an absolute nullity,' and Mendelssohn's complete failure that same year to persuade the orchestra even to rehearse the great C major Symphony for one of the Philharmonic Society's concerts in London has been discussed. John Ella performed the 'Death and the Maiden' Quartet and the two PF. Trios, Opp. 99 and 100, at the 'Musical Union' Concerts of 1848, and occasionally an Impromptu or one of the 'Moments Musicaux' was included in the programmes of London pianists. But it is depressing to come across a very denigatory account of his pianoforte works by J. Davison in the 'Musical World' of 9 February 1850. This is full of the usual clichés of the partially informed writer on Schubert, and is particularly hard to stomach in its context—an adulatory discussion of the supremacy and eternal values of Mendelssohn's 'Songs without Words'. Joachim wrote from London on 22 May 1852 to Liszt:

> Schubert is regarded here as an upstart in instrumental composition and people are inclined to doubt his fitness for work in this branch.

When August Manns undertook the conductorship of the concerts given in the Crystal Palace, in 1856, he decided to introduce

Y   B.S.

the great C major Symphony to the English public. It was given
in two parts on 5 April and 12 April 1856. The programme announced this dichotomy with these words:

> Though often performed and much admired in Germany Schu-
> bert's Symphony is never heard in this country; the cause is, doubt-
> less, its great length. In order that this may not be felt, the first three
> movements only will be given today, and on Saturday next the
> *Andante* and *Scherzo* will be repeated with the closing movement of
> the composition.

August Manns persuaded the secretary of these concerts to come
and listen to the music of the symphony at rehearsal, and that was
how George Grove first heard the music of Schubert, and when it
first took hold of his imagination and won his allegiance.

In France both chamber music and songs obtained a fairer
hearing than in England. As early as September 1830 the *Trout*
Quintet was performed in Paris. The two great string quartets,
and the PF. Trios were heard there before they were in England.
The songs also were much more popular in Paris than in London.
This was due in part to the singing of the famous tenor Adolphe
Nourrit, who had been first attracted to Schubert in 1833 by
hearing Liszt perform his arrangement of the *Erlking*. Nourrit
sang Schubert's songs in the Paris salons for the next five years
until his death in 1839, and won countless admirers for them.
Nourrit was a friend of Chopin. At his funeral service in Mar-
seilles, Chopin, returning from the ill-fated sojourn in Majorca,
played the Schubert song *Die Gestirne* on the cathedral organ. In
that same year the Paris firm Simon Richault published an 'Album
musicale de François Schubert' and another publisher, Maurice
Schlesinger, started a series of song-volumes on 7 July 1839. By
17 December, when Volume 8 appeared, the total number of
songs published was 185. Schubert's 'Lieder' were considered in
those days by Parisian critics to have killed the 'Chanson' or
'Romance'. This assertion, very debatable then, is today no longer
true. The 'Lied', originating in Schubert and culminating in Hugo
Wolf, is nowadays a dead form, and the 'Chanson', the 'Romance'

and the 'Ballad', so vigorous before Schubert, are as vigorous today.

It is ironical to have to record the fact that much of the continuing popularity of the Schubert songs in France during the 1840's was due to the song *Adieu!* This had been composed by August von Weyrauch and published in Paris in 1824; but somehow or other it had become associated with Schubert's name, and although it was of the very type of 'Chanson' already considered as 'killed' by Schubert, its popularity was widespread. The words are excessively sentimental and well calculated to appeal to the shallower type of music-lover. Weyrauch re-published *Adieu!* in Berlin in 1846 with an indignant preface calling attention to the misattribution of his song; he added that the style of the melody alone should have been enough to make it readily identifiable as *his* work and not Schubert's!

By 1850 the number of songs printed in Paris reached the astonishing total of 367; this was keeping pace with Germany and Austria and there must, by then, have been simultaneous publication in all three countries. But no greater success attended the attempts in those days to procure a performance of the C major Symphony in Paris; at rehearsals conducted by Habaneck in 1842, the orchestra simply refused to go on with the work. Not until 23 October 1851 was the symphony given in Paris. This was, at least, five years before the London performance, but even so, later than two already given in America: Boston, in 1849, and New York, in the spring of 1851.

In Vienna a plaque had been affixed to the walls of the Birthplace. The ceremony took place on 7 October 1858 and was organised by the 'Männergesangverein'. Ferdinand died a few months afterwards on 26 February 1859 and his death again brought to public notice the large amount of unpublished work passing into the keeping of his nephew Eduard Scheider. In the October of 1863 the bodies of Beethoven and Schubert were disinterred, their remains were measured and photographed and they were re-buried side by side (but still in the Währingerstrasse Cemetery). The biography of Kreissle, the discovery of the 'Unfinished' Symphony, its subsequent performance, and the publication of the important Mass in E flat: all these incidents were cumulative. The forty years of obscurity and neglect and hard won recognition for anything but his most popular songs were over. During the next forty years the light brightens and his reputation gathers strength and stature in overwhelming measure.

V

The appearance of Kreissle's great book produced a spate of reminiscences by all kinds of people who had known Schubert, and who felt, possibly, that their knowledge of him had not been sufficiently drawn upon for the compilation of the composer's biography. Often the connection between Schubert and these tellers of tales was extremely tenuous and in a few cases has been greatly exaggerated. Moreover, if the truth be told, many of their anecdotes were inventions, and can be demonstrated as false by comparison with associated documentary evidence. Since the many biographers of the composer, writing between 1864 and 1947 (the date when Deutsch published his Schubert 'Documents') have, in all innocence, woven these anecdotal reminiscences into the fabric of Schubert's life, it is proposed to deal here with the false informants and their inventions. There are six chief offenders: the brothers Hüttenbrenner, Anselm and Josef, Franz Lachner, Josef Doppler, Anton Schindler and Benedikt Randhartinger. The two Hüttenbrenners have figured in earlier chapters and have made there a poor showing as custodians of Schubert manuscripts. The fundamental trouble lay in Anselm's deep-seated jealousy of Schubert's growing reputation, and resentment at what he considered the musical world's perverse unawareness of his own gifts. The ambivalent relationship—a professed veneration and love for a composer who was his friend, and the unspoken envy of that composer's gifts and the spread of his reputation, produced a morbid, unbalanced state of mind. Josef, fond of his older brother, and loyal to his aspirations as a composer, shared Anselm's resentment and sometimes spoke bitterly against the love shown for Schubert's songs when his brother's, he held, were equally admirable. Towards the end of his life Josef became weak in mind, but continued to write about Schubert and Anselm, his brother, in letters which are almost incoherent. From Anselm Hüttenbrenner we have the fantastic story of Schubert's visit to the dying Beethoven in March 1827. The composer, from his deathbed, is supposed to have said: 'Anselm you have my mind (Geist), but Franz has my soul (Seele)'. Schubert's visit to Beethoven is recorded by two untrustworthy witnesses and there is no other evidence that he was ever in the company of Beethoven. On the contrary, Schubert's own statement has been mentioned in an earlier chapter—he told Spaun that he had never met, nor spoken to, Beethoven. Hüttenbrenner's story was designed to boost his own status. It was related in a biographical sketch of him written by Karl von Leitner, the poet, and published in the Graz 'Tagespost' of June 1868. Most of his reminiscences of Schubert, written for Liszt's and Luib's projected biographies, must be checked against existing documents before being accepted: they are all subtly coloured by the prevailing desire to deflate Schubert and inflate himself, although both processes are carried through with a deceptively mild pen.

Josef is responsible for the story, already quoted, that Schubert composed the Overture in F, Op. 34, in his rooms in three hours; and that on the manuscript (non-existent today) Schubert recorded the fact and added '. . . and dinner missed in consequence'. There are more fanciful decorations to this story. Josef also reported Schubert's great admiration for various compositions by his brother Anselm, the Requiem Mass in C minor, for example, which was chosen for performance in the Memorial Service after Schubert's death.

More seriously misleading than the Hüttenbrenner anecdotes however, because they have affected the attitude towards Schubert's compositional methods, are those of the other men. Josef Doppler, a friend of Schubert's youth, with whom he had little to do after 1818, was in touch with Kreissle and passed on several rather sensational stories based on half-remembered reports of carelessly told news. He gives another version of the anecdote mentioned above concerning the hastily written overture, cheapened by circumstantial additions. The composer is supposed to be returning from a performance of 'Tancredi'. He resents his friends' praise of Rossini's music, saying that it is the easiest thing in the world to write overtures like Rossini's. His friends take him at his word, and promise him a glass of good wine if he will write such an overture. Thereupon he sits down . . . and so on. This time, however, it was the 'Italian' Overture in D major which he produced. Doppler, of course, had no realisation of the craft of composition, and no idea of Schubert's seriousness of purpose in his vocation. He is responsible for the similar story of the composition of *Hark! Hark! the Lark!* in the beer-garden at Währing. This 'dashing-off' of songs and overtures is the non-musical person's idea of how a composer goes to work. Doppler's story of the break between Schubert and Salieri is as follows. Salieri cut out and corrected all the passages in the Mass in B flat which reminded him of Mozart and Haydn. Schubert came to Doppler with the defaced manuscript of the Mass, flung it down angrily, and said as he did so that he would have nothing more to do with Salieri as a teacher. The Mass was written in 1815; the manuscript is in the British Museum, available for anyone to see that there are no alterations or defacements of the nature indicated by the story. There was no 'break' with Salieri; the association merely ended as all pupil-teacher relationships eventually end. And that was certainly later than 1815. Schubert was, of course, not aware of how Doppler would one day tell these stupid tales, but some words he once wrote to Ferdinand have, to our ears, an ironic ring:

> I merely marvel at the blind and wrong-headed zeal of my rather clumsy friend Doppler, whose friendship does me more harm than good. (29 October 1818.)

Benedikt Randhartinger attended the *Stadtkonvikt* in the years following Schubert's leaving it. He claimed a much closer relationship with the composer than he actually enjoyed and decorated it with fanciful stories. The best known one deals with the inception of the song-cycle 'Die schöne Müllerin'. According to this, Schubert called on Randhartinger, then the secretary of Count Ludwig Széchényi, and being left alone for a moment, picked up a book of poems. He became interested, pocketed the book, and left before Randhartinger returned. The next morning he proffered several of the 'Müllerin' songs, already completed, as a peace-offering for what he had done. Here are the facts: the first songs of the 'Müllerin' cycle were composed in the summer (probably August) of 1823; Randhartinger's appointment as the Count's secretary was in 1824. The two dates cannot be reconciled to give the story any veracity. In the same way Randhartinger invented the account of Schubert's composing *Der Zwerg* in the few minutes while he kept his friend waiting for a walk. Another story of those 'dashed-off' compositions which will not bear the light of truth.

Either from Randhartinger, or from Franz Lachner, came the tale of the toast drunk at the 'Mehlgrube' inn on the night of Beethoven's funeral. It was first recorded in Kreissle's biography (Vol. II, page 269). Schubert's true movements on that memorable evening are recorded in the diaries of the Hartmann brothers. He was not at any time in the company of Randhartinger nor Lachner, nor did he visit the 'Mehlgrube' inn. Lachner, an associate of the composer in the years between 1823 and early 1828, wrote in 1881 some dubious stories about the composer, and passed on several more, by word of mouth, to Grove. His written reminiscences contain an absurd anecdote. It tells how Schubert was inspired by the sound of a coffee-mill to write the first theme of the D minor String Quartet. This, wrote Lachner, was early in 1826. Again, incompatible dates give him the lie. He based the date of his story, naturally, on the date given everywhere in 1881 for the commencement of the string quartet. Schubert's manuscript, discovered years afterwards, shows the beginning of the quartet to date from March 1824.

Lachner is responsible, too, for the 'locked drawer'—a story of Schubert's composing, thrusting the finished work in a drawer, locking it, and then forgetting all about it. It is an apt story of a man like its inventor, whose composition was a mere decoration of a busy musical life, but utterly unbelievable of a working composer like Schubert, who lived by selling his work. In the late 1870's (probably 1878) Grove's friend C. A. Barry visited Munich.

Grove begged him to get all the information on Schubert he could from 'old Lachner', who was then conductor of the Court Opera. The tales Barry received included the one just mentioned, another that Haslinger paid Schubert 10d. for each of the 'Winterreise' songs, and that he received from the publisher H. A. Probst, of Leipzig, the sum of 17s. 6d. for the PF. Trio in E flat, Op. 100. But Lachner's crowning effort is his statement to Barry about the compositions of the first twelve of the 'Winterreise' songs. 'Half-a-dozen', he remembered, 'were written in one morning.' This, after fifty years, shows a good memory. It is true that Schubert composed six or seven songs on one day in his 'teens. They were short, very lyrical songs, of no great moment. Examination of the autograph manuscript of the 'Winterreise' songs in question reveals a very different state of affairs and suggests days of work.

Several 'incidents' in early biographies of the composer originate with Anton Schindler. He was much addicted to the 'Romantic' period's ideal of a composer: a divinely-inspired, Byronic figure, who could strike noble attitudes of defiance, or prophetic utterance, or even, on occasion, of self-abnegation. His story, for example, of Weber giving the score of 'Euryanthe' to Beethoven, and praying him to make 'such alterations as he pleased' has been quite discredited. Yet his similar inventions about Schubert still linger on in modern biographies of the composer. The distorted story of Schubert and the Kärntnertor Theater conductorship is gradually disappearing; not so the visit to Beethoven in 1822 with the score of the 'Variations on a French Air', Op. 10, under his arm. We need not discuss whether or not Beethoven, as Schindler said, pointed out a fault in the harmony to the utter discomfiture of Schubert, for we know that the two composers never met. And Schindler's invention here is probably matched by a similar invention over the alleged remark of Beethoven: 'Truly in Schubert is the divine spark!' A favourite anecdote, first told by Schindler, tells of the efforts of Schubert's friends to persuade him to prepare and revise his compositions more thoroughly, more in the manner of Beethoven with sketches and modifications. Their efforts on the stubborn composer, applied evening after evening, were in vain. Schubert would sit down and resentfully say to them: 'Go it, I beg you!', implying that he was ready to suffer, but would ignore, their imprecations. This is the way in which Schindler tries to account for what he considered the lack of 'science' in Schubert's work, a view so dear to mid-nineteenth-century opinion. Who among Schubert's friends, one might ask, would have done this upbraiding? And there is another question that suggests itself: Was anyone, outside of Beethoven's closest circle, aware of his compositional methods in the early 1820's? It is extremely doubtful if any of Schubert's friends and associates knew of them. Schindler knew nothing of Schubert's own methods and preparation. He, like Lachner, was inclined to exaggerate the closeness of his friendship with Schubert, and some such thought was at the back of his mind when he invented the incidents connected with the composition of the songs in the 'Schwanengesang'. Details were given in the previous chapter, but the continuation of Schindler's story shows its falsity. Two days after he received the poems, Schubert took the completed settings of *Liebesbotschaft*, *Kriegers Ahnung* and *Aufenthalt* to Schindler, so we read. These songs were completed in August 1828, when Schindler was living at Pest.

There are other stories, too numerous to mention, which bear the same stamp of spuriousness. But one of these stories must, in concluding the dismal count, be refuted. It originated with Baron Schönstein. He said that Vogl took a recently composed song of Schubert's, transposed it into a more suitable key, and a fortnight afterwards put it in front of the composer. They tried it over together and at the close Schubert is supposed to have said: 'A good song. Whose is it?' Schönstein told the story to illustrate the popularly held idea that Schubert was 'clairvoyant', by which was meant that he composed in a state of hyper-physical, trance-like excitement: a kind of unknowing vehicle for the Muses who forgot his work when it was out of his system. It is a view commonly held amongst the more primitive music-lover, and even fostered by the more theatrical type of composer. It is perhaps hardly necessary to add that Schönstein, when pressed, could not remember *which* song it was. I have suggested elsewhere that if there is any truth in the incident at all, then Schubert was uttering a mild rebuke. He well knew what Vogl's 'transpositions' entailed: embellishments, and ornamentation of all kinds in the vocal part. 'Whose is it?' in that case would mean: 'Is the song mine—or yours?'

These tales are, in themselves, trivial and each alone not worth bothering about. But the cumulative effect of them is tremendous. What a picture they create: a composer who could throw off composition after composition without thought or revision, in a transport, and who would listen to nothing or nobody in his obstinate determination to pursue his own course. It is a false picture, and against it Schubert's true friends continued to protest in vain.

VI

Kreissle's catalogue of unpublished works brought about a result which Ferdinand Schubert, Schumann and other friends, urging the point in the 1840's, were unable to do. It awakened people's interest in the 'rich treasure' which Grillparzer, in his epitaph for Schubert, said was buried with the composer. He was almost telling the truth. The store was yielding, year by year, its 'rich treasure', and after the discovery of the 'Unfinished' Symphony and its subsequent publication, things at last began to move. One of the most amazing events in the record of Schubert's posthumous recognition is the outburst of publication and republication in Leipzig in the years 1868–1870. Leipzig had always been favourable to Schubert. From the days when Fink reviewed his songs in 1827 and 1828, on to the performance of the C major Symphony, and, later, to Schumann's warm-hearted advocacy of his songs and sonatas, there had always been a welcome there for his work. In 1868 every music publisher in Leipzig—and there were many such—began a series of song-volumes, besides republishing the three song-cycles. Piano arrangements of his symphonies and chamber music, and re-issues of that chamber music, were on sale, and liberally advertised in all the journals. New compositions, as well as old, were published, and these include 'Lazarus' (1866), the 'Quartettsaatz' in C minor (1870), the 'Arpeggione' Sonata, the String Quartets in D (D. 94) and G minor (D. 173) (1871), the Mass in A flat (1875).

In 1874 Gustav Nottebohm published his famous 'Thematic Catalogue' of Schubert's works. It was claimed to be 'of the printed works' ('Thematisches Verzeichniss der im Druck erschienenen Werke von Franz Schubert') but there were substantial supplements giving the unpublished works as well. The book was in three main sections, (a) Works with opus numbers, 1 to 173: (b) the 'Posthumous Musical Poems', fifty volumes; (c) Works published without opus numbers. The third part of a supplementary section gave a fairly full list of the yet unpublished music, based mainly on Kreissle's lists. There were also lists of Schubert's publishers, portraits, and books about him. It was an invaluable reference-book for the Schubert student and presented in an easily accessible form the material collected by three predecessors in that field—Diabelli's catalogue of 1851, Kreissle's, in the biography, of 1864, and the lists given by Reissmann in his biography of 1873. Nottebohm performed his task admirably, and today his book is only superseded because of the fuller, more accurate, and chronologically ordered catalogue of Otto Erich Deutsch.

The decade between 1880 and 1890 was the period of the 'Critically Revised Complete Edition' (the 'Gesamtausgabe'). Breitkopf & Härtel of Leipzig had produced these editions of the works of Beethoven, Mozart, Haydn, Schumann and Chopin and other less considerable figures. In 1884 the decision was taken to produce a similar 'Collected Edition' of the works of Schubert. It was a vast undertaking since much of the work would be published for the first time, and for sheer bulk it would exceed all the others. An editorial board was formed including such men as Brahms, Hellmesberger, Ignaz Brüll and so on, and, as a kind of 'General Secretary', Eusebius Mandyczewski. This was a most happy choice, for Mandyczewski was a musicologist, thorough, capable and industrious. Between 1884 and 1895 the volumes were slowly published, and Masses, Operas, Symphonies were at long last available in print. The supreme achievement of the edition, and it is due to Mandyczewski's efforts, is the ten volumes of songs. These, in spite of certain opinions to the contrary, were given chronologically, and whenever Mandyczewski found more than one version of a song he published it. The amazing number of Schubert's songs—already a source of wonder in the volumes published by other firms, which included as many as 367—was now found to be 603: two hundred or so published for the first time.

For the centenary of Schubert's birth, 1897, Breitkopf & Härtel published a 'Supplement' Volume which brought the total number of volumes to thirty-nine. The 'Supplement' contained all kinds of compositions, some fragmentary, some which had turned up after the appropriate volume had been published, for instance, the String Trio in B flat of 1817, some which were alternative versions of works already included in previous volumes, and some which were sketches for finished work. It is, for the Schubert student, a fascinating collection of pieces.[1]

Although arrangements of the early symphonies for PF. Duet had been published in the 1860's, no curiosity or desire to hear them in their original form was aroused. The fourth symphony, in C minor, because of its title 'Tragic', inevitably won more attention than the rest. The slow movement was published in score, and the whole work had been performed in Leipzig on 19 November 1849—a death anniversary—from manuscript parts. The sixth symphony, the 'Little' C major, had been performed as early as 1828 and it, too, was given in Leipzig soon after the performance of the 'Tragic' Symphony. In the case of the 'Little' C major Symphony it was felt, no doubt, that being the last of the early symphonies it was therefore the best: a surmise, unfortunately, which the merits of the work do not confirm. The general inferiority of these two best known symphonies produced the same effect upon public opinion as, earlier, the PF. Trio in E flat had done, and no attempt was made to perform the other four early symphonies. Brahms was 'Artistic Director' of the 'Musikverein' in 1873, when the famous 'World Exhibition' took place in

[1] The full story of the 'Complete Edition' of Schubert's works is given by O. E. Deutsch in 'Music & Letters', July 1951, page 226.

Vienna. He was invited to conduct a Schubert concert as part of the Festival activities, but he declined to do so. It would be strange, he said, excusing himself, to fill a concert with the works of one composer and besides, there were very few works by Schubert suitable for performance 'en grand style'. But Manns and Grove in England, their enthusiasm aroused during rehearsals of the 'Great' C major Symphony in 1856, eventually obtained the manuscript parts of all the early symphonies of Schubert. The honour of first performing them belongs to England, for Manns conducted the whole series during the seasons of the 'Crystal Palace Concerts'. The dates on which these symphonies were performed are these: no. 1, in D major, 30 January 1880; no. 2, in B flat, 20 October 1877; no. 3, in D major, 19 February 1881; no. 5, in B flat, 1 February 1873. The symphonies never became really established in the concert repertoire; in the closing decades of the nineteenth century, contemporary music, as represented by the work of Wagner, Strauss, Brahms, Tchaikowsky and others, was popular in a degree which we cannot imagine today. The comparative rarity of concerts, and the vast amount of music to be drawn upon, completely excluded the early Schubert symphonies. Only with the coming of broadcasting, and the multiplicity of concerts which resulted from it, did these early works win a hearing and, more than that, enable the Fifth Symphony, in B flat, to endear itself to the musical public as a thoroughly worthy forerunner of the two later symphonies, the 'Unfinished' and the 'Great' C major.

The operas were not so fortunate. They, with the exception of 'Die Verschworenen', have never been performed. So called 'first performances' of 'Alfonso und Estrella', 'Fierrabras', and others, are nothing of the kind. Liszt wrote enthusiastic letters about 'Alfonso und Estrella'—'cette charmante musique ... le succès, et un succès populaire et productif, est indubitable ...'; he wrote thus to Escudier on 21 January 1854. But he gave a severely cut version at Weimar five months after this, and it won, in that form, no success at all. The travesty of the opera published in vocal score by Haslinger in J. N. Fuchs arrangement has been discussed already. Today the full length operas are still unperformed, and judgements on their merits or otherwise, should remain in abeyance until they are given in their entirety, in a first class production.

VII

Schumann's famous visit to Vienna in 1839 can be paralleled by Grove's in October 1867. Ferdinand showed the amazed Schumann the store of accumulated manuscripts in his possession; the same store, only slightly diminished, was shown by Ferdinand's nephew, Dr. Schneider, to the equally astonished Grove. Just as Schumann returned to Leipzig, full of enthusiasm for what he had seen, arranged for a performance there of the C major Symphony, and wrote ardently in his journal of the composer and his music, so Grove returned to London, laden with the missing 'Rosamunde' part-songs, primed with information about the early symphonies, and determined to obtain performances of the 'Rosamunde' and other orchestral music. He too wrote of what he had found. When Arthur Duke Coleridge published in 1869 an English translation of Kreissle's 'Schubert', Grove wrote for the second volume a masterly appendix describing his Vienna visit and giving a *catalogue raisonné* of all the symphonies, including the E minor and major sketch, then in his possession. Eventually his researches and the accumulated experiences of his concert activities and his abiding love for Schubert produced the 'Life' of Schubert which he wrote for the 'Dictionary of Music and Musicians', published in 1882.[1] His article has been translated into German, by Hans Effenberger, but never published there. Between Kreissle (1864) and Grove (1882) there were two major biographies of the composer. The first is the work of the Berlin composer and scholar, August Reissmann. He published his book 'Franz Schubert: sein Leben und seine Werke' in 1873. It contained, as supplements, about six unpublished works quoted in full; others, such as the Quintet Overture (D. 8) for 2 violins, 2 violas and 'cello, composed by Schubert in June and July 1811, were merely referred to and briefly quoted. Amongst these works

[1] The 'Dictionary' had been published in instalments; the work, in four volumes, was published as a whole in 1883.

is the String Trio in B flat (1817), and in view of this reference it seems inexcusable for the editors of the 'Gesamtausgabe' to have forgotten it; they were forced to include it in the 'Supplement' volume. Reissmann, writing before Nottebohm's 'Thematic Catalogue', is also the first scholar to give a comprehensive chronologically ordered list of Schubert's works. He perpetrated several errors, it is true, which were taken over by Nottebohm and persisted into the twentieth century: these mistaken dates have already been discussed; they concern the two quartets of Op. 125, the two mature quartets of 1824, the Sonatas in D major, Op. 53 and A major, Op. 120, and the PF. Duet Sonata in B flat, Op. 30. Grove, later on, gave a most admirable catalogue of this kind. At the close of his dictionary article he printed eleven columns of full, detailed information, listing there 1,131 compositions. It was an intolerable deletion when future editors of 'Grove's Dictionary' cut out this catalogue in favour of an abbreviated summary of contents from the 'Gesamtausgabe', especially as Grove's list was without its equal anywhere in Europe. The fifth edition of 'Grove', under the editorship of Dr. Eric Blom, gives a full, dated list of works arranged in categories, with detailed information of publication, first performances, text sources and the like.

The second biography of importance published in the years between Kreissle's and Grove's is that written by Constantin von Wurzbach as an entry in his famous 'Biographical Lexicon of the Austrian Empire', 1876.[1] His article was based largely upon Kreissle, and contained in addition some facts from Anselm Hüttenbrenner; but a few valuable references to contemporary publications provide documentary facts of some importance.

Beside the biographers, major and minor ones, there arose a body of Schubertians who were fired, like the original band of men round the composer himself, purely by love of his music. These men inspired performance, publication and scholarship; they prompted memorials and suggested commemorative plaques on the various residences of Schubert in Vienna and other buildings (the Liechtenthaler church, for example) connected with his activities there. They also collected and preserved his manu-

---

[1] 'Biographisches Lexikon des Kaisertums Oesterreich', Vienna, 1876.

scripts. An early collector of this kind was Karl Pinterics, a friend of Schubert who amassed invaluable memoranda, first editions and copies of unpublished songs. On his death in 1831 his collection passed to Witteczek who added it to his own. Although there were few original manuscripts in the collection there was a large number of copied songs the originals of which had been lost. On Witteczek's death, in 1859, the collection was bequeathed to Spaun who also possessed an individual collection of Schubertiana. When Spaun died, six years after Witteczek, his entire collection, fed by so many subsidiary libraries, passed into public ownership for he left it to the Library of the *Gesellschaft der Musikfreunde*. It was, of course, an important source for the 'Collected Edition'.

Two other men who were collectors of manuscripts, and who owned many of Schubert's pieces, were Ludwig Landsberg discussed earlier in this chapter, and Gustav Petter. But the greatest of all these collectors, a man to whom the world of Schubert scholarship owes an incalculable debt, was Nicolaus Dumba, a wealthy Viennese merchant of Greek descent, and a cultured musician. He bought the entire mass of manuscripts in Dr. Schneider's possession, and others belonging to various descendants of Schubert, adding to these, many manuscripts of already published works which he obtained from the original publishers. Not only did he urge forward the project of the 'Collected Edition', he also aided its inception by a gift of money. On his death, 23 March 1900, the manuscripts in his possession were bequeathed to 'his beloved city of Vienna', most of them going to the *Stadtbibliothek*; but the 'Unfinished' Symphony, together with the sketches for the work, was left to the *Gesellschaft der Musikfreunde*. He had purchased the Kupelwieser water-colours and these, too, went to the *Stadtbibliothek*.

The Schubert manuscripts in the Berlin Library were admirably listed and described by Robert Lachmann ('Zeitschrift für Musikwissenschaft', November 1928) although several more Schubert manuscripts have been acquired since then. The Paris 'Conservatoire' possesses a large number of autograph manuscripts by Schubert which were the gift of Charles Malherbe. He

FERDINAND SCHUBERT

Lithograph by Kriehuber, 1852   *Historische Museum, Vienna*

was the archivist at the Paris 'Opéra' and an ardent manuscript collector. This collection was catalogued in exemplary fashion by Jacques Gabriel Prod'homme, who published his account in the 'Revue Musicologique', November 1928. The most sizeable collection of Schubert manuscripts still in private possession belongs to Konsul Otto Taussig, of Malmö, Sweden. Many of his manuscripts have come from the residue of Diabelli's purchases in 1830, which passed to successive owners of the original firm; this residue is now jointly owned by the brothers Alwin and Albert Cranz, the first in Vienna, the second in Brussels. Herr Taussig's collection thus contains unpublished work. This great collector also owns many autographs of subsidiary interest, such as documents written by Schubert's father, copies of the songs made by Enderes and Stadler (the only sources in many cases, since Schubert's originals are lost), and the copies made by Schindler which the dying Beethoven saw.

VIII

Grove's advocacy of Schubert met with general success in England, but it was not quite unqualified. Prejudice died hard, and many factors had contributed to it. For so long had the composer been looked upon as a songwriter, who had failed in his attempts to master instrumental forms, that the musical world of the day was half-reluctant to accept Schubert as a writer of masterpieces in all other spheres. But gradually his music conquered. In 1870 the first of the succession of 'Schubert Societies' was founded in London and gave many concerts of obscure or little-known works. In Manchester Charles Hallé performed a series of eight sonatas and these were then published by Augener's in London. Further volumes of piano-music followed. The 'Octet' was given at the 'Popular Concerts', and in 1881 the whole cycle of eight symphonies was given at the Crystal Palace. Two years later, on 5 May 1883, Barnett's completion of the symphony-sketch in E was performed.

In France the initial burst of song performance and publication did not lead to an interest in Schubert's other work such had arisen in England; there was to be no French counterpart of Grove. The 'Unfinished' Symphony was performed for the first time in 1873, but it was not until 1897 that the C major Symphony received a second performance. The Sonata in G major, Op. 78, was performed in 1875 (it was pronounced 'too orchestral, too long'), and various chamber works, Op. 100 and the D minor String Quartet, appeared occasionally in Paris concerts of the 1870's, but the biographical article on Schubert, written for 'Larousse' of 1875, deals with him solely as a song-writer and ignores his instrumental music altogether. It was possible for Ernest Legouvé, a well-known French singer, to write in his 'Souvenirs', published in Paris in 1885: 'Today, Schubert is almost forgotten.' Schubert occupies in France a position similar to that of Bruckner in England. Lip service is paid to his eminence, but performance of his work is infrequent, and then more dutiful than desired. Occasionally there is an ardent tribute from a French musician but not all Schubertians, and certainly not all musicians, will agree with the following comment of L. A. Bourgault-Ducoudray in his book 'Les musiciens célèbres', although it may perhaps be quoted as an antidote to Legouvé's lugubrious remark above. This is what Ducoudray wrote in 1908:

> La musique de Schubert n'est pas faite pour provoquer la fine analyse d'un intellectuel, ou pour exercer le scalpel d'un dilettante. *C'est un cadeau fait par Dieu, en un jour de largesse*, qu'on accepte sans discussion et sans reflection.

In Vienna the 'Männergesangverein', pursuing its ardent course of homage to the composer, collected funds for a monumental statue to be erected in the *Stadtpark*. The park lies just beyond the Ringstrasse (that section of it now named 'Schubertring') and the statue was carved by Karl Kundmann. It is a seated figure, and Schubert is looking up, pen poised, in the act of composing. It was unveiled on 15 May 1872 and at the ceremony Dumba delivered the address of homage. On 22 June 1888 Schubert's body was again exhumed, for the last time, and re-buried in the 'Grove of Honour', in the Central Cemetery. A bas-relief of the composer, with one of the Muses holding a laurel-wreath above

his head, stands over his grave; the sculptor was again Karl Kundmann. Above the empty grave in the Währingerstrasse Cemetery,
called today the 'Schubertpark', a copy of Dialer's bust was
erected (1925); the original bust now stands in the Birthhouse, in
the 'alcove-room' where, according to tradition, he was born.

During those slow years when the song-writer was being revealed as so much greater an artist, worthy of being named in the
same breath as Mozart and Beethoven, critical opinion was likewise undergoing a peculiar transitional phase. Kreissle, for all his
enthusiasm and knowledge, is naturally unable to dissociate himself entirely from the opinions and attitudes of his contemporaries
and often pronounces judgements which seem strangely jarring
to our ears. After admitting that the last Mass, in E flat, is not
known outside Vienna, he gives, as his opinion, the view that the
noblest of the other five Masses is that in G major, Schubert's
second setting of the office. This short work has great charm, but
his placing of it above the later one in B flat, and the mature
fifth setting, in A flat, is hard to understand. He calls the *Trout*
Quintet 'mindless' ('geistlos') and leaves it at that; the first and
last movements of the 'Wanderer' Fantasia are 'uncouth' in construction; the finale of Op. 100 has a 'poor subject' and is worn
threadbare by exceeding length. On the other hand he praises
work such as the Fantasy for PF. and violin, Op. 159, and the
'Rondo' of Op. 145, in terms which would be considered nowadays as extravagant.

The reluctance in England to accept the great C major Symphony as a masterpiece of the first rank was not fully overcome
until well into the twentieth century. The critic J. W. Davison,
writing in the 'Musical World', seemed unable to appreciate any
music which was not by Beethoven or Mozart or Mendelssohn
(his especial favourite); his vitriolic attacks on Chopin were
notorious. After a performance of Schubert's symphony by the
Musical Society in London during the 1859 season, he wrote:

> The ideas throughout it are all of a minute character, and the
> instrumentation is of a piece with the ideas. There is no breadth,
> there is no grandeur, there is no dignity in either; clearness, and con-
> trast, and beautiful finish are always apparent, but the orchestra,

though loud, is never massive and sonorous, and the music, though always correct, is never serious or imposing.

Grove, quoting this passage, asks: 'Is it possible for criticism to be more hopelessly wrong?'

But Grove himself sometimes errs. It is not a congenial thing to have to say, but the nineteenth century's unanimous tributes to Grove's biographical article on Schubert cannot, in honesty, go unchallenged today. Grove's excellent researches led to the discovery of unpublished letters, unrecorded dates on manuscripts and much factual evidence which was new at that time, and all this is admirable. But not only was Grove, like Kreissle, unable to view Schubert apart from the prejudice and spirit of those times, his writing is also, in a rather disturbing way, coloured by the Victorian ideals and limitations of the 1880's. He is occasionally arch, occasionally facetious, and sometimes a little too much the 'English Gentleman'. A careful and close re-reading of his article will reveal at once that he was a generous and warm-hearted soul, but his drawing of Schubert's character, his accounts of Schubert's methods of composition, his description of the music itself, his portraits of the composer's friends, are all slightly false. From start to finish he just misses the mark of truth. He is uncertain when he comes to tackling the music of Schubert because he himself was not sure of technical facts. These criticisms can be illustrated by his own words: the following extracts are from his letter to Mrs. Edmond Wodehouse, written on 18 March 1882 while he was writing the discussion of Schubert's music which closes his biographical article.[1] He wished, he wrote to Mrs. Wodehouse,

> ... to bring out the fact that in listening to Schubert one never thinks of the cleverness or the contrivance, as one often does even in Beethoven, but simply of the music itself—the emotions it raises in you and the strong personal feeling it excites towards the composer. Easy enough to put it in that way, but hitherto impossible to work it out in proper terms. It's quite curious how innocent he is of innovation or experiment or of trying aesthetic contrivances as Schumann, Mendelssohn, Spohr, even Beethoven himself do. His sym-

[1] 'Life of Sir George Grove', Charles Graves, London, 1903, page 282.

phonies and sonatas are just in the old form as far as arrangement of movements go, etc., and in the construction of each movement, if he wanders from the form, it is not from any intention of neglecting it and setting up something fresh, but just because he goes on pouring out what he has to say and so gets into all kinds of irregular keys and excrescences.

This is bad enough, but worse follows:

> Remember the splendid effects, the beautiful instrumentation, &c., and then recollect that every piece was written without note or sketch as hard as his pen would go, and you form some idea of the skill and technical ability of the man with all his want of learning.

Is it to be wondered at, that if Grove adopted this line in discussing Schubert, and if, in addition, he quotes without question all the rather foolish anecdotes by Schubert's friends, that he was the cause of similar serious misunderstanding on the part of other music lovers? The dictionary article appeared in 1882 and in October 1883 it was reviewed in the 'Edinburgh Review'. The review is anonymous in the journal, but it was actually written by H. Heathcote Statham. It is a poisonous effort, and it deeply upset Grove, although he had only himself to blame. Statham draws from Grove's biography conclusions about Schubert based upon the anecdotal aspect already deplored: he finds Schubert to be a lower-class ruffian, uncouth, dirty in his habits (for, Statham asserts, if he wore his spectacles all night we know what that tells us about his habits of cleanliness), drunken, and one who merely played at his art. Grove wrote a letter of remonstrance to the editor of the 'Edinburgh Review', Henry Reeve. But Reeve replied to Grove that he agreed with Statham, and the review exactly expressed his own opinions. In his letter (26 October 1883) he continued:[1]

> No one admires his [Schubert's] natural genius and vocal power more than I do, but as your biography proves, it was genius growing in a Vienna beer-shop, with a slender amount of education, a low social standard, and more facility than application. Wonderful but incomplete. . . .

[1] *loc. cit.*, page 293.

Grove's account of the composer and his composing greatly influenced musical opinion in England during the years from 1890 onwards, and we see the outcome, even so late as 1928, from the pen of a man who, although he cared deeply for Schubert and sang his songs in an almost incomparable fashion, reveals by his writing on the composer that his first hand knowledge and true apprehension are lamentably weak. Here is Plunket Greene, and the hand of Grove lies heavily upon him:[1]

> He burned no midnight oil. There is hardly a correction in his Mss.; he dashed them off in the white heat of his genius. It is no exaggeration to describe him as the most inspired of all composers, for what he did he did almost in spite of himself. His technical equipment was comparatively limited (he had arranged to take lessons in counterpoint just before he died). His harmonic range was *small*. He had certain tricks which almost amount to *clichés*. He rang the changes on alternating minor and major so often as almost to render them suspect to our modern ears. . . .

The repeated assertion that Schubert never altered or corrected his manuscripts was made by people who seem to be unaware of the fact that fair copies rarely do show such alterations. These critics show no knowledge of the existence of the composer's very numerous sketches.

IX

1897 revealed to the musical world at the close of the nineteenth century the true greatness of Schubert, and pointed to the fuller appreciation of his genius which was to develop in the twentieth century. Publication of his work (with the exception of numerous minor pieces) was complete at last, performances of all his instrumental masterpieces, for piano, for orchestra and for chamber music combinations, were regular occurrences and many of these masterpieces were firmly established in the concert repertory. His songs had never suffered any eclipse, and although the tremendous possibilities which he had opened up by his exploration of the 'Lied' had been developed, in their individual fashions,

[1] 'Music & Letters', London, 1928, page 317.

by Schumann, Brahms and Hugo Wolf, none of these composers did more than follow out the implications in the Schubert 'Lied': none of them produced anything so original in song-form that it led to yet further developments. And the Schubert 'Lied' is as beloved today, and as frequently performed, as it was in the 'Schubertiad' evenings of old Vienna.

With the dawn of the twentieth century there arose in the field of Schubertian scholarship and criticism, a man whose character, percipience and industry produced the greatest contribution to that field of study which it had ever known. Otto Erich Deutsch, studying the art of Moritz von Schwind, was drawn to the work of Schwind's friend Schubert, the greater artist. That was how Deutsch's work on Schubert began. In 1905 his first book was published: it was a 'Schubert Brevier', a collection of the sayings, letters, documents, dates, of the composer's life. It was an omen. Deutsch has never been drawn to the aesthetic discussion of music. A child of his time, he has concentrated on the factual and documentary basis of a composer's life and music. In Schubert there was an enormous sphere for his activities. Anecdote was largely rejected. Instead, Deutsch collected all the appropriate documents he could lay his hands on. Published letters, poems, inscriptions in albums and manuscripts were first assembled. Then he got into touch with the descendants of Schubert's relatives, his friends, his biographers, his publishers, and collected from them diaries, reports, accounts, letters, photographs and pictures. All the accumulated manuscripts of the archives and offices of the City of Vienna were combed through, and the back numbers of journals and periodicals were ransacked for advertisements and reviews. The harvest was rich. Deutsch then did a surprisingly simple thing. He assembled all his documents in chronological order and let the results speak for themselves. His book was called 'Franz Schubert: die Dokumente seines Lebens', and published by Georg Müller, Leipzig, in 1914. It was intended to be the second in a series of four works; the first to be a German translation of Grove's biographical article, the third a pictorial book ('Sein Leben in Bildern'), the fourth a thematic catalogue. The pictorial volume was actually published first, in 1913; if readers do not know this volume, let me urge its value, importance and fascination. Copies are rare and expensive, but most of the bigger libraries contain a copy and it is worth going to some trouble to consult it; very few persons, places or things which one encounters in the Schubert story are without their representation in the book. Deutsch's work corrected all the established errors of chronology, and proved many of the old, favourite stories to be myths. His standard of accuracy, that ruthless objectivity where facts were concerned, placed him in the forefront of Schubert authorities. We are concerned here only with his work on Schubert; in other fields, research on Handel, Haydn and, particularly, Mozart, his renown is as great.

The fourth volume, the thematic catalogue, was published in England in 1951. It is a companion volume to the English translation of the 'Documents' which had appeared four years earlier.[1] The reason for this fortunate conjunction of two books so vital to the English Schubertian, was that Deutsch left Vienna because of the German *Anschluss* of Austria in 1938 and sought refuge in England; he settled eventually in Cambridge.

Between 1897 and 1928 biographies of the composer continued to appear, impelled by a new vigour from the fact that all his music was by then available in the 'Gesamtausgabe' volumes. Two were outstanding, not so much from a biographical point of view, as from the fact that both contained extensive reproductions of manuscripts and manuscript-sketches, which were new to the musical public, and from their excellent analytical treatment of the whole corpus of composition. They are 'Franz Schubert', by Richard Heuberger (Berlin, 1902), and 'Schubert', by Walter Dahms (Leipzig, 1912). If, biographically, they contribute nothing new, it is because Deutsch's work now sets a much higher standard in such matters.

Apart from his documentary books, Deutsch published between 1902 and 1928 many works by Schubert which had escaped the notice of the editors of the 'Gesamtausgabe' or which were

[1] 'Schubert: A Documentary Biography', translated by Eric Blom, London, 1947.

discovered in various odd and interesting ways in homes and museums all over Europe. A list of these works has never been given, and the one provided here is supplied with dates of publication:

1. Six Ländler in B flat (1816). Graz, 1902.
2. Four Ecossaises (1815). 'Die Musik', Berlin, 1912.
3. *Lied in der Abwesenheit*, song (1816); Two Ländler in E flat (?1820). 'Moderne Welt', Vienna, 1925.
4. Three Trios for men's voices, poems by Matthisson (1816):
   (*a*) *Andenken*,
   (*b*) *Erinnerungen*
   (*c*) *Widerhall*.   Vienna, 1927.
5. Psalm XIII, song, translation by Moses Mendelssohn (1819). Vienna, 1927.
6. Eight Ländler in F sharp minor (1816). Vienna, 1928.
7. 'Ungarische Melodie' in B minor, PF. Solo (1824). Edition Strache, Vienna, 1928.
8. Polonaise in B flat, violin solo and orchestra (1817). Edition Strache, Vienna, 1928.

Other scholars had published various unknown Schubert works in New York, Munich, Leipzig and Berlin. Chief amongst them are a 'Salve Regina' in F major, for soprano solo and orchestra (1812) published in Vienna in 1928, a Trio in one movement in B flat, for PF., violin and 'cello (1812), published in 1923, and a charming song *Jägers Abendlied*, a setting of the Goethe poem written in 1815, which Mandyczewski published in 'Die Musik', January 1907.

On 22 May 1908 the City Authorities of Vienna purchased the 'Birth-house' from its owner, Rudolph Wittmann, and the decision was taken to turn the first floor of the house into a Schubert museum. It was opened on 18 June 1912 and is today a worthy place of pilgrimage. The most precious exhibits are Dialer's bust of Schubert from the original memorial stone, Schwind's sepia drawing 'A Schubert Evening at Spaun's', and various articles from the original furnishings of the parental home, or from Ferdinand's apartment: things such as bureaus, tables, a pianoforte, all of which Schubert knew and possibly used. His spectacles are there, together with an inkstand said to be his, and sundry other possessions.

In 1928 came the centenary celebrations of Schubert's death. Apart from concerts and festivals of all kinds, the world over, there was in Vienna an important exhibition of his work. It included many manuscripts and first editions such as could not, earlier, have been seen assembled in one place, pictures and manuscripts of his friends, his poets, publishers and biographers. There were numerous pictures of old Vienna, and of associated subjects. The beautifully prepared catalogue of this exhibition is a useful item in the Schubertian bibliography and as such appears in all recent lists of this kind.

Publication of scholarly studies of his music appeared in all musicological journals of the world, some of them, indeed, preparing a special issue devoted exclusively to essays on various aspects of his work. From the mass of studies so written one or two emerge as vitally important. Two essays by Sir Donald Tovey can safely be said to voice in an authoritative manner the new appreciation and the new veneration for Schubert which had grown from its beginnings in 1897. The first is the essay on the composer's tonality, already quoted on several occasions in previous chapters of this book, and the other is a full length study of the music entitled 'Franz Schubert'.[1] Finally, the book on Schubert's songs by Richard Capell must be mentioned. This, like Tovey's essay on Schubert's tonality, has been frequently quoted here. It is an affectionately written, but penetrating study of the songs, and of all aesthetic studies of the composer, in any language, it gets nearest to the heart of Schubert. Again and again Capell says things about the songs and their composer, phrased in his incomparable fashion, which, being once said, bear the stamp of imperishable truth and endear themselves to the Schubertian as an inseparable comment on the particular song or feature of the song. His introductory remarks to the 'Winterreise' have no equal in the Schubertian literature.

[1] 'Heritage of Music', Oxford University Press, 1927.

X

The enormous number of essays and books written for the 1928 centenary can be assessed from Willi Kahl's catalogue of all the writings on Schubert between 1828 and 1928. The first hundred years, to the end of 1927, produced, according to Kahl, nearly 2,000 items. One year later, in December 1928, this had risen to over 3,000 items. An inevitable period of reaction set in, but not a prolonged one. In the 1930's, in spite of the growing tension and unrest in Europe, biographies, notably Walter Vetter's 'Franz Schubert' of 1934, discoveries of letters and manuscripts, and literary studies of his music, continued to enrich the Schubertian heritage. A collection of newly-found dance music, 'Deutsche Tänze', was published in Vienna in 1930, edited by Alfred Orel and O. E. Deutsch; the charming dances composed in October 1824 at Zseliz, were published in 1931 from the manuscript which Schubert gave to Karoline Esterházy; a 'Tantum Ergo' in C major, for chorus and orchestra, edited by Karl Geiringer, followed in 1935; the first movement of a String Quartet in C minor (D. 103) from which the other movements had been lost, was edited by Orel and published in Vienna in 1939. After the outbreak of war, in 1940, Orel's book, 'Der junge Schubert', appeared. It contained a large number of Schubert's settings of Metastasio texts, written as exercises for Salieri, the manuscripts having formed part of Dumba's great collection. The book usefully concentrated on Schubert's juvenilia, and catalogued them in careful detail.

In England, a thorough survey of his work in all categories, excluding biography and concentrating on the music alone, was written by a group of scholars and published under the editorship of Gerald Abraham in 1947. This was 'Schubert: a symposium' and in it, for the first time, a serious attempt to examine the music of the operas was made by A. Hyatt King. A similar approach, 'Works' without 'Life', was made by Alfred Einstein in 1951. His book, 'Schubert', is an objective study by a first-class scholar who was not, primarily, a Schubertian specialist. The book on Schubert which forms part of the 'Master Musicians' series is by Arthur Hutchings, a most attractively written and thoughtful study.[1]

Discoveries of his manuscripts still continue. The 'deep suspicion' of the 'Musical World' in 1844, at the fact that new songs by a composer sixteen years dead continued to be published, might well be felt by any journal today, for not a year goes by but a new manuscript of Schubert's is discovered somewhere; lost for a hundred and thirty years or so, and then found again on a library shelf, in a collection of old music, in the posthumous papers of a dead musician. Most of the recent discoveries have been already described in the appropriate place in earlier chapters.

Breitkopf & Härtel are eventually to publish a second supplementary volume to the 'Gesamtausgabe'. It will contain all the still unpublished work and in 'Appendix II' of this book the ideal form of the volume, not necessarily the one it will take, is suggested.

Another publication promised for the near future is Deutsch's collection of the Schubert 'Memoirs', a convenient though not particularly accurate term used to describe the writings and reminiscences of the men and women who knew Schubert, or who were closely associated with people who knew him. It will be an invaluable source-book, although calling for careful handling, for it records all the anecdotes, genuine and otherwise, which arose in the mid-nineteenth century.

In 1955 a facsimile reproduction of the autograph manuscript of 'Winterreise' was published in Cassel, Germany, by the Bärenreiter Verlag. The publication was reviewed by 'C. v. D.' (Charlotte von Dach) in 'Der Bund', Berne, Switzerland on 26 May 1955. The closing paragraphs of that review sum up, in a most admirable fashion, the attitude of the mid-twentieth century to that Viennese composer who lived so short a life, and died in obscurity and poverty completely oblivious of the immortal name he was leaving behind him.

> Perishable leaves, fading traces of work and of what were once the realities of a man's life: he who examines them with the heart,

[1] J. M. Dent & Sons Ltd., London, edited by Eric Blom.

and not with the clumsier outward intelligence, to him they are magic mirrors, in which such a thing as the creative spirit is to be perceived.

They are precious, they are lovely, these leaves; and they have also a great moral significance: they show us the places in a man's soul where spirit wrestles with matter; the eternal struggle towards the light, the sacred toil to shape the pure form of the Divine out of the transitoriness of the human spirit.

For that reason we shall love and reverence these pages of grey paper on which Schubert penned his 'Winterreise'.

APPENDIX I

THE 'GMUNDEN-GASTEIN' SYMPHONY

It is not possible to come to a definite conclusion when considering the problem of this alleged composition by Schubert. One can assemble pieces of evidence from existing documents and make some attempt to assess the merit, or force, of each one, in itself and in its relationship to the others. And in the attempt one must keep in mind such imponderable factors as Schubert's own methods of composition (especially the composition of symphonies), his friends' often hazy knowledge of what he was actually working on at any given period, and their even hazier knowledge of his particular methods of work.

But these scraps of evidence, considered as impartially as possible, incline one to believe that to the question: Did Schubert compose a symphony at Gmunden and Gastein in 1825?—neither the definite 'Yes' nor the definite 'No' would be a satisfactory answer.

There are, altogether, ten documents to be brought forward as witnesses, and they group themselves fairly neatly into four sections.

I

1. Schubert to Leopold Kupelwieser, 31 March 1824
This has been quoted in full on page 154. The revelant extract is as follows:

> I have tried my hand at several instrumental works, for I wrote two quartets for violins, viola and 'cello, and an Octet, and I want to write another quartet, in fact, I intend to pave my way towards grand symphony in that manner. . . .

2. Schwind to Leopold Kupelwieser, 31 May 1824
After telling Kupelwieser that Schubert had left Vienna for Zseliz, taking an opera libretto with him, Schwind adds:

> . . . he has also resolved to write a symphony.

3. Anton Ottenwalt to Spaun, 19 July 1825

This was written while Schubert was on holiday in Upper Austria. The composer had just arrived from Gmunden to stay in Linz, and Ottenwalt, his host, wrote enthusiastically of the pleasure his songs had given them all. Then Ottenwalt informs Spaun:

> By the way, he had worked at a symphony in Gmunden, which is to be performed in Vienna this winter. . . .

4. Schubert to his father and stepmother, 25 July 1825

The composer was at Steyr for a short while. He describes his days at Gmunden:

> I lived at Traweger's, very free and easy. Later, when Councillor von Schiller was there, who is monarch of the whole Salzkammergut, we (Vogl and I) dined daily at his house and had music there as we also often did at Traweger's house.

5. Schwind to Schubert, 14 August 1825

This was written from Vienna and Schubert received it at Gastein. Schwind refers to Schubert's symphony in these words:

> About your symphony we may be quite hopeful. Old Hönig is dean of the faculty of jurisprudence, and as such is to give a concert. That will afford a better opportunity of having it performed; indeed we count upon it.

These five passages give the preliminary references to the symphony, and we might pause here and consider what they imply. We find that Schubert intended to write a symphony, that he told his friends so, and that they discussed the matter amongst themselves. It is true that he wanted to write a third string quartet first, and that his resolve to compose the symphony at Zseliz in 1824 was not carried through, but the idea is in the air. A year later, at Gmunden, there is no question—he worked at this symphony and must himself have told Ottenwalt so.

But how seriously did he apply himself to the task in view of his own account of the way he passed his days at Gmunden in the letter to his parents? There is no word from the composer himself, in any of his letters written during the period (and they are not few), about the symphony. At least the work was not finished, for no concert in Vienna that winter contained the performance of a new Schubert symphony. It is fairly safe to conclude that at Gmunden he composed sketches for a symphony, and took them back to Vienna with him in the autumn. How substantial they were there is no means of knowing, but they were set aside for the time being.[1]

II

Reference must be made here to a batch of documents belonging to the autumn of 1826, when, it was known, Schubert had announced his intention of dedicating a symphony to the *Gesellschaft der Musikfreunde*. These documents concern the transactions between the *Gesellschaft* and Schubert, in connection with a gift of £10. It was a token of the Society's sense of obligation to the composer and a generous acknowledgement of his work. It was presented on 12 October 1826. Schubert wrote an official receipt and courteous thanks on 20 October 1826. It has been suggested, when this period of Schubert's life was discussed, that the whole simple business has been befogged by associating with those straightforward documents an *undated* letter from Schubert to the Society in which he 'dedicated' a symphony to it:

6. Schubert to the 'Gesellschaft der Musikfreunde', NO DATE
    To the Committee of the Austrian *Gesellschaft der Musikfreunde*.

> Convinced of the noble intention of the Austrian 'Musikverein' to support any artistic endeavour as far as possible, I venture, as a native artist, to dedicate to them this, my symphony, and to commend it most politely to their protection.
>
> With all my respects,
Your devoted
Franz Schubert

---

[1] The alternative possibility should be taken into account, that Schubert might have abandoned any idea of completing the symphony and used his material for the Sonata in D major, composed at Gastein in 1825 and published as Op. 53 the following year.

It seems from Schubert's words here, that the score of the symphony was dispatched with the note. The *Gesellschaft* has no record of receiving any such symphony in 1826, nor has it any symphony score from that year, nor, in the letter offering the gift of money, sent to Schubert by the President, Raphael Kiesewetter, is any thanks offered for the work, which would be an omission not to be credited. On the other hand, the Society did receive the score of the great C major Symphony in 1828, and recorded the fact (Catalogue mark: xiii. 8024). At rehearsals the work was found too difficult, whereupon Schubert withdrew the larger symphony and offered to the Society the smaller, 1818 work in the same key. The undated letter just quoted, one feels, *must* belong to 1828, and have accompanied the score of the great C major Symphony. One small factual piece of evidence might be mentioned. Schubert's undated letter is still extant and in the archives of the Society. All documents of those early years were given a consecutive numbering—no date was added. The original number on this letter has been altered, which has a faint suggestion that its position has been moved in the early files, possibly to bring it into line with the transactions over the donation to Schubert and the rumours that he intended to dedicate a symphony to the Society. It is now to be found in the 'October 1826' section, from which it is quoted in the Schubert 'Documents' (page 559); the attribution there 'Early October 1826' has, however, nothing to support it.

III

But it seems permissible to draw the conclusion that the gift of £10 from the *Gesellschaft*, together with the fact that in June 1827 he had been elected as a 'representative' of the Society, inclined Schubert's thoughts to the composition of a symphony, so long in his mind and now, at last, taken in hand. The third string quartet, which he had wished to write before undertaking the 'grand symphony', had been composed in July 1826. The symphony sketches started at Gmunden meant that the work had, at least, begun to take shape on paper. During the autumn of 1827, after his return from Graz, he may have worked on his sketches to their conclusion. Early in 1828 the work was finished (probably in draft) for he himself mentioned it in a letter.

7. Schubert to B. Schott's Sons, Mainz, 21 February 1828

The composer offered a number of his instrumental and vocal works to the publisher. He concludes with these words:

> ... this is the list of my finished compositions, excepting three operas, a Mass, and a symphony. These last compositions I mention only in order to make you acquainted with my striving after the highest in art.

The next month, in March, the fair copy of the C major Symphony was begun. On its completion it was sent to the *Gesellschaft* with the result already related.

IV

After Schubert's death there were references to the C major Symphony in two of his obituary notices. These tend to confirm the possibility that the sketches made at Gmunden and Gastein were afterwards worked up into the symphony intended for the *Gesellschaft*, and that in their complete form we have the great C major Symphony.

8. Josef Spaun's 'On Franz Schubert' in the Linz journal 'Oester-reichisches Bürgerblatt fur Verstand, Herz und gute Laune' of 27 and 30 March and 3 April 1829

Spaun writes the following words in the course of his biographical article:

> ... in 1825, at Gastein, a grand symphony for which the composer himself had a vast preference. ...

but he makes no subsequent reference to the C major Symphony of 1828. This would be incomprehensible if he knew of the two symphonies as separate works, and he certainly knew of the existence of the 1828 symphony. To him the '1828' symphony originated at Gastein. He gives '6 Symphonies' as the composer's total, and since neither he, nor any of Schubert's friends in Vienna, knew of the existence of the 'Unfinished' Symphony, then at Graz, it is pointless to try and identify the six of which he was thinking. Later on, he writes of this 'Gastein' Symphony as a most beautiful work, a judgement which he could not have passed upon it since it was unknown on paper and in performance. He was obviously referring to the 1828 work.

9. Eduard Bauernfeld's 'On Franz Schubert' in the 'Wiener Zeitschrift für Kunst' of 9, 11 and 13 June 1829

Bauernfeld, basing his account on Spaun's already published obituary, named the 'Gastein' Symphony as composed in 1825. He gives a short account of Schubert's operas, and then continues:

> To the larger works of the last years belongs further a symphony written at Gastein in 1825 for which its author had a special liking, and the Mass of the year 1828 . . . his last work.

He then goes on to discuss a Symphony in C major, but this turns out to be the earlier work, for Bauernfeld gives its date of composition, 1817. Then he concludes:

> Perhaps the 'Gesellschaft' will by and by make us acquainted with one of Schubert's later symphonies, possibly with the 'Gastein' Symphony.

His brief mention of a 'Last Symphony' in 1828, of which he says nothing at all in his article, occurs in his catalogue, and is clearly designed to amplify Spaun's; it is not based on his knowledge of two separate symphonies.

One significant fact, which is generally overlooked in discussions of this question, is that Ferdinand nowhere makes any reference to a symphony in the last six years of his brother's life, other than the great C major Symphony, which he assigns, of course, to 1828. If there had been a symphony other than this, from the weeks at Gmunden and Gastein, and if the existence of such a symphony had been vaguely known to Schubert's friends, it would surely have been known also to Ferdinand. But he makes no mention of it.

10. Thematic Catalogue: manuscript notes made in 1842 by Aloys Fuchs.

That the symphony which Schubert intended to dedicate to the

Gesellschaft der Musikfreunde was, in fact, the work of 1828, is proved by a reference in this catalogue of Fuchs. He compiled it in collaboration with Ferdinand Schubert. Against his entry of the Symphony in C major, 1828, he writes:

> ... for the Vienna 'Musikverein'.

This information must have been confirmed by Ferdinand and seems to represent the truth in the matter.

The acceptance of the last symphony as the only work in that form written in Schubert's mature years was general until Grove raised the matter in 1881. He was preparing to write his biographical article for the 'Dictionary' and during his preliminary work on the subject he had pondered over Bauernfeld's entry: '1825. Grand Symphony.' He came to the conclusion that a symphony had been written by the composer in that year and soon afterwards lost. He expressed his views in a letter to the 'Times' of 28 September 1881. The secretary of the *Gesellschaft* in those days, C. F. Pohl, misinterpreted a passage in Grove's letter as an accusation against the authorities of the Society for negligence and careless handling of a score entrusted to their care. Pohl wrote a protesting reply to Grove, denying the charge: his letter was published in the 'Neue Freie Presse' of 7 October 1881. He stated categorically that the symphony dedicated to the Society was not lost, being, in fact, the great Symphony in C of 1828. As for the 'Gastein' Symphony, he did not believe in its existence:

> ... it would have been entered at once, in 1826, in the Archive-Catalogue, considering the punctilious care of Baron von Knorr, then the Society's Archivist. ... neither Sonnleithner, the sisters Fröhlich, Baron Schönstein, Bauernfeld, Spaun, nor his own brother Ferdinand, ever heard of it. Especially as Dr. Leopold Sonnleithner was, in 1826, witness at all the meetings of the Society, it seems impossible to believe that that man who has earned such honour over Schubert should during forty-nine years (he died in 1873) have never remembered the existence of this symphony.

Pohl erred, we can see, in saying that Bauernfeld and Spaun knew 'nothing of the symphony', but as the facts quoted above make clear, their knowledge was extremely hazy compared with that of such a witness as Leopold Sonnleithner.

In a letter to the 'Times' of 17 October 1881, Grove made haste to correct Pohl's wrong impression, but the subject had, through this irrelevant exchange of letters, forcibly thrust itself on the attention of the musical world, and since that day there has been an inconclusive discussion of the pros and cons of the existence of an earlier symphony from 1825–1826.

The collecting of the documents above cannot, as was implied in the introductory paragraph, decisively settle the issue. Paradoxically the answer seems to be, after all, that Schubert did not write a symphony at Gastein and Gmunden, nor was it subsequently lost!

APPENDIX II

WORKS BY SCHUBERT NOT INCLUDED IN THE 'GESAMTAUSGABE'

Most of these compositions are still unpublished. The publication of the others has been either in the form of supplements to Austrian, German or Swiss periodicals, or from Continental publishing houses with only local reputations. Even the published works are therefore largely inaccessible. The works are classified here according to the general plan of the *Gesamtausgabe* ('Complete Edition)' of Breitkopf & Härtel, to which they could well form a second Supplementary Volume (Serie XXII). Short fragmentary compositions, unsuitable for publication, are given in a paragraph at the end of the list of works.[1]

A. ORCHESTRAL WORKS

(*a*) Overture in D major. Fragment. (?) 1812.

(*b*) Symphony in D major: first movement. *Adagio* leading to *Allegro con moto*. Fragment, based on the material of (*a*). 1812.

(*c*) Movement in D major. Fragment. 1813.

(*d*) Polonaise in B flat for solo violin and strings. September 1817.

(*e*) Symphony in D. Sketches in pianoforte-score for eight movements. May 1818.

(*f*) Symphony in E. Sketches for four movements in full-score. August 1821.

(*g*) Sketch for, and the partly completed full-score of, third movement of the 'Unfinished' Symphony. October 1822.

B. CHAMBER WORKS

(*a*) String Quartet in G major: first movement. Fragment. (?) 1810.

---

[1] The list is a revised version of my article 'Supplement no. 2 for the Schubert *Gesamtausgabe*', published in the 'Monthly Musical Record' of February 1954. The material of that article is used here with the kind permission of the editor.

(b) Overture in C minor, for String Quintet (2 violins, 2 violas, 'cello). 29 June/12 July 1811.

(c) *Allegro* for piano, violin and 'cello called by the composer 'Sonata'. 27 July/28 August 1812.

(d) Second and fourth movements of a string Quartet in C major. *Andante* (A minor) and *Allegro con spirito* (C minor/major). September 1812. (The first and third movements were published in the *Gesamtausgabe* as 'String Quartet no. 2': V, 2; part of the fourth movement is given in the *Revisionsbericht*.)

(e) Trio-section of a minuet for flute, guitar, viola and 'cello. February 1814. (The original contribution to the so-called 'Guitar' quartet.)

(f) String Quartet in C minor: first movement. *Grave* leading to *Allegro*. April 1814.

(g) String Quartet in C minor: slow movement in A flat. Fragment. (The second movement to the famous 'Quartettsatz'.)

C. PIANOFORTE DUET

(a) Three German dances (one in E minor, two in E major). Summer 1818. (The first dance has two Trios, and the one in G major is published in the *Gesamtausgabe*, XII, 10.)

D. PIANOFORTE SOLO

(a) Fantasia in C minor. (?) 1810.

(b) Two minuets: i. C major, ii. F major. (?) 1810.

(c) Two fugues for 4 voices: i. D minor, ii. B flat. 1813.

(d) Two minuets and four trios. November 1813. (Two minuets probably lost from the MS.)

(e) Trio-section in E major (for the Waltz, Op. 127: no. 3). 1815.

(f) Waltz in C sharp major. 1815.

(g) Trio-section in (?) F major (for the unfinished Sonata in C major). 1815.

(h) Eight Ländler in D major. January 1816.

(i) Eight Ländler in F sharp minor. 1816.

(j) Four écossaises (F major, B flat major, two in A flat major). 1816.

(k) Sonata in E minor: first movement. Fragment. (?) 1817.

(l) Sonata in E minor: second, third and fourth movements of the Sonata no. 6. June 1817. (First movement published in the *Gesamtausgabe*: X, 4.)

(*m*) Écossaise in E flat. 1817.

(*n*) Ländler in E flat. (?) 1820.

(*o*) Eight Ländler (various keys). (?) 1820.

(*p*) PF. arrangement of the Overture for 'Alfonso und Estrella'. November 1822.

(*q*) Écossaise in D major. January 1823.

(*r*) Ungarische Melodie in B minor. Zseliz, 2 September 1824. (PF. sketch of the *Allegretto* from Op. 54.)

(*s*) Three écossaises (B flat, two in D major). September 1824.

(*t*) Six German Dances (three in A flat, three in B flat). Zseliz, October 1824.

(*u*) Two German Dances (F major and G major). April 1825.

(*v*) Four Waltzes (A flat, B minor, two in G major). 1825–1826.

E. CHURCH MUSIC

(*a*) 'Salve Regina' in F major (Sop. solo, orch. and organ continuo). June 1812.

(*b*) *Kyrie* of a Requiem in E flat. Fragment. (July ?) 1816.

(*c*) 'Tantum ergo' in C major (Chorus, orch. and organ continuo). August 1816.

(*d*) German Requiem (author unknown) in G minor (four voices and organ accompaniment). Zseliz, August 1818.

(*e*) 'Tantum ergo' in B flat (Vocal quartet, chorus and orch.) August 1821.

(*f*) *Kyrie* of a Mass in A minor. Fragment. May 1822.

F. DRAMATIC MUSIC

(*a*) *Adrast* (text: Johann Mayrhofer). Six numbers unpublished in the *Gesamtausgabe*. (?) 1819.

(*b*) *Claudine von villa Bella* (text: Goethe). Arietta and duet. Both fragments. July 1815.

(*c*) *Sakuntala* (text: J. P. Neumann after Kalidasa). Sketches for Acts I and II. October 1820.

(*d*) Two arias (nos. 8 and 13) (from *Alfonso und Estrella*); (PF. accompaniment arranged by the composer). 1822.

(*e*) *Sofie* (?): sketches for Act I of an unnamed opera. (?) 1823.

(*f*) *Rüdiger* (author unknown). Aria with chorus: duet. May 1823.

(*g*) *Der Graf von Gleichen* (text: Bauernfeld). Sketches (short score) for Acts I and II. June 1827/1828.

G. CANTATAS AND PART-SONGS

(a) *Dithyrambe* (text: (Schiller). Tenor solo, mixed chorus, solo voices, PF. accompaniment. March 1813.

(b) *Ewig still steht die Vergangenheit* (text: Schiller). Canon for three voices. July 1813.

(c) *Die Schlacht* (text: Schiller). Male voices. First sketch. August 1815.

(d) *Trinklied* (author unknown). T.T.B.B. unacc. 1816. (The original PF. accompaniment is lost.)

(e) *Erinnerungen* (text: Matthisson). T.T.B. unacc. May 1816.

(f) *Widerhall* (text: Matthisson). T.T.B. unacc. May 1816.

(g) *Andenken* (text: Matthisson). T.T.B. unacc. May 1816.

(h) *Leise, leise, lasst uns singen* (author unknown). T.T.B.B. unacc. 1819.

(i) *Viel tausend Sterne prangen* (text: A. G. Eberhard). Mixed chorus, PF. accompaniment. 1819.

(j) *Linde Lüfte wehen* (author unknown). S.T., PF. accompaniment. Fragment. April 1812.

(k) *Mondenschein* (text: Schober). T.T.B.B.B., PF. accompaniment. January 1826. (The *Gesamtausgabe* gives the version without accompaniment.)

(l) *Das stille Lied* (text: J. G. Seegemund). T.T.B.B. unacc. Fragment. May 1827.

(m) Sketches for *Mirjams Siegesgesang* (text: Grillparzer). March 1828.

H. SOLO SONGS

(a) *Ich sass am einer Tempelhalle* (text: (?) Salis-Seewis). Fragment. 1811.

(b) *Jägers Abendlied* (text: Goethe). 20 June 1815.

(c) *Meeresstille* (text: Goethe). 20 June 1815.

(d) *Der Graf von Hapsburg* (text: Schiller). Fragment. 1815.

(e) *An den Mond* (author unknown). Fragment. 18 October 1815.

(f) *Lorma* (text: Ossian—trans. Harold). Fragment. 28 November 1815.

(g) *Gruppe aus dem Tartarus* (text: Schiller). Fragment. March 1816.

(h) *Lied in der Abwesenheit* (text: Stolberg). Fragment. April 1816.

(i) *Am ersten Maimorgen* (text: Claudius). 1816.

(j) *An Chloen* (text: Uz). Fragment. 1816.

(k) *Mailied* (text: Hölty). November 1816.

(*l*) *Song without title or words.* May 1817.

(*m*) *Der Leidende* (author unknown). 1817.

(*n*) *Psalm XIII* (trans. Moses Mendelssohn). June 1819. (The last six bars are missing.)

(*o*) *Abend* (author unknown). Fragment. 1819.

(*p*) *Greisengesang* (text: Rückert). First version, substantially differing from the well-known setting. (?) 1822.

(*q*) *O Quell, was strömst du?* (text: Schulze). Fragment. 1826.

(*r*) *Fröhliches Scheiden* (text: Leitner). Fragment. 1827.

I. MISCELLANEOUS WORKS

(*a*) Seven exercises in counterpoint. *c*, 1812.

(*b*) Multiple settings of four passages from Pietro Metastasio. Autumn 1812.

    i. 'Quell' innocente figlio' (the angel's aria from *Isacco*), for S., S.S., S.A.T., S.A.T., S.A.T.B., S.A.T.B., S.A.T.B.

    ii. 'Entra l'uomo' (Abraham's aria from *Isacco*), for S., S.A., S.A.T., S.A.T.B., S.A.T.B., S.A.T.B.,

    iii. 'Te solo adoro' (Achior's aria from *Betulia liberata*), for S.A.T.B.

    iv. 'Serbate, o Dei custodi' (chorus from *La Clemenza di Tito*), for S.A.T.B. (two versions: both in D major), S.A.T.B. (C major), Tenor with bass continuo (two versions: both in C major).

(*c*) i. Six Ländler in B flat. February 1816.

    ii. Four 'Komische Ländler' in D major. 1816. (The treble stave only of these ten dances is preserved.)

(*d*) Verses from St. John's Gospel (ch. vi, vv. 55–58), for Sop. solo and figured bass. 1818.

(*e*) i. Two Ländler (A major, E major). 1819.

    ii. Two Ländler (both D flat). May 1821. (The treble stave only of these four dances is preserved.)

(*f*) Canon for six voices. January 1826.

The following items are very fragmentary. The last one is given here for the sake of completeness since it certainly contains traces of original work by Schubert; it could hardly be published as his work.

1. 35 bars from the first movement of a String Quartet (? in F major). *c*. 1813.

2. Offertory in C major ('Clamavi ad te'). *c.* 1813. (The soprano part only is preserved. The fact that it was copied by Schubert from a completed work, now lost, is proved by his insertion of the number of 'rest' bars between the vocal phrases.)

3. Two fragmentary arias from an unnamed opera. 1814.

4. Sketch (6 bars) for the opening of a setting of Mignon's song *So lasst mich scheinen.* (A flat, 2/4). September 1816.

5. Fragment (11 bars) from a completed setting of Mignon's song *So lasst mich scheinen.* (G major, 4/4). September 1816.

6. Sketches for 3 Polonaises from Op. 75: nos. 2, 3 and 4. *c.* 1818.

7. Arrangement for voice and orchestra of Maximilian Stadler's setting of Psalm VIII for voice and PF. August 1823.

APPENDIX III

THE WORKS IN CHRONOLOGICAL ORDER

This list of Schubert's works, chronologically arranged, is based upon primary research, and in all cases where it departs from the 'Thematic Catalogue' of O. E. Deutsch, there are good reasons for the departures. They may be due to further information from Dr. Deutsch himself, to recent discoveries, or to my own examination of various Schubert manuscripts. The results of Dr. Fritz Racek's careful description of the Schubert manuscripts in the Vienna 'Stadtbibliothek'[1] are also incorporated here.

I have omitted from the list some fifty items which are given in the 'Thematic Catalogue'. They comprise those works which are irretrievably lost, arrangements by Schubert of his own or of other composer's works, small fragments, dubious compositions, and one or two duplicates which, by acquiring dates differing from their originals, are masquerading as independent works, e.g. the song *Widerschein*.

In order to preserve a realistic chronology an approximate date has been assessed to those works which cannot be dated with certainty. It has in every case been carefully indicated. By this means it has been possible to avoid placing a number of undated works at the end of the list and the final works there are, as they should be, the last the composer wrote. With a similar aim in view works whose only date is that of the *year* of composition have been placed in the middle of that year's work, not at the beginning or end. Since they must be placed somewhere it seemed less desirable, to give an actual example, to break the sequence of December 1815 and January 1816, than that of June and July 1816.

[1] 'Von der Schubert Handschriften der Stadtbibliothek,' Fritz Racek, in the 'Festschrift zum hundertjährigen Bestehen der Wiener Stadtbibliothek' ('Wiener Schriften', IV), Vienna, 1956.

1810
Fantasia in G, PF. Duet (8 April–1 May).

1811
Hagars Klage (Schücking) (30 March).
Des Mädchens Klage (Schiller) (? March).
Eine Leichenphantasie (Schiller) (? March).
Overture in C minor, Str. Quintet (29 June–12 July).
Fantasia in G minor, PF. Duet (20 September).
Der Vatermörder (Pfeffel) (26 December).

1812
Overture in D, Orchestra (26 June).
Salve Regina in F, Soprano, Orchestra, Organ (28 June).
Klaglied (Rochlitz).
Der Spiegelritter, Operetta in 3 acts (Kotzbue): 1 act written.
Overture in D, Orchestra (Introduction in D minor).
Der Geistertanz (Matthisson).
Quell' innocente figlio (Metastasio), various settings.
String Quartet ('mixed keys')
Movement in B flat for PF., vn. and 'cello (called *Sonata*) (27 July–28 August).
Viel tausend Sterne prangen (Eberhard) (? August).
Der Jüngling am Bache (Schiller) (24 September).
Kyrie for a Mass in D minor, Chorus, Orchestra, Organ (25 September).
Overture (?) in D, Orchestral fragment (? 1812).
Overture to 'Der Teufel als Hydraulicus' (Albrecht), Orchestra (? 1812).
String Quartet in C major (September).
Andante in C, PF. Solo (9 September).
Twelve 'Wiener Deutsche', PF. Solo.
Entra l'uomo (Metastasio) various settings (September–October).
Te solo adoro (Metastasio) (5 November).
Serbate, o Dei custodi (Metastasio) (10 December).
String Quartet in B flat (19 November–21 February 1813).

1813
Totengräberlied (Hölty) (19 January).
Kyrie for a Mass in B flat, unacc. Chorus (1 March).
String Quartet in C (March).

Dithyrambe (Schiller), mixed voices, Tenor, PF. (29 March).

Fantasia in C minor, PF. Duet (2 versions) (April–10 June).

Kyrie for a Mass in D minor, Chorus, Orchestra (15 April).

Die Schatten (Matthisson) (12 April).

Unendliche Freude (Schiller), T.T.B. (15 April).

Sehnsucht ('Ach! aus dieses Tales') (Schiller) (15–17 April).

Vorüber die stöhnende Klage (Schiller), T.T.B. (18 April).

Unendliche Freude (Schiller), Canon, T.T.B. (19 April).

Selig durch die Liebe (Schiller), T.T.B. (21 April).

Sanctus, canon with coda (21 April).

Hier strecket (Schiller), T.T.B., (29 April).

Dessen Fahne (Schiller), T.T.B. (May).

Verklärung (Pope, tr. Herder) (4 May).

Hier unarmen (Schiller), T.T.B. (8 May).

Ein jugendlicher Maienschwung (Schiller), T.T.B. (8 May).

Thronend auf erhabnem Sitz (Schiller), T.T.B. (9 May).

Wer die steile Sternenbahn (Schiller), T.T.B. (10 May).

Majestät'sche Sonnenrossse (Schiller), T.T.B. (10 May).

Schmerz verzerret (Schiller), T.T.B. (11 May).

Kyrie for a Mass in F, Chorus, Orchestra, Organ (12 May).

Frisch atmet (Schiller), T.B.B. (15 May).

Fantasia in C minor, PF. Solo (? 1813).

Overture in D, Orchestral fragment (? 1813).

Symphony in D, Orchestral fragment based on above (? 1813).

Liebe säuseln die Blätter (Hölty), vocal trio (? 1813).

Fugue, 4 voices, PF. Solo (? 1813).

Allegro moderato in C, Andante in A minor, PF. Duet (? 1813).

String Quartet in B flat (2 movements) (8–16 June, 18 August).

Variations in F major, PF. Solo (? 1813).

Totengräberlied (Hölty), T.T.B. (? 1813).

Ich sass an einer Tempelhalle (? Salis) (? 1813).

Twenty Minuets, PF. Solo.

Miserero pargoletto (Metastasio).

Dreifach ist der Schritt (Schiller), T.B.B.

Dreifach ist der Schritt (Schiller), canon à tre (8 July).

Ewig still (Schiller), canon à tre (8 July).

Die zwei Tugendwege (Schiller), T.T.B. (15 July).

Minuet and Finale in F, 2 ob., 2 cl., 2 hn., 2 bn. (18 August).

Thekla (Schiller) (22–23 August).

String Quartet in D (22 August–September).

Trinklied ('Freunde, sammelt') (?) (29 August).

Pensa, che questo istante (Metastasio) (13 September).

Der Taucher (Schiller) (17 September–5 April 1814).

Son fra l'onde (Metastasio) (18 September).

Eine kleine Trauermusik, 2 cl., 2 bn., db. bn., 2 hn., 2 trb. (19 September).

Kantate zur Namensfeier des Vaters (Schubert), T.T.B. and guitar (27 September).

Auf den Sieg der Deutschen (?), solo with 2 vn. and 'cello (Autumn).

Two Minuets, PF. Solo (? 1813).

Symphony no. 1, in D (finished 28 October).

Zur Namensfeier des Herrn Andreas Siller (?), solo with vn. and harp (28 October–4 November).

'Des Teufels Lustschloss', Opera in 3 acts (Kotzebue) (30 October–22 October 1814).

Minuet in D, strings (? November).

String Quartet in E flat, Op. 125: no. 1 (November).

Verschwunden sind die Schmerzen canon, T.T.B. (15 November).

Five Minuets (6 trios) for String Quartet (19 November).

Five 'German' dances (7 trios) with coda, for String Quartet (19 November).

Two Minuets (4 trios), PF. Solo (22 November).

Don Gayseros (Fouqué) (? 1813). ⎫
Nächtens klang die süsse Laute (? 1813) ⎬ *Don Gayseros*
An dem jungen Morgenhimmel (? 1813) ⎭

Allegro moderato in C, PF. Solo (? 1813).

Andantino in C, PF. Solo (? 1813).

Fugue, 4 voices, PF. Solo (? 1813).

1814

Trio of a Minuet for fl., va., guitar and 'cello (included in the so-called 'Guitar' Quartet). (26 February).

Trost. An Elisa (Matthisson) (? April).

Andenken (Matthisson) (April).

Geisternähe (Matthisson) (April).

Erinnerung (also called *Totenopfer*) (Matthisson) (April).

Grave and Allegro, String Quartet in C minor (23 April).

Die Befreier Europas (?) (16 May).

Mass no. 1, in F, S.A.T.B., Chorus, Orchestra, Organ (17 May–22 July).

Minuet in C sharp minor, PF. Solo (? June).

Salve Regina, B flat, Tenor, Orchestra, Organ (28 June–1 July).

Lied aus der Ferne (Matthisson) (? July).

String Quartet in D.

Adelaide (Matthisson).

Der Abend (Matthisson) (July).

Lied der Liebe (Matthisson) (July).

Wer ist gross? (?), Bass, T.T.B.B., Orchestra (24–25 July).

String Quartet in B flat, Op. 168 (5–13 September).

An Emma (Schiller) (17 September).

Erinnerungen (Matthisson) (mid September).

Die Betende (Matthisson) (mid September).

Das Fraulein im Türme (Matthisson) (29 September).

An Laura (Matthisson) (2–7 October).

Der Geistertanz (Matthisson) (14 October).

Das Mädchen aus der Fremde (Schiller) (16 October).

Gretchen am Spinnrade (Goethe) (19 October).

Nachtgesang (Goethe) (30 November).

Trost im Thränen (Goethe) (30 November).

Schäfers Klagelied (Goethe) (30 November).

Sehnsucht (Goethe) (3 December).

Am See (Mayrhofer) (7 December).

Ammenlied (Luibi) (December).

Symphony no. 2, in B flat (10 December–24 March 1815).

'Szene aus Goethe's "Faust" ' (12 December).

An die Natur (Stolberg) (? December).

Lied (*Mutter geht*) (Fouqué) (? December).

1815

Bardengesang (Ossian, tr. Harold) (20 January).

Trinklied ('Brüder, unser Erdenwallen') (Castelli) (February).

Auf einen Kirchhof (Schlechta) (2 February).

Minona (Bertrand) (8 February).

Als ich sie erröten sah (Ehrlich) (10 February).

Der Sänger (Goethe) (February).

Lodas Gespenst (Ossian) (February).

Sonata no. 1, in E major (11 February–21 February).

Das Bild (?) (11 February).

Ten Variations in F major (finished 15 February).

Écossaise in F, PF. Solo (21 February).

Am Flusse (Goethe), 1st setting (27 February).
An Mignon ('Ueber Tal') (Goethe) (27 February).
Nähe des Geliebten (Goethe) (27 February).
Sängers Morgenlied (Körner), 1st setting (27 February).
Sängers Morgenlied (Körner), 2nd setting (1 March).
Amphiaros (Körner) (1 March).
Mass no. 2, in G major, S.T.B., Chorus, Strings, Organ (2–7 March).
Begräbnislied (Klopstock), S.A.T.B., PF. (9 March).
Trinklied vor der Schlacht (Körner) (12 March).
Schwertlied (Körner), Solo with Chorus (12 March).
Gebet während der Schlacht (Körner) (12 March).
String Quartet in G minor (25 March–1 April).
Das war ich (Körner) (26 March).
Stabat Mater in G minor, Chorus, Orchestra, Organ (4–6 April).
Die Sterne (Fellinger) (6 April).
Vergebliche Liebe (Bernard) (6 April).
Adagio in G major, PF. Solo (8 April).
Liebesrausch (Körner) (8 April).
Sehnsucht der Liebe (Körner) (8 April).
'Tres sunt', Offertory in A minor, Chorus, Orchestra, Organ (10–11 April).
Die erste Liebe (Fellinger) (12 April).
Trinklied ('Ihr Freunde') (Zettler) (12 April).
'Benedictus es, Domine', Gradual in C, Chorus, Orchestra, Organ, Op. 150 (15 April).
Second 'Dona Nobis' for the Mass in F major, S.A.T.B., Chorus, Orchestra, Organ (25 April).
'Die vierjährige Posten', 1 act *Singspiel* (Körner) (8–19 May).
Des Mädchens Klage (Schiller), 2nd setting (15 May).
Der Jüngling am Bache (Schiller), 2nd setting (15 May).
An den Mond (Hölty) (17 May).
Die Mainacht (Hölty) (17 May).
Die Sterbende (Matthisson) (May).
Stimme der Liebe (Matthisson) (May).
Naturgenuss (Matthisson) (May).
An die Freude (Schiller) (May).
Rastlose Liebe (Goethe) (19 May).
Amalia (Schiller) (19 May).
An die Nachtigall (Hölty) (22 May).

2 B   B.S.

An die Apfelbäume (Hölty) (22 May).

Seufzer (Hölty) (22 May).

Mailied ('Gruner wird') (Hölty) 2 voices or 2 hn. (24 May).

Symphony no. 3, in D major (24 May–19 July).

Mailied ('Der Schnee zerinnt') (Hölty), 2 voices or 2 hn. (26 May).

Der Morgenstern (Körner), 2 voices or 2 hn. (26 May).

Jägerlied (Körner), 2 voices or 2 hn. (26 May).

Lützows wilde Jagd (Körner), 2 voices or 2 hn. (26 May).

Liebeständelei (Körner) (26 May).

Der Liebende (Hölty) (29 May).

Die Nonne (Hölty) (29 May: revised 16 June).

Der Liedler (Kenner) (June–12 December).

Klärchens Lied (Goethe) (3 June).

Adelwold und Emma (Bertrand) (5–14 June).

Der Traum (Hölty) (17 June).

Die Liebe (Hölty) (17 June).

Jägers Abendlied (Goethe) (20 June).

Meeresstille (Goethe), 1st setting (20 June).

Meeresstille (Goethe, 2nd setting (21 June).

Colmas Klage (Ossian) (22 June).

Grablied (Kenner) (24 June).

Das Finden (Kosegarten) (25 June).

'Fernando', 1 act *Singspiel* (Stadler) (27 June–9 July).

Mailied ('Grüner wird') (Hölty), T.T.B.

Mailied ('Der Schnee zerrinnt') (Hölty), canon à tre.

Ballade ('Ein Fraulein schaut') (Kenner).

Waltz in C sharp major, PF. Solo.

2nd Trio for the Waltz in E major, PF. Solo, Op. 127: no. 3.

Klage um Ali Bey (Claudius), S.S.A. with PF.

Der Mondabend (Kumpf).

Geistes-Gruss (Goethe).

Waltzes for Op. 127, PF. Solo.

Minuet in A, PF. Solo.

Eight écossaises, PF. Solo.

Der Graf von Hapsburg (Schiller) (? 1815).

'Totus in corde', Offertory in C, Op. 46: Sop., Orchestra, Organ.

Lacrimoso son io (?), 2 settings as canon à tre.

Lieb Minna (Stadler) (2 July).

Salve Regina in F major (Second Offertory), Sop., Orchestra, Organ,
    Op. 47 (5 July: revised 28 January 1823).

Wanderers Nachtlied ('Der, du von dem Himmel bist') (Goethe). (5 July).

Der Fischer (Goethe) (5 July).

Erster Verlust (Goethe) (5 July).

Idens Nachtgesang (Kosegarten) (7 July).

Von Ida (Kosegarten) (7 July).

Die Erscheinung (also called *Erinnerung*) (Kosegarten) (7 July).

Die Täuschung (Kosegarten) (7 July).

Das Sehnen (Kosegarten) (7 July).

Hymne an den Unendlichen (Schiller), S.A.T.B. with PF. (11 July).

Der Abend (Kosegarten) (15 July).

Geist der Liebe (Kosegarten) (15 July).

Tischlied (Goethe) (15 July).

Abends unter der Linde (Kosegarten), 1st setting (24 July).

Abends unter der Linde (Kosegarten), 2nd setting (25 July).

Das Abendrot (Kosegarten), Vocal Trio with PF. (25 July).

Die Mondnacht (Kosegarten) (25 July).

'Claudine von Villa Bella' (Goethe), 3 act *Singspiel* (started 26 July)

Huldigung (Kosegarten) (27 July).

Alles um Liebe (Kosegarten) (27 July).

Das Geheimnis (Schiller), 1st setting (7 August).

Hoffnung (Schiller) (7 August).

Das Mädchen aus der Fremde (Schiller) (12 August).

Trinklied in Winter (Hölty), T.T.B. (? August).

Frühlingslied (?), T.T.B. (? August).

Willkommen, lieber schöner Mai (Hölty), 2 settings as canon àtre (? August).

An den Frühling (Schiller) (August).

Die Bürgschaft (Schiller) (August).

Die Spinnerin (Goethe) (August).

Lob des Tokayers (Baumberg) (August).

Punschlied (Schiller) (18 August).

Der Gott und die Bajadere (Goethe) (18 August).

Der Rattenfänger (Goethe) (19 August).

Der Schatzgräber (Goethe) (19 August).

Heidenröslein (Goethe) (19 August).

Bundeslied (Goethe) (19 August).

An den Mond (Goethe), 1st setting (19 August).

Wonne der Wehmut (Goethe) (20 August).

Wer kauft Liebesgötter (Goethe) (21 August).

Die Fröhlichkeit (Prandstetter) (22 August).

Der Morgenkuss (Baumberg) (22 August).

Cora an die Sonne (Baumberg) (22 August).

Abendständchen: an Lina (Baumberg) (23 August).

Morgenlied (Stolberg) (24 August).

Trinklied ('Auf! Jeder sei nun froh') (?), T.T.B.B., with PF. (25 August).

Bergknappenlied (?), T.T.B.B., with PF. (25 August).

Das Leben (Wannovius), S.S.A., with PF. (25 August).

An die Sonne (Baumberg) (25 August).

An die Sonne (Tiedge) (25 August).

Der Wieberfreund (Abraham Cowley, tr. Ratschky) (25 August).

Lilla an die Morgenröte (?) (25 August).

Tischerlied (?) (25 August).

Totenkranz für ein Kind (Matthisson) (25 August).

Abendlied (Stolberg) (28 August).

Punschlied (Schiller), T.T.B., with PF. (29 August).

Cronnan (Ossian, tr. Harold) (5 September).

An den Frühling (Schiller), 2nd setting (6 September).

Lied ('Es ist so angenehm') (Schiller) (6 September).

Furcht der Geliebten (Klopstock) (12 September).

Selma und Selmar (Klopstock) (14 September).

Vaterlandslied (Klopstock) (14 September).

An Sie (Klopstock) (14 September).

Die Sommernacht (Klopstock) (14 September).

Die frühen Gräber (Klopstock) (14 September).

Dem Unendlichen (Klopstock) (15 September).

Lied nach dem Falle Nathos (Ossian, tr. Harold) (September).

Sonata in C major (September).

Das Rosenband (Klopstock) (September).

Das Mädchen von Inistore (Ossian, tr. Harold) (September).

Shilric und Vinvela (Ossian, tr. Harold) (20 September).

Namensfeier (Vierthaler): or *Gratulations-Kantate*, S.T.B., Chorus, Orchestra (27 September).

Hoffnung (Goethe) (? September).

An den Mond (Goethe), 2nd setting (? September).

Twelve écossaises, PF. Solo (3 October).

Liane (Mayrhofer) (October).

Lambertine (Stoll) (12 October).

Labetrank der Liebe (Stoll) (15 October).

An die Geliebte (Stoll) (15 October).

Wiegenlied (Körner) (15 October).

Mein Gruss an den Mai (Kumpf) (15 October).

Skolie (Deinhardstein) (15 October).

Die Sternenwelten (Fellinger) (15 October).

Die macht der Liebe (Kalchberg) (15 October).

Das gestörte Glück (Körner) (15 October).

Nur wer die Sehnsucht kennt (Goethe), 1st setting (18 October).

Hektors Abschied (Schiller) (19 October).

Die Sterne (Kosegarten) (19 October).

Nachtgesang (Kosegarten) (19 October).

An Rosa I (Kosegarten) (19 October).

An Rosa II (Kosegarten) (19 October).

Idens Schwanlied (Kosegarten) (19 October).

Schwanengesang (Kosegarten) (19 October).

Luisens Antwort (Kosegarten) (19 October).

Der Zufriedene (Reissig) (23 October).

Kennst du das Land? (Goethe) (23 October).

Hermann und Thusnelda (Klopstock) (27 October).

Erlking (Goethe) (October).

Ländler and écossaises from Op. 18 (October).

Klage der Ceres (Schiller) (9 November: finished June 1816).

Mass no. 3, in B flat, S.A.T.B., Chorus, Orchestra, Organ, Op. 141 (started 11 November).

Harfenspieler: Wer sich der Einsamkeit ergibt (Goethe) (13 November).

'Die Freunde von Salamanka' (Mayrhofer), *Singspiel* in two acts (18 November–31 December).

Lorma (Ossian, tr. Harold), 1st setting (28 November).

Die drei Sänger (?) (23 December).

Das Grab (Salis), 1st setting (28 December).

1816

Eight Ländler in F sharp minor, PF. Solo (January).

Eight Ländler in D major, PF. Solo (January).

Four 'Komische' Ländler in D major (? PF. Solo) (January).

Six Ländler in B flat, (? PF. Solo) (February).

Der Tod Oskars (? Ossian, tr. Harold) (February).

Lorma (Ossian, tr. Harold), 2nd setting (10 February).

Das Grab (Salis), 2nd setting (11 February).

Eight Ländler in B flat, PF. Solo (13 February).

Salve Regina (German text) in F major, S.A.T.B., Organ (21 February).

Three Minuets for PF. Solo (Trio to the third unfinished) (22 February).

Morgenlied (?) (24 February).

Abendlied (?) (24 February).

Stabat Mater (Klopstock) in F minor, S.T.B. soli, Chorus, Orchestra (28 February).

Salve Regina in B flat, Chorus, Organ (March).

Sonata ('Sonatina') in D major, PF. and vn., Op. 137: no. 1 (March).

Sonata ('Sonatina') in A minor, PF, and vn., Op. 137: no. 2 (March).

Frühlingslied (Hölty) (13 March).

Auf der Tod einer Nachtigall (Hölty) (13 March).

Die Knabenzeit (Hölty) (13 March).

Winterlied (Hölty) (13 March).

Ritter Toggenburg (Schiller) (13 March).

'Die Schlacht' (Schiller), Cantata, PF. (March).

Laura am Klavier (Schiller) (March).

Des Mädchens Klage (Schiller), 3rd setting (March).

Die Entzückung an Laura (Schiller), 1st setting (March).

Die vier Weltalter (Schiller) (March).

Pfügerlied (Salis) (March).

Die Einsiedelei (Salis), 1st setting (March).

Gesang an die Harmonie (Salis) (March).

Lebensmelodien (Schlegel) (March).

Der Flüchtling (Schiller) (18 March).

Lied: In's stille Land (Salis) (27 March–April).

Wehmut (Salis) (End of March–April).

Der Herbstabend (Salis) (End of March–April).

Abschied von der Harfe (Salis) (End of March–April).

Der König in Thule (Goethe) (? April).

Jägers Abendlied (Goethe), 2nd setting (? April).

An Schwager Kronos (Goethe) (? April).

Sonata ('Sonatina') in G minor, PF. and vn., Op. 137: no. 3 (April).

Die verfehlte Stunde (Schlegel) (April).

Sprache der Liebe (Schlegel) (April).

Daphne am Bach (Stolberg) (April).

Stimme der Liebe (Stolberg) (April).

Entzückung (Matthisson) (April).

Geist der Liebe (Matthisson) (April).

Klage (Matthisson) (April).

Lied der Abwesenheit (Stolberg) (April).

Symphony no. 4, in C minor ('The Tragic') (finished 27 April).
Stimme der Liebe (Stolberg) (29 April).
Julius an Theone (Matthisson) (30 April).
'Die Bürgschaft' (?), Opera in 3 acts (unfinished) (started 2 May).
Klage an den Mond (Hölty) (12 May).
Twelve 'German' dances ('Deutsche'), PF. Solo (? May).
Six écossaises, PF. Solo (May).
Naturgenuss (Matthisson), T.T.B.B. (May: PF. acc. in February 1822).
Andenken (Matthisson), T.T.B. (May).
Erinnerungen (Matthisson), T.T.B. (May).
Trinklied im Mai (Hölty), T.T.B. (May).
Widerhall (Matthisson), T.T.B. (May).
Minnelied (Hölty) (May).
Die Erwartung (Schiller) (May).
Die frühe Liebe (Hölty) (May).
Blumenlied (Hölty) (May).
Der Leidende (?), 1st setting (May).
Der Leidende (?), 2nd setting (May).
Klage ('Trauer umfliesst mein Leben') (?) (May).
Seligkeit (Hölty) (May).
Erntelied (Hölty) (May).
Rondo in A major, Vn. solo and str. orch. (June).
An die Sonne (Uz), S.A.T.B., with PF. (June).
Chor der Engel (from Goethe's 'Faust'), S.A.T.B. (June).
Cantata for the 50th Jubilee of Salieri (Schubert.
    1st setting, T.T.B.B., Ten., PF. (? June).
    2nd setting, T.T.B., Ten., PF. (June).
Das grosse Halleluja (Klopstock) (June).
Schlachtgesang (Klopstock) (June).
Die Gestirne (Klopstock) (June).
Edone (Klopstock) (June).
Die Liebesgötter (Uz) (June).
An den Schlaf (? Uz) (June).
Gott im Frühlinge (Uz) (June).
Der gute Hirt (Uz) (June).
Fragment aus dem Aeschylus ('Oreste', tr. Mayrhofer) (June).
'Prometheus' (Dräxler) [Lost]: Cantata, Soli, Chorus, ? PF. (17 June).
Mass no. 4, in C major, S.A.T.B., Chorus, Orchestra. Organ, Op. 48 (June–July).

Der Entfernten (Salis), T.T.B.B. (? 1816).

Minuet in E major (two Trios), PF. Solo (*c*. 1816).

Die Einsiedelei (Salis), T.T.B.B.

An den Frühling (Schiller), T.T.B.B.

An mein Klavier (Schubart).

Allegretto in C major, PF. Solo (? 1816).

Der Entfernten (Salis) (? 1816).

Fischerlied (Salis) (? 1816).

Licht und Liebe ('Nachtgesang', Collin) (? 1816).

String Quartet in E major, Op. 125: no. 2

Trinklied ('Funkelnd im Becher') (?), T.T.B.B., with PF.

Gold'ner Schein (Matthisson), canon à tre.

Die Nacht (Uz).

An Chloen (Uz).

Am Bach in Frühling (Schober).

Waltzes from Op. 127 and Op. 9.

Romanze (Stolberg).

Fischerlied (Salis), T.T.B.B.

Freude der Kinderjahre (Köpken) (July).

Ländler PF. Solo (publ. 'Gesamtausgabe', XII, 10).

Requiem Mass (*Kyrie*) in F major, S.A.T.B., wind band (? July).

Osterlied (Klopstock), S.A.T.B. with PF. (? 1816).

Grablied auf einen Soldaten (Schubart) (July).

Das Heimweh ('Th. Hell'—K. G. Winkler) (July).

An die untergehende Sonne (Kosegarten) (July–May 1817).

Aus Diego Manzares (Schlechta) (30 July).

An den Mond (Hölty) (7 August).

Sonata in E major (publ. as 'Fünf Klavierstücke') (August).

Adagio in C major, PF. Solo (? August).

'Tantum ergo' in C major, Chorus, Orchestra, Organ (August).

'Tantum ergo' in C major, S.A.T.B., Chorus, Orchestra (August).

An Chloen (Jacobi) (August).

Hochzeitlied (Jacobi) (August).

In der Mitternacht (Jacobi) (August).

Litanei auf das Fest Aller Seelen (Jacobi) (? August).

Trauer der Liebe (Jacobi) (August).

Die Perle (Jacobi) (August).

Pflicht und Liebe (Gotter) (August).

Overture in B flat, Orchestra (September).

Andante in A major, PF. Solo (? September).

String Trio in B flat, one movement (September).
Symphony no. 5, in B flat (September–3 October).
Cantata (for Josef Spendou), S.A.T.B. soli, Chorus, Orchestra, Op.
    128 (September).
Liedesend (Mayrhofer) (September).
Abschied: nach einer Wallfahrtsarie (Mayrhofer) (September).
Rückweg (Mayrhofer) (September).
Alte Liebe rostet nie (Mayrhofer) (September).
Orpheus (Jacobi) (September).
Harfenspieler I: Wer sich der Einsamkeit ergibt (Goethe) (September).
Harfenspieler II: An die Türen (Goethe) (September).
Harfenspieler III: Wer nie sein Brot (Goethe),
    1st setting (September).
    2nd setting (September).
Nur wer die Sehnsucht kennt (Goethe),
    2nd setting (? September).
    3rd setting (September).
Der Sänger am Felsen (Karoline Pichler) (September).
Lied: Ferne von der grossen Stadt (Pichler) (September).
Magnificat in C major, Soli, Chorus, Orchestra, Organ (15 or 25
    September).
Adagio and Rondo concertante in F major, PF., vn., va., 'cello (called
    'Klavier-Konzert') (October).
'Auguste jam coelestium', in G major, Sop., Ten., Orchestra (Octo-
    ber).
Der Wanderer (Schmidt von Lübeck) (October).
Der Hirt (Mayrhofer) (October).
Lied eines Schiffers an die Dioskuren (Mayrhofer) (? October).
Geheimnis: an Franz Schubert (Mayrhofer) (October).
Zum Punsche (Mayrhofer) (October).
Am ersten Maimorgen (Claudius) (? November).
Mailied ('Grüner wird') (Hölty) (November).
Der Liedende (?), 3rd setting (? November).
Konzertstück in D major, Vn. solo and Orchestra (? November).
Lied: Ich bin vergnügt (Claudius), 1st setting (? November).
Phidile (Claudius) (November).
Lied: Ich bin vergnugt (Claudius), 2nd setting (November).
Bei dem Grab meines Vaters (Claudius) (November).
An die Nachtigall (Claudius) (November).
Abendlied (Claudius) (November).

Am Grabe Anselmos (Claudius) (4 November).
Der Geistertanz (Matthisson), T.T.B.B. (November).
Abendlied der Fürstin (Mayrhofer) (November).
Wiegenlied: Schlafe, schlafe, holder, süsser Knabe (?) (November).
Herbstlied (Salis) (November).
Rondo in E major, PF. Solo, Op. 145 (the finale of the Sonata in E
   major, 1817) (? December).
Skolie (Matthisson) (December).
Lebenslied (Matthisson) (December).
Leiden der Trennung (Metastasio, tr. H. v. Collin) (December).
Vedi, quanto adoro (Metastasio: Didone's aria) (December).

1817

Frohsinn (?) (January).
Jagdlied (Werner) (January).
Die Liebe (Leon) (January).
Trost ('Nimmer lange weil ich hier') (?) (January).
Der Alpenjäger (Mayrhofer) (January).
Wie Ulfru fischt (Mayrhofer) (January).
Fahrt zum Hades (Mayrhofer) (January).
Schlaflied (Mayrhofer) (January).
Augenlied (Mayrhofer) (? January).
Sehnsucht (Mayrhofer) (? January).
La pastorella al prato (Goldoni) (January).
La pastorella al prato (Goldoni), T.T.B.B., with PF. (? January).
Fischerweise (Schlechta) (? January).
Die Blumensprache (Platner) (? January).
Eight écossaises, PF. Solo (February).
Écossaise in E flat, PF. Solo.
An eine Quelle (Claudius) (February).
Der Tod und das Mädchen (Claudius) (February).
Das Lied vom Reifen (Claudius) (February).
Taglich zu singen (Claudius) (February).
Die Nacht (?, tr. Harold) (February).
Lied: Bruder, schrecklich brennt (?) (February).
Sonata in A minor, Op. 164 (March).
Gesang der Geister über den Wassern (Goethe), T.T.B.B. (March).
Der Schiffffer (Mayrhofer) (? March).
Am Strome (Mayrhofer) (March).
Philoktet (Mayrhofer) (March).

Memnon (Mayrhofer) (March).
Antigone und Oedip (Mayrhofer) (March).
Auf dem See (Goethe) (March).
Mahomets Gesang (Goethe) (March).
Ganymed (Goethe) (March).
Der Jüngling an den Tod (Spaun) (March).
Trost im Liede (Schober) (March).
An die Musik (Schober) (March).
Orest auf Tauris (Mayrhofer) (March).
Der entsühnte Orest (Mayrhofer) (? March 1817).
Freiwilliges Versinken (Mayrhofer) (? March 1817).
Die Forelle (Schubart) (? April).
Pax vobiscum (Schober) (April).
Hänflings Liebeswerbung (Kindl) (April).
Auf der Donau (Mayrhofer) (April).
Uraniens Flucht (Mayrhofer) (April).
Song: no title, no words (? May).
Overture in D major, Orchestra (May).
Sonata in A flat (May).
Liebhaber in allen Gestalten (Goethe) (May).
Schweizerlied (Goethe) (May).
Der Goldschmiedsgesell (Goethe) (May).
Nach einem Gewitter (Mayrhofer) (May).
Fischerlied (Salis), 2nd setting (May).
Die Einsiedelei (Salis), 2nd setting (May).
Gretchens Bitte (Goethe) (May).
Sonata in E minor (June).
Sonata in D flat (June).
Sonata in E flat, Op. 122 (revised and transposed version of previous sonata) (June).
Der Strom (?) (? June).
Das Grab (Salis) (intended for male voices) (June).
Die abgeblühte Linde (Széchényi) (? 1817).
Der Flug der Zeit (Széchényi) (? 1817).
Der Schäfer und der Reiter (Fouqué).
An den Tod (Schubart).
Sonata in F sharp minor. (July).
Lied im Freien (Salis), T.T.B.B. (July).
Iphigenia (Mayrhofer) (July).
Sonata in A major, PF. and vn. (called 'Duo'), Op. 162 (August).

Sonata in B major, Op. 147 (August).

Thirteen Variations on a theme by Anselm Hüttenbrenner in A minor, PF. Solo (August).

Die Entzückung an Laura (Schiller), 2nd setting (August).

Abschied von einem Freunde (Schubert) (24 August).

Polonaise in B flat, vn. solo, str. orchestra (September).

String Trio in B flat, vn., va., 'cello (September).

Gruppe aus dem Tartarus (Schiller) (September).

Elysium (Schiller) (September).

Atys (Mayrhofer) (September).

Am Erlafsee (Mayrhofer) (September).

Wiegenlied: Der Knabe in der Wiege (Ottenwalt) (September–November).

Der Alpenjäger (Schiller) (October).

Symphony no. 6, in C major (October–February 1818).

Overture (in the Italian style) in D major, Orchestra (November).

Overture (in the Italian style) in C major, Orchestra (November).

Six 'German' Dances, PF. Solo (XII, 13).

Three 'German' Dances, PF. Solo (XII, 15).

Two 'German' Dances, PF. Solo (XII, 17).

Scherzo in B flat, PF. Solo (November).

Scherzo in D flat, PF. Solo (November).

Der Kampf (Schiller) (November).

Thekla (Schiller), 2nd setting (November).

Lied eines Kindes (?) (November).

Das Dörfchen (Bürger), T.T.B.B. (December: revised and lengthened *c.* 1819).

1818

Lebenslust, S.A.T.B., with PF. (January).

Trio in E major, PF. Solo (for an unidentified Minuet) (February).

Auf der Riesenkoppe (Körner) (March).

Sonata in C major (First movement and Finale) (April).

Adagio in E major, PF. Solo (probably the slow movement of the previous item) (April).

An den Mond in einer Herbstnacht (Schreiber) (April).

Symphony sketches (D major): eight movements sketched (May).

Grablied für die Mutter (?) (June).

Four Polonaises, PF. Duet, Op. 75 (? July).

Three Marches: B minor, C, D, PF. Duet, Op. 27 (? July).

Introduction and variations on an original theme in B flat, PF. Duet, Op. 82: no. 2 (posth.) (? July).

Fantasia in C major, PF. Solo (? 1818).

March in E major, PF. Solo.

St. John's Gospel, vi. 55–8, Sop., with figured bass.

Sonata in B flat, PF. Duet, Op. 30 (? August).

'German' Dance with two trios and coda, PF. Duet (? August).

Einsamkeit (Mayrhofer) (August).

Deutsche Trauermesse ('German Requiem') (?), S.A.T.B., Organ (August).

Der Blumenbrief (Schreiber) (August).

Das Marienbild (Schreiber) (August).

Eight variations on a French air, in E minor, PF. Duet, Op. 10 (September).

Sonata in F minor (September).

Adagio in D flat (slow movement of preceding sonata).

Rondo in D major ('Notre amitié est invariable'), PF. Duet, Op. 138 (? September).

Blondel zu Marien (?) (September).

Allegretto in A flat (no. 6 of the 'Moments musicaux'), PF. Solo (? October).

Das Abendrot (Schreiber) (November).

Sonnet I (Petrarch, tr. Schlegel) (November).

Sonnett II (Petrarch, tr. Schlegel) (November).

Sonnett III (Petrarch, tr. Gries) (December).

Waltzes and écossaises from Op. 9 and Op. 18, PF. Solo.

Lob der Thränen (Schlegel) (? December).

Blanka (Schlegel) (December).

Vom Mitleiden Mariae (Schlegel) (December).

1819

Die Gebüsche (Schlegel) (January).

'Die Zwillingsbrüder' (Georg v. Hoffman), 1 act *Singspiel* (finished January).

'Adrast' (Mayrhofer), Opera, text lost: (unfinished) (? February).

Overture in E minor, Orchestra (? for 'Adrast') (February).

Der Wanderer (Schlegel) (February).

Abendbilder (Silbert) (February).

Himmelsfunken (Silbert) (February).

Das Mädchen (Schlegel) (February).

Berthas Lied in der Nacht (Grillparzer) (February).

An die Freunde (Mayrhofer) (March).

Sonata in C sharp minor (First movement: unfinished) (April).

Nur wer die Sehnsucht kennt (Goethe), T.T.B.B.B. (April).

Ruhe, schönstes Gluck der Erde (?), T.T.B.B. (April).

Marie (Novalis) (May).

'Hymnen: I, II, III, IV' (Novalis) (May).

Psalm XIII (tr. Moses Mendelssohn) (June).

Sonata in A major, Op. 120 (? July).

Two Ländler (? PF. Solo).

Der Schmetterling (Schlegel).

Die Berge (Schlegel).

Ruhe (?), T.T.B.B.

Sehnsucht ('Ach, aus dieses Tales Gründen') (Schiller).

Hoffnung (Schiller).

Der Jüngling am Bache (Schiller), 3rd setting.

'German' Dance in C sharp minor, PF. Solo.

Écossaise in D flat, PF. Solo.

Cantata (for J. M. Vogl's birthday), S.T.B., with PF., Op. 158 (publ. as 'Der Frühlingsmorgen') (August).

PF. Quintet in A major (*The Trout*), Op. 114 (started September).

Overture in G minor, PF. Duet (October).

Beim Winde (Mayrhofer) (October).

Die Sternennächte (Mayrhofer) (October).

Trost (Mayrhofer) (October).

Nachtstück (Mayrhofer) (October).

Die Liebende schreibt (Goethe) (October).

Prometheus (Goethe) (October).

Widerschein (Schlechta).

Overture in F minor and major, PF. Duet, Op. 34 (November).

Salve Regina in A major (Third Offertory), Op. 153, Sop., Orchestra (November).

Die Götter Griechenlands (Schiller) (November).

Mass no. 5, in A flat, S.A.T.B., Chorus, Orchestra, Organ (November– September 1822).

1820

Nachthymne (Novalis) (January).

Vier Canzonen (Vitorelli and Metastasio) (January).

'Lazarus: the Feast of Resurrection' (Niemeyer), Cantata in 3 acts (2 only finished), S.A.T.B., Chor., Orch. (February).

Die Vögel
Der Knabe
Der Fluss   }(Schlegel) (March).[1]
Der Schiffer

Die Sterne (Schlegel) (? March).

Namenstaglied (Stadler) (March).

Six Antiphons for Palm Sunday, Chorus (April).

Five écossaises in A flat, PF. Solo (May).

'Die Zauberharfe' (Hofmann), incidental music to a 3 act play (June, July ?).

Ueber allen Zauber Liebe (Mayrhofer).

Morgenlied (Werner).

Twelve Ländler (E flat and D flat), PF. Solo.

Liebeslauschen (Schlechta) (September).

Frühlingsglaube (Uhland).

'Sakuntala', Opera in 3 acts: sketches only (Neumann) (October).

Der Jüngling auf dem Hügel (H. Hüttenbrenner) (November).

String Quartet in C minor, 1 movement ('Quartettsatz') (December).

Gesang der Geister über den Wassern (Goethe), male voice octet, 2 va., 2 'cello. Sketch. (December).

Gesang der Geister über den Wassern (Goethe), T.T.B.B., with PF. Sketch. (December).

Psalm XXIII (tr. Moses Mendelssohn), S.S.A.A., with PF., Op. 132 (December).

Der zürnenden Diana (Mayrhofer) (December).

Im Walde ('Waldesnacht') (Schlegel) (December).

1821

Die gefangenen Sänger (A. W. v. Schlegel) (January).

Der Unglückliche (Pichler) (January).

Gesang der Geister über den Wassern (Goethe), 4 T., 4 B., 2 va., 2 'cello, D.B., Op. 167 (February).

Versunken (Goethe) (February).

'German' Dance in G flat, PF. Solo (8 March).

Grenzen der Menschheit (Goethe) (March).

Suleika I ('Was bedeutet?') (Goethe) (March).

Suleika II ('Ach um deine feuchten Schwingen') (Goethe) (? March).

[1] These four songs may have been composed in March 1823.

Geheimes (Goethe) (March).

Mahomets Gesang (Goethe) (March).

Variation in C minor on the Diabelli Waltz, PF. Solo (March).

Frühlingsgesang (Schober), T.T.B.B. (PF. acc. added in 1822).

Im Gegenwärtigen Vergangenes (Goethe), T.T.B.B., with PF.

Aria and Duet, T. and T.B., Orchestra: for Hérold's 'La Clochette' (Spring).

Die Nachtigall (Unger), T.T.B.B. (April).

Linde Lüfte wehen (?), Mezzo Sop. and Ten., PF. (April).

Heiss mich nicht reden (Goethe), 1st setting (April).

So lasst mich scheinen (Goethe), 1st setting (April).

Johanna Sebus (Goethe) (April).

Der Jüngling an der Quelle (Salis).

Atzenbrügger 'German' Dances, Op. 18 (July).

Symphony in E minor and major: sketch (August).

Tantum ergo in B flat, S.A.T.B., Orchestra (16 August).

Der Blumen Schmerz (Mayláth) (September).

'Alfonso und Estrella' (Schober), Opera in 3 acts (20 September–27 February 1822).

1822

Geist der Liebe (Matthisson), T.T.B.B. (January).

Am Geburtstag des Kaisers (Deinhardstein), S.A.T.B., Orchestra (January).

Epistel: Herrn Josef Spaun (M. v. Collin) (January).

Tantum ergo in D major, Chorus, Orchestra, Organ (20 March).

Die Liebe hat gelogen (Platen) (Spring).

Nachtviolen (Mayrhofer) (April).

Heliopolis I: Im kalten rauhen Norden (Mayrhofer) (April).

Heliopolis II: Fels auf Felsen (Mayrhofer) (April).

Kyrie for a Mass in A minor (May).

Three 'German' Dances (XII, 14) (? 1822).

Four quartets, T.T.B.B., Op. 17 (? 1822).

> i. *Jünglingswonne* (Matthisson),
> ii. *Liebe* (Schiller),
> iii. *Zum Rundentanz* (Salis).
> iv. *Die Nacht* (? Krummacher).

Der Wintertag (?). T.T.B.B., Op. 169 (PF. acc. lost (? 1812).

Three Military Marches, Op. 51, PF. Duet.

Der Wachtelschlag (Sauter).

Galop and eight écossaises, Op. 49, PF. Solo.

Tantum ergo in C major, Chorus, Orchestra, Organ, Op. 45.

Sixteen Ländler and two écossaises, Op. 67, PF. Solo.

An die Leier (Bruchmann).

Im Haine (Bruchmann).

Am See (Bruchmann).

Du liebst mich nicht (Platen) (July).

Gott in der Natur (Kleist), S.S.A.A., with PF. (August).

Todesmusik (Schober) (September),

Wer nie sein Brot (Goethe), 3rd setting (? October).

Symphony in B minor (The 'Unfinished') (October–November).

Fantasia in C major (The 'Wanderer'), PF. solo, Op. 15 (November).

Schatzgräbers Begehr (Schober) (November).

Schwestergruss (Bruchmann) (November).

Des Tages Weihe (?), S.A.T.B., with PF., Op. 146 (22 November).

Sei mir gegrüsst (Rückert).

Selige Welt (? Senn).

Schwanengesang (Senn).

Ihr Grab (Engelhardt).

Die Rose (Schlegel).

Der Musensohn (Goethe) (December).

An die Entfernte (Goethe) (December).

Am Flusse (Goethe), 2nd setting (December).

Willkommen und Abschied (Goethe) (December).

1823

Twelve écossaises, PF. Solo (January).

Écossaise in D major, PF. Solo (January).

'German' Dances, and two écossaises from Op. 33 (January).

Der Zwerg (M. v. Collin) (? January).

Drang in die Ferne (Leitner) (? January).

Wehmut (M. v. Collin) (? January).

Sonata in A minor, Op. 143 (February).

Waltzes from Op. 127, PF. Solo (February).

Two 'German' Dances (XII, 18), PF. Solo.

Dass sie hier gewesen
Du bist die Ruh } (Rückert) (? February)
Lachen und Weinen
Greisengesang

Waltzes from Op. 50, PF. Solo (? February).

Der zürnende Barde (Bruchmann) (February).

Viola (Schober) (March).

Abendröte (Schlegel) (March).

Die Verschworenen (later: *Der häusliche Krieg*) (Castelli), 1 act *Singspiel* (March–April).

Lied: Des Lebens Tag ist schwer (Stolberg) (April)

Pilgerweise (Schober) (April).

Twelve 'German' Dances, Op. 171, PF. Solo (May).

'Rüdiger', Opera sketches (?) (May).

Opera sketches (unnamed: 'Sofie' (?)) (May).

Vergissmeinnicht (Schober) (May).

Das Geheimnis (Schiller), 2nd setting (May).

Der Pilgrim (Schiller) (May).

Two 'German' Dances in D flat, (XII, 17), PF. Solo (? 1823).

'German' Dance in D major, PF. Solo (XII, 20) (? 1823).

Three 'German' Dances, PF. Solo (XII, 16) (? 1823).

Wanderers Nachtlied: Ueber allen Gipfeln (Goethe).

'Fierrabras' (Kupelwieser), 3 act Opera (May–October).

Die schöne Müllerin (Müller), song-cycle, (August–early 1824).

  i. *Das Wandern.*

  ii. *Wohin?*

  iii. *Halt!*

  iv. *Danksagung an den Bach.*

  v. *Am Feierabend.*

  vi. *Der Neugierige.*

  vii. *Ungeduld.*

  viii. *Morgengruss.*

  ix. *Des Müllers Blumen.*

  x. *Thränenregen.*

  xi. *Mein!*

  xii. *Pause.*

  xiii. *Mit dem grünen Lautenbande.*

  xiv. *Der Jäger.*

  xv. *Eifersucht und Stolz.*

  xvi. *Die Liebe Farbe.*

  xvii. *Die böse Farbe.*

  xviii. *Trockne Blumen.*

  xix. *Der Müller und der Bach.*

  xx. *Des Baches Wiegenlied.*

Allegro moderato in F minor (no. 3 of the 'Moments musicaux'), PF.
Solo.

Auf dem Wasser zu singen (Stolberg) (? autumn).

'Rosamunde', Play in 4 acts (Helmina v. Chézy), incidental music
(November).

1824

Introduction and variations in E minor on 'Trockne Blumen', Fl. and
PF., Op. 160 (January).

String Quartet in A minor, Op. 29 (? January).

Two 'German' Dances, PF. Solo (XII, 18) (? January).

Octet in F major, Strings and wind, Op. 166 (February–1 March).

Der Sieg (Mayrhofer) (March).

Abendstern (Mayrhofer) (March).

Auflösung (Mayrhofer) (March).

Gondelfahrer (Mayrhofer) (March).

Der Gondelfahrer (Mayrhofer), T.T.B.B., with PF. (March).

String Quartet in D minor ('Death and the Maiden') (March).

Salve Regina in C major, T.T.B.B., Op. 149 (April).

Waltzes from Op. 50, PF. Solo.

Waltzes from Op. 127, PF. Solo.

'German' Dances from Op. 33 (May: arr. for PF. Duet in July).

Dithyrambe (Schiller).

Sonata in C major, PF. Duet ('Grand Duo'), Op. 140 (June).

Eight variations on an original theme in A flat, PF. Duet, Op. 35
(July).

Four Ländler, PF. Duet (XII, 27) (July).

Gebet (Fouqué), S.A.T.B., with PF. (September).

Three écossaises, PF. Solo (September).

Ungarische Melodie in B minor, PF. Solo (2 September).

Divertissement à la hongroise in G minor, PF. Duet, Op. 54 (September).

Six Grand Marches, PF. Duet, Op. 40 (October).

Six 'German' Dances, PF. Solo (October).

Sonata for PF. and Arpeggione (in A minor) (November).

'German' Dances from the set published as *Gesamtausgabe*, XII, 10,
orig. for PF. Duet (November).

Lied eines Kriegers (?), Bass and Chorus (31 December).

1825

Lied der Anne Lyle (Scott) (? January).

Gesang der Norna (Scott) (? January).

Des Sängers Habe (Schlechta) (February).

Wehmut (Hüttenbrenner), T.T.B.B. (February).

Nacht und Träume (M. v. Collin).

Die junge Nonne (Craigher).

Im Abendrot (Lappe) (February).

Der Einsame (Lappe) (February).

Im Walde (Schulze) (March).

Der blinde Knabe (Colley Cibber, tr. Craigher) (April).

Bootgesang, T.T.B.B., with PF.

Coronach, S.S.A., with PF.

Ellens Gesang I: Raste Krieger ⎬(Scott) (Spring).

Ellens Gesang II: Jäger, ruhe

Ellens Gesang III: Ave Maria

Lied des gefangenen Jägers (Scott) (4 April).

Two 'German' Dances, PF. Solo (April).

Albumblatt: Waltz in G major, PF. Solo (16 April).

Totengräbers Heimwehe (Craigher) (April).

Sonata in A minor, Op. 42 (April).

Sonata in C major ('Reliquie') (April).

Normans Gesang (Scott) (? June).

Trinklied aus dem XVI. Jahrhundert (Latin text), T.T.B.B. (July).

Nachtmusik (Seckendorf), T.T.B.B. (July).

Sonata in D major, Op. 53 (August).

Cotillon in E flat, PF. Solo.

Waltz in A flat, PF. Solo.

Das Heimweh (Pyrker) (August).

Die Allmacht (Pyrker) (August).

Auf der Bruck (Schulze) (August).

Fülle der Liebe (Schlegel) (August).

Wiedersehen (A. v. Schlegel) (September).

Abendlied für die Entfernte (A. v. Schlegel) (September).

Florio

Delphine ⎬from the play 'Lacrimas' (Schütz) (September).

Six Polonaises, PF. Duet, Op. 61 (Autumn).

Divertissement in E minor, PF. Duet, Op. 63: no. 1 and Op. 84: nos. 1 and 2 (Autumn).

'Abschied von der Erde', musical monologue (Pratobevera) (Autumn).

Grande Marche funèbre (on the death of Alexander I) in C minor, Op. 55 (December).

An mein Herz
Der liebliche Stern }(Schulze) (December).
Um Mitternacht

1826

Tiefes Lied (Schulze) (January).
O Quell, was strömst du (Schulze) (January).
Mondenschein (Schober), T.T.B.B.B., with PF., Op. 102 (January).
Four songs from 'Wilhelm Meister' (Goethe), Op. 62 (January):
    i. *Mignon und der Harfner* (*Nur wer die Sehnsucht*),
    ii. *Heiss mich nicht reden,*
    iii. *So lasst mich scheinen,*
    iv. *Nur wer die Sehnsucht keent.*
Canon à sei (January).
Am Fenster
Sehnsucht: Die Scheibe friert }(Seidl) (March).
Im Freien
Im Frühling (Schulze) (March).
Lebensmut (Schulze) (March).
Ueber Wildemann (Schulze) (March).
Twelve 'Valses Nobles', PF. Solo, Op. 77 (? 1826).
Waltz in G major, PF. solo (? 1826).
Two waltzes (G major, B minor), PF. Solo (? 1826).
Grande Marche heroïque (for the coronation of Nicholas I), in A minor, PF. Duet, Op. 66 (Spring).
Two 'Marches caractéristiques' in C major, PF. Duet. Op. 121 (Spring)
String Quartet in G major, Op. 161 (20–30 June).
Come thou Monarch of the Vine
Hark! Hark! the Lark! }(Shakespeare) (July).
Who is Silvia?
Hippolits Lied (Gerstenbergk) (July).
Widerspruch (Seidl), T.T.B.B., with PF. (? 1826).
'Four refrain-songs' (Seidl), Op. 95 (? 1826).
    i. *Die Unterscheidung,*
    ii. *Bei dir allein,*
    iii. *Die Männer sind méchant,*
    iv. *Irdisches Glück.*

Wiegenlied (Seidl) (? 1826).

Der Wanderer an den Mond (Seidl).

Das Zügenglocklein (Seidl).

Totengräber-Weise (Schlechta).

Das Echo (Castelli).

Nachthelle (Seidl), Ten. solo., T.T.B.B., with PF., Op. 134 (September).

Grab und Mond (Seidl), T.T.B.B. (September).

Sonata in G major, Op. 78 (October).

Deutsche Messe (including 'The Lord's Prayer') (Neumann), Chorus, wind band, Organ (late Autumn).

PF. Trio in B flat, Op. 99 (end of 1826?).

Adagio in E flat, PF., vn., 'cello ('Notturno'), Op. 148 (end of 1826 ?).

Rondo in B minor, PF. and vn., Op. 70 (December).

1827

Romanze des Richard Löwenherz (*Ivanhoe*: Scott) (January).

Zur guten Nacht (Rochlitz), Bar. solo, Male voices with PF. (January).

Alinde (Rochlitz) (January).

An die Laute (Rochlitz) (January).

Der Vater mit dem Kind (Bauernfeld) (January).

Eight variations on a theme from Hérold's 'Marie', in C major, PF. Duet, Op. 82 (February).

Jägers Liebeslied (Schober) (February).

Schiffers Scheidelied (Schober) (February).

'Winterreise' (Müller), song-cycle (Book I, February: Book II, October).

i. *Gute Nacht,*	
ii. *Die Wetterfahne,*	
iii. *Gefror'ne Thränen,*	
iv. *Erstarrung*	
v. *Der Lindenbaum,*	
vi. *Wasserflut,*	Book I
vii. *Auf dem Flusse*	
viii. *Rückblick,*	
ix. *Irrlicht*	
x. *Rast,*	
xi. *Frühlingstraum,*	
xii. *Einsamkeit,*	

xiii. *Die Post,*

xiv. *Der greise Kopf,*

xv. *Die Krähe,*

xvi. *Letzte Hoffnung,*

xvii. *Im Dorfe,*

xviii. *Der stürmische Morgen,*

xix. *Täuschung,* } Book II

xx. *Der Wegweiser,*

xxi. *Das Wirtshaus,*

xxii. *Mut,*

xxiii. *Die Nebensonnen,*

xxiv. *Der Leiermann.*

Schlachtlied (Klopstock), Double Male-voice Chorus, (28 February).

Nachtgesang im Walde (Seidl), T.T.B.B., 4 hn. (April).

Frühlingslied (Pollak), T.T.B.B. (April).

Frühlingslied (the above arr. for voice and PF.) (April).

Allegretto in C minor, PF. Solo (27 April).

Das Lied im Grünen (Reil) (June).

'Der Graf von Gleichen' (Bauernfeld), 3 act Opera (sketches started mid-1827).

Ständchen (Grillparzer)

i. Contralto solo, T.T.B.B., with PF. (July).

ii. Contralto solo, S.S.A.A., with PF. (July).

Gott im Ungewitter (Uz), S.A.T.B., with PF. (? 1827).

Gott der Weltschöpfer (Uz), S.A.T.B., with PF. (? 1827).

Wein und Liebe (Haug), T.T.B.B.

Four Impromptus, Op. 90, PF. Solo (Summer ?).

Allegretto in C minor, PF. Solo (XXI, 16).

Three Italian Songs (first two: Metastasio, third: ?), Op. 83.

Heimliches Lieben (Klenke) (September).

'Edward: eine altschottische Ballade' (Percy, tr. Herder) (September).

Twelve 'Grazer' Waltzes, Op. 91, PF. Solo (September).

'Grazer' Galop, PF. Solo (September).

Kindermarsch in G major, PF. Duet (11 October).

Das Weinen.

Vor meiner Wiege }(Leitner) (? October).

Fröhliches Scheiden.

PF. Trio in E flat, Op. 100 (November).

Der Hochzeitsbraten (Schober), S.T.B., with PF. (November).

Der Wallensteiner Lanzknecht (Leitner) (November).

Der Kreuzzeug (Leitner) (November).

Des Fischers Liebesglück (Leitner) (November).

Moments musicaux, nos. 1, 2, 4 and 5, Op. 94 (? November).

Fantasia in C major, PF. and vn., Op. 159 (December).

Four Impromptus, Op. 142, PF. Solo (December).

Cantata ('for the recovery of Irene v. Kiesewetter') (?), S.A.T.T.B.B., with PF. Duet (26 December).

1828

Der Tanz (Schnitzer), S.A.T.B., with PF. (? January).

Der Winterabend (Leitner) (January).

Die Sterne (Leitner) (January).

Fantasia in F minor, Op. 103, PF. Duet (January: finished April).

Symphony in C major (the 'Great') (February: finished March).

Mirjams Siegesgesang (Grillparzer), Sop. solo, S.A.T.B., with PF. (March).

Auf der Strom (Rellstab), acc. for PF. and hn. (March).

Lebensmut (Rellstab) (? March).

Herbst (Rellstab) (April).

Drei Klavierstücke, PF. Solo (XI, 13) (May).

Hymn an den heiligen Geist (Schmidl), T.T.B.B., with Male-voice Chorus (May).

Allegro in A minor ('Lebensstürme'), Op. 144, PF. Duet (May).

Fugue in E minor, Op. 152, PF. or Organ Duet (3 June).

Mass no. 6, in E flat, S.A.T.B. soli, Chorus, Organ (June).

Rondo in A major, Op. 107, PF. Duet (June).

Psalm XCII (Hebrew text), Bar. solo, S.A.T.B. Chorus (July).

Glaube, Hoffnung, Liebe (Reil), S.A.T.B. Chorus, with wind band (August).

Glaube, Hoffnung, und Liebe (Kuffner) (August).

'Schwanengesang', song 'cycle':

    i. *Liebesbotschaft,*

    ii. *Kriegers Ahnung,*

    iii. *Frühlingssehnsucht,*

    iv. *Ständchen,*   }(Rellstab) (August).

    v. *Aufenthalt,*

    vi. *In der Ferne,*

    vii. *Abschied,*

viii. *Der Atlas,*

ix. *Ihr Bild,*

x. *Das Fischermädchen,*

xi. *Die Stadt,* }(Heine) (August).

xii. *Am Meer,*

xiii. *Der Doppelgänger*

xiv. *Die Taubenpost* (Seidl) (October).

String Quintet in C major (2 vn., va., 2 'cellos) (September).

Sonata in C minor,

Sonata in A major, }(September)

Sonata in B flat major.

Second 'Benedictus' for Mass no. 4, in C major, S.A.T.B., Chorus, Orchestra, Organ (October).

Tantum ergo in E flat, S.A.T.B., Chorus, Orchestra (October).

Offertory in B flat ('Intende voci'), Ten. solo, Chorus, Orchestra (October).

Hymnus an den heiligen Geist (Schmidl), double Male-voice Chorus, Soli and Chorus, with wind band, Op. 154 (October).

Der Hirt auf dem Felsen (Müller and H. v. Chézy), with acc. for PF. and cl., Op. 129 (October).

(i) GENERAL INDEX

Abraham, Gerald, 209, 351, (362)
Adamsberger, Antoine, 247
Adieu (Weyrauch), 327
Advokaten, Die, 261
Aeschylus, 92, 282
Albert, Prince Consort, 300
'Album Musicale', 152
Aristophanes, 129
Arnold, Matthew, 230
Artaria (Vienna), 25, 160, 239, 243, 251, 287, 318
Atzenbrugg, 102, 107, 109, 116
Augener (London), 341

Bach, 3, 217, 256, 283, 301
    48 Preludes and Fugues, 158, 283
Barbaja, Domenico, 128
Barnett, John Francis, 110, 112, 341
Barry, Sir Charles A., 331
Barth, Gustav, 47, 321
Barth, Josef, 47, 235, 321
Bates, Ralph, 8
Bauernfeld, Eduard, 10, 113, 153, 162, 170, 173, 237–9, 241–2, 245, 247, 263, 280–1, 285–6, 307, 322, 323, 359–60
Beethoven, 2, 3, 5, 12, 16, 17, 22, 36, 37, 51, 53, 64, 87, 91, 93, 146, 155, 185, 187, 196, 197, 209, 216, 226, 229, 231, 234, 256, 258–60, 264, 275, 280, 288, 293, 301, 303, 308, 322, 327, 329, 331, 332, 335, 343, 344
    'Diabelli' Variations, 189–90
    Fidelio, 12
    PF. Concerto in G major, 275
    Septet, 182
    Sonata in F sharp major, 119
    Symphony no. 3, 197
    Symphony no. 5, 225

Symphony no. 7, 185
Symphony no. 9, 199
Beethoven, Karl, 100
Berg, Isaak, 217, 268
Berlioz, 3, 4, 300
Bernhardt, J., 145, 173
'Biedermeier' Period, 9
Blahetka, Josef von, 83
Blahetka, Leopoldine von, 83, 153
Blom, Eric, 42, 97, 301, 339, 348, 352
Blumenthal, Jacob, 174
Boccherini, Luigi, 293
Bocklet, Karl von, 249, 251, 270, 282
Bogner, Ferdinand, 51, 133, 146
Böttger, Adolf, 190
Bourgault-Ducoudray, Louis, 342
Brahms, 112, 122, 143, 181, 200, 204, 234, 270, 335, 336, 337, 347
Breitkopf & Härtel (Leipzig), 104, 239, 243, 265, 299, 315, 319, 335–6, 352, 362
British Museum, 112, 246
Bruchmann, Franz, 12, 108, 109, 149
Bruchmann, Justina, 108
Bruckner, Anton, 256, 302, 342
Brüggemann, Karl (Halberstadt), 290
Brüll, Ignaz, 335
Burg Theater, Vienna, 14, 51, 163, 164
Bürger, Gottfried, 94

Capell, Richard, 35, 170, 223, 232, 268, 301, 350
Cappi & Co. (Vienna), 173, 175, 239
Cappi & Diabelli (Vienna), 50, 99, 105–6, 124
Carse, Adam, 122
Castelli, Ignaz, 10, 129–30, 134
Chézy, Wilhelm von, 322
Chézy, Wilhelmina von, 135, 148, 294

Chopin, 129, 153, 199, 227, 249, 270, 311, 326, 335, 343
Claudius, Matthias, 76
Clementi, Muzio, 65
Clodi, Florian, 167
Clodi, Max, 165
Clodi, Therese, 165, 167
Cobbett, William: 'Cyclopedia of Chamber Music', 97
Coleridge, Arthur Duke, 112, 338
Collin, Heinrich von, 10
Collins, Anthony, 187
Cooper, Fenimore, 307
Cranz, Albert & Alwin, 317, 341
Crystal Palace Concerts, 23, 110, 123, 325, 337
Czerny, Joseph (Vienna), 98, 235, 309
Czerny, Karl, 174, 242, 311

Dach, Charlotte von, 352
Dahms, Walter, 114, 131, 352
Dale, Kathleen, 63
Dante, 230
Davison, James William, 325, 343
Dean, Winton, 206
Deutsch, Otto Erich, 25, 37, 39, 70, 81, 83, 115, 126, 156, 229, 240, 250, 252, 261, 320, 328, 336, 347-8, 351, 368; see also under 'Schubert: Thematic Catalogues'
Diabelli, Anton, 68, 294
Diabelli & Co. (Vienna), 53, 74, 80, 128, 173, 174, 186, 240, 248, 269, 270, 283, 286, 290, 309, 314-17, 319, 323, 341
Dialer, Josef Alois, 310, 343, 349
Dietrichstein, Moritz von, 104, 105
Doblhoff, Anton von, 134, 145
Doppler, Josef, 4, 51, 82, 153, 242, 328, 329-30
Dräxler, Phillip, 37
Dresdel, Otto, 87
Dumba, Nikolaus, 108, 317, 340, 342, 351
Dürer, Albrecht, 138
Dussek, Jan Ladislav, 65, 95
Dvořák, Anton, 51

Ebner, Leopold, 14
'Edinburgh Review', 345
Effenberger, Hans, 338, (347)
Einstein, Alfred, 90, 123, 229, 269, 351
Ella, John, 325
Enderes, Karl von, 163, 240
Esterházy family, 156-7, 233
Esterházy, Count Johannes, 25, 50, 82, 152, 155
Esterházy, Countess Rosine, 82
Esterhàzy, Albert, 82
Esterhàzy, Karoline, 82, 85, 159-60, 268, 313, 351
Esterházy, Marie, 82, 85, 268
Eybler, Josef, 236

Fallersleben, Hoffmann von, 264
Farrer, J. H., 316
'Faust', 285
Fellner, Alois, 114
Fétis, François Josef, 2
Fink, Gottfried, 271, 291, 334
Fischer, Anton, 261
Field, John, 227
Fitzwilliam Museum, Cambridge, 190
Ford, Walter, 231
Förster, Christian Friedrich, 310
Frankl, L. A., 21
Franz, Robert, 87, 318
Friedländer, Max, 47, 104, 116, 132, 140, 257
Fries, Moritz von, 105
Frischling, Franz, 50
Fröhlich, Anna, 103, 104, 262-3, 283, 310, 313, 323, 360
Fröhlich, Barbara, 104, 146
Fröhlich, Josefine, 104, 263, 283
Fröhlich, Kathi, 104, 262
Fruhwirthaus, Vienna, 161
Fuchs, Alois, 36, 57, 320, 322-3, 359
Fuchs, Johann Nepomuk, 137-8, 265, 337

Gahy, Joseph von, 81, 86, 173, 250, 254, 282, 313
Gänsbacher, Johann Baptist, 38

Gastein, 5, 156
Geiringer, Karl, 351
Geist der Welt, Der (Schubert), 320
Gesellschaft der Musikfreunde (Vienna), 36, 61, 67, 245, 247, 251, 255, 258, 262, 270, 283, 299, 310, 317, 323, 340, 356–60
Glock, William, 184
Gluck, 12
Goethe, 10, 12, 34, 35, 40, 41, 42, 45, 49, 76, 93, 139, 165, 230, 247, 262, 282, 290, 325
Gosmar, Louise, 262–3, 284
Gotthard (Vienna), 315
Graves, Charles, 344
Graves, Robert, 41
Gray, Cecil, 16
Greene, Plunket, 346
Greipel, Josef, 80, 316
Grillparzer, Franz, 10, 104, 247, 250, 262, 283, 310, 322, 334
Grob, Heinrich, 27
Grob, Therese, 27, 34, 313
Grove's Dictionary, 144, 338, 339, 345
Grove, Sir George, 4, 16, 111, 112, 123, 136, 207, 299, 317, 318, 326, 331, 337, 338, 341, 344–6, 360–1
Gründwedel, Auguste, 254
Gymnich, August von, 104
Gyrowetz, Adalbert, 12

Habaneck, François, 299, 327
Hallé, Charles, 341
Handel, 283
'Harmonicon' (London), 251, 270
Hartmann, Franz von, 132, 162, 237, 250, 253, 259, 260, 282, 285–6, 331
Hartmann, Fritz von, 132, 161, 162, 237, 251, 253, 259, 262
Haslinger, Karl (Vienna), 269
Haslinger, Tobias (Vienna), 260–1, 266, 267, 269, 271, 283, 288, 290, 291, 309, 318, 332, 337
Hassak, Heinrich, 166

Hatwig, Otto, 51
Hauer, Anton, 14
Hauer, Josef, 235
Haydn, 2, 5, 12, 20, 22, 26, 51, 65, 93, 198, 216, 229, 330, 335
The Seasons, 26
Haydn, Michael, 93
Heine, Heinrich, 149, 282, 288, 292, 305
Hell, Theodor, 148
Hellmesberger, Johann Georg, 153
Hellmesberger, Josef, 321, 335
Henneberg, 53
Herbeck, Johann, 118, 317
Herder, Johann Gottfried von, 19, 42, 266
Hérold, Ferdinand, 10, 269, 291
La Clochette, 107
Herz, Heinrich, 174
Hess, Ernst, 122
Heuberger, Richard, 248
Hill, Ralph, 296
Hiller, Ferdinand, 260
Hoffmann, Georg von, 85
Holmes, Edward, 1, 260
Hölty, Ludwig, 43, 44
Holzapfel, Anton, 14, 125
Holzer, Michael, 13, 313
Hönig, Anna, 109, 239, 242, 280
Hönig, Karl, 12, 108, 109
Hönig, Ludwig, 355
Hortense, Queen, 86
Hugo, Victor, 138
Hummel, Johann Nepomuk, 2, 12, 53, 65, 124, 182, 200, 260, 292, 319
PF. Quintet, Op. 87, 95
Hutchings, Arthur, 352
Hüther, Franz, 174
Hüttenbrenner, Andreas, 117
Hüttenbrenner, Anselm, 53, 80, 104, 117, 120, 236, 259, 265, 312, 328, 339
Hüttenbrenner, Josef, 26, 80, 89, 105, 117, 120, 127, 134, 233, 259, 307, 312, 323, 329

Indy, Vincent d', 195–6

Jacobi, Johann, 42
Jaeger, Fritz, 85
Jaell, Eduard, 83
Jagor'sche Saal, Berlin, 165
Jenger, Johann Baptist, 86, 117, 247, 264, 267, 285, 287, 290, 309, 310
Joachim, Josef, 112, 187, 325
'July 1815': calendar, 39

Kahl, Willi, 97, 179, 351
Kalbech, Max, 141
Kalkbrenner, Friedrich, 255
Karlskirche, Vienna, 161, 234, 249
Kärntnertor Theater, Vienna, 16, 54, 85, 101, 128, 164, 238, 251, 322
Kenner, Josef, 14, 109, 126
Kiesewetter, Rafael von, 247, 357
King, A. Hyatt, 351
Kinsky, Princess Charlotte, 291
Kleist, Heinrich von, 282
Klemm, C. A. (Leipzig), 57
Kleyle, Sofie, 251, 253
Klier, Karl, 168
Klopstock, Friedrich, 42
Knorr, Baron von, 360
Kobald, Karl, 143
Koller, Josefine von, 67, 69, 85
Költzsch, Hans, 63
Konvikt, see Stadtkonvikt
Körner, Theodor, 139
Kosegarten, Ludwig, 43, 44
Kotzebue, August von, 10, 23, 100, 138, 285
Kozeluch, Leopold Anton, 2
Kreissle von Hellborn, Heinrich, 4, 16, 33, 55, 68, 112, 118, 153, 207, 242, 318, 322–4, 327, 329, 338, 343–4
Křenek, Ernst, 190
Kreutzer, Conradin, 200
Kriehuber, Josef, 162
Kuhlau, Friedrich, 65
Kundmann, Karl, 342–3
Kupelwieser, Josef, 131
Kupelwieser, Karl, 108, 154, 158
Kupelwieser, Leopold, 108, 148,

153–5, 160, 163, 170, 173, 178, 244, 250, 340, 354
Kupelwieser, Paul, 244

Lablache, Luigi, 269
Lachner, Franz, 4, 86, 235, 262, 264, 285, 286, 290, 307, 328, 331–2
Lachmann, Robert, 340
'Lacrimas' (Schütz), 172, 177
Landsberg, Ludwig, 317, 340
Lang, Franz Innocenz, 13, 18, 22
Lang, Paul Henry, 17, 197, 200
Lanz, Josef, 307
Lappe, Karl, 177
Larousse: 1875, 342
Lászny, Katherina von, 164, 173, 260
Legouvé, Ernest, 342
Leidesdorff, Maximilian, 154, 291
Leitner, Karl von, 42, 267, 268, 282, 329
Lerchenfeld Kirche (Vienna), 116
Lessing, Gotthold, 10
Lewy, Josef, 284
Liebenberg de Zsettin, Emanuel von, 124
Leichtentaler Kirche, Vienna, 5, 6, 8, 13, 26, 313, 339
Liechtental district, Vienna, 5, 8
Lied der Trennung (Mozart), 44
Liedertafel, 93
Ligne, Prince Charles Joseph de, 11
Linke, Josef, 147, 270, 282
Linz Music Society, 134, 158
Liszt, 3, 47, 118, 126, 141, 325, 329
    Wanderer Fantasia arrangement, 125, 188
    Erlking arrangement, 326
Loewe, Karl, 266, 318
Luib, Ferdinand, 69, 95, 126, 268, 323, 329
Lutz, Johanna, 149, 163, 244

Mackworth-Young, Gerard, 92
Malherbe, Charles, 340
Mandyczewski, Eusebius, 208, 257, 259, 335, 349
Männergesangverein (Vienna), 47, 321, 327, 342

Manns, August, 23, 325, 337
Matiegka, Wenzel, 25
Matthisson, Friedrich von, 44
Mautner-Markof, Frau, 244
Mayrhofer, Johann, 32, 38, 46, 49, 75, 84, 91, 113, 115, 139, 140, 144, 176, 257, 281, 286, 322
McNaught, William, 296, 299
Meangya family, 27
Mein Gebet (Schubert), 320
Mendelssohn, Felix, 3, 110, 160, 196, 199, 299, 300, 319, 325, 343, 344
   Songs without words, 325
Mendelssohn, Moses, 103, 349
Mendelssohn, Paul, 111, 112
Menz, Ignaz, 293
Metastasio, Pietro, 15, 351
Metternich, Prince Clemens, 10
Meyerbeer, Giacomo, 265
Milder-Hauptmann, Anna, 42, 164–5, 175, 294, 319
Mohn, Ludwig, 108, 149, 158
'Monthly Musical Record', London, 266, 307, 362
Mosel, Ignaz von, 12, 104, 127
Mosewius, Johann Theodor, 291
Mozart, 2, 5, 12, 16, 20, 22, 44, 51, 52, 65, 73, 75, 93, 197, 198, 216, 226, 227, 229, 231, 293, 330, 335, 343
   Abendempfindung, 93
   Magic Flute, The, 172
   Veilchen, Das, 93
Müller, Sophie, 163–4, 235, 240, 247
Müller, Wilhelm, 10, 133, 202, 256–7, 267, 294
'Music & Letters', London, 42, 156, 168, 199, 231, 304, 336, 346
'Music Review', London, 119
'Musical Examiner', London, 325
'Musical Quarterly', New York, 17, 320
'Musical Union' Concerts, 325
'Musical World', London, 324–5, 343, 352
Musikverein, see *Gesellschaft der Musikfreunde*

My Dream (Schubert), 114–15, 320

Nachgelassene musikalische Dichtungen, see 'Posthumous Musical Poems'
Nachtschmetterling, Der, 164
Nägeli, Hans Georg, 93, 242, 246, 290
Napoleon, 9
Nationalbibliothek, Vienna, 80, 240, 316
Neumann, Johann Phillip, 249, 313
Neumann, Ludwig, 322–3
Niemeyer, August Hermann, 100
Nourrit, Adolphe, 47, 326
Nowak, Leopold, 81, 144

Orel, Alfred, 351
Ottenwalt, Anton, 168, 195, 355
Ottenwalt, Marie, 168

Pachler, Faust, 265–6, 267
Pachler, Karl, 264, 266
Pachler, Marie, 264–5, 267, 279, 285, 287, 309
Paganini, Nicolo, 249, 284
Pálffy, Count Ferdinand von, 88
Panofka, Heinrich, 264, 288
Parry, Hubert, 195, 208, 209
Passini, Johann Nepomuk, 175
Paumgartner, Sylvester, 85, 95, 98, 132, 182
Pennauer, Vienna, 166, 173, 239, 248
Peters, Leipzig, 294
Peterskirche, Vienna, 80, 282, 316
Petter, Gustav, 36, 340
Pichler, Karl, 313
Pichler, Karoline, 205
Piledrivers' Song (Gmunden), 167
Pinterics, Karl, 340
Pixis, Johann Peter, 174
Pohl, Carl Ferdinand, 360–1
Pope, Alexander, 19
'Posthumous Musical Poems', 315, 321, 335
Pound, Ezra, 41
Preiger, Emil, 62
Pritchard, T. C. L., 119

Probst, H. A., Leipzig, 243, 255, 262, 268, 289, 292–3, 332
Prod'homme, Jacques Gabriel, 341
Pyrker, Johann Ladislaus, 170, 177

Racek, Fritz, 368
Racine, Jean, 10
Raimund, Ferdinand, 10
Randhartinger, Benedikt, 4, 14, 133, 144, 328, 330–1
Ratz, Erwin, 60
Reading Parties, 148, 154, 163, 282
Reeve, Henry, 345
Rehberg, Walter, 56, 65
Reichardt, Johann, 93
Reissmann, August, 4, 123, 207, 338
Rellstab, Ludwig, 287–8
Richault, Simon (Paris), 326
Rieder, Wilhelm August, 162, 175
Rinna, Ernst, 289, 307
Rischl, Thorwald, 25
Rochlitz, Johann, 42
Rockstro, William, 112
'Roman Emperor' Hall, Vienna, 71
Roner, Franziska, 282
Rosa, Kunigunde, see Vogl, Kunigunde
Rossau, Vienna, 82, 115, 127, 234
Rossini, 12, 70, 72, 217
   Tancredi, 330
Royal College of Music, London, 112
Rückert, Friedrich, 144
Ruczicka, Wenzel, 14, 46

St. Pölten, 112
Salieri, Anton, 14, 15, 26, 34, 36, 80, 94, 195, 217, 236, 330, 351
Salis-Seewis, Johann von, 44
Salomon, Karl, 187
Sauer & Leidesdorff, Vienna, 88, 148, 151, 152, 173, 239, 248
Schaeffer, Erwin, 257
Schechner, Nanette, 238, 241
Scheibler, Ludwig, 57, 65, 69, 81, 323
Schellmann, Albert, 42
Schikh, Johann, 284–5

Schiller, 10, 36, 40, 44, 76, 138, 140, 179
Schiller, Councillor Franz von, 355
Schindler, Anton, 15, 53, 88, 238–9, 258, 262, 288, 292–3, 322–3, 328, 332–3
Schlechta, Franz von, 37, 38, 350
Schlegel, Friedrich von, 171
Schlesinger, Paris, 326
Schmidl, (?Adolf), 295
Schmidt, Georg Philipp (of Lübeck), 40, 50
Schmidt, Klamer, 44
Schneider, Eduard, 136, 317, 327, 338, 340
Schneider, Georg Abraham, 155
Schneidl, Herr, 83
Schober, Axel von, 33, 77
Schober, Franz von, 21, 32, 38, 49, 54, 56, 76, 102, 108, 109, 113, 115, 126, 133, 134–5, 147–9, 152, 157, 159, 161, 164, 170, 173, 207, 237, 241–2, 246, 248, 254, 259, 280, 281, 291, 307–8, 310, 312, 313
Schober, Katherina von, 33
Schönberg, Arnold, 204
Schönstein, Baron Karl von, 152, 161, 313, 333, 360
Schott's Sons, Mainz, 53, 283, 289, 290, 292, 358
Schottentor, Vienna, 117
Schraub, Franz, 93
Schröder-Devrient, Wilhelmina, 324
Schubart, Christian, 76
SCHUBERT:
   Applications for posts, 34, 236, 238
   Birthplace, 6, 327, 343, 349
   Catalogues (1) Deutsch, 39, 70, 81, 102, 147, 335, 348, 368
      (2) Diabelli, 261, 335
      (3) Fuchs, 57, 322
      (4) Grove, 339
      (5) Kreissle, 322, 334, 335
      (6) Nottebohm, 335, 339
      (7) Reissmann, 335, 339
      (8) Schindler, 323
      (9) Schubert, Ferdinand, 320

Conscription, 22
'Documentary Biography', 239, 251, 259, 280, 328, 348, 357
Dream, My, 114–15, 320
Diary, 36, 37, 152
Gesamtausgabe, 20, 89, 90, 239, 265, 294, 315, 316–17, 318, 335, 339, 340, 348, 362
Poems: *Abschied*, 77
  Geist der Welt, Der, 320
  Mein Gebet, 320
Schubertiads, 108, 113, 149, 162, 164, 173, 240, 245, 250, 254, 260, 282
Spectacles, 109, 345, 350
Schubert, Elisabeth (mother), 5, 114
Schubert, Elisabeth (sister), 6
Schubert, Ferdinand, 6, 12, 16, 68, 70, 98, 110, 116, 127, 143, 158–9, 190, 281, 289, 291, 294, 299, 306–9, 312–17, 319–20, 322, 327, 334, 338, 350, 359–60
Schubert, Franz (of Dresden), 104, 243
Schubert, Franz Theodor (father), 5–8, 13, 16, 82, 114, 150, 157, 171, 234, 245, 308, 355
Schubert, Ignaz, 6, 12, 16, 27
Schubert, Josefa, 307
Schubert, Karl (brother), 6
Schubert, Karl (Ferdinand's son), 116, 313, 317
Schubert, Maria Theresa, 6, 7, 13, 236, 317
Schubert, Therese, 307
Schultz, Johann Abraham, 93
Schulze, Ernst, 157, 171, 176, 234, 240
Schumann, Clara, 186
Schumann, Robert, 4, 124, 160, 186, 190, 199, 201, 226, 227, 229, 269, 270, 287, 292, 299, 318, 319–21, 334, 335, 338, 344, 347
Schuppanzigh, Ignaz, 146–7, 150, 153, 182, 270, 282
Schuster, Vincenz, 156

Schütz, Wilhelm von, 172
Schwind, Moritz von, 6, 10, 11, 109, 113, 133, 134, 135, 137, 147, 150, 154, 157, 159, 161–3, 164, 169, 173, 237, 239, 241, 245, 250, 259, 263, 286, 308, 347, 349, 354, 355
Scott, Sir Walter, 86, 138, 167, 176, 290
Sechter, Simon, 15, 306–7
Seckendorff, Karl, 166
Seidl, Johann, 42, 245, 288
Senn, Johann, 14, 100
Seyfried, Ignaz von, 137
Shakespeare, 10, 113, 230, 267
Shaw, George Bernard, 16
Shelley, 37, 41
Sibelius, Jean, 4, 200
Siboni, Giuseppe, 54
Silbert, Johann Peter, 92
Slavík, Josef, 240, 249, 251, 270
Sonnleithner, Ignaz von, 37, 99, 104, 108
Sonnleithner, Josef von, 37, 247
Sonnleithner, Leopold von, 37, 51, 99, 105, 127, 146, 217, 263, 268, 320, 322, 360
Spaun, Anton von, 126, 172, 240
Spaun, Josef von, 12–15, 32, 34, 45, 46, 55–6, 81, 85, 104, 108, 113, 115, 126, 127, 134, 143, 150, 161, 168, 195, 207, 235, 237, 240, 241, 247, 250–1, 254, 258, 259, 264, 281, 289, 307, 312, 322–4, 340, 355, 358, 360
Spina, C. A., Vienna, 182, 240, 293
Spohr, Louis, 200, 344
Stadler, Albert, 14, 22, 67, 69, 95, 125, 138, 169, 172, 312, 323
Stadler, Maximilian, 132
Stadtbibliothek, Vienna, 35, 59, 81, 144, 257, 317, 323, 340
Stadtkonvikt, Vienna, 13–18, 21, 22, 31, 46, 93, 114, 159, 169, 225, 246, 297, 320, 330, 368
Stanford, Charles, 77
Statham, H. Heathcote, 345

Stiebar, Freiherr von, 313
Stiernblad, Axel, 33
Stockhausen, Margarete, 325
Stolberg, Count Leopold, 144
Storck, Adam, 163
Strauss, Johann, 5, 123
Strauss, Richard, 244, 337
Streinsberg, Josef von, 313
Styrian Music Society, Graz, 117, 158, 265
Sullivan, Arthur, 112, 136, 317
Széchényi, Count Ludwig, 330

Taussig, Konsul Otto, 20, 259, 341
Tchaikowsky, 337
Teltscher, Josef, 265
Thayer, Alexander Wheelock, 101
Theater an der Wien, Vienna, 16, 85, 88, 102, 137
Thomas, Dylan, 41
Tieck, Ludwig, 282
Tietze (or Titze), Ludwig, 255, 282, 284
Tomašek, Václav, 227
Tovey, Donald, 187, 199, 223, 274, 304, 350
Traweger, Eduard, 167
Traweger, Ferdinand, 166, 167, 285, 355
Trauttsmandorff, Prince Ferdinand, 236
Troyer, Count Ferdinand, 146–7, 182, 243
Truscott, Harold, 63

Umlauff, Johann, 108–9
Unger, Johann Karl, 153
Uz, Johann Peter, 42, 77

Vering, Josef von, 307
Vetter, Walter, 351
Vienna City Library, see Stadt-bibliothek
Vogl, Kunigunde, 240, 264
Vogl, Michael, 12, 33, 54–5, 69, 76, 85, 99, 101, 104, 105, 108, 126, 162, 164, 165, 207, 240, 242, 245, 247, 250, 259, 260, 284, 294, 333, 355

Wagner, 3, 4, 92, 160, 199, 234, 337
  Lohengrin, 12
  Siegfried, 101
  Tristan und Isolde, 92, 229
  Walküre, Die, 101
Währing, nr. Vienna, 241, 308
Walcher, Ferdinand, 237, 251, 253, 255–6, 313
Walker, Frank, 307
Watteroth, Heinrich, 32, 35, 37, 249
Watteroth, Wilhelmina, 35
Weber, 127, 148, 257, 332
  Euryanthe, 134
  Freischütz, Der, 12, 134
Weigl, Josef, 12, 16, 237
Weigl, Thaddeus, Vienna, 161, 239, 248, 269
Weingartner, Felix, 110
Weintridt, Vincentius, 114
Weiss, Franz, 174
Weissenwolf, Countess Sofie, 168–9, 172
Werner, Theodor, 203
Werner, Zacharias, 49
Wessel & Co., London, 324
Westrup, Jack A., 198
Weyrauch, August von, 327
Whistling, Leipzig, 62, 190, 317
Whistling's Handbuch, 93
Wieck, Friedrich, 287
Wilder, Victor, 130
Windsor Castle, 300
Winkler, Karl, 148
Wisgrill, Johann, 307
Witteczek, Josef, 32, 35, 61, 63, 68, 240, 250, 260, 267, 313, 340
Wittmann, Rudolph, 349
Wodehouse, Mrs. Edmond, 344
Wolf, Hugo, 92, 204, 326, 347
Wolzogen, Karoline von, 40
Worzischek, Johann, 227
Wurzbach, Konstant von, 118, 339

Zedlitz, Johann von, 42
Zelter, Karl Friedrich, 93
Zseliz, 67, 82, 84, 91, 156–61, 313, 354
Zuckmantel, 5

(ii) INDEX OF WORKS

1. VOCAL MUSIC

Abend, Der, 24
Abendbilder, 91
Abendlied, 313
Abendrot, Das, 313
Abschied, 288
Adelaide, 24
Adrast, (Opera), 140
Alfonso und Estrella (Opera), 113,
   127, 134, 135, 137, 141, 160,
   164, 218, 265–6, 312, 320,
   337
   Overture, 225, 239, 251, 316
Allmacht, Die, 170, 177, 255, 261
Alpenjäger, Der, 12
Altschottische Ballade, Eine, 266
Am Erlafsee, 78
Am ersten Maimorgen, 27
Am Flusse (I), 45, 203–4
Am Flusse (II), 203–4, 213
Am Meer, 204, 208, 305
Am See (Mayrhofer), 32
Amalia, 36
Amphiaros, 46
An Chloen, 42
An den Mond (Goethe) (I), 35, 41
An den Mond (Goethe) (II), 41
An den Mond (Hölty), 43, 215
An den Mond in einer Herbstnacht, 91
An den Tod, 76, 152
An die Dioskuren, 49, 271
An die Freunde, 91
An die Laute, 261
An die Musik, 77
An die untergehende Sonne, 44
An mein Herz, 306
An Mignon, 34, 173
An Rosa (I) and (II), 44
An Schwager Kronos, 12, 45, 128,
   173, 251

An Sie, 42
Andenken, 24
Andenken (Part-song), 349
Annot Lyle's Song, 236, 290
Antigon und Oedip, 75
Atlas, Der, 288, 305
Atys, 78
Auf dem Flusse, 301
Auf dem See, 290
Auf dem Strome, 284
Auf dem Wasser zu singen, 144, 223,
   255, 261, 269
Auf der Bruck, 171
Auf der Donau, 76, 271
Aufenthalt, 203, 288, 304, 333
Auflösung, 176
Augenlied, 55, 259
Ave Maria, 50, 166, 247, 256, 324

Benedictus (for the C major Mass),
   294
Berthas Lied, 313
Blinde Knabe, Der, 260
Blondel zu Marien, 313
Blumenbrief, Der, 313
Blumensprache, Die, 313
Bootgesang (Part-song), 169
Bundeslied, 35, 45
Burgschaft, Die (Opera), 140

Cantata for Salieri's Jubilee, 37
Canzonets, IV, 313
Claudine von Villa Bella (Opera), 83,
   139, 312
Come, thou Monarch of the vine, 241
Coronach (Part-song), 169, 176

Dass sie hier gewesen, 144, 223, 247
Delphine, 172, 219

Dioskuren, Die, see *An die Dioskuren*
Doppelgänger, Der, 176, 181, 204, 205, 212, 288, 290, 304–5
Dörfchen, Das (Part-song), 94, 114
Du bist die Ruh', 247

Edit Nonna (Part-song), 166
Edone, 42
Edward (*Eine altschottische Ballade*), 266–7
Eifersucht und Stolz, 133
Einsame, Der, 174, 177, 251
Einsamkeit, 91
Enchanted Rose, The, 157
Entsühnte Orest, Der, 75, 159
Entzückung, 44
Epistel, Die, 313
Erinnerung, 153
Erinnerung (Part-song), 349
Erlking, 34, 45–7, 49, 104, 165, 176, 212, 235, 243, 324
Erster Verlust, 34, 45, 181

Fahrt zum Hades, 75
Fernando (Opera), 138–9
Fierrabras (Opera), 113, 131, 133, 141–2, 158, 280, 337
   Overture, 214, 316, 325
Fischer, Der, 34
Fischermädchen, Das, 288, 305
Fischers Liebesglück, Des, 268
Florio, 172
Forelle, Die, 12, 76, 80, 102, 174, 205, 312, 313, 324
Fragment aus dem Aeschylus, 49
Freiwilliges Versinken, 75
Fremdling, Der (*Der Wanderer*), 50
Freunde von Salamanka, Die, 139, 140, 184, 186
Fröhliches Scheiden, 205
Frühen Gräben, Die, 42
Frühlingsglaube, 144
Frühlingssehnsucht, 287
Frühlingstraum, 205
Fülle der Liebe, 171

Ganymed, 55, 76, 173
Gebet (Part-song), 313
Gefangenen Sänger, Die, 116

Geheimnis: an Franz Schubert, 38
Geheimnis, Das, 159, 313
Geist der Liebe (Part-song), 114
Geisternähe, 24
Geistertanz, Der (Part-song), 94
Geistes-Gruss, 34, 290
Gesang der Geister über den Wassern (Part-song)
   (I), 94
   (II) Sketch: 103
      Complete version, 316
   (III) Sketch: 103
Gesang der Norma, 290
Gestirne, Die, 326
Glaube, Hoffnung und Liebe (Part-song), 285
Gondelfahrer, Der (Part-song), 150, 151
Gott in der Natur (Part-song), 313
Gott und die Bajadere, Der, 35, 45
Götter Griechenlands, Die, 92, 179, 184, 186
Grab, Das, 313
Grab und Mond (Part-song), 245
Grablied für die Mutter, 313
Graf von Gleichen, Der (Opera sketches), 137, 146, 237–8, 242, 264, 280, 307
Grenzen der Menschheit, 144
Gretchen am Spinnrade, 12, 25, 28, 34, 45, 47, 49, 105, 177, 206, 306, 325
Gretchens Bitte, 76
Gruppe aus dem Tartarus, 12, 76, 78, 205, 220
Gute Nacht, 256

Hagars Klage, 15, 18
Hark! Hark! the Lark!, 50, 224, 241, 330
Harper's Songs from *Wilhelm Meister*, 12, 45, 106
   (I) *An die Türen*, 48
   (II) *Wer sich der Einsamkeit ergibt*, 48
   (III) *Wer nie sein Brot*, 48, 247
Häusliche Krieg, Der, see *Verschworenen, Die*

Heidenröslein, 12, 34, 45
Heimliches Lieben, 266–7
Heimweh, Das (Hell), 148
Heimweh, Das (Pyrker), 170, 177, 261
Heliopolis, I, and II, 144
Herbst, 287, 288
Herbstabend, Der, 45
Hirt auf dem Felsen, Der, 294
Hymn to the Holy Ghost (1828), 295

Ihr Bild, 288
Im Abendrot, 177–8, 207, 254
Im Freien, 260, 261
Im Frühling, 202, 240
In der Ferne, 288
Intende Voci, 294
Irrlicht, 301

Jägers Abendlied (I), 349
　(II), 34
Jägers Liebeslied, 313
Junge Nonne, Die, 163, 174, 177, 203, 235, 251, 288, 324
Jängling an der Quelle, Der, 45

Kampf, Der, 313
Klage, 27
Klage an den Mond, 43
Klagelied, 19
König in Thule, Der, 34, 105
Kreuzzug, Der, 268
Kriegers Ahnung, 287, 333

Lachen und Weinen, 247
Lady of the Lake, The (songs), 163, 166, 169, 172, 176, 236, 239, 258
Lazarus (Cantata), 100, 334
Lay of the imprisoned huntsman, 167
Lebenslied, 63
Lebensmut (Rellstab), 287, 288
Liedende, Der, 135
Leiermann, Der, 208, 257, 290
Letzte Hoffnung, 214
Liebe (Part-song), 94
Liebe hat gelogen, Die, 219
Liebe schwärmt auf allen Wegen, 140

Liebende schreibt, Die, 92
Liebesbotschaft, 287, 333
Lied (Schiller), 40
Lied (Stolberg), 144
Lied der Anne Lyle, see *Annot Lyle's Song*
Lied eines Schiffers an die Dioskuren, see *An die Dioskuren*
Lied im Grünen, Das, 261
Lied in der Abwesenheit, 349
Lied: in's stille Land, 45
Linde Lüfte wehen, 106, 116
Lindenbaum, Der, 202, 301
Litany for All Souls' Day, 43
Lob der Tränen, 81
Lorma (II), 66
Luisens Antwort, 44

Mädchens Klage, Des, 19
Magnificat in C, 316
Mahomets Gesang, 76
Mailied, 6, 27
Mainacht, Die, 43
Masses:
　F major, 26, 263
　G major, 236, 343
　B flat major, 66, 236, 319, 330
　C major, 173, 313
　A flat major, 116, 142–4, 335
　E flat major, 2, 142, 220, 222, 226, 287, 300–1, 302, 327, 343
　Deutsche Messe, 249, 313
Meeresstille, 34, 45
Memnon, 75, 223
Mignon's songs:
　(a) *Kennst du das Land?*, 47
　(b) *Nur wer die Sehnsucht kennt* (1815), 35, 47
　(c) *Nur wer die Sehnsucht kennt* (Part-song), 94, 312
　(d) *So lasst mich scheinen*, 48
Mignon und der Harfner, 261
Miriam's Song (Cantata), 283, 310, 319
Mondenschein (Part-song), 290
Mondnacht, Die, 44
Morgenlied, 105
Musensohn, Der, 290

Nacht, Die (Part-song), 94
Nacht und Träume, 163, 174, 254
Nachtgesang, 35, 360
Nachthelle (Part-song), 245, 255
Nachthymne, 220
Nachtigall, Die (Part-song), 114, 153
Nachtmusik, Die (Part-song), 166
Nachtstück, 91, 173
Nachtviolen, 144
Nähe des Geliebten, 34
Nebensonnen, Die, 257, 267
Norman's Song, 258, 265
Nur wer die Sehnsucht kennt, see under
Mignon's songs

Orest auf Tauris, 75

Pause, 227
Pax vobiscum, 308
Perle, Die, 43
Philoktet, 75
Post, Die, 257, 290
Prometheus, 92, 101
Prometheus (Cantata), 37, 263, 320
Psalm XIII, 349
Psalm XXIII (Part-song), 103, 251,
258, 306, 313, 319

Rastlose Liebe, 34, 45, 49
Rattenfänger, Der, 35, 45
Rosamunde (Incidental music), 100,
102, 123, 134–7, 146, 147,
186, 338
Overture, 71, 102, 141
Romanze ('Der Vollmond
strahlt'), 135, 148
Rose, Die, 236, 261
Rosenband, Das, 42
Rüdiger (or *Rüdigers Heimkehr*),
(Opera sketches), 130
Ruhe, schönstes Glück (Part-song),
312

Salve Regina (1812), 349, (1815), 27,
173
Sänger, Der, 35
Scene in the Cathedral (*Faust*), 30
Schäfer und der Reiter, Der, 105

Schäfers Klagelied, 30, 34, 55, 85
Schlachtgesang (Part-song), 284
Schöne Müllerin, Die (Song-cycle),
130, 133, 144, 150, 151–2,
203, 219, 330
Schwanengesang (Song collection),
288–9, 292, 304–6, 309, 318,
333
Sehnen, Das, 44
Sehnsucht (Goethe), 35
Sei mer gegrüsst, 203, 270
Seligkeit, 43
Serenade (Part-song: Grillparzer),
263, 284
Serenade (Rellstab), 50, 288
Shepherd on the Rock, The, see *Hirt
auf dem Felsen, Der*
Sieg, Der, 176
Sofie(?) (Opera sketches), 131
Sommernacht, Die, 42
Sonnett III (Petrarch), 221
Spiegelritter, Der, (Opera), 18, 312
Spinnerin, Die, 34, 45
Stadt, Die, 288, 304–5
Ständchen, see *Serenade* and *Hark!
Hark! the Lark!*
Sterne, Die (Leitner), 282
Stimme der Liebe (Stolberg), 220
Strom, Der, 313
Suleika (I), 106, 144, 149, 164–5
(II), 144, 174

Tantum ergo (I) (1816), 313
(II) (1816), 351 (1828), 294
Tubenpost, Die, 288, 294, 295, 306
Teufels Lustschloss, Des, 23, 113,
127, 140, 312
Thekla, 313
Tischlied, 35
Tod und das Mädchen, Der, 77, 105,
186
Todtenkranz für ein Kind, 44, 224
Totengräberlied (Part-song), 94
Totengräbers Heimweh, 177
Trockne Blumen, 133, 146
Trost im Liede, 77, 262
Trost in Tränen, 35
Trout, The, see *Forelle, Die*

Über Wildemann, 240, 274, 291
Um Mitternacht, 176
Ungeduld, 224, 313
Unglückliche, Der (*Der Wanderer*), 50
Unglückliche, Der (Pichler), 205

Vergissmeinnicht, 130
Verklärung, 19
Verschworenen, Die (Opera), 129, 138, 142, 155, 337
Vierjährige Posten, Der (Opera), 139
Viola, 258
Vor meiner Wiege, 267

Wachtelschlag, Der, 261
Waldesnacht (*Im Walde*), 208, 313
Wallensteiner Lanzknecht, Der, 268
Wanderer, Der (Schmidt), 40, 49, 50, 109, 324
Wanderer an den Mond, Der, 260
Wanderers Nachtlied (I), 34
Wanderers Nachtlied (II), 159

Wegweiser, Der, 301
Weinen, Das, 267
Wer kauft Liebesgötter?, 35
Wetterfahne, Die, 257, 301
Widerhall (Part-song), 349
Widerschein, 102, 368
Wiedersehn, 172
Winterabend, 282
Winterreise, 10, 181, 202, 206, 253, 256–8, 267, 290, 291, 292, 301, 304, 308, 318, 332, 350, 352–3
Wohin soll ich mich wenden?, 250
Wonne der Wehmut, 34

Zauberharfe, Die (Opera), 71, 101, 137, 140
Zügenglöcklein, Das, 260
Zürnenden Diana, Der, 173, 258
Zwerg, Der, 144 251, 331
Zwillingsbrüder, Die (Opera), 85, 101, 140–1
Zwillingssterne, Die, see *An die Dioskuren*

2. INSTRUMENTAL MUSIC

Adagio in D flat, PF. Solo, 315
Adagio in E major, PF. Solo, 78
Adagio and Rondo in E major, Op. 145, 62, 321
Adagio and Rondo in F major, PF. Quartet, 314
Allegretto in C minor, 256, 313
Andante in A major, 70
Andantino varié, PF. Duet, 248
'Arpeggione' Sonata, 156, 313, 335
Atzenbrügger Deutsche, 107

Ballet Music (*Rosamunde*), 135–6

Concerto in D major, Vn. & Str. Orch., 314
Cotillon in E flat, 75

Deutsche (German Dances):
  Op. 33, 173
  Deutsche Tänze (published 1930), 351
  'October 1824', 351
Divertissement à l'hongroise, Op. 54, 160, 164, 186, 217
Divertissement on French themes, Op. 63: no. 1, 248
  Op. 84, 269
Drei Klavierstücke, 227
Duo, Grand, *see* 'Sonatas'
Duo in A major, Vn. & PF., *see* 'Sonatas'

Écossaises (1815), 349
Entr'actes (*Rosamunde*)
  in B minor, 123, 135

Entr'actes (*Rosamunde*) (*cont.*)
in B flat major, 135, 179, 269

Fantasias for PF. Solo:
in C major (The *Wanderer*), Op.
15, 124, 180, 187, 343
in C minor, 19, 315
Fantasies for PF. Duet:
in G major, 18
in G minor, 18
in C minor, 18, 312
in F minor, Op. 103, 217, 268,
282, 286, 301, 319
Fantasia in C major, Vn. & PF.,
Op. 159, 217, 270, 343
Fünf Klavierstücke, 57
Fugue in E minor, Org. or PF. Duet,
285, 314

'Gastein' Symphony, *see under* 'Symphonies'
Grand Duo, *see under* 'Sonatas'
Grätzer Gallop and *Walzer*, 266
'Guitar' Quartet (spurious), 25

Impromptus, PF. Solo, 227, 318, 325
Op. 90, 230, 261, 269
Op. 142, 269–70

Kindermarsch, 266, 312

Ländler, PF. Solo:
Op. 67, 254
6 in B flat, 2 in E flat, 8 in F sharp
minor, 349
Lebensstürme, PF. Duet, 187, 286, 301

Marches, PF. Duet:
Marches heroïques, 88, 151
Marches militaires, 114, 248
Grandes marches, 160, 164, 173,
186, 250
Marches caractéristiques, 240, 319
Funeral March for Alexander I,
187, 239, 241, 248
Coronation March for Nicolas I,
241, 248
Marcia on French themes, Op. 84,
248
Kindermarsch, 266, 312

Moments musicaux, PF. Solo, Op.
94, 88, 152, 227, 255, 291,
325

'Notre amitié est invariable', PF.
Duet, 80
Notturno, PF. Trio, Op. 148, 168,
217
Noturno (Matiegka) (spurious), 25

Octet in F major, Op. 166, 147, 155,
178, 197, 201, 215, 243, 260,
314, 321, 341
Overtures for orchestra:
Der Teufel als Hydraulikus, 316
D major (sketch), 316
B flat major, 70
D major (1817), 70, 316
D major ('in the Italian style'), 70,
78, 85, 102, 316, 330
C major ('in the Italian style'), 70,
78, 85, 316
E minor, 89–91
For Opera Overtures: *see under the
work in* 'Vocal Music'
Overtures for PF. Duet:
D major (arr. from the 'Italian'
overture), 72, 313
C major (arr. from the 'Italian'
overture), 72, 313
G minor, 88
F minor/major, 36, 89, 169, 173,
182–5, 329

Pianoforte Quintet ('The Trout'),
95, 98, 103, 182, 227, 318,
326, 343
Pianoforte Trios:
B flat ('Sonata'), 18, 349
B flat, Op. 99, 168, 199, 227, 243,
272, 277–8, 252, 325
E flat, Op. 100, 12, 74, 119, 199,
201, 208, 217, 227, 268, 270,
272, 278–9, 284, 290, 291,
292, 310, 313, 325, 332, 342,
343
Adagio in E flat, *see Notturno*

Polonaise in B flat, Vn. & orch., 349
Polonaises, PF. Duet, Op. 75, 87, 269

'Reliquie' Sonata, *see under* 'Sonatas'
Rondeau brillant, PF. & Vn., 249, 251
Rondo in E major, Op. 145, 315, 343
Rondos for PF. Duet:
  in D major, Op. 138, 80, 87
  in A major, Op. 107, 287, 318, 319

Scherzo in D flat major, PF. Solo, 64
Sehnsucht Waltz, 53, 80
Sonatas for PF. & Vn.:
  D major, Op. 137: no. 1, 74, 314, 319
  A minor, Op. 137: no. 2, 74, 314, 319
  G minor, Op. 137: no. 3, 74, 314 319
  A major ('Duo'), 74, 75, 96, 216, 314
Sonatinas for PF. & Vn., *see above* Sonatas for PF. & Vn.
Sonata for PF. & Arpeggione, 156
Sonatas for PF. Duet:
  B flat major, Op. 30, 88, 89, 323, 339
  C major (Grand Duo), 88, 160, 186–8, 254, 319, 320
Sonatas for PF. Solo:
  1. E major (1815), 56
  2. C major (1815), 56
  3. E major (Fünf Klavierstücke), 57, 70
  4. E minor (fragment), 58
  5. A minor, Op. 164, 60, 67, 315
  6. A flat major, 61, 315
  7. E minor (1817), 61–3, 317
  8. D flat major, 63
  9. E flat major, Op. 122, 63, 78, 319
  10. F sharp minor, 64
  11. B major, Op. 147, 66, 69, 315, 321

  12. C major (1818), 78
  13. F minor, 67, 221
  14. A major (1819?), 68, 85, 243, 319, 339
  15. A minor, Op. 143, 67, 128, 209, 223, 243, 315
  16. A minor, Op. 42, 12, 166, 173, 188–90, 199, 239, 242, 271, 276
  17. C major ('Reliquie'), 188, 190–1, 317, 322
  18. D major, Op. 53, 12, 169–70, 192, 239, 251, 314, 339, 356
  19. G major, Op. 78, 12, 119, 243, 246, 254, 260, 271, 274–7, 304, 318, 342
  20. C minor (1828), 2, 292, 303–4, 320
  21. A major (1828), 64, 292, 302–4
  22. B flat major (1828), 196, 199, 223, 246, 292, 301, 302–4, 319
String Quartets:
  C major (1812), 20, 225, 315
  B flat major (1812–13), 15, 315
  C major (1813), 20, 315
  B flat major (1813), 20, 211, 315
  D major (1813), 15, 18, 20, 29, 151, 315
  E flat major, Op. 125: no. 2, 20, 23, 156, 319, 323, 339
  D major (1814), 26, 315, 335
  B flat major, Op. 168, 20, 24, 26, 210, 322
  C minor (1814), 315, 351
  G minor (1815), 72, 315, 335
  E major, Op. 125: no. 1, 2, 72, 156, 319, 323, 339
  C minor (Quartett-Satz), 103, 180, 228, 334
  A minor, Op. 29, 12, 92, 147, 150–1, 155, 178–80, 184, 196, 217, 321, 339
  D minor ('Death and the Maiden'), 2, 71, 147, 151, 180–2, 184, 196, 210, 217, 219, 223, 227, 235, 243, 319, 321, 325, 326, 339, 342

String Quartets (*cont.*)
  G major, Op. 161, 151, 156, 181, 193, 198, 211, 219, 240, 243, 249, 268, 271–4, 284, 315, 321, 357
String Quintets:
  'Overture' in C minor, 18, 338
  C major, Op. 163, 74, 181, 196, 199, 226, 258, 292, 301, 314, 321
String Trios:
  B flat major (1816), 72–3
  B flat major (1817), 72–3, 314, 336, 338
Symphonies:
  D major (sketch), 316
  1. D major, 22, 225, 337
  2. B flat, 50, 51, 337
  3. D major, 50, 52, 337
  4. C minor ('Tragic'), 50, 52, 336
  5. B flat, 50, 51, 62, 317, 337
  6. C major (the 'Little'), 78, 110, 117, 295, 299, 336, 357
  7. D major (sketches), 79, 110, 208, 211, 217, 314
  8. E minor/major (sketches), 90, 109, 211, 225, 338, 341
  9. B minor (the 'Unfinished'), 3, 5, 51, 52, 103, 110, 116–24, 178, 196, 197, 199, 206, 208, 217, 225, 312, 314, 318, 327, 334, 337, 340, 342, 358
  10. C major (the 'Great'), 2, 5, 51, 53, 71, 184, 197, 198, 210, 212, 222, 225, 258, 274, 282, 292, 295–300, 301, 319, 320, 325–6, 327, 337, 338, 342, 343, 357–61

'Gmunden-Gastein' Symphony, 167, 175, 187, 248, 354–61

Trauerwalzer, 53, 80

'Unfinished' Symphony, *see above* 'Symphonies: B minor'
Ungarische Melodie, 349

Variations:
  Ten Variations in F major, 57, 314, 315
  on a Hüttenbrenner theme, 80, 312
  on *Die Forelle*, 85, 95
  on a French Air, Op. 10, 86, 105, 332
  on an original theme in B flat, Op. 82, 87
  On *Der Wanderer*, 124
  on *Trockne Blumen*, 133, 146
  on a waltz by Diabelli, 152, 190
  on an original theme in A flat, Op. 35, 158, 160, 166, 173, 186, 190, 197, 254, 282
  on a theme from Hérold's 'Marie', 269, 291
  on *Sei mir gegrüsst*, 270

Waltzes, PF. Solo:
  Op. 9, 105, 223
  Op. 18, 213
  Op. 33, 129, 213
  Op. 171, 129, 213, 220, 230
  'Johanna Lutz', 244
  'Grätzer Walzer', 266
  see also under *Trauerwalzer* and *Sehnsucht* Waltz

PRINTED IN GREAT BRITAIN BY ROBERT MACLEHOSE AND CO. LTD
THE UNIVERSITY PRESS, GLASGOW